All THE RULES

Time-tested Secrets for Capturing the Heart of Mr. Right

**ELLEN FEIN
AND SHERRIE SCHNEIDER**

GC

**GRAND CENTRAL
PUBLISHING**

NEW YORK   BOSTON

Grand Central Publishing
Hachette Book Group USA
237 Park Avenue
New York, NY 10017
Visit our Web site at www.HachetteBookGroupUSA.com

Grand Central Publishing is a division of Hachette Book Group USA, Inc. The Grand Central Publishing name and logo is a trademark of Hachette Book Group USA, Inc.

Printed in the United States of America

Originally published in hardcover by Hachette Book Group USA
First mass market edition: February 1996, September 1998
First compilation edition: January 2007

12 11 10 9 8 7 6 5 4

The Rules: Book I _____

Contents

The Rules: Book II _____

Contents

The Rules

Book I

To our wonderful husbands
and great kids
Special thanks to our agent,
Connie Clausen

Chapter I _____

The History of *The Rules*

No ONE SEEMS to remember exactly how *The Rules* got started, but we think they began circa 1917 with Melanie's grandmother, who made men wait nervously in her parents' parlor in a small suburb of Michigan. Back then, they called it "playing hard to get." Whatever you call it, she had more marriage proposals than shoes. Grandma passed on her know-how to Melanie's mother, who passed it on to Melanie. It had been a family treasure for nearly a century. But when Melanie got married in 1981, she freely offered this old-fashioned advice to her single college friends and coworkers, like us.

At first, Melanie whispered *The Rules*. After all, modern women aren't to talk loudly about wanting to get married. We had grown up dreaming about being the president of the company, not the wife of the president. So, we quietly passed *The Rules* on from friend to friend, somewhat embarrassed because they seemed so, well, '50s. Still, we had to face it: as much as we loved being powerful in business, for most of us, that just wasn't enough. Like our mothers and grandmothers before us, we also wanted husbands who would be our best friends. Deep inside, if the truth be told, we really wanted to get married—the romance, the gown, the flowers, the presents, the honeymoon—the whole package. We didn't want to give up our liberation, but neither did we want to come home to empty apartments. Who said we couldn't have it all?

If you think *The Rules* are crazy, don't worry, so did we. But after much heartache we came to believe that *The Rules* aren't immoral or outlandish, just a simple working set of behaviors and reactions that, when followed, invariably serve to make most women irresistible to desirable men. Why not admit it? We needed *The Rules*! Nineties women simply have not been schooled in the basics—*The Rules* of finding a husband or at least being very popular with men.

Soon, we got bolder and began to talk louder. These *Rules*—they worked! Although they were old-fashioned and unflinching, they were extremely effective!

At first, we were uncomfortable with some of the premises which seemed to fly in the face of everything we'd been taught about male-female relations; but—there was no getting around it—success talked. We swallowed some of our preconceived theories, followed *The Rules* faithfully, and watched as so many of us got married (along with being career women or whatever else we were).

There we were—a secret underground, sharing the magic, passing it on, doing what historically women have done for each other since the world began—networking for success. This time, though, the stakes were larger and the victories sweeter than any corporate deal. We're talking marriage here—real, lasting marriage, not just loveless mergers—the result of doing *The Rules*. The simple *Rules*. The How-to-Find-a-Swell-Husband *Rules*.

For years, we had been sharing them with the women we knew, both at home and at work. For years, women had been calling us to check up on points: "Did you say that you have to end the date first or he does? I forget."

Then one night, during a Chinese dinner in Manhattan with a few of our single friends, we heard Cindy mention something about these . . . er, *Rules* . . . that she'd heard about from a friend in California. We knew it! There could be no mistake. These were the same *Rules* one of us had followed in New York to find her wonderful husband. *The Rules* had crisscrossed the country, bouncing from woman to woman, from suburb to city, until here they came right back to us over egg rolls in Manhattan!

But—and here's the catch—Cindy got them wrong!

"*The Rule* says men have to end the date first so that they're in charge," said Cindy.

"No, no, no. WRONG. *The Rule* is *you* end the date first so that you leave him wanting you more," we explained.

It was then that we decided to write *The Rules* down so that there would be no mistakes.

What Are *The Rules*?

HOW MANY TIMES have you heard someone say, "She's nice, she's pretty, she's smart . . . why isn't she married?" Were they talking about you, perhaps? Ever wonder why women who are not so pretty or smart attract men almost effortlessly?

Frankly, many women we know find it easier to relocate to another state, switch careers, or run a marathon than get the right man to marry them! If this sounds like you, then you need *The Rules*!

What are *The Rules*? They are a simple way of acting around men that can help any woman win the heart of the man of her dreams. Sound too good to be true? We were skeptical at first, too. Read on!

The purpose of *The Rules* is to make Mr. Right obsessed with having you as his by making yourself seem unattainable. In plain language, we're talking about playing hard to get! Follow *The Rules*, and he will not just marry you, but feel crazy about you, forever! What we're promising you is "happily ever after." A marriage truly made in heaven.

If you follow *The Rules*, you can rest assured that your husband will treat you like a queen—even when he's angry with you. Why? Because he spent so much time trying to get you. You have become so precious to him that he doesn't take you for granted. On the contrary, he thinks of you constantly. He's your best friend, your Rock of Gibraltar during bad times. He's hurt if you *don't* share your problems with him. He is always there for you—when you start your new job, if you need surgery. He even likes to get involved in mundane things, such as picking out a new bedspread. He always wants to do things *together*.

When you do *The Rules*, you don't have to worry about him chasing other women, even your very attractive neighbor or his bosomy secretary. That's because when you do *The Rules*, he somehow thinks you're the sexiest woman alive! When you do *The Rules*, you don't have to worry about being abandoned, neglected, or ignored!

A woman we know who followed *The Rules* is now married to a wonderful man who doesn't try to get rid of her to go out with the guys. Instead, he becomes slightly jealous when she does her own thing. They are very good friends, too.

Men are different from women. Women who call men, ask them out, conveniently have two tickets to a show, or offer sex on the first date destroy male ambition and animal drive. Men are born to respond to challenge. Take away challenge and their interest wanes. That, in a nutshell, is the premise of *The Rules*. Sure, a man might marry you if you don't do *The Rules*, but we can't guarantee that yours will be a good marriage.

This is how it works: if men love challenge, we become challenging! But don't ask a man if he loves challenge. He may think or even say he doesn't. He may not even realize how he reacts. *Pay attention to what he does, not what he says.*

As you read this book, you may think that *The Rules* are too calculating and wonder, "How hard to get do I have to be? Am I never to cook him dinner or take him to a Broadway show? What if I just feel like talking to him? Can't I call? When may I reveal personal things about myself?"

The answer is: Read *The Rules*. Follow them completely (not à la carte) and you will be happy you did. How many of us know women who never quite trust their husbands and always feel slightly insecure? They may even see therapists to talk about why their husbands don't pay attention to them. *The Rules* will save you about $125 an hour in therapy bills.

Of course, it's easy to do *The Rules* with men you're not that interested in. Naturally, you don't call them, instantly return their calls, or send them love letters. Sometimes your indifference makes them so crazy about you that you end up marrying one of them. That's because you did *The Rules* (without even thinking about it) and he proposed!

But settling for less is not what this book is about. The idea is to do *The Rules* with the man you're *really* crazy about. This will require effort, patience, and self-restraint. But isn't it worth it? Why should you compromise and marry someone who loves you but whom you're not crazy about? We know many women who face this dilemma. But don't worry—this book will help you marry only Mr. Right!

Your job now is to treat the man you are really, really crazy about like the man you're not that interested in—don't call, be busy sometimes! Do all of this from the beginning—from day one! Do it from the second you meet him—or should we say, the second he meets you! The better you do *The Rules* from the beginning, the harder he will fall for you.

Keep thinking, "How would I behave if I weren't that interested in him?" And then behave that way. Would you offer endless encouragement to someone you didn't really like? Would you stay on the phone with him for hours? Of course not!

Don't worry that busyness and lack of interest will drive him away. The men you don't like keep calling after you've turned them down, don't they?

Remember, *The Rules* are not about getting just any man to adore you and propose; they're about getting the man of your dreams to marry you! It's an old-fashioned formula, but it really works!

We understand why modern, career-oriented women have sometimes scoffed at our suggestions. They've been MBA-trained to "make things happen" and to take charge of their careers. However, a relationship with a man is different from a job. In a relationship, the man must take charge. He must propose. We are not making this up—biologically, he's the aggressor.

Some women complain that *The Rules* prevent them from being themselves or having fun. "Why should dating be work?" some ask. But when they end up alone on Saturday night because they did not follow *The Rules*, they always come back to us saying, "Okay, okay, tell me what to do."

Doing what you want to do is not always in your best interest. On a job interview, you don't act "like yourself." You don't eat cake if you're serious about losing weight. Similarly, it is not wise to let it all hang out and break *The Rules* as soon as you begin dating a man.

In the long run, it's not fun to break *The Rules*! You could easily end up alone. Think long term. Imagine a husband you love, beautiful sex, children, companionship, and growing old with someone who thinks you're a great catch.

Think about never having to be alone on Saturday nights or having to ask your married friends to fix you up. Think about being a couple! Unfortunately, however, you must experience some delayed gratification in the first few months of the relationship to achieve this marital bliss. But has wearing your heart on your sleeve ever gotten you anywhere?

There are many books and theories on this subject. All make wonderful promises, but *The Rules* actually produce results. It's easy to know what's going on when you do *The Rules*. It's very simple. If he calls you, pursues you, asks you out, it's *The Rules*. If you have to make excuses for his behavior—for example, he didn't call after the first date because he's still hung up on his ex-girlfriend—and you have to think about every word he said until your head hurts and you call him, it's not *The Rules*. Forget what he's going through—for example, "fear of commitment" or "not ready for a relationship." Remember, we don't play therapist when we do *The Rules*. If he calls and asks you out, it's *The Rules*. Anything else is conversation.

Chapter III

Meet a *Rules* Girl

IF YOU HAD EVER met Melanie, you wouldn't have thought she was extraordinarily pretty or smart or special, but you might have noticed that she had a way of behaving around men that put prom queens to shame. Melanie did the best with what she had: she wore makeup and clothes well, and acted elusive. Unlike other, prettier girls who ran after men or made themselves available every time a man called, Melanie acted indifferent—sometimes aloof, sometimes nice, but always *happy and busy*. She didn't return their calls, didn't stare at them (a dead giveaway of interest, see *Rule #3*), and always ended phone conversations first. "I've got a million things to do" was her favorite closing line. Melanie's boyfriend eventually proposed to the one girl he thought he would never get—her!

Who hasn't met a Melanie? Haven't we all known women who seemed to be experts around men? Men don't appear to unnerve these women or trip them up. They have a certain self-confidence around men that has nothing to do with their looks or their jobs. Melanies simply feel *good* about themselves—they can take or leave men—which makes men have to have them. Call it reverse psychology or whatever you want, but Melanies always get their man.

When you meet a Melanie, especially a plain and simple Melanie, you want to go up to her and ask, "What is it, what are you doing that make men run after you? What's your secret? What am *I* doing wrong?" A genuine Melanie would probably say without too much thought, "Oh, it's really nothing." The born-again Melanies—former *Rules* breakers who have learned their lesson after being burned by chasing men—would probably say, "Yes, there is a secret. Men love a challenge. Don't talk to them first, be busy sometimes, turn them down once in a while (nicely!)."

You will find Melanies everywhere you go. Watch them carefully. Observe how they have made self-contentment and independence an art form. They don't look wildly around to catch men's eyes. They don't say hello first. They just go about their business.

It would probably be good practice the next time you are at a social event to stand back and watch the Melanies and *The Rules* breakers. Compare how the two types of women behave around men and notice the results. Notice how the Melanies intentionally don't carry a pen with them in order to give men their phone numbers and they don't rush to give their business cards. Notice the way they move around the room while

The Rules breakers stand too long in one place, look anxious, or talk too long to one man. They make it too easy for men to ask them out—and, as you will read in this book, that's a big mistake.

One day, after years of watching girls like Melanie snag the men of our dreams, we asked Melanie how she got such a great catch. She took pity on us and told us about *The Rules*. She said that we were nice but we talked too much and were overly eager, and that we mistakenly tried to be "friends" with men rather than elusive butterflies, or, as she put it, "creatures unlike any other" (see *Rule #1*).

Needless to say, we were offended by what seemed to us to be downright trickery and manipulation. *The Rules* would send women back twenty-five years. What would the feminists say? On the other hand, Melanie had what we wanted: the husband of her dreams who adored her. It made sense to rethink our offended psyches!

Melanie assured us that plain-looking women who followed *The Rules* stood a better chance of being happily married than gorgeous women who didn't. Thinking back on our own dating history it did appear that the men we really wanted didn't necessarily want us. We'd be ourselves, friendly and supportive, and they thought we were great—but it ended right there. And, come to think of it, the ones we didn't particularly care for, the ones we didn't notice, maybe even snubbed, were the ones who didn't stop calling, the ones who were crazy about us. There was a message here somewhere: treat the men we *wanted* like the men we *didn't* want.

Simple, but not easy. But what did we have to lose? We wanted what Melanie had. So we did what she did, and—it worked!

Chapter IV

But First the Product—You!

BEFORE *THE RULES* can be applied for the best, most unbelievable results—the man of your dreams asking you to marry him—you have to be the best you can be. Certainly not perfect or gorgeous, but the best you can be, so . . .

Look your best! The better you look, the better you will feel, and the more desirable you will become to him. Maybe other men will start finding you more attractive and asking you out. You will no longer feel that the man you're currently dating is the only man on earth. You'll be less anxious and more confident. And when you look and feel good, you're less likely to break *The Rules*.

We are not nutritionists, but we do know that eating right—protein, fruits, and vegetables— makes you feel good. And that exercise releases endorphins which make you feel happier and more energetic. So, in addition to a healthy diet, we strongly suggest that you shake your buns! Join a gym, buy an exercise video, or go jogging in a nearby park (also a great place to meet men who are jogging or walking their dogs). Make exercise exciting by playing music while you do sit-ups.

Diet and exercise and *The Rules* have a lot in common. Both require putting long-term goals before short-term gratification. You will have to experience a certain amount of discomfort when you can't eat a cookie and you can't call a man. But you want to be fit and you want to get married, so you do what you have to do. Make friends with a woman in the same predicament and jog together, go to dances together, and reprimand each other when either of you is tempted to break *The Rules*. You don't have to do all this hard work alone!

If you are serious about finding a husband, then you must change your definition of gratification. Gratification is a man calling you, pursuing you, and asking you to marry him. Gratification is *not* a hot fudge sundae or a hot date where you break *The Rules*!

Self-improvement will help you catch and keep a man. So try to change bad habits like slovenliness if you expect to live with a man. Men like women who are neat and clean. They also make better mothers of their children—the kind who don't lose their kids at the beach.

Now a word about clothes. If you walk around in any old clothes on the theory that what counts is only what's inside, not your outside, think again! Men like women who wear fashionable, sexy clothes in bright colors. Why not please them?

If you don't know a lot about clothes, read fashion magazines like *Cosmopolitan*, *Vogue*, *Glamour*, and *Mirabella* and books on the subject; consult a friend whose taste you admire; or enlist the help of a personal shopper at a department store. Trying on clothes by yourself in a dressing room can be overwhelming and confusing—not to mention painful if you are out of shape—so it's always good to get a second opinion. Why not a professional one? Personal shoppers can help you find clothes that look good on you and that hide your flaws, as opposed to clothes that are perhaps trendy but not flattering.

Always remember when you are shopping that you are unique, a creature unlike any other, a woman. Don't aspire to the unisex look. Buy feminine-looking clothes to wear on the weekends as well as during the work week. Remember that you're dressing for men, not other women, so always strive to look feminine.

While it's good to keep up with the times, don't be a fashion slave. Don't spend a month's salary say, on bell bottoms and clogs just because they happen to be in vogue this year. First of all, they may not be around next season, and, more importantly, you may not look good in them! We know women who have gone overboard with one look—be it man-tailored suits or oversized crocheted sweaters—and ended up looking overdressed, trendy, and not at all sexy. Be a smart shopper, not a runaway spendor! Buy a few good classics and mix them with cheaper items.

Keep in mind that just because something is in

vogue doesn't mean that it will look good on you or appeal to men. Men don't necessarily care for the "waif" look or like it when women wear long granny dresses and combat boots, however popular the look may be. They like women in feminine clothes. Wear a short skirt (but not too short), if you have the legs for it.

Also, don't feel that you have to wear designer clothes to attract men. Men don't care whose label you're wearing, just how your clothes look and fit on you. It's better to buy a no-name brand that looks stunning and hides your hips than a designer outfit that doesn't.

While you're shopping in a department store, stop by a cosmetics counter and treat yourself to a makeover. We can all look better than we do. Many of us don't realize our potential until we get a makeover, which, by the way, is often given for free with a minimal purchase. Pay attention to which colors are good for you and how the makeup artist applies them. Buy whatever he or she suggests that you can afford and go home and practice putting it on. Don't leave the house without wearing makeup. Put lipstick on even when you go jogging!

Do everything you possibly can to put your best face forward. If you have a bad nose, get a nose job; color gray hair; grow your hair long. Men prefer long hair, something to play with and caress. It doesn't matter what your hairdresser and friends think. You're certainly not trying to attract them! Let's face it, hairdressers are notorious for pushing exciting, short haircuts on their clients; trimming long hair is not fun for them. It doesn't matter that short hair is easier to wash and dry or that your hair is very thin. The point is, we're girls! We don't want to look like boys.

It will be easier to feel like a creature unlike any other if you follow good grooming. Manicures, pedicures, periodic facials, and massages should become part of your routine. And don't forget to spray on an intoxicating perfume when you go out—just don't overdo it.

Now that you look the part, you must act the part. Men like women. Don't act like a man, even if you are head of your own company. Let him open the door. Be feminine. Don't tell sarcastic jokes. Don't be a loud, knee-slapping, hysterically funny girl. This is okay when you're alone with your girlfriends. But when you're with a man you like, be quiet and mysterious, act ladylike, cross your legs and smile. Don't talk so much. Wear black sheer pantyhose and hike up your skirt to entice the opposite sex! You might feel offended by these suggestions and argue that this will suppress your intelligence or vivacious personality. You may feel that you won't be able to be yourself, but men will love it!

In addition, don't sound cynical or depressed and tell long-winded stories of all the people who have hurt you or let you down. Don't make your prospective husband a savior or a therapist. On the contrary, act as if you were born happy. Don't tell everything about yourself. Say thank you and please. Practice this ladylike behavior with waiters, doormen, and even cab drivers who take the long way to your destination. This will make it easier to be ladylike on dates.

If you never meet men accidentally, go to everything—dances, tennis parties (even if you don't play tennis), Club Med. Just go, go, go—show up! Put a personal ad in a magazine, answer ads, ask people to set you up. Don't shy away from singles events with the rationalization that "The men who go there aren't my type." Remember, you are not trying to find large groups of men who are your type, just one! Don't lose sight of this concept. It will keep you going on those bad days when you are convinced that true love is just never going to happen to you!

Last but not least, trust this process. You may not meet your husband immediately after you have gotten in shape, bought some terrific outfits, and practiced *The Rules* on three eligible men. It may not be your time. But it is our experience that if you continue to do *The Rules* at every opportunity and pray for patience, you will eventually meet and marry the man of your dreams.

Be a "Creature Unlike Any Other"

BEING A CREATURE unlike any other is a state of mind. You don't have to be rich, beautiful, or exceptionally smart to feel this way about yourself. And you don't have to be born with this feeling either. It can be learned, practiced, and mastered, like all the other rules in this book.

Being a creature unlike any other is really an attitude, a sense of confidence and radiance that permeates your being from head to toe. It's the way you smile (you light up the room), pause in between sentences (you don't babble on and on out of nervousness), listen (attentively), look (demurely, never stare), breathe (slowly), stand (straight), and walk (briskly, with your shoulders back).

It doesn't matter if you're not a beauty queen, that you never finished college, or that you don't keep up with current events. You still think you're enough! You have more confidence than women with MBAs or money in the bank. You don't grovel. You're not desperate or anxious. You don't date men who don't want you. You trust in the abundance and goodness of the universe: if not him, someone better, you say. You don't settle. You don't chase anyone. You don't use sex to make men love you. You believe in love and marriage. You're not cynical. You don't go to pieces when a relationship doesn't work out. Instead, you get a manicure and go out on another date or to a singles dance. You're an optimist. You brush away a tear so that it doesn't smudge your makeup and you move on! Of course, that is not how you really *feel*. This is how you *pretend* you feel until it feels real. *You act as if!*

On a date, you never show that getting married is foremost on your mind. You're cool. He may think you've turned down several marriage proposals. You sip—never slurp—your drink and let him find out all about you, instead of the other way around. Your answers are short, light, and flirtatious. Your gestures are soft and feminine. When your hair falls in front of your face, you tilt your head back and comb back your hair with your hand from the top of your head in a slow, sweeping motion.

All your movements—the way you excuse yourself to use the ladies' room or look at your watch to end the date—are fluid and sexy, not jerky or self-conscious. You've been on many dates before; you're a pro. That's because you take care of yourself. You didn't lie in bed depressed, eating cookies before the date. You took a bubble bath, read this book, and built up your soul with positive slogans like, "I'm a beautiful woman. I am enough." You told yourself that you don't have to do anything more on the date than show up. He'll either love you or not. It's not your fault if he doesn't call again. You're beautiful, inside and out. Someone else will love you if he doesn't. All that matters is that you end the date first (see *Rule #11*).

When you go to singles dances or parties, you pump yourself up. You pretend you're a movie star. You hold your head high and walk in as if you just flew in from Paris on the Concorde. You're only in town for one night and if some lucky hunk doesn't swoop down and grab you it'll be his loss!

You get a drink, a Perrier perhaps, even if you're not thirsty. It keeps your hands busy so you don't bite your nails or twirl your hair out of nervousness. You don't show that you're nervous, even if you are. That's the secret: you act as if everything's great, even if you're on the verge of flunking college or getting fired. You walk briskly, as if you know where you're going, which is just around the room. You keep moving. You don't stand in a corner waiting for anyone. They have to catch you in motion.

If you think you aren't pretty, if you think other girls are better dressed or thinner or cooler, you keep it to yourself. You tell yourself, "Any man would be lucky to have me," until it sinks in and you start to believe it. If a man approaches you, you smile and answer his questions very nicely without saying too much. You're demure, a bit mysterious. You leave him hungry for more, as opposed to bored. After a few minutes you say, "I think I'll walk around now."

Most women hang around men all night waiting to be asked to dance. But you do *The Rules*. If he wants to be with you or get your phone number, he'll search the crowded room until he finds you. You don't offer him *your* pen or business card. You don't make it easy for him. Don't even carry them with you or you may be tempted to "help him out." The reason is that *he* has to do all the work. As he scrambles around begging the coat-check girl for a pen, you stand by quietly. You think to yourself, "*The Rules* have begun!"

It's that simple. You do *The Rules* and trust that one day a prince will notice that you're different from all other women he's known, and ask for your hand!

Rule #2

Don't Talk to a Man First (and Don't Ask Him to Dance)

NEVER? NOT EVEN "Let's have coffee" or "Do you come here often?" Right, not even these seemingly harmless openers. Otherwise, how will you know if he spotted you first, was smitten by you and had to have you, or is just being polite?

We know what you're thinking. We know how extreme such a rule must sound, not to mention snobbish, silly, and painful; but taken in the context of *The Rules*, it makes perfect sense. After all, the premise of *The Rules* is that we never make anything happen, that we trust in the natural order of things—namely, that man pursues woman.

By talking to a man first, we interfere with whatever was supposed to happen or not happen, perhaps causing a conversation or a date to occur that was never meant to be and inevitably getting hurt in the process. Eventually, he'll talk to the girl he really wants and drop you.

Yet, we manage to rationalize this behavior by telling ourselves, "He's shy" or "I'm just being friendly." Are men really shy? We might as well tackle this question right now. Perhaps a therapist would say so, but we believe that most men are not shy, just not *really, really* interested if they don't approach you. It's hard to accept that, we know. It's also hard waiting for the right one—the one who talks to you first, calls, and basically does most of the work in the beginning of the relationship because he must have you.

It's easy to rationalize women's aggressive behavior in this day and age. Unlike years ago when women met men at dances and "coming out" parties and simply waited for one to pick them out of the crowd and start a conversation, today many women are accountants, doctors, lawyers, dentists, and in management positions. They work with men, for men, and men work for them. Men are their patients and their clients. How can a woman not talk to a man first?

The Rules answer is to treat men you are interested in like any other client or patient or coworker, as hard as that may be. Let's face it, when a woman meets a man she really likes, a lightbulb goes on in her head and she sometimes, without realizing it, relaxes, laughs, and spends more time with him than is necessary. She may suggest lunch to discuss something that could be discussed over the phone because she is hoping to ignite some romance. This is a common ploy. Some of the smartest women try to make things happen under the guise of business. They think they are too educated or talented to be passive, play games, or do *The Rules*. They feel their diplomas and paychecks entitle them to do more in life than wait for the phone to ring. These women, we assure you, always end up heartbroken when their forwardness is rebuffed. But why shouldn't it be? Men know what they want. No one has to ask *them* to lunch.

So, the short of it is that if you meet men professionally, you still have to do *The Rules*. You must wait until he brings up lunch or anything else beyond business. As we explain in *Rule #17*, the man must take the lead. Even if you are making the same amount of money as a man you are interested in, he must bring up lunch. If you refuse to accept that men and women are different romantically, even though they may be equal professionally, you will behave like men—talk to them first, ask for their phone number, invite them to discuss the case over dinner at your place—and drive them away. Such forwardness is very risky; sometimes we have seen it work, most of the time it doesn't and it *always* puts the woman through hell emotionally. By not accepting the concept that the man must pursue the woman, women put themselves in jeopardy of being rejected or ignored, if not at the moment, then at some point in the future. We hope you never have to endure the following torture:

Our dentist friend Pam initiated a friendship with Robert when they met in dental school several years ago by asking him out to lunch. *She spoke to him first*. Although they later became lovers and even lived together, he never seemed really "in love" with her and her insecurity about the relationship never went away. Why would it? *She spoke to him first.* He recently broke up with her over something trivial. The truth is he never loved her. Had Pam followed *The Rules*, she would never have spoken to Robert or initiated anything in the first place. Had she followed *The Rules*, she might have met someone else who truly wanted her. She would not have wasted time. *Rules* girls don't waste time.

Here's another example of a smart woman who broke *The Rules*: Claudia, a confident Wall Street broker, spotted her future husband on the dance floor of a popular disco and planted herself next to him for a good five minutes. When he failed to make the first move, she told herself that he was probably shy or had two left feet and asked him to dance. The relationship has been filled with problems. She often complains that he's as "shy" in the bedroom as he was that night on the dance floor.

A word about dances. It's become quite popular these days for women to ask men to dance. Lest there is any doubt in your mind, this behavior is totally against *The Rules*. If a man doesn't bother to walk across the room to seek you out and ask you to dance, then he's obviously not interested and asking him to dance won't change his feelings or rather his lack of feelings for you. He'll probably be flattered that you asked and dance with you just to be polite and he might even want to have sex with you that night, but he won't be crazy about you. Either he didn't notice you or you made it too easy. He never got the chance to pursue you and this fact will always permeate the relationship even if he does ask you out.

We know what you're thinking: what am I supposed to do all night if no one asks me to dance? Unfortunately the answer is to go to the bathroom five times if you have to, reapply your lipstick, powder your nose, order more water from the bar, think happy thoughts; walk around the room in circles until someone notices you, make phone calls from the lobby to your married friends for encouragement—in short, anything but ask a man to dance. Dances are not necessarily fun for us. They may be fun for other women who just want to go out and have a good time. But you're looking for love and marriage so you can't always do what you feel like. You have to do *The Rules*. That means that even when you're bored or lonely, you don't ask men to dance. Don't even stand next to someone you like, hoping he'll ask you, as many women do. You have to *wait* for someone to notice you. You might have to go home without having met anyone you liked or even danced one dance. But tell yourself that at least you got to practice *The Rules* and there's always another dance. You walk out with a sense of accomplishment that at least you didn't break *The Rules*!

If this sounds boring, remember the alternative is worse. Our good friend Sally got so resentful of having to dance with all the "losers" at a particular party that she finally decided to defy *The Rules* she knew only too well and asked the best-looking man in the room to dance. Not only was he flattered, but they danced for hours and he asked her out for the next three nights. "Maybe there are exceptions to *The Rules*," she thought triumphantly. She found out otherwise, of course. It seems Mr. Right was in town for just a few days on business and had a girlfriend on the West Coast. No wonder he hadn't asked anyone to dance that night. He probably just went to the party to have fun, not to find his future wife. The moral of the story: don't figure out why someone hasn't asked you to dance—there's always a good reason.

Unfortunately, more women than men go to dances to meet "The One." Their eagerness and anxiety get the best of them and they end up talking to men first or asking them to dance. So you must condition yourself not to expect anything from a dance. View it simply as an excuse to put on high heels, apply a new shade of blush, and be around a lot of people. Chances are someone of the opposite sex will start to talk to *you* at some point in the evening. If and when he does, and you're not having such a great time, don't show it. For example, don't be clever or cynical and say, "I would have been better off staying home and watching *Seinfeld*." Men aren't interested in women who are witty in a negative way. If someone asks if you're having a good time, simply say yes and smile.

If you find all of this much too hard to do, then

don't go to the dance. Stay home, do sit-ups, watch *Seinfeld*, and reread *The Rules*. It's better to stay home and read *The Rules* than go out and break them.

Rule #3

Don't Stare at Men or Talk Too Much

LOOKING AT SOMEONE first is a dead give-away of interest. Let him look at *you!* If he doesn't notice you first, he's probably not interested. Keep walking, someone else will notice you.

Did you know that there are workshops designed to teach women how to make eye contact with men they find attractive? Save your money. It is never necessary to make eye contact. What about letting men know you're receptive? We suggest simply smiling at the room (or the universe, if you will) and looking relaxed and approachable. That's how to acknowledge a man's attention, not by staring at him. Don't look anxiously around for "The One." That is certain to make anyone look the other way. There is nothing attractive about anxiety.

On the first date, avoid staring romantically into his eyes. Otherwise, he will know that you're planning the honeymoon. Instead, look down at the table or your food, or simply survey the crowd at the restaurant. It's best to seem generally interested in life, in others, in your surroundings, in the paintings on the wall, as opposed to this live prey. He will feel crowded and self-conscious if you gaze at him too much. Restrain yourself. Let him spend the evening trying to get *your* attention.

One of the hardest aspects of dating is figuring out what to say. Do you talk about the weather or politics? Should you be intellectual or girlish? If you're smart, you'll stay cool and just listen to what he says. Follow his lead. If he wants to talk about dance clubs, tell him which ones you've been to and which ones you like. We're not suggesting that you be an airhead. On the contrary! It's just that you're easy to be with. When appropriate, show him that you keep up with current events and have interests.

Early dating is *not* the time to tell him about your job problems. In general, don't be too heavy. But don't be funny if he's serious. Just go with the flow.

Needless to say, there will be moments on a date when neither of you has anything to say. Don't feel the need to fill in these silences. You'll end up saying something stupid and forced. Sometimes men just want to drive in silence without saying a word. Let them. Maybe he's thinking about how he's going to propose to you one day. Don't ruin his concentration.

Don't feel you have to be entertaining or have interesting conversation all the time. He will think you are trying too hard. Just be there! Remember, men fall in love with your essence, not with anything in particular you say.

If anything, men should be the ones scrambling their brains to come up with clever lines, asking you a lot of questions, and wondering whether or not they're keeping you interested. Besides, most men find chatty women annoying. We know one man who stopped calling a woman he was physically attracted to because she simply didn't stop talking. Don't be like that. As a woman, you probably like to talk, *especially* about the relationship, but you must hold your tongue. Wait until the date is over and then you can call ten girlfriends and analyze the date for hours.

On the date itself, be quiet and reserved. He'll wonder what you're thinking, if you like him, and if he's making a good impression. He'll think you're interesting and mysterious, unlike many of the women he's dated. Don't you want him to think about you like that?

Don't Meet Him Halfway or Go Dutch on a Date

MEN LOVE A challenge—that's why they play sports, fight wars, and raid corporations. The worst thing you can do is make it easy for them. When a man is trying to set up a date to meet you, don't say, "Actually, I'm going to be in your area anyway"; don't offer the names of restaurants between your place and his, unless he asks. Don't say much at all. Let him do all the thinking, the talking, let him flip through the Yellow Pages or magazine listings and call a couple of friends for suggestions to come up with a place convenient for you. Men really feel good when they work hard to see you. Don't take that away from them.

The Rule is that men are supposed to rearrange their schedules around you, pursue you, take cabs and trains to see you. For example, on their second date, Charles drove forty miles out of his way to see Darlene because she was spending the weekend at her mother's. Most girls would have left their moms in the lurch so that their date wouldn't have to be inconvenienced. But Darlene was schooled in *The Rules* and knew the right thing to do. The extra miles only made Charles more determined to see her.

Friends and colleagues meet halfway. Men (real men) pick up women at their apartments or offices for dates. Always make the place convenient for you. We don't care where you live.

Invariably, we find that men who insist that their dates meet them halfway or (worse) on their own turf, turn out to be turds—inconsiderate, uncompromising, and even miserly. Jane recalls that after cabbing from Greenwich Village to Brooklyn Heights to meet Steve (a blind date) at his favorite brunch place, he suggested they split the check.

Jane, a truly nice person, agreed that it was only fair to pay her share. After all, she made a considerable amount of money as a lawyer and felt it would be "unfair" for Steve to "absorb" the entire cost of the date. Why should he have to pick up the whole tab? That was very nice of Jane, but we assure you that had she insisted that they meet at a place near her, perhaps just for a drink (especially if she didn't feel right spending his money), Steve would have treated her like a princess, not a coworker. But since Jane made everything so easy for him, he didn't treat her well, lost interest, and eventually stopped calling.

It's not that women aren't capable of taking subways and paying for themselves. It's just chivalrous, hence *The Rules,* for men to pick up their dates and pick up the checks. Equality and dutch treat are fine in the workplace, but not in the romantic playing field. Love is *easy* when the man pursues the woman and pays for the woman most of the time. He feels that the money he spends on the food, the movie, and the cabs is the price of being with you and it's worth every penny. You should feel honored, happy, not guilty.

But if part of you feels uncomfortable about him paying for everything, offer to leave the tip or, if the night is a long one—say, dinner, a show, and three cab rides or parking—pay for something small along the way. But don't pay for anything on the first three dates. Later on, you can reciprocate in your own way: cook him dinner at your place or buy him a baseball cap. If he's on a tight budget or is a student and you're worried about him spending tuition money, still don't split the check. Instead, suggest inexpensive places to eat and have a hamburger. Don't order appetizers or more than one drink. There's always pizza or Chinese food. Suggest movies, museums, and cheap outdoor concerts, not Broadway plays.

It's nice of you to care about his finances, but remember that he is deriving great pleasure from taking you out. Why deprive him of the joy of feeling chivalrous? Actually, the best way you can repay him is by being appreciative. Say thank you and please. Don't criticize the place or the food or the service, even if they are plain awful. Be positive. Look for the good in everything. We know one man who became even more enamored of a girl on their second date because she didn't complain one word when he couldn't remember where he parked at a football game. For the whole hour during which they pounded the pavement looking for his car, he kept thinking, "What a great girl!"

Many things can go wrong on a date, especially when a guy is so eager to impress you that he ends up making more mistakes—locking his keys in the car, forgetting the theater tickets, and so on. Never use these blunders to make him feel bad. Instead, see all the effort and expense he is putting into the date. Being a good sport could make the difference between being just another date and his future wife.

Don't Call Him and Rarely Return His Calls

IF YOU ARE following *The Rules* religiously, there is no reason to call him. He should be calling you, and calling you again and again until he pins you down for a date.

To call men is to pursue them, which is totally against *The Rules*. They will immediately know that you like them and possibly lose interest! Another reason not to call men is so you don't catch them in the middle of something—watching a football game, paying bills, entertaining a friend, or even sleeping—when they may not be in the mood to talk to you. Why take a chance?

Invariably, when *you* call him, he will get off the phone first or quickly and you might misinterpret his busyness as disinterest. *You* may even think that he's with another woman! Understandably, you feel empty and nervous for the rest of the day or evening or until you hear from him again. This nervousness might make you call him *again* to ask, "Is everything okay?" or "Do you still love me? miss me?" And, you end up breaking more rules!

So, if you don't want a man to know how much you like him, or that you feel empty and insecure, don't call him. If he leaves a message on your machine to return his call, try not to. Only call him back right away if it's a scheduling change regarding an upcoming date or event, not just to chat.

Not calling will leave him desiring you more, make him want to see you again and call you again. It prevents him from getting to know all about you much too quickly and getting bored. Besides, when you call only once in a while, it becomes special.

Don't worry about seeming rude. When he loves you or wants to get in touch with you badly, he won't think you're rude, just busy or hard to get—and men always call again.

Have you ever noticed that the conversation is always better when men call you? That's because when they call you, they're doing the dialing, they want you, miss you at that moment, and can't wait to hear your voice. When they call you, they're the aggressor, they've thought about what they're going to say and have made the time to say it. They're available!

The Rules work for you when they call you because you may not be home and they'll wonder where you are or have to call again. When they call you, you might be busy and have to nicely cut the conversation short. It will be easier to do *Rule*

#6: *Always End Phone Calls First,* when you let them call you.

But none of us are saints and the reality is that we sometimes have to call men back. Not call them, mind you, just call them back. If, for whatever reason, you have to return a man's calls, try to wait. Don't call right back. When you do, keep the conversation short and sweet. Don't tell his machine what time and what nights you can be reached or volunteer any additional information about how he can reach you. That would be making it too easy for him and you will appear too eager. Let him figure it out! Remember, you're a *Rules* girl and you're very busy! A *Rules* girl typically comes home to many messages on her answering machine from men trying to fill up her weekends.

Now what if he leaves a message on your machine on Tuesday night and you're dying to get a Saturday night date out of him? Do you call back Tuesday night? *The Rules* answer is no because it will seem obvious that you are probably calling to get a Saturday night date. Better that *he* call *you* again by Wednesday night (the absolute cutoff) for a Saturday night date. Better not to have a date on Saturday night than to get in the habit of calling him. *The Rules* are not about getting a date, but a husband. Don't win the battle and lose the war.

Remember, *The Rules* are also about not getting hurt or dumped. We never want you to go through unnecessary pain. Life has enough pain without our adding man pain to it. We can't control cancer or drunk drivers, but we can restrain ourselves from dialing his number. If you call him and he doesn't return your call or doesn't ask you out, you'll be crushed. If you call him, he'll think you're not so elusive and he won't have to work so hard. If you call him, he won't get trained to ask you out at the end of each date. He has to learn that if he doesn't ask you out when he sees you, he might not reach you on the phone so soon and not see you for a week or two. It's not that you're *impossible* to get, you're just *hard* to get. Remember, you're very busy with activities and other dates and you make plans ahead of time. But don't reprimand him for not calling sooner by saying, "If you had called earlier . . ." Just say, "Really, I'd love to, but I can't." (He'll figure out he has to call sooner.)

If he's in love with you, he'll start calling Monday or Tuesday for Saturday night. If he doesn't love you, then he won't call you again and again until he pins you down.

However, don't be surprised if a man takes a week or two after the first date to call. He may have a lot of things going on, or he may be dating other women. He may be trying to fit you into his schedule but just isn't sure how to do it. Remember, he had a life before he met you! Don't flip out! Just get busy (so you don't think about him twenty-four hours a day). Give him space, wait for *him* to call.

Here's a good example of how to handle such a situation: Our friend Laura waited two and a half weeks after her first date with David to hear from him. David was newly divorced and needed time to think before jumping into another relationship. A *Rules* girl, Laura gave him time and space. Unlike most women, she didn't call to "see how he was doing" or with some other excuse like, "Didn't you say you needed the name of my financial planner?" Sure, Laura was hurt, but she made plans with friends and went on blind dates. She had a pragmatic attitude. She knew that if he liked her, he'd eventually call; if he didn't, it was his loss! *Next!* When David finally called she was nice and friendly. She didn't demand to know why he didn't call sooner and want to *talk* about it. They dated for ten months and are married now.

One last thought about the phone: sometimes we want to call a man we are dating not to speak to him, but just to hear his voice. We feel that we are simply going to die if we don't hear his sexy voice this minute! That's understandable. We suggest you call his home answering machine when he's at work. Hang up before the beep. It really works!

Rule #6 _____

Always End Phone Calls First

DON'T CALL MEN (see *Rule #5*), except to occasionally return their calls. When a man calls you, don't stay on the phone for more than ten minutes. Buy a timer if you have to. When the bell rings, you have to go! That way you seem busy and you won't give away too much about yourself or your plans (even if you don't have any plans). By ending the conversation first, you leave them wanting more. Good conversation enders are: "I have a million things to do," "Well, it's been really nice talking to you," "Actually, I'm kinda busy right now," and "My beeper's beeping, gotta run!" Remember to say these things in a very nice way.

Women love to talk. And one of their biggest faults is talking to men as if they were their girl-friends, therapists, or next-door neighbors. Remember, early on in a relationship, the man is the adversary (if he's someone you really like). He has the power to hurt you by never calling again, by treating you badly, or by being around but indifferent. While it's also true that you can reject him, the fact is that it's the man who notices you, asks you out, and ultimately proposes marriage. He runs the show. The best way to protect yourself from pain is to not get emotionally involved too quickly.

So don't stay on the phone for an hour or two recounting your feelings or every incident of the day. You'll become transparent very quickly and run the risk of making him tired or bored. He does not want to date his crazy younger sister, his chatterbox mother, or his gossipy next-door neighbor. He wants to talk to a girl who's friendly, light, and breezy. By getting off the phone first, you don't have to wonder if you've kept him on too long, bored him, or revealed too much about yourself. Because it can be very difficult to monitor the amount of time you spend on the phone when you are "in like" or in love, we again suggest using a timer or stopwatch. When the bell rings, you sweetly say, "I really have to go now." A timer is objective; you are not.

It doesn't matter if you're having a great conversation and you want to tell him all about what happened to you between the ages of five and six that shaped your life. When the bell rings, the conversation is over. Remember, you always want to be mysterious. Having to get off the phone first creates a certain amount of mystery in his mind. He'll wonder why you have to go so soon, what you're doing, and if you're dating someone else. It's good for him to wonder about you. *The Rules* (and a timer) will make him wonder about you a lot.

You may think that men will find your abruptly ending a phone call rude and won't call again. On the contrary, just the opposite often happens simply because men are irrational when it comes to love. For example, our friend Cindy set her timer to four minutes one evening. "Gotta go," she said at the sound of the bell. Five minutes later he called back to insist that they start seeing each other twice a week instead of once a week. The four-minute call worked like a charm, bringing him closer to her, not (as you would expect) farther away.

If you're a genuinely nice person, you will probably feel cruel when you do *The Rules*. You will think you are making men suffer, but in reality you are actually doing them a favor. By doing *The Rules*, you make men want to spend more time with you on the phone and in person. They get to experience longing! Tell yourself you are doing them a favor when you feel heartless about doing *The Rules*!

Another tip for driving a man to madness is to turn off your answering machine on a Sunday afternoon, and see if he doesn't go crazy trying to pin you down. When Cindy tried this tactic, her boyfriend ended up calling so many times that day that he activated her answering machine. (Some machines will automatically turn on after fourteen rings. Can you imagine him letting it ring fourteen times?!) When he finally got her on the phone that night, he possessively asked, "Where have you been? I wanted to take you for a drive in the country." It's good when men get upset; it means they care about you. If they're not angry, they're indifferent, and if they're indifferent, they've got one foot out the door. Getting off the phone after a few minutes is not easy, but it works.

Our friend Jody felt that she was "losing" Jeff, her boyfriend of three months, when after a Saturday night date he said good-bye very casually and told her, "I'll call ya. I'll let you know what's a good night for *me* next week." Jody felt the tables turning and took an extreme but necessary *Rules* action. She didn't answer her phone the night he usually called. She just listened to it ring and ring. When he finally reached her the next day at work, he was a little less cocky and somewhat nervous. He asked her what night would be good for *her*! The phone strategy worked—he never pulled another stunt like that again.

Here's another phone tip: if you're home on a Friday night because you're tired or don't have a date, leave the answering machine on or have your mom or roommate say you're not home. That way, if by some chance he calls you on a Friday night because he's not doing anything either, he'll think you're not home. The worst thing you can do is give him the impression that you aren't busy and sought after by other men. Don't let him think that you're a couch potato, even if you are. Don't think playing games is bad. Sometimes game playing is good. Men like to think that they are getting the prom queen. Show him that you have a full life, that you are independent.

On any other night when he calls and you pick

up the phone, don't feel you have to tell him exactly what you are doing. After a few minutes, just say you're busy (nicely) and can't talk anymore. You won't be lying because sometimes you *are* busy—doing the laundry; just don't tell him you're doing the laundry. Never let him think, even if it's true, that you are home thinking about him and making the wedding guest list. Men love the seemingly unattainable girl!

Lest you think this advice is old-fashioned, remind yourself that you are a very fulfilled person— stable, functional, and happy—with a career, friends, and hobbies, and that you are perfectly capable of living with or without him. You are not an empty vessel waiting for him to fill you up, support you, or give you a life. You are alive and enthusiastic, engaged in work and in living fully on your own. Men like women who are their own person, not needy leeches waiting to be rescued. *The Rules* are not about being rescued!

In fact, the biggest mistake a woman can make when she meets a man she wants to marry is to make him the center of her life. She may jeopardize her job by daydreaming at her desk about Prince Charming rather than rolling up her sleeves and working. All she thinks about and talks about is him. She bores her girlfriends to death with details about every date. She is constantly looking for ties to buy him or clipping newspaper articles that he would find interesting. Not only is such behavior unhealthy, but also it's the surest way to lose him.

First of all, he may be overwhelmed by all the

attention. Second, he may never propose. And third, he may never rescue you emotionally and financially in the way you think. Even if he marries you, he may always have that night out with the boys, his hobbies, or that Sunday morning basketball game. And he may want a working wife. So better get used to the idea now that you *must* have a life of your own—a job, interests, hobbies, friends that you can fill up on in between dates and even when you are married. The worst thing you can do when dating is to expect him to be your entertainment director. Don't call him just because you're bored or want attention. Be happy and busy. He should always be catching you coming or going.

We hear again and again about women whose worlds shrink when they meet Mr. Right. When you meet Mr. Right is precisely the time to take up tennis, get an MBA, or go on that camping trip with your friends.

Don't Accept a Saturday Night Date after Wednesday

IT'S QUITE COMMON these days for men to ask women out for the same night or the very next day. And it's equally common for women to accept such casual, last-minute invitations out of fear that it will be the best offer they get that week. But this is not a *Rules* date. The man who eventually wants to marry you will not wait until the last minute to ask you out. On the contrary, he is kind, considerate, thoughtful and also afraid that if he doesn't pin you down five days in advance, he may not see you for another week. And when he is in love with you, a week will feel like eternity!

Needless to say, men don't always know that they shouldn't be calling you on Thursday or Friday night for a Saturday night date. Other women have spoiled them by accepting last-minute offers. As we've stated, ideally he should ask you out at the end of your last date or call you as early as Monday or Tuesday for the next

Saturday night. *The Rules* will make you foremost on his mind, the first thing he thinks about in the morning. And if you are always on his mind, he won't want to wait until Thursday to call you.

It may be a telltale sign of how a man feels about you if he doesn't call you early in the week. The best way to encourage him to phone sooner is to turn him down when he calls on Thursday for Saturday night. Hopefully, he will get the hint. This is not a game. It is essential that men ask you out early in the week because, as a *Rules* woman, you simply can't put your life on hold until Thursday or Friday! You have friends and lots of things to do. You need to know ahead of time if you're going to have a date Saturday night or go to the movies with the girls. When men are calling you as late as Thursday, you become a nervous wreck. You're frenetically checking your answering machine, or if you live at home, you're constantly asking your mother if he called. Basically, you're living on the edge. *Rules* girls don't live on the edge. They have plans.

If he hasn't called by Wednesday night, make other plans for the weekend. Then you must politely decline if he calls Thursday and nonchalantly asks, "Hey, hon, what are you doing Saturday night?" Practice the following answer in the nicest voice possible: "Oh, I'm so sorry, but I've already made plans." Don't break down and go out with him even though you'd much rather do that than hang out with the girls or go out with another man you don't like as much. And don't counteroffer by saying, "But I'm free Monday." Men have to ask you out without your help. *But don't reprimand him for calling so late in the week*. Be very nice, but very firm when you say no. Also, don't say what your plans are because it doesn't matter. What matters is the message you're sending, which is: If you want to get a Saturday night date with me, you must call on Monday, Tuesday or Wednesday.

Now you may be saying to yourself, "This is all so rigid, lots of men make plans when the mood strikes them, what's wrong with spontaneity?" These arguments sound convincing, but the reality is not so pleasant. When Ted first called our friend Beth on a Thursday night for a Saturday night date, she said yes right away. That set a bad precedent for him calling her at the last minute for future dates. Although they went out for a few months, he never thought that much about her during the week and she felt confused by the relationship because she was never sure if she was going to see him Saturday night.

Remember, *The Rules* are about the long haul. The way a man behaves—rather, the way you *allow* him to behave toward you—during your courtship is usually the way he will behave during your marriage. For example, if he's last minute about dating you, he'll be last minute and inattentive about you in other ways. That's why last-minute dates are just unacceptable. Men who call ten minutes before they're going to be in your neighborhood to see you may be terrific dates, but how busy and hard to get are you if they can see you in ten minutes? If you give in, these men will end up treating you like someone they *can get* in ten minutes.

But remember to be very nice when you say no. Don't think negatively, "This man doesn't think much of me to call right before he wants to see me," or scream, "No, I'm busy," and slam down the phone. He isn't thinking that at all. He isn't thinking that he's not treating you like a creature unlike any other. Give him a break. *Rules* girls are an unusual breed. As we've suggested, nicely say, "No, wow, I wish I wasn't busy!" Then sigh and get off the phone. He will soon realize that you simply want to be asked in advance for a date. Again, men are not trying to hurt you when they call at the last minute. Don't be offended, just train them to call earlier without actually *demanding* it of them.

Spontaneity is not "Hi. Want to see a movie this afternoon?" That call might have come out of boredom or the fact that the woman he really wants to be with is busy. He didn't call you in advance, dream about you for a week, and get all excited about putting his arm around your shoulders during the movie. He didn't think of your date together as something precious that must be scheduled in advance like a reservation at a very exclusive restaurant. Spontaneity is fine, but it should happen *during* the date, such as an unexpected drive to the beach after dinner.

We often hear about "spontaneous" women who go out with men on twenty-four hours' notice. We wish them luck. When a man knows he can have you five minutes after his last girlfriend gave him the boot, he'll call you because he's lonely or bored, not because he's crazy about you. In such cases, buyer beware: it won't last. Free spirits might object to what we are saying, but for long-lasting results we believe in treating dating like a job, with rules and regulations. Just like you have to work from nine to five, no matter how you *feel*, we believe you have to silently train men to make plans with you (elusive, busy, happy you!) ahead of time. When you do *The Rules*, what you're really doing is giving men the secret, silent code that they understand very well. If you make it too easy for men, they're certain to take advantage and then you can forget about getting a *Rules* marriage.

We realize that the days in between dates with the man you are crazy about can be long and excruciating; but, remember, it's worse to say yes indiscriminately whenever he wants to see you and risk him getting bored. If you play your cards right, he will reach the conclusion that the only way to see you whenever he wants, at the last minute, is to marry you!

Fill Up Your Time before the Date

MOST WOMEN GO on dates with a lot of expectations. They want the man to find them beautiful, to ask them out again, and to father their children. Needless to say, these women are usually disappointed. That's why we have found it very helpful—in fact, essential—to be booked up as much as possible before the date. It's best to be busy right up until the doorbell rings so that you're slightly breathless and brimming with energy when you finally see him.

Here are some suggestions for what to do on the day of the date:

1. To relieve anxiety, go to the gym, get a manicure, or take a long hot bubble bath.
2. Buy a new shirt or a bottle of perfume. Get a makeover. Treat yourself.
3. Take a nap. If you're the type who gets drowsy at 10 P.M., a good nap will keep you going.

4. Go to the movies (see a comedy, not a romance, so love isn't too much on your mind), read the newspaper or a book to fill your head with something other than how your first name sounds with his last name. If you're busy all day, you won't be so needy and empty when he picks you up.

Here's what *not* to do:

1. Don't talk to your girlfriends all day long about the date, about how his astrological sign and yours go together, about how you know he's "The One," or about relationships in general. You really shouldn't be thinking about the date at all.
2. Don't see your mother, grandmother, or anyone who absolutely can't wait for you to get married and have children. Being around them might make you reek of desperation on the date. You might inadvertently mention the *M* word (marriage) and scare him away.
3. Don't write your name and his in all different combinations, such as:

> Susan Johnson
> Susan Dobbs Johnson
> Susan D. Johnson

Don't you have better things to do?

How to Act on Dates 1, 2, and 3

IF YOU ARE ANYTHING like us, you've thought a lot about how much the two of you have in common before he even arrives to pick you up. And you've named the children before he says hello. This type of seemingly innocuous day-dreaming before the date is dangerous, possibly the worst thing you can do short of professing love to him during dessert. This kind of fantasizing leads to unfulfilled longing and to unrealistic expectations of romance and passion that makes you prone to say foolish things like, "I have two tickets to a concert," after the first date. (Yes, you can reciprocate but much later—see *Rule #4*).

If at all possible, don't think of him before he arrives—it isn't necessary for the first three dates. Be busy right up until the minute he buzzes you from downstairs. (Don't have him come up to your apartment on the first date. Preferably, meet him in the lobby of your apartment building or at a restaurant. *Rules* girls play it safe.) On these three dates, don't tell him all about your day as if you've known each other for years, thinking that it will bring you closer. Don't be too serious, controlling, or wifey. Don't mention the M word, not even to mention that your brother recently got married.

Remember that you are a creature unlike any other, a beautiful woman, inside and out. So don't feel that you have to fit in a love seminar or last-minute therapy session to be in good form. You should feel no pressure whatsoever.

In fact, all you really have to do on the first three dates is show up, relax, pretend you're an actress making a cameo appearance in a movie. Reread *Rule #1: Be a "Creature Unlike Any Other."* Be sweet and light. Laugh at his jokes, but don't try too hard. Smile a lot, and don't feel obligated to fill up the lulls in the conversation. In general, let him do all the work—pick you up, pick the restaurant, open the door, and pull out your chair. Act nonchalantly at all times, as if you're always on dates and it's nothing out of the ordinary (even if you haven't had a date in years). If you have to think about something, think about your date with another man that week. You should always try to date other people so that you never get hung up on one man at any time.

End the date first (see *Rule #11*), especially if you like him. Glance at your watch after two hours (for a drink date) or three or four hours (for a dinner date), simply sigh, and say, "Gee, this was really great, but I've got a really big day tomorrow." Don't say what it is you're doing tomorrow. At the end of the first date, you can accept a light peck on the cheek or lips even though you're dying to do more.

Don't invite him up to your place at the end of the first date. After all, he's still a stranger at this point. He should only see the lobby of your apartment building. This is both for safety and *The Rules*. By not letting him into your apartment or agreeing to go to his, you drastically reduce your chances of any sort of problem occurring. If you meet someone at a bar or party, the same rule applies. Don't get into his car for any reason (or you might end up in his trunk!). Don't invite him to go to your apartment or go to his that night. It's a crazy world out there. Play it safe!

On the second date, use your judgment. If you feel comfortable with this man, he can pick you up at your apartment and you can invite him up for a drink at the end of the night. But when in doubt, meet him in the lobby of your building and say good night there as well. *Rules* girls don't take chances!

We know we're asking you to go against your feelings here, but you want to get married, don't you? Anyone can get a one-night stand. In summary, the first three dates should be like "being and nothingness." Dress nice, be nice, good-bye and go home. Not too much feeling, investment, or heart. You're probably wondering how long you can keep up this act, right? Don't worry, it gets easier!

Rule #10

How to Act on Dates 4 through Commitment Time

ON THE FIRST three dates, you showed up and acted sweet. On the fourth date, you can show more of yourself. You can talk about your feelings, as long as you don't get too heavy, or play therapist or mother. Exhibit warmth, charm, and heart. If his dog died or his baseball team lost, express sympathy. Look into his eyes, be attentive and a good listener so that he knows you are a caring human being—a person who would make a supportive wife. Still, don't mention words like *marriage, wedding, kids,* or *the future.* Those are subjects for *him* to bring up. He *must* take the lead. Talk about something outside your relationship, like your favorite sport, TV show, a great movie, the novel you just finished, an interesting article from Sunday's *New York Times*, or a good museum exhibition you just saw. You get the idea!

Don't tell him what your astrologist, nutritionist, personal trainer, shrink, or yoga instructor thinks about your relationship with him.

Don't tell him what a mess you were before you discovered seminars and gurus, as in, "My life was *such* a mess before The Forum (or est)."

Don't tell him he's the first man to treat you with respect. He'll think you're a loser or a tramp.

Don't give him the third degree about his past relationships. It's none of your business.

Don't say, "We've got to talk" in a serious tone, or he'll bolt from the bar stool.

Don't overwhelm him with your career triumphs. Try to let him shine.

Don't plague him with your neuroses!!

Remember, you won't have to keep such things to yourself forever. Just for the first few months . . . until he says he's in love with you. Eventually you will become more yourself. It's the first impressions from the first few months of dating that men remember forever.

If you find it hard to keep up this act, then end the date early or see less of him. Letting it all hang out too soon is counterproductive to your goals. Many women are conditioned in therapy to open up very soon. This is fine for therapy or with a girlfriend, but don't do this on a date. *The Rules* are about opening up slowly so that men aren't overwhelmed by us. It's rather selfish and inconsiderate to burden people with our whole lives on a three-hour date, don't you think? Remember, *The Rules* are innately unselfish.

But not so unselfish that you feel you have to answer any question you regard as too personal or none of his business just yet. Don't tell him anything that you will regret. Some men like to pry secrets out of women. Women sometimes reveal more than they really care to, hoping that their revelations will draw a man closer to them—but afterwards they feel naked, as well as tricked and cheated. Better to smile when asked a question that is too personal, and say, "Oh, I'd rather not talk about that right now."

Of course, personal matters may come up. Be careful how you answer his questions. If he asks you how long you are planning to live in your apartment, say you're renewing your lease. Don't say, for example, that you've been hoping to meet a man soon so that you can get a bigger apartment with him when your lease is up. Even if that is in fact your true hope and desire, don't say so or your date will run to the nearest exit.

Act independent so that he doesn't feel that you're expecting him to take care of you. That's as true on the first date as the fiftieth. Jill remembers that when she went bed shopping for herself with Bruce, her boyfriend of six months, she deliberately bought a single bed rather than a queen-size bed. It killed her to have to do this as she was hoping he was "The One" and knew if they were to get engaged and married she would have no use for the bed. But the fold-out couch she'd been sleeping on was broken. Rather than consulting Bruce on the bed purchase—asking him what kind of bed he liked and what size he liked, as if to suggest that this might be the bed they would be sharing one day—she bought the single bed as if she had no intention of getting married soon.

It was important not to let Bruce know that she was buying a bed with him in mind, when they weren't married and might never be. Of course, the single bed hasn't gone to waste: Jill's in-laws (Bruce's parents) now keep it as a spare in their guest room.

Always End the Date First

IF YOU HAVE NOT been living by *The Rules*, then you probably didn't know that the first date or two should last no more than five hours. A good way to end the date is to nonchalantly glance at your watch and say something like, "Gosh, I really must be going now. I have such a busy day tomorrow." (As we said before, don't say what you're doing. It doesn't matter and it's none of his business.)

Ending the date first is not so easy when you really like him and want to marry him, and you're both having a great time. But it must be done because you must leave him wanting more of you, not less. If he wants to know more about you as the date is ending, he can always call you the next day or ask you out again when he drops you off. It is our experience that men will want to see you a lot, sometimes every day in the beginning, and then grow very bored very quickly. So abide by *The Rules* and he'll stay smitten.

Not ending the date first is bad enough. What's *worse*, however, is prolonging the date once it should have been over. Randy felt that she was "losing" Bob at the end of their second date (dinner and movie), so she suggested that they go dancing. Bob didn't want to hurt her feelings so he said okay, then he never called again. Of course, Randy should have ended the date right after the movie, but she thought she could excite Bob with her great disco dancing.

Other women try to prolong a first or second date, for example, by inviting the man up to her apartment for a drink or coffee so that he'll fall in love with her decorating, or her home-brewed decaf. No! First of all, it should be *the man* trying to prolong the date, not you. He should be suggesting dancing, drinks, or a café where the two of you can get dessert and cappuccino. If he didn't suggest it, then it's not supposed to happen. Instead of worrying about making the date interesting or longer, just make sure you end it first.

Rule #12 _____

Stop Dating Him if He Doesn't Buy You a Romantic Gift for Your Birthday or Valentine's Day

WHAT KIND OF present can you expect to receive on your birthday when a man is in love with you? Ideally, jewelry, but any romantic gift will do. Now don't get us wrong. This is not a rule for gold diggers; it's just that when a man wants to marry you, he usually gives you jewelry, not sporty or practical gifts like a toaster oven or coffee maker. It is not how expensive the item is, but the *type* of gift it is. A typewriter can cost more than an inexpensive pair of earrings, and a computer, one would think, connotes love, being such a costly item; but such presents come from the head, not the heart, and are not good signs of love at all. Therefore, *The Rule* is that if you don't get jewelry or some other romantic gift on your birthday or other significant occasion, you might as well call it quits because he's not in love with you and chances are you won't get the most important gift of all: an engagement ring.

No one knows this rule better than Susan, who received a Sergio Tacchini sweat suit for Valentine's Day from Brian, her boyfriend of three months. When we told her the romance was over, she argued that the suit costs almost two hundred dollars and is very cool at the better country clubs. But we knew that Susan would have been better off with candy or flowers. Why? Because even though Brian's gift was expensive, it was not romantic. When men are in love, they give love objects even if they are on a tight budget. Flowers, jewelry, poetry, and weekend trips to the country are the kinds of gifts given by men in love. Sweat suits, books, briefcases, toasters, and other practical gifts are the kinds of things men give when they like you, care about you (like a sister), but don't really want to marry you. (Sure enough, Brian dropped Susan a few months later.)

Remember, gift giving has nothing to do with money. We know a poor student who could only afford a $1.50 greeting card for his girlfriend on Valentine's Day. He then spent four hours writing a beautiful love poem to her in it. A *Rules* present if there ever was one! As most women know, the time a man spends on anything is virtually priceless.

One more point about greeting cards: check to see if he signs "love." A man may sometimes send a greeting card with very casual intentions. If he doesn't sign it "love," don't assume he does. When Bobby was dating Cheryl, he signed his cards, "Yours, Bobby." (I just *know* he loves me, she'd tell her friends.) They eventually had "a talk," and he told her he wasn't in love with her. So don't assume anything. Just read what's written!

Furthermore, while a romantic gift is a must for birthdays, Valentine's Day and anniversaries, a man who is crazy about you will give you all kinds of things all the time. You're always on his mind, so you might get a stuffed animal he sees at a street fair or something kooky that's just perfect for you. For example, when Patty expressed an interest in biking, her boyfriend Mike bought her a fancy helmet. If he didn't love her, he would have given her the helmet on her birthday, but being in love, be gave her a necklace and flowers on her birthday and the helmet to celebrate their six-month anniversary

When you do receive gifts, don't overreact. When Lori received roses from Kevin on their third date she was absolutely ecstatic. She rarely had gotten flowers from anyone she liked, but she did *The Rules* thing to do, she smiled, nonchalantly put them in a vase, and said, "Thank you!"

In general, *The Rule* is that when a man loves you he just wants to give you things. Anything. If your glass is empty in a restaurant, he wants to give you water or promptly asks the waiter to get it. If you can't see the screen in the movie theater, he asks five people to move over to give you another seat. If he sees you digging in your bag for a pen, he lends you his and then tells you to keep it. Basically, he notices everything about you, except anything bad. If you're ten pounds over-weight, he doesn't think you're overweight, he thinks you're cute. But if your girlfriend (whom he is not in love with) is the same size, he thinks *she's* fat. When a man is not in love with you, he notices nothing or only the bad. For example, he might say, "Lose weight and I'll take you on va-cation." You feel you have to earn his love. That's not *The Rules*, that's conditional love and not what we're after.

Again, this is not about being gold diggers or princesses wanting to be doted on all the time. It's about determining whether a man is truly in love with you and, if not, going on to the next. If you end up marrying a man who gives you a briefcase instead of a bracelet on your birthday, you may be doomed to a life of practical, loveless gifts and gestures from him such as food processors, and you may spend thousands of dollars in therapy trying to figure out why there's no romance in your marriage.

Rule #13

Don't See Him More than Once or Twice a Week

MOST MEN FALL in love faster than women. They also fall out of love faster. They may want to see you two or three times a week, some even every day, in the beginning. If you give in and see them every time, eventually they get restless and irritable, and then stop calling. They seem moody a lot and say things like, "I don't know what's wrong. I just have a lot going on right now."

To keep a man from getting too much too soon, don't see him more than once or twice a week for the first month or two. Let him think you have "other plans," that he is not the only man or interest in your life. When we hear someone say that she just met the greatest man and sees him every day, we think, "Uh oh, this isn't going to turn out so well." A woman *must* pace the relationship slowly. Don't expect a man to do it.

We know how painful this can be. It's only natural that when you meet a man you like who also likes you, you want to see him all the time. You want to know all about him—his favorite color, his past relationships, what he eats for breakfast, everything—almost overnight. So it's hard for you to say no when he asks you out for Saturday night, Sunday brunch, and a Monday night dinner and movie all in one breath. But, girls, you must put your foot down! Don't make seeing you so easy. Men like sports and games—football, tennis, blackjack, and poker—because they love a challenge. So be a challenge!

Remember, this *Rule* is not forever. After seeing him once a week for the first month, you can see him twice or three times a week during the second month, and three to four times a week in the third month. But never more than four or five times a week unless you're engaged. Men must be conditioned to feel that if they want to see you seven days a week they have to marry you. And until that blessed proposal occurs, you must practice saying no to extra dates even though you're dying to spend more time with him and even though you've mentally said to yourself, "This is The One."

If, for example, after kissing you passionately at the end of your first or second date he says, "So what are you doing tomorrow?," summon up your sweetest voice and say, "I'm sorry. I already have plans." Stick to your ground, even if you feel intoxicated by the smell of his cologne on your neck. And, of course, don't say what your plans are or include him in them.

A man who is in love with you and hopes to marry you won't be put off by the once-to-twice-a-week dating structure you set up in the beginning. We find that only men who are just with you for fun or sex are likely to get angry or impatient. Don't be fooled if these men say the kinds of things that make you believe they want to marry you. It happens all the time. It's called Standard Operating Procedure.

On the first date, such a man might point to a restaurant and say, "That's where my father proposed to my mother," leading you to think that he will propose to you there one day. Or he might talk about the future, saying something like, "In the summer we can go to Connecticut and I'll take you to this great seafood place." You are naturally in heaven, thinking that this man has plotted out your lives forever. It might all be true and he may call again and ask you out. But it might be a ploy to get you into bed on the first or second date.

If you fall for his lines and see him every night that week—after all, you think he is serious about you—he might take you out a couple of times and have sex with you. But he may never call again or worse, he may continue to date you, but you'll end up watching his interest fade away. (A very painful thing. Watching someone falling "out of love" is really awful!) If you follow *The Rules* and slow down the process, forcing him to get to know you and *really* fall in love, this will not happen.

The Rules will make you harder to get so that a man who doesn't really like you won't waste his or your time. So do yourself a favor and do *The Rules*. Don't see him more than once or twice a week!

No More than Casual Kissing on the First Date

IT'S COMMON KNOWLEDGE that men want as much as they can get on the first date. It's your job to slow them down. Let him kiss you on the first date, but nothing more. Keeping it to a kiss will force him not to think of you as just a physical object. If a *Rules* relationship is to develop, he must fall in love with your soul, your whole being, not just your body. So the less you do physically, the better. Besides, it's easier to stop something if you don't let things get too hot and heavy right away.

We know this is not an easy *Rule* to follow, particularly when you're out with someone really cute and he's driving fast in his sports car and kissing you at every red light. He's a great kisser and you wonder what else he's great at. This is when you have to brace yourself and say, "*The Rule* is no more than casual kissing on the first date. No, don't invite him up to the apartment. No, don't let his hands go everywhere." If you're getting too excited, end the date quickly so you don't do anything you'll regret. If he wants more of you, let him call you and ask you for a second date.

Some men might make you feel that you're being old-fashioned or prudish. Some might make fun of you or even get angry. Let them know as nicely as you can that if they don't like it, they can get lost! If a man pressures you, then he's not someone you want to date. Keep telling yourself that other women have spoiled men by sleeping with them on the first date, but you're a *Rules* girl and you take your time. If he really cares about you, he will respect your boundaries. If he's a gentleman, he'll let the physical part of the relationship develop at your pace and never force anything on you. Forget all the "free love" theories from the swinging sixties. Besides, it's not spontaneous or cool to have an unwanted pregnancy or a disease.

In addition, if you are following *Rule #9: (How to Act on Dates 1, 2, and 3)*, things should not get out of hand. As we said earlier, you should be talking about politics, real estate, good movies, not marriage, kids, love, former boyfriends and girlfriends, and sexual positions. The conversation should be cordial, not steamy, so you don't end up in bed after dessert. Besides, if you really like him, just kissing can be a lot of fun!

Don't Rush into Sex and Other *Rules* for Intimacy

WHEN IS IT OKAY to have sex? *The Rule* depends on your age and personal feelings. If you're eighteen and a virgin, you will want to wait until you are in a committed relationship. If you're thirty-nine, waiting a month or two can be fine. Of course, if you feel strongly against premarital sex, you should wait until you're married. If he loves you, he'll respect *whatever* decision you make.

But don't be surprised if the man you're dating gets very angry when you kiss him good night in the lobby at the end of your second date rather than invite him up to your apartment for a drink. He has probably been spoiled by other women who slept with him on the first or second date and now he feels he's being denied this pleasure. But don't worry. Anger indicates interest, and you might be surprised, for he will probably call you again!

But what if you like sex a lot too, and denying

yourself is just as hard as denying him? Does that mean you can sleep with him on the first or second date? Unfortunately, the answer is still no. You will just have to exercise a bit of self-restraint and character building here and trust that if you hold off for a few weeks or months, you won't be sorry. Why risk having him call you easy (and think of you that way) when he's talking to his buddies in the locker room the next day? Better that he be angry and strategizing ways of seducing you on the next date than moving on to the next girl. Making him wait will only increase his desire and create more passion when you finally have sex whenever you're ready.

We know it can be excruciating to put sex off with someone you're attracted to, but you must think long term here. If you play your cards right, you can have sex with him every night for the rest of your life when you're married!

Now you might argue that you don't mind having sex with him on the first or second date and taking your chances, that it's okay with you if he doesn't call again because you're both grown-ups and you can take your lumps. We know from experience, of course, that most girls who say this are lying to themselves. Deep down inside it's not okay with a woman if she sleeps with a man and he doesn't call. Every woman wants the man she just slept with to call her, that is, if she really likes him—and hopefully she likes the man she's sleeping with. Every woman we know who said it was okay if a man didn't call after sex was actually *not okay* when he didn't call. When you sleep with him on the second date, you don't really know if he's going to be a gentleman or a creep. *Rules* girls don't take risks. We wait until we're sure before having sex.

Let's say that now, hopefully, you've held off for a while and are ready to have sex with him. What *Rules* should you follow in bed? First and foremost, stay emotionally cool no matter how hot the sex gets. The fact is, most women turn men off not only because they sleep with them too soon, but because they talk too much about it in bed. They try to exploit the physical closeness of sex to gain emotional closeness, security, and assurances about the future. The theories of Masters and Johnson (who are now divorced) are not to be ignored, but please wait a good amount of time before you begin holding lengthy seminars about your needs during sex or after sex. Don't be a drill sergeant, demanding that he do this or that. You have to trust that if you relax and let him explore your body like unchartered territory you will have fun and be satisfied. Being with you in bed should not be difficult or demanding. Don't bring anything—red lightbulbs, scented candles, or X-rated videos—to enhance your sexual experience. If you have to use these things to get him excited, something's wrong. He should be excited about just sleeping with you.

While you're snuggling in bed after great sex is not the time to say, "So, do you want me to make room in the closet for your clothes?" or "I put a toothbrush in the bathroom for you." Don't bring up marriage, kids, or your future together, not in bed (or out). Remember, these are *your* needs you are concerned about filling, and *The Rules* are a selfless way of living and handling a relationship. Men merely want to lie down next to someone they care about when they are feeling strong emotions. Women are more curious, wanting to know, "Now that we've slept together, where is this relationship going?" or "What is the meaning of what we've just done?" While all these thoughts are whirling through your head and your desire to own this man is mounting from minute to minute, try to relax and think about nothing.

Don't cling to him if he has to leave that night or the following morning. Be casual and unmoved about the fact that the date is over. With that attitude, chances are he will be the one hanging on. Don't try to keep him there longer by suggesting brunch or sweet rolls and coffee in bed. If you do, he'll probably run to the nearest coffee shop for breakfast. Instead, go quietly about your business—brush your hair and your teeth, do some sit-ups and stretches, brew coffee—and chances are he'll start massaging your shoulders and suggesting morning sex or a great brunch place.

It's only fair that if you're dating a man for a month or two and don't plan to sleep with him for a while to let him know. Otherwise, you're being a tease. On the other hand, what if *you're* more into sex than he is? *The Rules* answer is, if you don't want to feel insecure, then don't initiate sex. After you're in a committed relationship, when you know he is crazy about you, you can occasionally and playfully make an overture.

Last but not least, whenever you do have sex, always use a condom. Don't cave in when a man says, "Just this once." Remember, you're a *Rules* girl and you take good care of yourself.

Rule #16

Don't Tell Him What to Do

IF YOUR BOYFRIEND wants to join the new "in" health club where all the leggy model types work out, don't tell him to jog on the street or exercise at home. Say, "That's great!" and go about your business. Don't show that you are jealous or insecure. If he loves you, it won't matter how pretty the girls at the gym are.

If he'd rather go camping with his friends on the weekends than be with you, either let him or break up with him, but don't tell him what to do. Our friend Marcy was seeing Joe for a couple of months when he suddenly started to make weekend plans with his friends. Conditioned by her therapist to be honest and up front about her feelings, Marcy told Joe that she felt abandoned. He immediately started making weekend plans with her. She was ecstatic. But after a month of togetherness, he suddenly stopped calling. She never heard from him again.

The moral of the story: don't play social director. If Joe didn't want to spend weekends with Marcy, being asked to wasn't going to change his mind. Men do what they want to do. If they can't live without you, it's very clear. If they can live without you, it's also clear. Don't be dense. Read the tea leaves and move on to the next man if necessary!

If, after dating you for months, he has never introduced you to his parents or friends, that means he doesn't want you to meet his parents or friends. He may simply be shy about the whole thing. Don't be pushy and suggest meeting them if he doesn't bring it up. We don't force ourselves on the family. We don't make friends with his roommate or take his mother to lunch so that she'll tell him to marry us. No one can make him marry us. Either accept the situation as it is and be patient, or date others, but don't force anything to happen.

Finally, don't try to change his life in any way. Don't go through his closets and throw out his favorite but disgusting old jeans and then suggest you and he go shopping for new ones. Don't try to turn him on to tennis when he loves drinking beer and watching football. Don't sign him up for career counseling courses because *you're* unhappy with his current job. Don't push your interests on him either. If he loves steak, don't preach the virtues of vegetarianism. You don't own him. Don't fix him. You will end up emasculating him and he will come to see you as a domineering shrew. He wants someone who makes him feel good or better, not inadequate. So leave him alone. When he *asks* you what to wear or how to play tennis, you can help him. Until then, just be there.

Rule #17 _____

Let Him Take the Lead

DATING IS LIKE SLOW dancing. The man must take the lead or you fall over your feet. He should be the first one to say "I love you," "I miss you," "I've told my parents so much about you. They can't wait to meet you."

He should be an open book, you should be a mystery. Don't tell him he's the first person you've felt this way about in a long time, or that you never thought you'd fall in love again.

Remember, let him take the lead. He declares love first, just as he picks most of the movies, the restaurants, and the concerts the two of you go to. He might sometimes ask you for your preference, in which case you can tell him.

You should meet his parents before he meets yours unless, of course, he picks you up at your parents' house. Let your mother or father open the door, but don't let them hang around too much. Tell your mother not to smile at him as if he were her son-in-law and don't let her mention your sister's upcoming wedding. Remember, mothers can get quite anxious about your dating life. So be ready to go—don't be in the bathroom applying more mascara—when he arrives so that your parents don't spend too much time with him alone, asking him questions like, "How's business?" or "So what are your intentions?"

The same rule applies to your friends. He should introduce you to his friends before you introduce him to yours. You should double with his married or dating friends before you double with yours.

Reciprocate when you feel quite secure about the way the relationship is going and don't tell your friends too much about him because they might inadvertently blab when they do meet him. If you can't trust them to be quiet and discreet, then say nothing. The last thing you need is a well-meaning, but not too smart friend, saying something like, "Oh, it's nice to meet you. Sheila has told me so much about you."

Don't worry. After he proposes, he will eventually meet all your friends and family. Until then, just follow his lead!

Don't Expect a Man to Change or Try to Change Him

LET'S SAY YOU HAVE met the man of your dreams—almost. There are a couple of things you wish were different. What do you do? Nothing! Don't try to change him because men never *really* change. You should either accept certain flaws or find someone else. Of course, it all depends on what it is about him that bothers you.

If he is fanatically neat, chronically tardy, hates Chinese food (your favorite) and disco dancing (you love it), or he won't part with his childhood baseball card collection, but he loves you to death, consider yourself lucky. These are annoying but relatively harmless vices, which we classify under category A.

On the other hand, if he flirts with other women in front of you at parties, exhibits violent behavior at times, pays no attention when you are telling him something important, or forgets your birthday, then he is into category B (bad) behavior and you have some heavy-duty thinking to do.

In the case of A, pray for acceptance and don't nag him. It won't work anyway. Just be ready at 9 P.M. when he says he'll be over at 8.

When it comes to B-type behavior, such as infidelity and lack of consideration, seriously think about ending the relationship. People don't change that much and you can't *count* on it happening. What you see is what you get. If a man cheated on you during your courtship, he may do so during your marriage. He might be on best behavior for a while after you catch him the first time. But don't delude yourself. Old habits die hard.

You must decide if you can live with him. Whether or not he ever cheats on you again, realize that the thought will always cross your mind. You might find yourself checking his shirt collar for lipstick stains and his pockets for little pieces of paper with women's phone numbers on them, or calling him at the office when he says he's working late. Is that how you want to live? If it is, *Rules* women make up their minds and live with it. The key to a successful marriage is to be happy with the way things are, not the way they could be *if only* he changed.

Of course, a playboy type who falls in love with you because you did *The Rules* will automatically mend his ways. He will want to be monogamous because you, unlike other women he's dated, are busy, don't call him, make him wait for sex, and don't bring up marriage or the future. Therefore, his object in life is to win you over. He has very little interest in other women because he has no time for them! Thoughts of how to conquer you consume most of his waking hours. You have become the biggest challenge in his life. Do *The Rules* and even the biggest playboy can be all yours!

Deciding whether or not you can live with a man's bad habits or his past (ex-wives and children) is not easy. Also, some character traits don't fall so easily into either category A or B. For example, your man may be someone who doesn't live up to his earning potential. Whether you can live with him depends on how important money, career, status, and a big house are to you.

In all such cases, you must sit quietly with yourself and ask for guidance to do the right thing. Consulting others helps, but remember *you* have to live with these things yourself. Ask yourself if you can really marry an ex-womanizer or a recovering alcoholic. Can you really live with the possibility that he may cheat or drink again? Ask yourself if you can live with stepchildren or past infidelity. If the answer is yes, great. But if you are too troubled by his past or current behavior, you might have to do *The Rules* thing and walk away. Taking him to couples therapy in the hopes of changing him can take forever, rarely works, and some things just cannot be changed.

Whatever you do, don't nag him or he's sure to resent you for it. So think long and hard, but don't waste too much time deciding. Remember, there are lots of men out there!

Don't Open Up Too Fast

DATING IS NOT THERAPY. There are many ways to kill a relationship. Getting heavy and examining everything is certainly one of them. Conditioned by therapy and self-help books to tell all, women tend to overdo it on first dates, bringing up past relationships, their hurts and fears, their alcohol or drug problem—all in an attempt to bond with this new man. This is deadly and boring. Be intelligent but light, interesting yet mysterious. That's why we have suggested not opening up too fast. (See also *Rule #9: How to Act on Dates 1, 2, and 3.*) The first date should be short, so you don't say too much. Remember, the person who talks the most has the most to lose.

By the end of the first date, he should know just a few facts, such as your name, your profession, how many siblings you have, where you went to college, where you grew up, and your favorite restaurants. By the end of the first date, he should not know your dating history. Don't reprimand him for picking you up thirty minutes late and then tell him you were afraid he would never show up, that you felt abandoned, and explain that "abandonment" is one of your issues in therapy. Don't tell him that his behavior reminds you of your ex-boyfriend who was also never on time. Even if this is true, don't tell him. Don't worry. By doing *The Rules*, you will automatically attract a loving, attentive husband who will be around so much that you won't have time to think about your abandonment issues!

If you have a burning desire to tell him a secret, *The Rules* credo is "Haste makes waste." It's always better to wait before telling someone something that you might feel ashamed or nervous about. Wait at least a couple of months. Better yet, wait until after he says "I love you." Unless he loves you, it's none of his business anyway!

Too many women tell intimate details of their lives far too soon. This is not only unwise, but also it doesn't work. No man wants to be the recipient of a therapy session upon first meeting you. No man wants to hear how wrong or messed up your life has been before he *really* loves you.

You are not on this date to get sympathy but to have a nice evening and get him to call you again. Remember *Rule* #9—that the first three dates are about being light and charming, like a summer breeze. Men must always remember you as mysterious on the first three dates. Their initial impression tends to go a long way. If and when things get serious, you can casually tell him about your difficult childhood and some of your fears. Even then, tell him in an easy, short, simple way.

Don't be dramatic about your past. Don't go into long details. Don't be burdensome.

Let's say you are a recovering alcoholic. He takes you out for a drink on your first date and to dinner on the second. He notices you only ordered club soda both times. He is about to order a bottle of wine and wants to know if you'll join him. Don't say, "No, I *never* drink. I hit a terrible bottom with drugs and alcohol two years ago and now I'm sober in AA." Just say, "No, thanks," and smile. After a couple of months when he's madly in love with you and you feel that he would not judge you for your drinking problem, you can tell him something like, "I used to drink a lot in college. It really made me sick. Now I'm in AA and I don't drink anymore. I feel better." Then smile and go on to other, more pleasant conversation. If be loves you, he will not make you feel bad. He won't argue with you or try to encourage you to "just have one." He might even start drinking less himself to make you feel better. He might even say that he's proud of your sobriety and discipline.

If you've had a serious illness and you're embarrassed about obvious scars from your surgery, wait until you're about to be intimate with him and then casually mention, as you take your clothes off in the dark, that you had an illness. If he loves you, he will kiss and caress you. Don't bring up the illness in a serious, heart-to-heart talk on your first date. Remember, especially in the beginning, don't be too intense about anything or lay all your cards on the table. In general,

the less tragic you are about your life circumstances, the more sympathy you will probably
get. Ask for sympathy and you never get it.

If you don't know how to hold on to a dollar,
don't balance your checkbook, have an answering machine filled with calls from bill collectors
leaving threatening messages, don't tell him what
a mess you are with finances and that you got it
from your father who once gambled away your
college tuition. Now you might feel that we are
asking you to act casually about your problems,
but the fact is, you are bad with money and he
will soon see that. But does he really have to
know about the creditors and your canceled
credit cards? No, all he has to know is that
money is not your strong suit.

We are not suggesting that you hide or lie
about bad things in your life, just that you not
burden him with all the gory details too soon.
Does he really have to know that your last
boyfriend dropped you for your best friend?
Can't you just say, if he asks, that your last relationship "just didn't work out?"

He should always feel that he's in love with the
girl of his dreams, not someone damaged. If you
feel damaged (many of us do in some way), read
Rule #1 again and again. Remember, you are a
creature unlike any other! It's when and how you
tell him your darkest secrets, not the secrets themselves, that matter.

By the time you are engaged, he should know
all that really matters about you and your family
and your past. *The Rules* are truthful and spiri-

tual in nature. It is morally wrong to accept an engagement ring without revealing whatever truths about yourself you need to share. Tell him these things in a calm, nondramatic manner and don't, as some women do, surprise him with these skeletons after you're married. That's not the time to tell him that you were previously married or never finished college. It's not fair to him and not good for a *Rules* marriage.

Be Honest but Mysterious

MEN LOVE MYSTERY! Fifty years ago it was easier to be mysterious with men. Women lived at home and their mothers answered the phone and never told the men who else called their daughters. Dates didn't see women's bedrooms so soon. Today, men pick up women at their apartments, see their lingerie in the bathroom, their romance novels in the living room, and hear their phone messages. While such openness is good for marriage, it's important to project a certain amount of mystery during the dating period.

We are all looking for someone to share our lives, thoughts, and feelings with, but as we suggested in *Rule #19* wait until he says he loves you to share your innermost secrets. When he is in your apartment, don't listen to your answering machine. Let him wonder who called you besides him! You might know that the messages are probably from girlfriends feeling suicidal about their dating situations, but he doesn't!

If your date is at your place and one of your

friends calls and asks how everything is going, don't say, "*Scott*'s over. I can't talk." That means you've been talking about Scott to your friends and he's somehow important. Even if that is the case, Scott should not know that he is the subject of your thoughts and conversations or he might think he doesn't have to work so hard to get you. Simply say, "I can't talk right now. I'll call you later." After you hang up, don't tell him who called or why.

Before he comes to your apartment, tuck this book away in your top drawer and make sure any self-help books are out of sight. Have interesting or popular novels or nonfiction books in full view. Hide in the closet any grungy bathrobes or something you don't want him to see, such as a bottle of Prozac.

In general, don't give away any information that is not absolutely necessary. If you are busy on the night he asks you for a date, don't tell him what you are planning to do. Just say you are busy. If he asks you out for the weekend, don't say, "I'm visiting my brother this weekend. His wife just had a baby." Simply say, "I'm sorry, but I already have plans." Less is more. Let him wonder what you are doing. You don't have to be an open book. This is good for him and it's good for you. It keeps the intrigue going. You don't want to make dating you so easy and predictable that he loses interest in you. Always remember that in time you will be able to tell him just about anything!

On the other hand, *Rules* girls don't lie either.

Don't tell a Mel Gibson–type guy that you love hiking and shop at L.L. Bean all the time when you can't stand trees, insects, and backpacks. And certainly don't tell your boyfriend that you love and want children because he does when you really don't. Take our advice. Don't lie. It's a law of the universe.

Accentuate the Positive and Other *Rules* for Personal Ads

PERSONAL ADS HAVE become a popular way to meet men. But many women shy away from ads because they feel it smacks of desperation. Don't worry! We know lots of women who've placed and answered ads without seeming desperate or too interested. That's because they wrote or responded to ads in a *Rules* way.

1. How to Write a Personal Ad

Ads can be expensive, so make yours no more than four or five lines. Ads that run on and on are a waste of money and seem desperate. (Why else would anyone spend six hundred dollars for one ad?) Not surprisingly, they contain too much information that no one cares about, and too much lovey-dovey stuff (of course you like walks on the beach, who doesn't?). Most people skim or ignore long ads and rarely respond to them. Think of advertising campaigns ("It takes a tough man to make a tender chicken," "Maybe she was born with it. Maybe it's Maybelline") when you write an ad. It should be short, upbeat, and flirtatious—a pleasure to read. It should contain facts only about height, hair color, religion, sex, and profession. Don't mention marriage or kids. Don't refer to your past—for example, divorced or newly available since your last breakup. Don't say things like, "I'm not into makeup or superficiality" or "I'm happily overweight." Perhaps a man will not mind your extra twenty pounds when he sees your beautiful face, but chances are he won't answer such a candid ad.

Many ads are a turnoff because they look for sympathy. The writers hope to hook you in by telling you that they are human and damaged. For example, "Ex-wife of alcoholic seeks nonabusive soul mate." It's honest but a bit depressing, don't you think? I mean, would you answer a man's ad that said, "Unemployed executive looking for understanding wife?" Thus, *The Rule* is that as long as you don't outright lie, you needn't be honest to a fault either. Just leave things out—for example, don't say you're slim if you're fat. Simply leave out your weight entirely and accentuate your blue eyes and long blond hair.

Don't be shy! It's perfectly okay to ask for exactly the kind of man you want. We know one woman who said only men with Porsches need apply. You might think she had a lot of nerve, or that men might be turned off by such an ad because the woman comes across as a gold digger.

The fact is that this woman received dozens of letters with photos of men in front of their Porsches and she married one of them. Another woman wanted only the kind of man who would write poetry. Dozens of men sent her poems. Men like to be challenged in an ad and like impressing women, so let them. Ask for what you want—just don't say you want to get married.

When you receive responses, sort them out into yes, no, and maybe piles. Don't rule out letters without photos. Men are often lazy about such things. If you like their note and the sound of their voice on the phone, agree to a drink date. But be wary if a man doesn't mention certain critical facts in his letter. You don't want too many surprises on the first date.

2. How to Answer an Ad

Get some plain white stationery the size of a telephone memo pad, don't perfume it or seal it with a kiss and *never* include your address—you don't want any crazies stalking you at your apartment. (More about safety at the end of this chapter.) Write a flirtatious note with the essential facts. If his ad said, "Marriage-minded, Tom Cruise look-alike," you could start your note off with: "Dear Tom" or "Dear T. C." Never mention marriage, even though he brought it up in boldface.

Remember, you're just doing this for fun, to meet some nice men. Notes that talk about marriage, kids, and commitment make most men run the other way even when they want it. Just start out with something easy like, "Your ad caught my eye." (That makes it sound like you were casually reading XYZ magazine. He needn't know that your Monday night ritual is poring over personal ads looking for your husband or that you answered twenty other ads that week.)

Don't try to be different. Don't send a sleazy photo or a collage from a fashion magazine with your face over Cindy Crawford's body. All of that is sophomoric. It also shouts desperation. The best way to respond is to dash off a cute note in five minutes while watching the 11 o'clock news. Less is more. Remember, he has a lot of other letters to read. End the note by saying something like, "Well, I'm off to my aerobics class. Hope to hear from you soon." Keep it light!

The photo is actually the most important part of the package. Most men decide to call you based on your photo, not your note. They either like your looks or they don't, so spend the extra time getting the right photo. It should be about 3x5, no posters or photo-booth photos, preferably of you alone and smiling. Don't send photos of you holding your one-year-old niece or in a bikini or with a girlfriend.

Don't be surprised if you only get one or two replies for every twenty ads you respond to. Men typically receive hundreds of responses from women. Some take weeks and months to call. When you do get a call, try to make the date for only a quick drink. You have no idea what he looks like and he may have been exaggerating about how handsome he is. On the other hand, he could very well be Kevin Costner's twin. A short drink date will give you enough time to decide if he's for you, which is all that matters.

A word of caution: dating via personal ads involves taking risks that dating by introduction usually doesn't. You don't know this man from a hole in the wall!—so be careful! When he calls you to set up a date, don't feel you have to go out with him if he sounds weird, angry, or rude. But if you do like him and the sound of his voice, agree to meet at a restaurant near your apartment. *Never* give him your address or meet him at your apartment, and *never* let him pick you up in his car to drive to a restaurant. If he gets very angry because you won't let him pick you up at your apartment, or makes you feel that you're being paranoid, say "Maybe this isn't going to work out" and get off the phone. But if everything is okay, make sure to get his telephone number, saying you want it in case you need to cancel or reschedule. Then call the number to make sure it's his. Hang up when he or his answering machine answers. Give your mother or a friend the number before the date so someone can track you down if anything happens. We know all this precaution seems very unromantic, but *Rules* girls don't take unnecessary risks!

Don't Live with a Man (or Leave Your Things in His Apartment)

To LIVE TOGETHER or not to live together? Is that a question you're grappling with now? Your friends (not knowing *The Rules*) might say, "Do it." Your parents (being conservative) will no doubt say, "No." *The Rules* answer is: "Move in only if you've set a wedding date." In other words, the only reason to live with someone is if you're planning the wedding and you don't want to pay two rents.

Contrary to popular belief, living together is not a trial period for him to see how he feels about you. He either loves you or he doesn't, and playing house and cooking him a lot of breakfasts won't change a thing. In fact, sometimes the best way for him to see how he feels about you is to not see you at all. You may have to dump him if he can't commit. If he really loves you, he'll beg you to come back. If he doesn't, you've lost nothing, saved time, and can now go on to someone else.

Women who think that commitment will come *after* they shack up often learn the hard way that this is not the case. Of course, by the time the lesson is learned, their self-esteem is shattered and they're two or three or four years older. Does this scenario sound familiar? After dating Mitch for a year and a half, Wendy wanted a ring. Mitch wouldn't budge. They decided to live together to see if they could "work it out" (his idea and word choice). Nothing changed. When he went away on business trips he didn't call or think about her that much. Nine months and a lot of wasted time later, he was still not in love, and so he moved out. Wendy attributed the breakup to his parents' messy divorce, which he was working out in therapy. The truth is, she should have just ended it sooner when he wouldn't commit.

If you operate under the delusion that living together without a real commitment will somehow bring you closer together, you should know that many women tell us that their husbands proposed after they *moved away from, not toward,* the relationship. One woman booked a trip to Club Med with a girlfriend after dating her boyfriend for a year, another started getting very busy and unavailable on weekends, and a third talked about taking a job in another city. Then, their husbands proposed.

Remember, men don't necessarily propose when you're cuddled up on the couch watching a rented video, but do so when they're afraid of losing you. In *Love Story*—a movie you should study like the Bible—Oliver proposes to Jenny (a *Rules* girl, if there ever was one) after she says she's planning to take a scholarship in France and after suggesting that their opposite (rich/poor) backgrounds would not mix well. Jenny wasn't grateful or loving at that moment—she almost broke off their relationship. (You don't have to go that far!) But be a *little* distant and difficult. The unobtainable is always more exciting; men very often want something more just because they can't have it.

If you are following *The Rules* (particularly *Rule #13: Don't See Him More than Once or Twice a Week*), you can't possibly live with him, by design or by accident. Women who tell us that they moved in with a man accidentally, as a result of spending long weekends with him, obviously broke a few rules along the way. You stay over a lot and one thing leads to another. First you get a drawer, then a shelf, and then a closet of your own. Before you or he realize it, you're having your mail delivered to his apartment and your friends are leaving messages on his tape machine.

Needless to say, this should not be happening. If you are doing *The Rules*, you never need a closet full of clothes and accessories at his place. Don't leave your toothbrush or bathrobe there. He should be begging *you* to leave things in his apartment and going out of his way to make shelf space. This invasion of space should not come from you. You are independent, you are not a crasher, you are always ending the evening (or the morning) first. (Besides, the less he sees of some of your less glamorous habits, like the way you floss your teeth or the sound you make when you slurp your coffee, the better.)

Is there any reason to live with a man if you haven't set a wedding date? Yes, and that's when *he* wants to and you don't! He's crazy about you and you're not so sure about him. In this case, he's taking the risk, not you. Still, proceed with caution. Living with him may prevent you from dating others and meeting someone you're crazy about, so how smart is it?

Rule #23

Don't Date a Married Man

DATING MARRIED (or unavailable) men is not only an obvious waste of time, but also it's dishonest and stupid. So why do so many women do it? Some feel it's better than dating no one, some find the very wrongness and danger of it (the secret hotel rendezvous) fun and exciting, and some hang on to the hope that one day the men will leave their wives for them.

All these women suffer from low self-esteem, or why would they settle for so little? We are not big advocates of therapy, but we believe it would be worth $125 an hour to find out why you would do this to yourself.

When you date a married man, you basically spend your life waiting for him to get separated. The deadline keeps changing from Thanksgiving to Christmas, then Easter, then Labor Day. You wait and you sit by the phone on the off chance that his wife took the kids to her parents' house and he can spend an hour or two with you. And you cry when he can't see you on Valentine's Day or on his wedding anniversary or his wife's birthday. You are always second. In the beginning, affairs are full of promise and great sex. By the end, you are always crying on the shoulders of girlfriends and wishing his wife would die.

You will not get much sympathy from us. Dating married men is dishonest and totally contrary to *The Rules*. We do not take what is not ours. We don't date married men because then we get a reputation for it and no one will trust us around their boyfriends or husbands.

If you have recently met a married man that you are mad about, then you must practice self-restraint. If he is everything you ever wanted in a husband, be friends with him and hope he gets divorced. Until then, you must say to yourself that a single man like him exists somewhere out there for you. Then you must get busy, go to a singles dance, answer a personal ad or put one in a magazine, ask your friends to fix you up with someone. Take action. Join a gym, a church, or synagogue, or do volunteer work at a hospital. Never sit around dreaming about him or you might end up acting on your thoughts.

Dating a married man is easy because you can fantasize about his future availability. But, at the risk of sounding preachy, it bears repeating that you won't be at peace if you date a married man. Even if he leaves his wife, how do you know he'll actually marry you?

You're a *Rules* girl! Your life is never on the edge because of a man. Either a man is available and in love with you or he's taken and you have nothing to do with him romantically. You are not desperately waiting in the wings for his situation to change. You are not someone who waits and hopes while he takes his wife and kids to Disney World. You have a life of your own.

Lest you think we are being naive, we know that extramarital affairs happen all the time and that married men do at times divorce their wives and marry the girl they've been seeing on the side. We know one such woman who waited five years for a man to break up with his wife. They are now very happily married. She was very lucky. Are you willing to take that chance?

Rule #24 _____

Slowly Involve Him in Your Family and Other *Rules* for Women with Children

IF YOU ARE A DIVORCED or single woman with children, you should follow all *The Rules*. In addition, be especially careful when dating not to go on about all the pain from your first marriage or talk too much about your children.

When you meet a man at a dance or social situation, it isn't really necessary to mention your children at all. Let him take your phone number, then wait until he calls for you to gently weave it into the conversation. Don't say in a serious tone, "I need to tell you something." Remember in *Rule #19: Don't Open Up Too Fast*, we advise you to tell him about yourself very informally. Just casually say, "Oh, that's my son playing the piano" or something like that.

If and when he does ask you out for Saturday night, don't say, "Nine on Saturday is great, but I'll have to call the baby-sitter." Don't fill him in on details of raising children or how your ex-husband was supposed to baby-sit and is just so unreliable! It isn't necessary for a man to know you haven't gotten your alimony payments for the last three months and Tommy really needs new sneakers. Simply say, "Saturday at nine is great." At this point he is interested in *you*, not your family or your problems.

Please do not take this advice the wrong way. We are not telling you to be ashamed of your past or your children. Just wait a while before involving him. On your first few dates, it would be wise to meet your date in the lobby of your building or a restaurant so you don't have to introduce him to your children. This is as much for your date's sake as your child's. Your child should not have to meet every Tom, Dick, and Harry you date, only the serious contenders. Let the man be the one to bring up meeting your children. Make him curious about seeing them. Meeting your children should be an honor, not a routine occurrence. Just the way you hold back on other things in the beginning of your relationship, this too should take time. Make him work (again? yes) for the privilege of meeting your loved ones.

On the other hand, don't use motherhood as an excuse not to get out there and mingle. Having a child often means being in situations with married people and you might feel like a fifth wheel among all the couples you meet at PTA meetings and Little League. But remember that there are plenty of single fathers out there who want to remarry. So go to PTA meetings with a smile on your face and wearing a nice outfit. Socialize wherever you go with your child. You never know.

Practice, Practice, Practice! (or, Getting Good at *The Rules*)

How DOES ONE get good at *The Rules*? Unfortunately, the same way one gets good at playing the piano or tennis or anything else. Practice, practice, and more practice!

Once you're truly convinced you need *The Rules*, you should read this book over and over again until you've practically memorized it, then practice the principles as much as possible. Don't expect to get them right the first time or every time. We didn't. We broke rules, got hurt, and then eventually got serious and did *The Rules* as they are written.

Don't be discouraged. Just keep practicing! Try *The Rules* on all men at all times. Don't even say hello first to your doorman or the butcher at the deli. Let them say hello to you first and then just smile. Don't ignore them or anyone else, just practice *responding* rather than starting any conversation. Then later, when a man says to you, "I can tell you were the prom queen," and you weren't even asked to go, you will instinctively smile and say nothing. If, however, you are so used to blabbering all the time, then you might start explaining that you were thirty pounds heavier in high school and never really went out. If he is planning to marry you, you will eventually tell him all about your unpopular days, and by that time it won't really matter. We find that most women regret spilling their innermost feelings and thoughts on the first few dates. There will be less to regret if you learn to be quiet and mysterious more often. Reread *Rules #19* and *#20*.

When the urge to call him comes, call a friend, your mother, the weather channel, walk the dog, write a letter, answer a personal ad, anything, until the urge passes, and it will. Call a friend who recently broke *The Rules* to remember how painful it is to chase a man. If you must call a man, better that you call a friendly ex-boyfriend than the current man of your dreams. The old relationship is over and there's not much to lose, but your new flame may lose interest in you if you pursue him.

The good news, girls, is that the more you practice *The Rules*, the easier it gets. If it's painful, remember, none of us do them perfectly. But try to do the best you can. Ending a phone conversation after ten minutes seemed cruel and impossible for us in the beginning, but the more we used a timer and did it anyway, the more natural it became to say, "It's been nice talking to you, but I really have to run."

It's not necessary to have a high IQ to do *The*

Rules, just a certain degree of determination. In fact, highly educated girls have the hardest time with *The Rules*. They tend to think all this is beneath them. They'll say, "I went to graduate school, I'm not playing these games" or "I'm in management. I believe in being up front with men about my needs, my opinions, and who I really am. I refuse to be demure and smile when I don't *feel* like it."

If you think you're too smart for *The Rules*, ask yourself, "Am I married?" If not, why not? Could it be that what you're doing isn't working? Think about it.

But even if you're not desperate to get married right away, you never know when you'll change your mind. We've all met women who are certain in their twenties that they don't want two kids and a house with a picket fence. They tell us that their career, friends, and assorted romantic relationships are fine with them. So they don't bother to play hard to get when they meet men. They treat men like women—as friends. Then one day they meet a handsome man with gorgeous eyes. Suddenly they not only want him but want to have his children. These women either don't know about *The Rules* or have never practiced them. This is why you should always do *The Rules*. You never know when you'll want to get married.

Another reason to do *The Rules* is so that people—men, women, bosses, parents—treat us well. When we don't do *The Rules*, we inevitably get hurt. When we do *The Rules*, we find out who really loves us. The answer might be painful, but better to weed out the uninterested parties than to carry on unsatisfying relationships. For example, you ask a man out and he says no, or he says yes to be polite and never calls again. You're hurt. But had you not initiated the date, he would never have hurt you. You have no one to blame but yourself! Or let's say your neighbor only comes by to borrow milk or when he's bored. You wish he would invite you to dinner. He doesn't. So you suggest dinner. He makes excuses. You're hurt. Again, situations of our own making! If someone is not asking you out, then they don't want to be with you. Go about your business and trust you will meet other people who genuinely like you and want to be with you. You might feel lonely and hurt for a while, but better that than being rejected.

The Rules can be used in many life situations. For example, if you love your sister too much, but she doesn't act particularly warm or nurturing toward you, don't call her every day. Just return her calls. Stop trying to "work things out" or go over childhood feelings. Just get a life so that your relationship with her is not the main thing on your mind. Be busy and when she finally calls you, be friendly. No one likes talking to someone who is angry or depressed.

You may be thinking, "But without so-and-so, I wouldn't have a friend to go to singles dances with or a summer house to visit." We know how you feel, but maybe you're supposed to go to dances by yourself or you're supposed to let go of so-and-so to make room for better friends. Just do *The Rules*. Don't think about the short-term results. Trust that you will find other ways to fill the emptiness. Maybe you'll take up running and meet someone on the track. Looking back, whenever we did *The Rules* and lost a relationship, we got a better one.

You see, whenever you love someone more than that person loves you, you are in a position to get hurt. *The Rules* way of thinking and acting protects you from unnecessary pain. It's a law of the universe that the more you try to get the love and attention of someone who doesn't naturally want you, the more frustrated and unhappy you will be. When we do *The Rules*, we give up the struggle. We accept that some people don't want us and we go on to the next. We don't force people to love us.

We had to change our definition of gratifying relationships. A gratifying relationship is long lasting and mutual, not short term and hurtful!

When we do *The Rules* in life, whether or not we want to get married, we create boundaries with people. Some of us get so overly friendly with our secretary, baby-sitter, or cleaning lady that they take advantage of us and don't do their jobs. We should be friendly but always remain the boss. We say yes to last-minute dates or let men get off the phone first, and then we wonder why we feel so empty. At work, we try too hard to make our coworkers like us, but they sense our motives and find us annoying.

The Rules are even useful in the business

world. If your boss ignores you or isn't particularly fond of you, don't try to ingratiate yourself by making unnecessary conversation, asking about his or her weekend, suggesting lunch or bringing in homemade cookies. If your boss doesn't take you out to lunch, he or she doesn't want to. If your desks are near each other, don't constantly stare at him or her to make eye contact. Keep your eyes glued to your computer screen or the papers on your desk.

Everyone hates a brownnoser, so be professional and businesslike. Just do your work quietly and efficiently. Don't tell him or her how hard you work; don't stay late at the office to impress people. Don't look haggard or disheveled from having come in to the office early or stayed late the night before. Coworkers and bosses are actually more impressed by well-rounded people who get their work done during business hours and have a healthy social life. Dress as if you have a date after work.

If you think of *The Rules* as a manual for life rather than simply as rules for getting married, you might do them more often. Then, when you meet the man of your dreams, you'll have had plenty of *Rules* practice.

Even if You're Engaged or Married, You Still Need *The Rules*

IDEALLY, WE DO *The Rules* from the minute we meet a man until he says he loves us and proposes. But if you were not lucky enough to learn about *The Rules* before reading this book, we suggest you do the best you can right now. Better to do *The Rules* now than not at all.

However, if you did not know about *The Rules* until now, don't think you can totally erase the way you related to your fiancé or husband from the beginning of your courtship. For example, if you initiated the relationship, called him up, asked him out, and so on, in order to make the relationship work, he'll always expect such things from you. He didn't worry about getting you to marry him, he knew he had you, you told him so with every word and gesture, so on some level he may take you for granted. And chances are you still make things happen by initiating sex and/or romantic dinners, asking him about his feelings for you, wishing he would spend less time in the office or with his friends and more time with you. You might even wonder from time to time if he's having an affair.

If you didn't do *The Rules* at the beginning of your relationship, your husband might ignore you, talk to you rudely, or treat you badly. You might wonder, "Is his behavior the result of bad upbringing or something in his past?" Maybe. But we believe it's because you didn't do *The Rules*. He never needed to treat you like his dream girl. The same man who would act indifferent or ignore a wife who pursued him wouldn't dream of it with the woman who did *The Rules*.

Abuse doesn't happen in a *Rules* relationship because when you play hard to get and he works like hell to get you, he thinks you're the most beautiful, wonderful woman in the world, even if you're not. He treats you like a precious jewel.

But don't despair. Start doing *The Rules* now as best you can and he may notice a difference in your behavior and want you more. Here are five suggestions:

1. Don't call him at work so often. When you do, keep it brief and practical ("What time is the movie?"). Don't call saying, "I miss you. Let's make love tonight." He should be calling you to express those sentiments.

2. Don't initiate sex, even if you want it badly. Let him be the man, the aggressor in the bedroom. Biologically, the man must pursue the woman. If you bring up sex all the time, you

will emasculate him. Act as if you're a *Rules* girl on a first date. Be coy. Flirt when he tries to kiss you or bite your neck. This will turn him into a tiger.

3. Dress better, a little sexier. No man likes coming home to a woman wearing sweatpants or a bathrobe all the time. Try wearing tight jeans, a miniskirt, or a deep V-necked shirt in a bright color. Put on some makeup and perfume. Wash your hair. Pretend you're dating him.

4. Act independent. Always be *coming* or *going*. Don't sit on the couch waiting for him to come home. Don't bore him with details about your day or your aches and pains. Make lots of plans with friends, your kids, the neighbors. Go to the movies, to the shopping mall. Just go. This will make him desperate to catch a minute of your time. He will want to corner you in the kitchen for a kiss if he senses you're not around much. He'll get mad if you're on the phone when he's home because he'll want you all to himself. This is how it is when you do *The Rules*. He'll feel as if he can never get enough of you. He'll start calling you from work to suggest dinners alone or a weekend getaway. This is what you want. Men love independent women because they leave them alone. They love chasing women who are busy. It gives them a thrill, as big as a touchdown or a home run.

5. Take up a hobby. Most men are content to sit around in a recliner on a Sunday afternoon and drink beer and watch football. Some bring work home from the office and spend the entire afternoon on the computer. Women tend to feel empty when their boyfriends or husbands don't include them in their plans or pay attention to them. It's imperative that you don't nag him to give up his hobbies, friends, or work because you're bored. You'll get more attention from him if you get even busier than he is. Make play dates for the kids, go out for a run or take an aerobics class at a gym. That will not only keep you busy but also will get you in shape, making you all the more attractive to him. He may wonder if other men are looking at you in your Lycra. That will be good for the relationship. It will make him want to turn off the TV or computer and be alone with you. You might get involved in a charity, read a book, take up a sport. The key here is to keep yourself independent and busy. This way you're not hanging around him complaining that he's not paying enough attention to you!

Unfortunately, doing *The Rules* sometimes means acting single (even if you're married with children) all over again. Just be grateful you're not!

Do *The Rules*, Even when Your Friends and Parents Think It's Nuts

REMEMBER YOUR REACTION when you first heard about *The Rules* or read this book? No doubt you thought the idea was crazy, dishonest, or extreme. "Why can't love be more natural? Why can't I ask a man out? After all, we're approaching the 21st century." But because your way didn't work, you became open-minded rather quickly. Something deep down inside you said *The Rules* just might be the answer.

Well, don't be surprised if the people around you don't support your new philosophy. Don't be surprised if they think you're nuts or question every move you make or don't make. When a man you're dating calls and leaves a message with your mother, don't be surprised if she hovers over you like a bee nagging you to call him back right away. Rather than say, "I can't call him back. I'm doing *The Rules*," just say, "Okay, Mom, later, after I wash my hair." Keep postponing any *Rule*-breaking activity.

Your mother may hassle you, but it's your girlfriends that will probably give you the hardest time, possibly because they're not doing *The Rules* themselves. Don't be surprised if they take your devotion to *The Rules* as antifeminist. They may say things like, "You know, marriage isn't the answer. No man is going to fix you. There has to be a 'me' before a 'we.' You don't need *The Rules*. You need some good analysis to find out why you want to get married so much!" Don't say, "If I don't get married I'm going to kill myself" or "In Noah's ark, they went in twos." Just smile and change the subject.

Your friends might tell you that *The Rules* are dishonest, that you should let a man know exactly who you are, that it's rude not to call him or call him back. Unless they want to do *The Rules* themselves, don't argue with them or explain what you are doing. Just do *The Rules* quietly and let the results speak for themselves. The fact is that your friends and others might not have that burning desire to get married and have babies. They may be perfectly content in their careers and hobbies. You, on the other hand, can't imagine life without a husband. Neither could we. That's why we did *The Rules*—to ensure that the right man didn't get away.

We suggest you find like-minded women who believe in *The Rules*, want to get married, and support each other much like any support group. Call *them* when you want to call him. Don't bother asking your male friends if they like being pursued by women. They might say one thing and believe another. They will probably tell you that they're flattered to be called and asked out by women. What they won't say is that these are not the women they end up marrying or even dating.

Don't take a poll of men, or of married people for that matter. Your married friends or relatives might tell you, "I didn't do *The Rules* and I got married." They will poke holes into every rule, one telling you that she asked him out for the second date, and the other that she paid for the third dinner date. Don't argue with these people. Don't tell them you're doing *The Rules* because nothing else has worked. Just smile and say, "Oh, it's just for fun" and change the subject. Don't stop doing *The Rules* because married women tell you they didn't. How do you know what their marriage is like? How do you know that, because she pursued him, he isn't always neglecting her or spending too much time at the office? You want a *Rules* marriage, not just any marriage.

If you can't find any like-minded women to support you in doing *The Rules*, just read this book a lot, carry it around in your purse to refer to on long supermarket lines, and practice what you read as much as possible. Believe us, if you do *The Rules*, you'll be too busy dating your future husband to care or even think about what anyone else is doing or what anyone else thinks of what you are doing.

Be Smart and Other *Rules* for Dating in High School

REMEMBER JANIS IAN'S SONG, "I learned the rules at seventeen, that love was meant for beauty queens?" The fact is, unless you look like Brooke Shields, high school can be very rough. There's acne and not fitting into the "in" crowd, not to mention having to go to the prom with a group because you don't have a date. Our *Rules* for high school won't guarantee you a date for the prom, but they will bring out the very best in you and make you more attractive to the opposite sex.

1. If you have really bad acne, go to a dermatologist. Cut out the greasy foods—pizza, potato chips, french fries—that make your face oily. Eat fruits and vegetables and drink six to eight glasses of water a day. It also goes without saying that you should never spend Saturday nights lying on your bed. Have fun,

make plans. Start believing now that you are a creature unlike any other! (See *Rule #1.*)

2. Spend your baby-sitting money on manicures and some pretty clothes. Wear makeup, but not too much. The idea is to look pretty, not overdone.

3. If you have a crush on a boy, your older brother's friend perhaps, don't act like one of the boys with him. Don't wear a baseball cap and sit around watching a ball game with the group. If he happens to be around, don't talk to him first. Be reserved and slightly mysterious. Let *him* notice you.

4. Always be out, mingling, not indoors, worrying. Go out to the beach, to the movies, to parties, not in your room dwelling on your flaws or quoting Sylvia Plath. When you go to parties, dances, or the beach, don't look wildly around for a boy to talk to you or ask you to dance. Don't chew gum and cackle. Walk erect as if you were balancing a book on your head, look directly in front of you, and seem self-contained even if you're lonely and bored to death.

5. If you have decided to have sex, wait until you are in a steady relationship. Use birth control, specifically a condom. You don't want to end up with an unwanted pregnancy or disease. Impulsive and irresponsible behaviors are not *The Rules*. In the '90s, it can be even cooler and safer to simply wait until you're more mature.

6. Don't smoke, take drugs, or drink alcohol, even if a very cool and good-looking boy is pressuring you to do so. Cigarettes are unhealthy, drugs and alcohol are mind altering and addictive and might make you do something that you don't want to do (like sleep with him on the first date). To do *The Rules* you must always be one step ahead. Drugs and alcohol make you messy and stupid—definitely not *Rules* behavior.

7. High school is a good time to take up sports like jogging, aerobics, swimming, or tennis. This is not only good for your body, but also for your social life. Lots of socializing goes on at running tracks and tennis courts. A healthy hobby will give you something to do in the summer. If you have the money, you might think about going to tennis camp where you can meet athletic boys your age. If you spend the summer working, on your days off make sure you go to the beach, get a (safe) tan, wear short shorts and bikinis, and go swimming, play tennis, or go Rollerblading.

8. *Act* confident even if you don't *feel* it. Notice what kinds of clothes, shoes, bags, jewelry, and hairstyles the most popular kids in high school are wearing. Don't try to be too different or frugal in this area. You'll feel lousy, so it's not worth it. To see what's hot and not, subscribe to *Seventeen* and *Glamour*. Don't let your mind tell you that all of this is superficial and beneath you. (Save your mind

for final exams and the SATs.) Don't you like boys who wear Polo shirts and cowboy boots when that's in fashion? Well, they like girls who wear what's on MTV and in *Seventeen*.

9. If the boy you like doesn't ask you to the prom, don't ask him. Better that you go with someone else who asks you or with a group. Start being a *Rules* girl now!

10. If you are lucky enough to have a boyfriend during high school, let *him* be the one to worry about the future. Choose a college that's good for you, not necessarily the one he is going to. (Who knows? You could follow him all the way to college only to have him dump you for a prettier girl in his dorm.) Go to whatever college you like and if he wants to see you, let him travel to *your* campus. Let him call and write you. Unless you're engaged, date others. Don't spend every weekend with your high school boyfriend, as some girls do who have a hard time separating. If you're meant to marry your high school sweetheart, it will happen despite the distance between you and despite any other men you meet in college.

Take Care of Yourself and Other *Rules* for Dating in College

IF YOU'RE GOING to college soon, we'd like to save you about four years of heartache. Here are seven mistakes not to make, now that *The Rules* are part of your curriculum.

1. Don't look up his class schedule and follow him around campus hoping he will eventually notice you. It's great exercise; otherwise, don't bother. Either he noticed *you* or he didn't.

2. Don't hang out in the dining hall for all three dinner shifts hoping to spot him at some point between 4:30 P.M. and 8:00 P.M., and end up gaining the "freshman twenty-five pounds" instead. (Do you really want to spend your college career in the cafeteria wondering, "When will so-and-so walk in?")

3. Don't have your girlfriend talk to his best friend and find out how he feels about you or

if he even knows who you are, and/or become best friends with his fraternity or the girl on his floor, or do favors for anyone he knows. (Don't waste your time. No one, not even his best friend, can make him like you.)

4. Don't find out what his favorite albums or CDs are and play them all the time and don't wear, say, a Grateful Dead T-shirt if that's his favorite rock group. (Strange how women think that men are attracted to women who dress like men—sporty and even grungy. Yet, it's always the girls with cute jeans and fashionable shirts that get the guys.) *The Rule* is don't wear clothes to copy men, but to attract them.

5. Don't become a cheerleader or sports fanatic simply because he's on the football team. The same goes for taking up smoking or drinking because he does those things. Many women we know sipped Perrier on dates with men who drank alcohol and smoked and are now married to them. When it comes to habits, be yourself.

6. Don't offer to help him with Shakespeare if literature is not his strong suit or type his papers, hoping he'll date you. He either wants to or doesn't.

7. Don't be stupid about safety! Date rape has become quite rampant in college these days. Be wary. Study in a lounge or library rather than alone with him in his dorm room or off-campus apartment. *Always* tell someone your whereabouts so they can keep track of

you. *Rules* girls don't take chances. Don't take date rape lightly!

Now that you know what *not* to do, what *should* you do to attract your man on campus?

1. Study! After all, that's what you're there for! Smart is sexy!
2. Eat sensibly, even when your friends are gorging on unlimited cafeteria food and having pizza delivered to their rooms at midnight. We suggest you take fruit from the dining hall to save as a midnight snack. Tell yourself during the pizza party that your jeans will fit tomorrow. Remember, overweight is *not The Rules*.
3. Wear makeup. Read *Glamour* and other popular fashion magazines.
4. Get involved in some extracurricular activity, preferably one that you're interested in and where you can meet men naturally.
5. Don't sit in your room alone on Friday and Saturday nights reading Jean-Paul Sartre. Friday and Saturday nights are for mingling. You can read Sartre on Monday.
6. Pick a major and a career goal. College is not about picking up your MRS degree, although you may very well meet your future husband on campus. Still, you must exercise your brain, both for his sake and yours. Don't be a ditz!

Next! and Other *Rules* for Dealing with Rejection

LIFE IS NOT always fair. Fortunately, *The Rules* will help ensure that you are never unnecessarily hurt by a man. By behaving around men in a *Rules* way—independent and busy, not needy or aggressive—we do not put ourselves in a position to be hurt.

However, we cannot make a certain man like us or prevent a man from meeting someone else he likes better and consequently dropping us. And we can't stop an ex-girlfriend from winning him back. So what do we do when we get dumped?

Our natural reaction may be to stagnate and isolate, wish we were dead, not wash our hair or wear makeup, cry, sleep a lot, play sad love songs, and swear we'll never meet anyone as perfect as him again. We might find consolation in the refrigerator or talk nonstop about him to our friends. Obviously, this is ridiculous. Allow yourself about two days of such behavior, and then go on.

The Rules recipe for rejection is to wear a great

dress and flattering makeup and go to the *very* next party or singles dance and tell your friends you're available for blind dates. Hopefully, you've been diligent about *The Rules* up to the breakup, and your social calendar is already full of dates. Remember, until the ring is on your finger or you're exclusive—by exclusive, we mean he's serious about marrying you and it's just a matter of time before he pops the question, as opposed to he's dating you until someone better comes along—you should be dating others. Nothing is better for cushioning the blow than the adoring attention of other men.

Whatever you do, don't lose your cool over this man. Now is the time to acquire faith, to believe in abundance. Tell yourself he is not the last man on earth, there are many others and certainly at least one out there for you. Talk to women friends who were dumped and then met "The One." They will tell you how happy they are now that so-and-so broke up with them, even though they didn't realize it at the time. Comfort yourself with uplifting slogans like, "When one door closes, another one opens" and any other positive philosophies you can think of.

Remember, *Rules* girls don't get hung up on men who reject them. They say, "His loss" or "Next!" They carry on. They don't tear themselves apart and wish they had done this differently or said this and not that. They don't write men letters offering to change or make things work out. They don't call them or send messages via friends. They accept it's over and get on with it. They don't waste time.

Don't Discuss *The Rules* with Your Therapist

YOU'RE USED TO TELLING your therapist everything, so it's only natural that you want to tell him or her about *The Rules*. We strongly suggest you don't go into great detail for the following reasons:

1. Some therapists will think that *The Rules* are dishonest and manipulative. They will encourage you to be open and vulnerable in your relationships with men, to talk things out, not to keep your feelings of love or hurt inside. That, of course, is the basis of the therapeutic process. It's great advice for resolving issues with family and friends, but it doesn't work in the initial stages of dating. Unfortunately, you have to be mysterious in the beginning of a romantic relationship, not an open book.

2. Some therapists don't realize women's capacity for forcing themselves on men who don't

want them and/or trying to make relationships happen. If they only knew how we wandered around campus hoping to run into men. If they only knew about the love poetry we've sent men, the interests we've pretended to have in order to make men like us (of course that never works), and if only they knew the lengths we've gone to get friendly with men's parents so that they would make their sons propose. If any therapist knew all these things—perhaps we never told them the whole story—they too would encourage us to focus on ourselves and not force things to happen. A woman in love with a man who is not in love with *her* can be dangerous to herself and him. Her only hope is to do *The Rules*.

3. Another reason not to discuss this book with your therapist is that you don't want to debate the merits of doing or not doing *The Rules*, otherwise you might lose your resolve to do them. It's hard enough to do *The Rules* when you believe in them, it's even harder when you talk to people who are downright against them. You should also not read any books that go counter to this philosophy or preach another method, particularly books that encourage women to pursue men or express their inner child.

Self-improvement is great—we all can be better in many areas. But self-improvement still won't get you the relationship you want. You may feel "whole" and "ready" after years of inner work and wonder why you still haven't snagged Mr. Right. The reason is you're not doing *The Rules*! Simply being a better person won't get you the man of your dreams. You have to do *The Rules*!

We suggest you try *The Rules* for six months before doing anything else. You can't do *The Rules* and something else at the same time. It just doesn't work!

If there's anything your therapist should be helping you with regarding *The Rules*, it's helping you develop the discipline and self-control necessary to do them!

Don't Break *The Rules*

IF YOU BREAK *The Rules*, will he still marry you?

Women are always asking us this question. They do *The Rules* for a month or two and then stop. He still hasn't said "I love you," much less proposed; yet, these women are now asking him out, bringing up marriage, and in some cases cleaning and decorating his apartment. They don't realize that *The Rules* way is not a hobby, but a religion. We keep doing *The Rules* until the ring is on our finger!

Let's take the case of our good friend, Candy. We told her about *The Rules* and she admitted she pursued men and they never proposed. She finally became willing to do everything we suggested for the first month or so of dating a hard catch named Barry. *The Rules* worked so well for Candy that after two months Barry took her to Jamaica for a week. That's when Candy went back to her old ways, ignoring our suggestions. She didn't think she had to do them anymore!

During their vacation, Candy asked for assurances about their future and acted more amorously than he did by leaving love poetry on his pillow and initiating sex. When they returned to New York and continued dating, she suggested they get together during the week as well as on weekends. Whenever he kissed her good night, she suggested they have sex or rent a movie or do some other thing to prolong their time together. He finally told her, "I love you, but I'm not *in* love with you. It's really strange because in the beginning there was something about you I had to get to know, but then it changed for me." Sure, all that love poetry!

Candy had the strength to end the relationship shortly after he told her he didn't love her and didn't want to marry her. Men don't lie! When they say they are not in love, they mean it. They are giving you a hint to break it off and look elsewhere, which most women don't heed. More often than not a woman will stay put, wasting precious time and hoping against hope that a man will change his mind. Have you ever gone through this? Aren't you tired of the pain? After Candy and Barry finally broke up, she *never* broke *The Rules* again. We are happy to report that she recently got married by doing *The Rules* as they are written, which should give all women hope, as many women break *The Rules* before they finally do them!

Rules girls don't hang around where they are not wanted. They don't try to revive a love gone sour. If you've broken *The Rules* to the point where he's convinced he's out of love with you, don't stick around hoping for a second chance. Remember, sometimes distance and time can make a man realize he's made the biggest mistake of his life. He can always call you—he has your phone number! Your part is to move on. Better that you do *The Rules* perfectly in your next relationship than to hang around, tolerating the loveless feelings of your current flame. So the answer to the question, "Will he still marry me if I break *The Rules*?" is, sorry to say, "Maybe yes, but most likely, no." So why take a chance?

That's why we strongly suggest that you don't break *The Rules* at all. Of course, you might make mistakes as you practice them. If you have chased men your whole life, you can consider it progress if you stop writing men love letters but call them once in a while. However, we believe in striving for perfection. When you do *The Rules* perfectly, you don't have to worry about second chances because he won't fall out of love with you. When you break *The Rules*, you automatically take away the pleasure men get from pursuing you, and they end up resenting you for it. Then they treat you badly and you're left wondering if it was something you said, did, didn't say, or didn't do that caused the problem. The answer is simple: you broke *The Rules*.

Prepare yourself for the fact that you will usually want to break *The Rules* after you have been dating someone for a couple of months. You may feel that the relationship is slowing down or going nowhere. He starts calling less often or still hasn't brought up marriage. Your girlfriends are planning the wedding and you still haven't met his parents. You feel anxious. Naturally, you want to shake things up or move things along. You are tempted to send him heavy-handed greeting cards from the "relationship" section of the card store or a love letter telling him how much you care about him to bring him closer to you. Without his permission, you want to throw out his old leather jacket and buy him a new one. You act as if you are his wife and feel entitled—after all, he sees you every weekend and bought you flowers twice. You may even decide to try to patch things up between him and his dad, who haven't spoken for a while. Let's face it, you are out of control!

Persist in this kind of behavior only if you want to destroy any chance of his proposing! *The Rules* action to take when things slow down is more of the same: reread how to behave on the first few dates (see *Rules* #9 and #10). Just *hang out*, trust in the process, be patient, don't nag him, and don't make anything happen. If you still feel frustrated after a few weeks, then get moving yourself! Rent that summer share with your girlfriend rather than waiting for him to suggest plans, or sign up for tennis lessons with that new instructor at your health club. Don't hone in on the man you are dating—he will feel smothered, not loved. Move away, get busy and elusive, and he will either miss you or not. Best to find out now rather than later if he can live without you.

There are many ways to break *The Rules* in the

early stages of a relationship. Here's another example:

After dating Ken for a month, Nicole decided to discard *The Rules*, which she had followed faithfully on the first four dates, and do what she *felt* like doing. If Ken was going to be her husband and father her children one day, she reasoned, why shouldn't she show him her true self? (Have you ever thought like Nicole?) So, for his birthday, she planned a big surprise party, partly as a ploy to meet his family and friends.

Not a weekend went by that Nicole's feelings didn't get the best of her. Once when they passed a playground, she suggested that they ride on the see-saw and swing on the swings, hoping to make him think about children. Ken found her behavior obvious and boring. The relationship went downhill from there. Nicole suggested couples therapy. He decided to break up with her and find someone else to date.

The lesson here is simple: don't break *The Rules*.

Don't make him a birthday party or give him an expensive gift, don't mention children, don't patch things up with his family, don't ask him out, and try not to call him very often. Basically, don't push yourself into his life or you won't be his wife!

When we pursue a man, a bell goes off in his head. *The challenge is over*, and his feelings start to fade. Suddenly, the romance turns to mud. Whatever he found adorable about you, he finds annoying. You're no longer his dream girl. It's as if you picked up the check or opened the door for him. You've taken his job away, you've done him a disservice.

So when you think that not calling him and other *Rules* are rude and hurtful, remember you are in fact helping him want you more. *The Rules* are actually *good* for him. So don't go by your feelings, just do *The Rules*.

The good news is that when a man is in love with you, he is not afraid to make a fool of himself by calling you five times in one day to tell you little, stupid things. (Yes, *he* can call you five times a day, but you can't or he'll think you're crazy!) *You* don't need to call him five times a day because when you do *The Rules* you have peace of mind. You don't need to call him for reassurance about the relationship because you're secure. And you don't have to stay up until 2 A.M. making excuses about why he hasn't called in two weeks because when you do *The Rules* he calls every week, sometimes every day!

Rules girls don't fret too much. They do *The Rules* and, in return, men give them that secure, snug feeling of being loved and being asked out for Saturday night early in the week or, better yet, at the end of their last date.

Now we all know women who broke *The Rules* and got married anyway. We know one *Rule* breaker who is always initiating intimacy with her husband. He says he loves her, but he never pinches her bottom in the kitchen and would rather watch the 11 o'clock news alone in his reclining chair than cuddle in bed with his wife.

So if you break *The Rules*, at least muster the courage to end the relationship when he says he is not in love and it's over. It will save you a lot of time. It's a spiritual axiom that when you feel someone slipping away, let the person go. Don't try to find out why he doesn't love you or what you could have done better. That's begging and, frankly, it's beneath a *Rules* girl to do. Be firm when it's over, knowing that you'll be able to break down and cry with your girlfriends later.

Even if you think you could have done *The Rules* better, don't blame yourself. Just love yourself and do them better the next time. Don't call him, don't talk to his friends about it, don't try to be buddies. It's over. Next! The relationship was not meant to be. There is somebody better out there for you. In the meantime, lining up a few dates is the best thing to do (and the best revenge).

Rule #33

Do *The Rules* and You'll Live Happily Ever After!

WHAT CAN YOU expect to get when you do *The Rules*? The answer is total adoration from the man of your dreams. Otherwise, why else would we do them?

Let's face it, many of the things we ask you to do or not do in this book are downright difficult. Not calling him, not being intimate too soon, not bringing up marriage or children, and ending the date first require a great deal of self-restraint, patience, and determination. Sometimes we thought we would simply *die* at the thought of holding off having sex. And the agony of not calling him! There were many days when we just had to hear his voice.

So what kept us going? What made us continue doing *The Rules*? The incredible, unbelievable pay-offs, twenty of which are listed below. So when you find yourself resisting doing a certain *Rule* (maybe you don't want to end the phone call after five or ten minutes because you're afraid he'll think you're rude and never call again), read this list and summon the courage. Remember, men want you more when you do *The Rules* and lose interest quicker when you don't!

1. The biggest payoff first: he wants to marry you! Most women bring up marriage or the future after a couple of weeks or months of dating a man. They want to know where the relationship is going. Most likely, it's going nowhere because men don't want to be pushed into proposing. As a *Rules* girl, you've been trained not to bring up marriage or kids. You talk about books, business, politics, football, and the weather. When you do *The Rules*, he ends up proposing.

2. When you are seated at a booth in a restaurant, he slides over and sits next to you. Sitting opposite you is just *too far away* when he's truly in love.

3. He sends you roses after you have sex.

4. He writes love notes or poetry for you and tapes them on the refrigerator door.

5. He finds your idiosyncrasies harmless rather than annoying. You never have to worry that he'll leave you if you don't change a bad habit. He doesn't like it—but he doesn't leave you because of it.

6. He calls to see how your doctor's visit went.

7. He gives you little presents, jewelry, and flowers on every possible occasion.

8. He gets angry when you don't pay attention to him. He wants your constant attention

and companionship. He doesn't ignore you. He's always walking into whatever room you're in. You are never a "football widow." He wants to take you to the football game (even if you don't like the sport or understand it) in order to spend more time with you. He wants to do everything with you!

9. He is always ready to make up after a fight.
10. He gets involved in every aspect of your life. You don't bore him.
11. If you call him at work, he'll always want to talk to you even if he is busy. He calls you from work a lot anyway.
12. He doesn't like to work late because he wants to see more of you.
13. When you have a cold or become ill, he still wants to be with you.
14. He always wants the phone number of where you are so he can get in touch with you.
15. He watches out for you.
16. He doesn't like it when you go to bachelorette parties.
17. He *listens* when you talk to him.
18. When you walk around the house with very little on, he whistles, as though you were a babe on the beach.
19. Your picture is on his desk in the office and in his wallet. He always wants to look at you.
20. When he loves you, he loves your kids.

Hopefully, some or all of the above promises will motivate you to do *The Rules*. Still another incentive for doing *The Rules* is what you *won't* get:

1. No messy divorce. Instead, you have one of those made-in-heaven marriages. He'll take care of you when you're old. He really, really loves you. A *Rules* marriage is forever.

2. No outside counseling. He has no interest in couples therapy. When you do *The Rules*, he doesn't have big issues with you. He doesn't wish you were this, that, or different. His love for you is unconditional. Sure, he might wish you balanced your checkbook, lost ten pounds, or cleaned the house more often, but he is not seriously annoyed or upset about it. He finds it all amusing. Ultimately, he finds most things about you adorable. He doesn't feel the need to consult a professional to talk about his feelings. He's busy planning your next vacation or chasing you around the house for a quick kiss.

3. No anxiety. You're not walking on eggshells. You're not always wondering if you hurt his feelings or said the wrong thing. You know that he will always forgive you, not hurt you, that he is ready to make up with you at a moment's notice.

4. No physical abuse. When you do *The Rules*, he treats you like a fragile, delicate flower. He cups your face, rubs your back when you've had a hard day, and strokes your hair as if it were silk. You don't have to worry about being battered.

5. No cheating. When you do *The Rules*, he thinks you're more beautiful than other women (even if you're not). He doesn't want to have sex with anyone but you; he can't get enough of you and even wants to build up his biceps for you. You can leave him in a room full of gorgeous women and not worry. When he loves you, he loves you!

Love Only Those Who Love You

ONE OF THE greatest payoffs of doing *The Rules* is that you grow to love only those who love you. If you have been following the suggestions in this book, you have learned to take care of yourself. You're eating well and working out. You're busy with interests and hobbies and dating, and you're not calling or chasing men. You have high self-esteem because you are not sleeping around or having affairs with married men. You love with your head, not just your heart. You are honest; you have boundaries, values, and ethics. You are special, a creature unlike any other. Any man would be lucky to have you!

Because you love yourself, you are no longer interested in men who ignore you, cheat on you, hurt you either physically or emotionally, and, of course, any man who can live without you. The kind of men who once nauseated you because they were open books, called too much, wrote mushy cards, and told their friends and parents about you long before you said anything to your friends and parents, you now find attractive and desirable. Of course, we don't mean to suggest that you love someone simply because he loves you. No, you love whom you love. But when a man you are interested in is crazy about you, you are happy about it. You are not bored or turned off. You don't think, "Gee, this is too easy." *Love should be easy!*

As a result of doing *The Rules*, you have a new attitude. You love being loved. You think that anyone who thinks you're great is great, not a jerk. You have no desire to chase someone who hasn't noticed you, sought you out, or dialed your number and asked you out. Love is finally simple and sweet, not heart-wrenching and hard.

You might be saying to yourself, "But of course!" Yet, you'd be surprised how many of us only went after men who didn't want us. We thought it was our mission in life to reform men, make men who preferred blondes (if we are brunette) interested in us. We thought we had to *work* at making men love us. If love came easily, we were bored. Now we like love to be easy. We go to a dance or a party and we don't have to work at all. We just show up, do *The Rules*, and whoever likes us, likes us, and who doesn't? We accept whatever happens. We're laid back and confidant. We don't struggle.

You're living painfree. No more lonely Saturday nights, no more waiting for the phone to ring, no more fantasizing about the man who got away or wanted your best friend, no more jealous tantrums, no more checking his desk drawers or coat pockets for incriminating evidence. To be adored and secure at last! That's the incredible payoff you get when you do *The Rules*, and you're going to love it!

Be Easy to Live With

THE RULES ARE about playing hard to get. Once you've got him, it's about being easy to be with.

Many things can go wrong in the first few months or year of marriage. You might have fights about where you'll live. There may be money problems or family problems. You thought you wouldn't have to work so hard, that you could work part-time and start planning for kids. He says he wants you to work full-time and have kids later. He thought you would make him home-cooked meals like his mother made his father and gets angry every time you open a can of tuna.

There may be more serious problems—for example, loss of job or illness. What is *The Rule* now?

The Rule is that as hard as you worked to play hard to get is how hard you must work to be easygoing! Be kind, considerate, and patient; try to overlook his faults and build up his ego—tell him how good *he* looks, try to see things *his* way.

Don't expect him to see things *your* way all the time.

It's natural to want to fly off the handle every time something goes wrong in the love kingdom—we all have fantasies of marital bliss. But you must try to be serene and unselfish, or you won't be a happy princess.

Let's say you've cooked him his favorite dinner, but he calls at the last minute to say he's working late and that you should eat without him. You're mad and want to scream into the phone, "But I cooked a special meal just for you!" Instead, take a deep breath and say something sweet like, "You've really been working hard lately. I'm so proud of you." Promise him a back rub when he gets home. Then get busy—read a book or clean the house. Don't tell him how disappointed you are and turn into a nag. Remember, he's working long hours for the both of you!

Or let's say it's your birthday and you know he's getting you something special but you have this thing about getting a dozen roses. So, you're on edge all day and wondering if you should give him a hint. You're also mad that you even have to say something!

So what do you do? Tell a friend, buy *yourself* flowers, and forget about it. Practice being happy with what you get instead of expecting him to fulfill your every romantic fantasy. Also, give it time. The roses will come. Life is long.

In general, remember that he works hard all day—whether or not you think he does. Don't hit him with every crisis the minute he walks in the door. And remember, small acts of kindness make for a great marriage.

This isn't always easy. Sometimes you just don't feel like shaving your legs, cooking him a hot meal, or being so sweet, kind, and loving. Your PMS might be in high gear. How do you keep yourself going?

We think it helps to use any stress busters—yoga, meditation, aerobics, running, biking, tennis, a spa weekend, and so on—to reenergize your batteries. True, it takes a lot more work to be a *Rules* wife than an ordinary one, but it's so much more rewarding in the long run, don't you agree?

You might also try reading spiritual literature, seeing a therapist, or joining a support group if things get too much for you or you find yourself constantly bickering with him about little things. But whatever path you choose, remember to keep the focus on *yourself*. Don't go into therapy or exercise with the idea of changing your husband or prodding him to get healthy, too. Change *yourself,* and your reaction to what he is or isn't doing.

On any given day, try to remember that an attitude of gratitude can go a long way. On bad days, try to remember the reasons you married your husband. In the middle of a fight with your husband, stop and recall all those bad blind dates, the seemingly endless search for Mr. Right. That should help you not say anything too mean in the middle of a fight like, "I wish I had never met you!" or "I should have married someone else." Don't dredge up the past or be mean-spirited and say things like, "Remember the time you were late for my sister's wedding?" Tell yourself, "I found Mr. Right—how important is this?"

If you want a happy *Rules* marriage, may we suggest a few more rules?

1. Don't go through his clothes, pockets, and drawers looking for anything—lipstick stains, women's phone numbers, hotel receipts, and such. Remember, if you're in a *Rules* marriage, he's not cheating on you. Then go about your business—read a book, exercise. Don't you have a letter to send or a drawer to clean out?

2. Don't open his mail unless it is specifically addressed to both of you. It is natural to think that what's his is yours, but that's not for you to decide. If he doesn't specifically show you something, or include you in certain things, it's none of your business. Besides, the less nosy you are, the more he will want to tell you—eventually.

3. Try not to raise your voice or scream too much. For some of us, who are more emotional than others, this is not always easy to do. For example, when he watches the ball-game on TV all afternoon instead of helping you clean the house, don't zap the tube off in a moment of anger. Nicely tell him you need his help. If he still insists on watching the game, leave him alone. Tell yourself, "No big deal." This kind of thing is not that impor-

tant. To lose your cool every time you don't get your way gets you nowhere.

4. Don't hold him back from doing something he really wants to do, such as a ski weekend with a bunch of friends. He should always feel free. He should not think of you as the kind of person who wouldn't want him to be happy because it means not being with you. If you feel you have to hold him back from anything, there's a problem in the relationship. Don't try to control him. Remember, we don't make things happen or stop them from happening! We're easy to be with, we go with the flow.

5. Always try to show utter contentment with him, yourself, the world. Be carefree. You'll get fewer wrinkles and backaches; you'll feel less stress. He'll want you more when you're the easygoing girl he dated—a creature unlike any other. Reread *Rule #1.*

6. If you're feeling weak about *The Rules* and start acting like your old pain-in-the-neck self—angry, needy, not so nice—reread *The Rules* from the beginning. It will inspire you to. act like a creature unlike any other, and will remind you of the benefits of doing so. Namely, your husband will find you irresistible all over again!

7. Make time for a healthy love/sex life and spend quality time together. We know that after a hard day of work, food shopping, aerobics, and so on, you may not want to have wild sex or go to the football game with him.

When you were dating you did things because you wanted to please him so that he would propose. Now that you have him, you think you don't have to try that hard.

True, you never have to do *The Rules* quite as hard as you did in the first three months of the relationship. But that doesn't mean you can be selfish or inconsiderate or lazy. Remember that if you want a good marriage, *The Rules* never really end!

Last But Not Least— 12 Extra Hints

1. When he asks you out, silently count to five before saying yes. It will make him nervous and that's good!
2. Don't call him even when you feel mean about not calling him. If he loves you, he'll call anyway. When he asks you to call him, call him once. Do the absolute minimum!
3. When he asks you out for ice cream, a drink, or to a football game when you wish you were going out for a fancy dinner, say "Sure!" Remember, you're hard to get but easy to be with! You'll go to an expensive restaurant another time.
4. When walking down the street, drop *his* hand first, ever so slightly.
5. *The Rules* are written in stone, but how you do them will depend on your temperament. If you're an overly nice, gushy girl, do *The Rules* like boot camp. The stricter, the better, that is, never call him, or return his phone calls very infrequently.

But if you're already cool or aloof by nature, be extra sweet when you do *The Rules*. Call him once for every five times he calls you. Be affectionate. As long as you're not asking him out or moving in or bringing up marriage, you can show him you like him a little more on each date.

6. If he's being a bad boy, taking you for granted, or you want to shake things up to make him propose faster, book a trip for a week. If things are going well but you still want to make him miss you, plan a weekend away with a girlfriend. Tell him a week before you go, in a very innocent, sweet voice, that you're going to Florida with your girlfriend to get a tan and relax. "Nothing serious, hon, just some R & R."

7. If you are unsure about him, double date with a *Rules*-minded friend. She will tell you whether he's planning to marry you or not.

8. Even men who are in love with you and want to marry you will occsaionally say things to irk you or make you nervous, such as, "I'll take you there if we're still seeing each other next year . . . you know how relationships go." Don't get paranoid, just ignore him. Most girls would make a big fuss about it and get mad. *Rules* girls stay calm when men tease them.

9. Don't let him know you're *afraid* to be alone, to be without a man. Women who let men know how much they need to be with some-

one invite bad behavior. Then he knows you'll put up with anything not to be alone.

10. Don't get angry if he's taking longer than you'd like to propose. Most women want to be proposed to *yesterday*. Whatever you do, don't blow up at him and press the issue. You've waited this long, hang in there. If you're doing *The Rules*, it will happen!

11. Don't get sloppy about your looks. Continue to exercise. Men don't leave women who put on twenty pounds after the wedding or the first baby, but if you want your fiancé or husband to keep drooling over you, keep fit.

12. Read the newspaper and books so you can talk to your life partner about things other than your work issues or dirty diapers. Men want wives who can fulfill them mentally as well as physically and emotionally.

The Rules-at-a-Glance

Rule 1   Be a "Creature Unlike Any Other"

Rule 2   Don't Talk to a Man First (and Don't Ask Him to Dance)

Rule 3   Don't Stare at Men or Talk Too Much

Rule 4   Don't Meet Him Halfway or Go Dutch on a Date

Rule 5   Don't Call Him and Rarely Return His Calls

Rule 6   Always End Phone Calls First

Rule 7   Don't Accept a Saturday Night Date after Wednesday

Rule 8   Fill Up Your Time before the Date

Rule 9   How to Act on Dates 1, 2, and 3

Rule 10   How to Act on Dates 4 through Commitment Time

Rule 11   Always End the Date First

Rule 12   Stop Dating Him if He Doesn't Buy You a Romantic Gift for Your Birthday or Valentine's Day

Rule 13   Don't See Him More than Once or Twice a Week

The Rules

Book II

Acknowledgments

We would like to thank our wonderful husbands and children for their love and support.

Special thanks, too, to our agent Stedman Mays at Connie Clausen & Associates.

A big thank you to everyone at Warner Books, in particular Chairman of Time Warner Trade Publishing Larry Kirshbaum, our Editor Caryn Karmatz Rudy, Senior Publicist Tina Andreadis, and Publicity Assistant Heather Fain.

And, of course, we owe our thanks to our mothers Sylvia and Margie, our friends, our staff, Rules contacts around the world, and the thousands of women who wrote and called and encouraged us to write *The Rules II*. Most of all, we dedicate this book to the memory of Connie Clausen, our literary agent and friend.

Ellen and Sherrie

Foreword: *The Rules* Phenomenon

Four years ago, when we set out to write *The Rules,* we knew that we had an important message to share. We believed in *The Rules.* We had seen them work time and time again in our own lives, in our close circle of girlfriends and an ever-widening circle of friends and acquaintances, as well as coworkers and relatives.

When our phones began ringing off the hook with dating questions and (eventually) success stories, we knew we had to write *The Rules* in book form to make it available to *all* women.

Lo and behold, *The Rules* became not just a best-selling book, but a phenomenon, revolutionizing dating practices both here in America and abroad.

In fact, *The Rules* became so popular that it achieved a kind of pop culture status. It was spoofed on *Saturday Night Live* ("Get the ring!"), used as the plot for several TV sitcoms, and also inspired a number of parody books including *Breaking the Rules* ("Stare straight at men and talk incessantly") and *Rules for Cats* ("Don't accept a trip to the vet after Wednesday").

Suddenly, *The Rules* was everywhere! A financial publication ran an article on the rules for investing ("Don't buy on Friday if your broker calls after Wednesday") and a political columnist wrote that one presidential candidate might have won the election if he had just tried to be a "creature unlike any other."

Why all the fuss? Why all the interest in *The Rules* when there are dozens of other dating books on the market? Why has *The Rules* become such a phenomenon?

The answer is simple: *The Rules* work! Unlike other dating books that are therapeutic and theoretical—that sound good, that give warm 'n fuzzy, meaningless, and misleading advice such as *be yourself, don't play games, tell a man how you feel,* but don't work in real life—*The Rules* tell the truth about dating and help you get Mr. Right!

The Rules take the analysis and angst out of dating. It's simple. If he calls you, he likes you. If he doesn't, *Next!* What does *be yourself* mean if that's calling a man three times a day or staying on the phone for three hours? Why would anyone want to read a dating book that didn't help you get the man you want to marry you?

Many people ask how we wrote a bestseller. To be honest, we were not trying to. We wrote *The Rules* to help women date with self-esteem and get married. Period.

While we are naturally thrilled by the success of the book, what's been even more rewarding is seeing how women of all ages and all walks of life use *The Rules* to love themselves and marry Mr. Right. After three decades of haphazard dating—dutch treat, sex on the first date, and living together—these women are delighted that such a dating book exists.

"I wish I had known about *The Rules* ten years ago," is the most frequent comment we hear.

"*The Rules* should be given out to all women at birth," wrote another *Rules* fan.

The book hit a chord not only with single women in their twenties, thirties, and forties, but with mothers and grandmothers. "She won't listen to me, maybe she'll listen to you," wrote one mom. Another mom told us she gave the book to her daughter and her daughter's friends.

While many readers thanked us for the general guidelines provided in *The Rules*, just as many wrote and called asking for more specific answers to dating situations and problems—for example, rules for long-distance relationships, rules for getting back an ex-boyfriend, rules for dating a celebrity, rules for dating a coworker, rules for turning a male friend into a boyfriend, rules for dating services and on-line dating, and for advice on how to start a *Rules* support group, among many other topics.

We wrote *The Rules II* to answer all these questions—and to clarify any confusion you might have about rules in the first book, such as, "How will he know the real me if I do *The Rules*?" and "Can I *ever* call a man?"

We have included some success stories in *The Rules II* that we hope will inspire you to do *The Rules*. We hope to publish many more—perhaps yours!—in the future.

We look forward to your comments, questions, success stories, and wedding invitations!

Ellen and Sherrie

Chapter 1

Why *The Rules* Work

WHY DO *THE RULES* work?

Because *The Rules* are based upon the basic truths of human nature! Everyone wishes we could be more open and honest with men in the early stages of dating or ask men out, but these wishes are pure fantasy. To think men and women should treat each other exactly alike, as platonic friends do—dutch treat, even steven, tit for tat—is unrealistic. In the *romantic* world, there's only one way that truly works. The man must be attracted to and then pursue the woman. It simply doesn't work any other way.

That doesn't mean we have to *like* it. Even *we* didn't want *The Rules* to be true. Who wants it to be true that a man's attraction to us doesn't grow? Who wants it to be true that a man might lose interest if we're too aggressive, too needy, or too predictable?

Everyone wishes certain things were different from what they are. Who wants war, crime, or bitter cold weather? Who wants to diet and exercise? Wouldn't it be great if we could eat whatever we wanted, whenever we felt like it and still be slim, fit, and have perfect thighs?

Rules girls are realists. They accept that men and women are different and act accordingly. They don't always *like* to do *The Rules*, but they do them anyway because they love the results.

Of course, as popular as *The Rules* has become, it has also been the subject of controversy—mostly by the media and the authors of other dating books, not by women who simply want advice about men. They just want to get married!

The Rules have been criticized for being old-fashioned and antifeminist, and for encouraging women to play games and get married at any cost ("get the ring"). We would like to examine these criticisms one by one and explain why they are unfounded.

Old-fashioned? Not really. While *The Rules* may sound like something your mother may have told you about, times and circumstances have completely changed. Women in the '90s need *The Rules*—not because pursuing men is morally wrong or scandalous, or any of the reasons your mother may have told you. No, *The Rules* tell us not to pursue men for one simple reason. It doesn't work!

Fifty years ago, women didn't call men or live with men before marriage because it was considered socially unacceptable. Fifty years ago, they didn't even need to think about "ending the date first." Their fathers ended it for them by requiring them to be home at a certain time, much like their great-grandfathers put an end to dates by holding up a shotgun on the front porch!

In addition, back then, women often had to get married in order to move out of their parents' house. Women were financially dependent on men, and once married they became full-time wives and mothers who, for the most part, did not pursue careers.

Compare that to '90s women. Many are financially self-sufficient. They can afford their own apartments, cars, vacations, wardrobes, and creature comforts. They can even have or adopt and support a child on their own. They no longer need men to get away from their parents or to have good or interesting lives. But the truth is they *want* men in their lives—as partners/friends, lovers, husbands/fathers. They can function without men, but they yearn for marriage and children and/or fulfilling relationships.

Their problem is *how* to get married or be in fulfilling relationships. The sexual revolution of the '60s proved to be filled with empty promises— sex and living together did not add up to commitment.

Who or what can women turn to for dating advice? They may or may not be able to relate to their mothers. Besides, some mothers, trying to be hip and modern or desperate for their daughters to get married and produce a grandchild, will give them bad advice and tell them to call men and pay their own way. ("Don't be so picky," they tell them.)

Their female friends, conditioned by the social

mores of today and with well-meaning intentions, may say "Oh, call him if you like him! What have you got to lose?" If he turns them down, "So, what?" they say.

Well, we say:

(1) Maybe if you don't call him, he'll build up a *real* desire and call you!

(2) A man who is receptive to your advances (without making any of his own) may date or even marry you at your suggestion, but down the road he'll be bored and ambivalent toward you.

Women have turned to *The Rules* because it's the only advice they can count on that works. They're not retro, they're fabulous!

Antifeminist? No, as far as we are concerned, there is no conflict between *The Rules* and feminism. *Rules* girls can be feminists. *We are feminists*. We believe in and are grateful for the advances women have made in the last century. How else could we have become authors and formed a company? All women have different definitions of feminism, but to us, it is about getting equal pay for equal work. It's about women being authors, astronauts, doctors, lawyers, CEOs, or whatever they want to be—getting promoted, being treated the same and paid as much as men!

Feminism is also about women believing in their own importance. It is about being fulfilled by our jobs, our hobbies, our friendships. It is knowing that the women in our lives are as important as the men—and treating our friends with respect and consideration to prove it!

But with all due respect, feminism has not changed men or the nature of romantic relationships. Like it or not, men are emotionally and romantically different from women. Men are biologically the aggressor. They thrive on challenge—whether it's the stock market, basketball, or football—while women crave security and bonding. This has been true since civilization began!

Men who respond to *The Rules* are not sick or stupid, but quite normal and healthy. Your average guy. What would be *sick* is if a man chased and chased a woman who clearly didn't want him, who repeatedly said "no" when he asked her out as early as Monday for Saturday night. But that's not what we're talking about. We're talking about a woman who says "yes" to dates when asked a few days in advance and is nice to men on dates. She's simply not too eager and doesn't drop everything to see him at a moment's notice. That way he respects her and wants to be with her and marry her.

Why men are naturally driven by challenge is not important. The point is to do what works to have a successful relationship, which is to let men do the pursuing . . . in other words, to follow *The Rules*.

After twenty to thirty years of do-what-you-feel and haphazard dating, most women we know are actually relieved to have rules and boundaries to live by. These women are happy that feminism has helped them get ahead in business and given them financial independence, but they agree that trying to be as aggressive in relationships with men as they are in their careers doesn't work.

Are we telling women to play games? Some people like to focus on the most superficial aspects in *The Rules*—the ones most likely to promote controversy—but the book is really about self-esteem, about setting boundaries. Yes, in some ways, you're playing a game. The game is called *liking yourself*! The game is not accepting just any treatment from a man. The game is being true to your heart. Everyone knows in their hearts that *The Rules* work, that this is the way it really is. But some people have to read the book a few times before they get the message that it's not just about egg timers, lipstick, and not returning calls.

The Rules is not an etiquette book—it's not about how to order wine on a date or which fork to use. While these niceties are important, they're not what *The Rules* focus on. *The Rules* are about saving women—and men, for that matter—heartache. There are many disastrous relationships out there because women either initiated relationships with men or kept them going long after they should have been over. A failed relationship is depressing, confidence-shaking, and altogether unpleasant. By following *The Rules*, you avoid these disastrous results—and these painful emotions.

We had to write *The Rules* strictly, like a strict diet book, because we knew women would break them. You always sneak in your favorite high-fat meal or a piece of chocolate cake on Saturday night. With such strict rules, even if women broke the occasional rule, they could still reap the benefits of doing the rest.

Even therapists, whom we were sure would find the "be mysterious" part of *The Rules* objectionable, are actually recommending the book to their clients (see Chapter 8). They agree that the openness and honesty so necessary in therapy do not work in the initial stages of dating.

Are *The Rules* too marriage-minded? No, just realistic. Many women want to get married, and why not? It's great to have a wonderful man to share your life with—end of story. We're not telling women they're nothing without a man. It's just that many women feel that if they don't marry a nice guy, they're missing something. It's a fact. This is how they really feel. It's not a moral issue. Can they be happy without a husband? Sure. Can you be happy without taking vacations? Sure, but why would you want to?

We are not advocating marriage at any cost. On the contrary, in Chapter 17, "Buyer Beware," we explain how to determine if he's Mr. Right. This is a thinking woman's guide to marriage. This is not about being a Stepford wife.

Indeed, *The Rules* represents a change in attitude about dating, a new spirituality that is sorely needed today. It's going against nature when you chase a man, sleep with him too soon, or beg him to marry you. He may end up mistreating you, even if he marries you. He may never forgive you for trapping him and treat you badly.

Conversely, when you do *The Rules* on a man

who initially showed interest, he gets to fall in love with you and value you. He does not take you for granted. Every phone call and date is precious. He never feels trapped or that you pressured him to marry you because *he* did the calling, the pursuing, the proposing.

Rules marriages are happy marriages. *Rules* husbands make wonderful partners for life. They are attentive and involved husbands and fathers. They change diapers, help the kids with their homework, and plan family vacations.

The Rules work. They really do. That's why women who want to be happily married—or at the very least, in a loving relationship—are living by *The Rules*—and loving the results!

Chapter 2

Rules for Turning a Friend Into a Boyfriend

YOU'VE BEEN FRIENDS for ages. Now, for whatever reason, you've decided he's The One. Can you turn a friend into a boyfriend?

Only if *he* really always liked you, but you or circumstances prevented the friendship from developing further. For example, *you* never wanted anything more until recently, or you were both dating other people. Maybe you couldn't imagine him as a boyfriend because of age differences (he's much older or younger than you), personality differences (he's artsy, you're a business-type), or you come from different backgrounds.

How can you be sure he always liked you as more than a friend if you've just been friends?

There are certain things a friend does or says when he is drawn to you. For example:

He always just happens to be in your neighborhood or business area. He likes to watch *Friends* in your apartment. He likes your TV set better. If you are coworkers, he's frequently drinking water from the fountain near your desk. If you're in college, he's always hanging out outside of your dorm room or is often at the dining hall when you're there.

The bottom line: when a man is attracted to you, he finds ways—excuses—to be near you. We're not exaggerating when we say, whoever's near you likes you! You don't have to look far or wide to find him. He's always hanging around. You can't get rid of him!

When a friend wants to date you, he doesn't talk about other women, even if he's dating someone else. He never seems to notice other women, even your very attractive friend. If, in fact, he is attracted to other women, he tells everyone but you. Around you, the words will just not come out, they stick in his throat.

While he's private about his own love life, he wants to know about yours and asks a lot of questions. He wants to know the type of guy you like to date and what you like to do on Saturday night. He makes it sound as if he's just curious, *no big deal, of course,* but he's really figuring out how he's going to use that information to make a move one day. He thinks anyone you're dating is not good enough for you. He'll even put them down ("His father got him the job.").

When a male friend is really interested in you, he tries to be helpful. He offers to show you how to play tennis or how to work the computer. He might help you move your stuff from one apartment to another or listen to your work or roommate problems without expecting anything in return. In fact, he never expects you to help him with anything, unless it's an excuse to stay connected to you.

If he likes you as more than a friend, he'll tease you, flirt with you, and make you laugh. He thinks your shortcomings are cute.

He means more than he says. He tries to be cool around you, but he's really quite nervous.

When a male friend is *not* interested in you romantically, he behaves quite differently. He's calm, rational, matter-of-fact. You can take everything he does and says at face value.

He asks you for advice about dating another woman because he *really* wants your advice! He's simply interested in a woman's perspective. He's not secretly in love with you or bringing it up to get closer to you. He talks freely about liking other women. He might even say in front of you, "She's really cute." He doesn't think he could be hurting your feelings because you're his friend. You're like his sister—there's no sexual undercurrent.

When a male friend likes you as a friend, he's not that interested in your love life. He's satisfied with your friendship. If you're not dating anyone, he might offer to fix you up with someone, but he doesn't want to go out with you himself. He doesn't want to start anything, he feels no spark.

If you're having a problem with the guy you're dating, he will try to help you "work it out," as opposed to helping you get out of the relationship! He's not angry if he sees you with other men because he's not interested in you romantically. He *wants* to see you happy. If he's a little jealous when you have a boyfriend, it's in the same way a close girlfriend might be. Your relationship reminds him of what he doesn't have and takes time away from your friendship with him. It's a friendship loss, not a romantic loss. This, however, doesn't mean he wants you. You'd know if he did—if you thought about it honestly or read this chapter.

When a male friend is just a friend, he helps you as much as you help him. He'll show you how to read a financial statement, you'll teach him how to cook. Everything's dutch treat. It's a mutually beneficial relationship.

A male friend might even be your best friend—someone who would be there in a pinch if you ever needed him. He would lend you money to pay your rent, visit you in the hospital if you had an accident, or come to the funeral if a family member died. *But he doesn't look down the street when you walk away, try to stare at you when you're not looking, or secretly dream about having sex with you. And such feelings on a man's part are essential in the beginning of a romantic relationship!*

If he likes you only as a friend, there is nothing you can do about becoming his girlfriend. Don't try to convince him by having a heart-to-heart talk about your feelings because it will probably put a strain on your friendship. He will feel awkward or sorry for you, but he still won't feel a spark. He may try a "let's sleep together" once or twice. But it won't mean much to him and you, if not both of you, will come to regret it.

Worse yet, the two of you may decide to date or even get married at *your* initiation. But because *he* never felt a spark, your marriage will be more of a friendship and if you want more than that you will constantly be unhappy. You will be doubting your looks and your sexuality and complain, "He never notices me." Your self-confidence really plummets when you sleep with or get involved with a man who only really wanted a friendship. It's a bad road to travel. Don't even try it.

Just do *The Rules*—not to get him to like you since you can't—but for *your* self-esteem. Do *The Rules* so that your whole life isn't about this unavailable friend. Don't call him. When he calls, get off the phone in ten minutes. Don't play therapist when he talks about his girlfriend problems. More important, try to meet other men. You're better off forcing yourself to go to social events to meet your possible husband than forcing yourself on this friend.

But if you think he may be interested in you, you can casually mention that you're having boyfriend problems, not seeing your boyfriend anymore or that you're not dating anyone in particular. See how he reacts. If he's interested, he'll ask you out, and then start doing *The Rules*.

Don't talk to him like a friend—like Elaine on *Seinfeld*—but be light, feminine, and mysterious. Don't tell him all your problems. Don't start pursuing him with calls, notes, and dinner invitations. Don't think you can say or do anything you want—call him whenever you feel like it or suddenly try to increase the time you spend together—

because you were platonic friends. Concentrate on making your relationship a *Rules* relationship. Keep in mind, the dynamics will be a little different now. For example, if he's from out-of-town and used to crashing on your couch when he visits you, now you should be the first to say, "It's been great, but I have a really big day tomorrow," and end the evenings first.

Now that you want him, you may be tempted to go to the other extreme—call him all the time, talk about your change of heart, refer to him as your soul mate, talk about marriage or the future—and drive him away. Men don't like to be overwhelmed, *even by women they like.*

Many women who wake up one day and decide that their male friend is their soul mate have been known to come on too strong and overwhelm their friend. Remember, part of the reason he liked you is that you didn't really notice him, and never pursued him! You've been a challenge—not because you were trying to do *The Rules*—but because you were truly not interested. You were naturally indifferent.

Therefore, when you start to date, you must not let the fact that he always liked you stop you from doing certain rules. For example, don't see him at the last minute or all the time. Don't start knitting him sweaters or talk about marriage or moving in. Okay, you've decided he's The One. But until he's decided you're The One and courts you and proposes, you have to do *The Rules*—or you might ruin a good thing!

Second Chances—*Rules* for Getting Back an Ex

IF YOU ARE SOMEONE who read *The Rules* and thought, "If only I had done *The Rules* on my old boyfriend" or "So that's why he wouldn't commit!" then this chapter is for you.

You may not have seen him in months or even years, but now you're convinced he could have been The One. You didn't know any better and you blew it . . . and now you could kick yourself! If only you had known *The Rules* back then!

You want him back. At the very least, you want to give the relationship a second chance. You want to do *The Rules* this time and see what happens. You're wondering if there's any hope. You want to know what to do next, if anything.

Before you make a move, take a deep breath, calm down, and forgive yourself. Realize that what you're going through is very common—regretting the past, wishing you had behaved differently with a certain man, thinking he's the one that got away and you'll never meet anyone better. We've received hundreds of letters from women that begin with: "I wish I had had this book ten years ago when I was dating (fill in the blank)." These women either just didn't know they should behave a certain way with men, or they instinctively knew they should but didn't have the strength to do it without specific guidelines and support.

Of course all you care about now that you've read *The Rules* is, can you get him back?

It depends.

If you initiated the relationship—spoke to him first, asked him out—and he eventually ended it, then it's not only over, *it was never meant to be*. Don't call him or write him or try to contact him in any way to say you've changed and want a second chance. He didn't really want you in the first place. Forget him and move on!

But if he pursued you and you broke rules—for example, you were possessive, saw him every night, or moved in with him and he broke it off because he felt suffocated—there may be hope. There's one way to find out and we call it "One Call for Closure."

Call him *once* when you're sure he's not home, so you get his answering machine. Calling when he's not in is crucial; you don't want to make him uncomfortable if he doesn't want to hear from you or is involved with someone else or even married. Leaving a message also allows him to call you if and when *he* wants to, which is the best start for any conversation between you. Your message gives him time to think and the option of not calling, which you must give him. Of course, if his answering machine says, "We're not home right now" and you hear a woman's voice chiming in, do not leave a message. Leave him alone and go on with your life.

Assuming he's not involved with someone, we suggest you leave the following message: "Hi, it's (your name). I just wanted to say hello, to see how you're doing. You can reach me at (phone number)." That's it!

If you don't hear from him, it's over. Don't call again to make sure he got the message. He got the message. His answering machine isn't broken. Don't write him or track him down at work, home, his favorite bar, or the gym. That's called stalking. Forget all about him and move on. You must work on accepting the way he feels and not dwelling on the past and what might have been. Don't berate yourself; if you were supposed to end up with him, you would have. Tell yourself there's someone else out there for you, try to date others, and keep doing *The Rules*.

If he does call, don't automatically assume he's rekindling the romance. He might just be returning your call, being polite, nothing deep. So try not to get too excited or show how happy you are to hear from him. Be cool, cordial. Say, "Oh hi. How are you?" Don't say, "I was hoping you'd call."

If he asks why you called, just say, "Oh, I just wondered how you were doing and wanted to say hello." Keep the conversation light . . . business, vacations, and so on. Don't ask him if he ever thinks about you or misses you, if he's seeing any-one new. After ten minutes, say, "Well, I have to get going. It was nice talking to you." Don't stay on the phone for thirty minutes or an hour, wait-ing and hoping he will suggest drinks. If he doesn't ask you out within ten minutes, he's not interested. Remember, if he is interested but needs more than ten minutes to ask out an ex-girlfriend, he can always call you again!

If he does ask you out, say yes if it's for a fu-ture date—it need not be a Saturday night the first time you meet, but it should be at least three days in advance. You want to let him know that your life didn't stop since the two of you split and that your calendar is full.

Your first date with an ex-boyfriend is very much like a first date with a man you just met. It's almost like a new relationship, so let him pick you up and take you out.

Look very, very good when you meet him. Extra care with your makeup, pretty outfit. Don't dress down as if it's your 200th date, even if tech-nically, it is. Be light, casual, upbeat. Needless to say, don't have a heavy discussion about your re-lationship or the past, unless he brings up the subject. Even if he talks about the way it was, try not to dwell on it. Discuss general topics such as what you have both been doing professionally, if he still runs three miles every morning, and so on. Keep the date on a "let's catch up" level, as op-posed to "what you've been through since the breakup" level. By the way, you should not tell him how much or how little you've dated since the breakup. Be honest, but mysterious.

Don't get terribly serious. Don't tell him that you now realize all the mistakes you've made since the relationship with him ended and how much you've changed and how you want another chance. It's too intense. Besides, it's easy to tell someone how much you've changed. The important part is actually *being* a changed person when he dates you!

Don't tell him that you've read *The Rules* and now realize what you did wrong—that you were too needy, that you shouldn't have gotten mad when he went out with the guys, and that you'll never be that way again. Simply be light. Try to be the girl he originally fell in love with.

End the date first.

Don't go back to his apartment or invite him up to yours or even think of having sex with him that night. *Remember, this is a first date. If anything, you must be extra strict with this man. He dumped you once, he can hurt you again.*

If this is to be a *Rules* relationship, he must call you and ask you out for Saturday night from now on. Seeing you either awakened a desire to date you again and to renew the relationship, or it didn't. The only way to find out is if he calls you and asks you out. You should not ask him if he missed you or if he wants to get back together. If he is to pursue you, he should not know exactly how you feel about him. He should think, "She called me one day. She might be interested, but I'm not sure. Maybe she was just bored or found an old photo of us." Remain mysterious—if he thinks that you've decided he's The One, he could get scared.

If he calls, you must do all *The Rules* outlined in our first book, specifically, "How to Act on Dates 1, 2, and 3" and "How to Act on Dates 4 through Commitment Time." Treat him like a new boyfriend—don't talk about the past or act too chummy. For example, you should not call his family, even if you met his parents and sister twenty times when you were dating. Remember, you've been apart. He has to invite you to any social events with his family and friends all over again.

If you meet him for dinner and he never calls again, he may not have felt a strong enough spark. Maybe he thought about it, but never got around to picking up the phone. Men can be that way. Maybe he's involved with someone else, but didn't tell you and met you for old times' sake.

We know of several women who contacted old boyfriends for various reasons—to make amends for the past, to discuss a business problem, or to try to start over. In each case, these men met them for drinks, said they had a great time and hoped they could stay good friends, and then never called again.

We can only say that if this happens to you, you must try to accept that it's over for him and move on.

Now what if this man happens to be your ex-husband and you've decided you want him back?

Again, it depends. If *he* initiated the divorce,

you can make "One Call for Closure" and then follow the plan (outlined above) for getting back an ex-boyfriend. But don't start making room in your closet. When a man initiates a divorce, he's usually gone! It's over and out.

However, if *you* initiated the divorce but are now sorry and miss him, there is hope, especially if you are still in contact with your ex and sense that he would be open to a reconciliation— maybe you have kids together and he lingers a while when he comes by on weekends to pick them up or just seems to find reasons to call you, to be friends, to be in your life. But you're wondering, how do you go about telling him you want him back without making a fool of yourself or risking rejection?

We suggest you simply weave the following question into a friendly conversation the next time you see him or he calls: "Have you ever had second thoughts about our divorce?" *That's it. Don't say another word.* Don't get sentimental and weepy and pour your heart out. He must take it from there, give you some indication that he would also like a reconciliation, whether it be then or at some point in the future when he's had a chance to sort it out. Whatever you do, don't rush him. Let him proceed at his own pace. He may suggest having dinner or drinks to talk things over, but these must be his overtures. You've done your part. Now it's up to *him*.

We've outlined our suggestions for getting back an ex. But don't be too upset if your old boyfriend or ex-husband just won't come back. Remember, there was a reason the relationship didn't work out before, so don't romanticize it. Also, comfort yourself with the knowledge that it's usually easier to do *The Rules* on a new man than an ex.

Sometimes trying to rekindle an old flame works, but frequently the best advice we can give a woman who thinks she's still in love with her ex is *Next!*

Chapter 4

Don't Waste Time on Fantasy Relationships

IF YOU HAVE A good rapport with your doctor, lawyer, or accountant, you may find yourself wondering if he is interested in you romantically. You're not alone, but you may not be seeing the situation for what it is. How can you know for sure? It's simple. Has he ever asked you out? Has he ever suggested having a drink, coffee, lunch, or dinner? If the answer is no, then he's not!

This may sound obvious, but you'd be surprised how many women tell themselves it's romance when a man pays them the slightest attention out of professional courtesy. We wrote this chapter to smash any delusions you might have about a fantasy relationship of your own. Unless he asks to spend time with you in a nonprofessional capacity, a relationship beyond business does not exist—and *Rules* girls don't waste their time on nonexistent relationships!

The fact is, when a man is interested in a woman—including a female patient or client, employer or employee—he finds some way to ask her out. He may invite her to work out at his gym, attend a fund-raiser with him, or to play tennis over the weekend. He may not necessarily ask her out for a Saturday night date since that might be too obvious, or awkward, or forward, but he'll figure out some way to see her outside of the office. This behavior is different from the professional courtesy of a physician or financial advisor, who might say, "Call me anytime," which women mistakenly interpret as romantic interest.

Let's examine three fantasy relationships and *The Rules*'s answers to remove any doubt you might have about a similar situation in your life.

Fantasy Relationship #1: Your internist of two years told you "beep me anytime" if your asthma acts up. He once told you to call him by his first name. He puts his arm around your shoulders when he escorts you out of his office. You just know he would ask you out if you weren't his patient. And, naturally, you want to have a "talk" with him or ask him out!

The Rules answer: If a doctor is friendly, affectionate, concerned, and kind, then he's doing his job. It's not a come-on for a doctor to tell a patient to beep him or call the office "day or night" if his patient has asthma—people can die of asthma, and it's his job to make sure his patients stay alive and well. Some doctors are informal (it's okay to call them by their first name) and others are touchy-feely (they kiss *all* their patients hello and good-bye). It's just good bedside manners—and good business—for a doctor to show warmth and caring. If he were romantically interested in you and uncomfortable about dating a patient, he would refer you to his associate and then ask you out.

Sure, it's a little more complicated for a doctor, lawyer, or CEO to pursue a patient, client, or associate. But it's not impossible. We've heard about bosses who've dated and even married their employees, even though it was frowned upon by the company. At first they kept the relationship a secret and then they voluntarily decided he or she would transfer to another division or another company so they could date freely.

Fantasy Relationship #2: Your accountant called you over the weekend to remind you to send in your tax forms before April 15. You think because he called you on Saturday at home instead of during the week at work there might be something there.

The Rules answer: Accountants work on the weekends, especially during the busy tax season. The lines between work and home, during the week, and weekends can be very blurry in business. Unless he suggested brunch, don't read into it.

Fantasy Relationship #3: You think the waiter at the restaurant you go to twice a week likes you because he always remembers how you like your eggs and that you take your coffee light with two sugars. You think he's more attentive to you than other customers—refills your coffee before you ask—and always makes conversation with you. You want to let him know you're not seeing anyone seriously and would go out with him if he asked. The problem is, he hasn't. What to do?

The Rules answer: Waiters are in the service business. It's normal for a waiter to remember a regular customer's preferences. He works for tips so it's in his interest to be friendly, make conversation, get your order right. If he liked you beyond this, however, he would suggest having drinks one night.

The point bears repeating: When a man is really interested in a woman, he figures out some way to ask her out.

Don't be insulted. We're not suggesting that your doctor, broker, or accountant isn't fond of you, just that it's not a *Rules* relationship until he asks you out.

Also keep in mind that many men, including professionals, like to flirt with women. Looking at lab results, contracts, and financial statements all day can get pretty boring, so it's fun for them to make small talk, notice your figure if you're in good shape, and compliment you on your new hairstyle. After all, they are men and they do like to look at women! It's also an ego boost for them to put on the charm, knowing that it gives some of their female patients/clients high school girl crushes. But it's all quite harmless, so don't take it seriously unless he asks you on a date.

We're not saying that you can't daydream about your sexy doctor or look forward to quarterly meetings with your handsome financial planner. Being a *Rules* girl doesn't mean you can't have obsessions, it means you don't act on them.

The danger lies in thinking there's a relationship there, and not being open to real relationships. Women who are absorbed in fantasy relationships usually don't have real ones!

Ask yourself, are you doing everything to meet men or are you living for the day when your dream lover asks you out? You're less likely to place a personal ad, sign up with a dating service, or take that singles ski trip if you believe you're in a relationship.

Remember, *Rules* girls know they're either dating a man or not. There's nothing in between.

So if you thought your broker or lawyer was interested in you, but after reading this chapter realize he may like you but not romantically, try to accept the truth instead of fighting it. Your first impulse may be to clear the air, be open and honest—ask him if he has feelings for you but isn't acting on them because of your professional relationship. You might want to write him a note or, worse, a long letter explaining how you feel.

Don't. First, that's not *The Rules*. He must initiate any such talk. Second, nothing good will come of it. If you talk to him and he tells you that you misread his politeness and that he's just as nice to every other client/patient, you'll feel foolish and hurt—not to mention embarrassed about seeing him again professionally.

If, on the other hand, he tells you he is attracted to you, but has decided not to pursue the relationship because he's involved with someone else or more interested in you as a client/patient than a lover, you're not much better off. You have the ego satisfaction of knowing that he's attracted to you, but so what? You still don't have a Saturday night date, much less a relationship. And it's a hollow victory anyway because if he was really *crazy* about you—and why would a *Rules* girl settle for anything less?—he would rather date you than just have a professional relationship with you.

So if you can't tell him how you feel, what can you do?

The Rules. Look your best whenever you see him, end all phone calls/meetings first, show no interest in him personally, don't send him holiday cards (if you mistakenly thought that would make him think about you in a different light) or invite him to your New Year's party to pave the way from a professional relationship to a social one. Don't buy him a tie for Christmas or bake him cookies for the holidays. Gifts don't make men think about women or ask them out. Try to treat him as you would an elderly or unattractive man—not the handsome hunk you think he is!—someone you wouldn't think twice about, much less bake brownies for!

Doing *The Rules* won't make him ask you out if he was never going to, but it will keep you from wasting time baking cookies and writing notes to men who aren't interested in you. You'll have more self-esteem.

Of course, the best thing you can do is try to meet other men, *men who do ask you out*. Nothing replaces a fantasy relationship better than a *Rules* one! So move on!

Chapter 5

Don't Stand by His Desk and Other *Rules* for the Office Romance

THE OFFICE IS ONE of the trickiest places to follow *The Rules* because if you are dating someone at work, your professional life and your love life may overlap to some extent. Therefore, you must do *The Rules* strictly so you don't place your job or your relationship (or both) in jeopardy.

Of course, the first rule is to figure out whether or not you are actually *in* an office romance. A lot of men like to flirt with women at the office. They don't think twice about it, it means nothing to them and it should mean nothing to you! (See Chapter 4: "Don't Waste Time on Fantasy Relationships.")

If you have a crush on someone in your office—a coworker, employee, or your boss—and he's never asked you out, don't try to get his attention. Some dating books have suggested you drink from the water cooler near his office or use the copier closest to his desk or even ask him out to lunch to discuss business. *The Rules* say, do your job and look your best. Don't look for excuses to talk to him or walk by his desk. (You shouldn't have to do any of these things to make him notice you. He either notices you or he doesn't!)

Don't tell yourself that he would have asked you out if you didn't work for the same company. There are enough office romances out there to refute that theory. As we have stated, if it is not a company code, bosses have no problem dating employees and even their own secretaries if they want to. On the other hand, don't count on working for the same company to be the spark that will unite you. Don't stay at the company hoping that one day he will notice you and ask you out. We know women who waited in vain for years for that to happen. *Rules* girls don't hold themselves back for a fantasy relationship.

Now assuming you are dating a coworker or even your boss, how should you act? Below are fourteen rules for office dating. Do them to the letter because you might have to see this man on a daily basis. There's nothing worse than having to work with a man you dread seeing or who dreads seeing you everyday because you broke rules—or working with him after he drops you! These rules are not just good for the relationship, but for your company and your career. You'll be a better worker if you're not figuring out ways to be with him all day!

1. Do not go to work everyday, motivated by the prospect of seeing him or spending time with him, or you might act out on your feelings. Go to work thinking, how can I work hard today and contribute to my company—or at the very least, how can I not break *The Rules*. Try to be busy, as opposed to daydreaming at your desk or, worse, finding reasons to talk to him or see him. (When the urge to stop by his office hits you, begin a new project or stop by a friend's desk to say hello.) If he stops by your desk, be nice, but end the conversation after five or ten minutes unless it's business-related. Just pick up the papers on your desk and say, "I'd better get back to work!"

2. Work hard, but don't be such a tireless worker that you don't care about your appearance. Don't spend so much time at the office that you have no time for such mundane tasks as taking your clothes to the dry cleaner or getting a manicure. We know women who are smart and attractive, but you can't help but notice the coffee stains on their blazers, their scruffy shoes, and untweezed eyebrows. Don't be like that. You're a *Rules* girl!

   Make sure you're wearing fashionable suits and shoes—you want to look as good as you can! Don't wear pantyhose with runs in them—keep extra pairs in your desk drawer in case they rip at work. Shine your shoes.

Wear makeup and perfume, but not too much. (It's an office, not a disco!) Remember, you're a creature unlike any other and you care about your looks. Do all of this for yourself, but also because you could run into him or someone else at the office.

3. Do not agree to see him on a moment's notice just because you work together. If he stops by your desk and casually asks you to have lunch with him that day or to have drinks after work that evening, say you'd love to, but can't. Even if you are free for lunch or drinks, don't see him on short notice. He should be asking you out in advance for the weekend.

   If you see him on a whim, the relationship will become too casual. He won't think you're special enough to plan in advance to see you. In addition, if you allow the relationship to be on a coworker level, it could take him years to propose. We know a very attractive woman who accepted last-minute dates from a man she worked with. Several times a week at 6:00 P.M. he would drop by her desk and suggest having drinks. She always said yes. He also couldn't commit to Saturday night dates until Friday or Saturday because he "wasn't sure what *he* was doing." She accepted his behavior because she didn't know there was a better way. It took him six years to propose and their marriage is troubled; he never seems to really make the effort, and she feels taken for granted.

So, just because you work at the same company doesn't mean he can see you whenever he feels like it. Don't make it so easy for him. He has to ask you out in advance—otherwise, you're busy! If you work closely together, you should sometimes disappear at lunch hour. Don't tell him where you're going. Remember, he works with you and dates you—that can get a little all-consuming, so you must be doubly careful to remain a little mysterious!

4. Be discreet. Don't talk about the relationship with coworkers. If anyone asks you what you did over the weekend, don't say, "David and I went hiking." Just say that *you* went hiking. Don't answer any questions with "we." It may hurt your career to be the subject of office gossip. It's not good for the relationship, either, since no man likes to date a big mouth. Men love privacy. Anything coworkers know about the relationship should come from him!

Likewise, don't volunteer information to him. For example, don't tell him where you're going on a business trip or who you're having a meeting with unless he specifically asks about either.

5. If you need to talk to the man you are dating about business—perhaps he's your boss—by

all means, talk to him! Always be professional and return his calls promptly if it is a business matter. Just check your motives. Is it really necessary to contact him, or are you looking for an excuse to be with him? For example, don't knock on his door to tell him about concert tickets or a lecture on personal growth! If it is work-related, keep the conversation brief and end it first.

If possible, leave the information with his secretary or in his "in box." Write any memos or notes in a businesslike manner. Do not leave love notes or cute Post-it's on his desk. If he needs to talk to you, he can always come to *your* office or leave you a note!

6. He can E-mail you as much as he wants, but don't E-mail him back every time unless it is business-related. On all nonbusiness E-mails, once for every four of his E-mails is a good rule of thumb. Remember, keep your E-mails brief and breezy and stick to business. This is important, because you never know who has access to your E-mail—it may be read by the head of the company, so keep all romance off the screen and save it for Saturday nights.

7. Don't snoop around his office. You shouldn't even be near his office! Don't ask his secretary who calls him or who he's having lunch with and where. It's none of your business. Besides, she might tell him and he will be annoyed and resent it.

8. Don't make your office a shrine to your relationship. Don't put his photo in a frame on your desk or keep the teddy bear he gave you for Valentine's Day in your office after February 14. It's best to be businesslike.

   Speaking of your office, be neat. Neat is sexy. No one likes to date a slob. So don't be a pack rat. Don't have piles of paper on your desk or stash half-eaten sandwiches in your desk drawer. Don't collect objects or hang memorabilia on the walls. Don't decorate your office like a college dorm room. Don't be cute or juvenile. Be professional.

9. Don't kiss or hold hands at the office. Not only is it unprofessional, it's not good for *The Rules*. He has to ask you out on a date to kiss you or spend quality time with you. Don't agree to go to a hotel with him during your lunch hour. That's not a date and he won't respect you (and you'll come back from lunch looking rumpled and unbusinesslike). No one wants a reputation—be careful that you don't earn one. Again, he has to ask you out for the weekend for you to take dating him seriously!

10. Don't sleep with your boss or coworker unless you're in a committed relationship—not just for sex and not to further your career. Bad motives tend to backfire.

    Keep in mind that *The Rules* don't stop because you're out of town. If you're on a business trip together and it would be easy to have sex because you're staying at the same hotel—still say no if you're not in a committed relationship. It may seem tempting—you are away from the office, and who will know? But remember, eventually you have to return home—back to reality—and you'll regret sleeping with him if he isn't serious about you or ignores you when you return to the office.

11. Don't hang out at the office at the end of the day or go to happy hour with the gang after work. You do not want to be thought of as the office party girl, but the kind of girl men marry. And of course don't get drunk at the office Christmas party or at any other party. It's hard to do *The Rules* when you're drunk!

12. If you work in different cities for the same company, let him travel to visit you three times before you visit him. If you're sent to his city on business, don't mention getting together. *He* must suggest making plans. If things do get serious, you shouldn't relocate until you have a commitment/wedding date.

13. Don't stay at the company just because he works there. If you are not happy with your job or are interested in other opportunities, pursue them. We don't hold ourselves back for a man. If it's good for your career to leave the company, go! Doing what's good for you

will also show him you're independent, not clingy. It might make him miss you and propose faster because he can't see you everyday.

14. Do not suggest commuting together even if you live near each other and work at the same company. It must be his suggestion and you should turn him down sometimes just so he doesn't take you for granted and so you can remain mysterious.

Married women have written to us asking how they should behave if they work with their husbands.

We hope they were either already working together when they met, or that it was their husband's idea to work together. Women should never suggest working with their husbands as a way of spending more time with them or checking up on them. It's not *The Rules,* and men hate it. You should only work with your husband if there is a legitimate reason to and/or it was his idea.

Regardless of why you are working together, here are five rules:

1. Do not suggest sharing an office or putting your desks near each other. Any togetherness must come from him.
2. Do not be the one to suggest commuting together.
3. Do not suggest having lunch together. You both need some time apart during the day.

4. Don't spy on him, don't ask his secretary who called, or get upset if he talks to other women.
5. Don't bring up personal business at the office and discourage him if he does. Be professional. Do your job!

Long-Distance Relationships. Part I: How They Should Start

MANY QUESTIONS ARISE in long-distance relationships that don't come up when dating a man closer to home. But before going into the specific rules for these relationships, it's important to talk about the mistakes women make when they first meet a man from out-of-town—mistakes that can easily prevent a long-distance *Rules* relationship from ever developing. As we have said before, it's the first encounter—who spoke to whom first, how long the conversation lasted, and who ended it first—that often determines whether it's a *Rules* relationship or not.

Let's look at some typical scenarios:

You meet a man at a mutual friend's wedding in Atlanta. You're from New York and he's from Chicago. He comes up to you and asks you to dance. It's *The Rules*! You like him a lot. You dance one dance and then another and then another. You feel glued to his side.

You know you should really walk away, say hello to some college friends you haven't talked to in years, but you don't. You figure the two of you live miles apart, who knows if you'll ever see him again, so what's the harm with spending five hours with him?

He asks you to join him for dessert. You say yes. Then he invites you to take a walk with him around the grounds. You agree. He takes your phone number at the end of the evening, kisses you good-bye, and says something about calling you in a few days, maybe visiting New York.

You're in love. You fly back home and tell your friends and your mother, and start thinking about your *own* wedding.

But because you broke *The Rules* by spending so much time with him, he either never calls, or calls after a week or two just to say hello but doesn't make plans to see you. Or he calls and asks you to fly to Chicago to see him, or makes plans to see you in New York but only because he's going to be there on business anyway. Naturally, you feel hurt and disappointed. Why doesn't he sound crazy about you? Why doesn't he want to jump on a plane and see you right away?

Looking back on the evening—and after reading *The Rules*—you realize that you didn't play hard to get. You spent five straight hours with him. He knew you liked him and the challenge was gone.

We're not saying that had you walked away or turned him down a couple of times for dances that he would definitely call and pursue a long-distance relationship. Maybe he has a girlfriend in Chicago, maybe he just wanted to have fun at the wedding—nothing more, nothing less.

But by *not* doing *The Rules*, you lessened your chances, you got your hopes up, and you got emotionally involved and hurt. If he was interested and you were more elusive, chances are he would have thought about you on the plane ride home, missed you in Chicago, called sooner, and made plans to see you in New York, even if he didn't have a business trip there.

In the future, when you meet someone at a wedding or party whom you may never see again, don't spend the entire evening with him. Talk to him for fifteen to twenty minutes, dance with him a couple of times, and then excuse yourself to use the ladies' room or say hello to a friend or just walk around for a while. He should be looking for you during the evening and trying to pin you down for another dance.

When you spend four or five hours with a man you just met, he no longer finds you as mysterious or interesting, even if he made the first move. When he goes back home, he may not think you're that special or dream about seeing you again because you were too available.

The same goes for meeting a man on a business trip. Let's say you meet a man at a conference. He notices you, strikes up a conversation, and asks you to have dinner with him that evening since he's leaving town the next morning. You say yes because he's cute and maybe something will start.

You tell yourself you may never cross paths again—he's from Boston and you're from San Diego—and you weren't going to do anything special for dinner anyway but order room service and HBO.

The Rules answer is to say, "Thank you, but I already have plans." Why? Because if you see him at the last minute, even if it's convenient for both of you, some of the challenge evaporates. If he's interested in you, let him call you and make special plans to visit you. If he can see you at a moment's notice, he won't have to long for you and pursue you and whatever interest he had in you may fizzle.

Don't think we're being overly strict about this. We see it happen time and time again. A woman meets a man at a business function or a party who says he's in town for just a few days and wants to take her to dinner that very night. He's totally charming and makes her feel special. She tells herself that she would really be missing something if she turned him down. He won't be in town again for another month.

He's a sexy movie producer or a plastic surgeon with offices on both coasts. She says yes— maybe it's just dinner, maybe she sleeps with him—and she thinks this is the beginning of a whirlwind bicoastal courtship.

The reality is, it may not be. He may be lying. He may be in town for another week, but figures this way he'll get what he wants right away. Or he may be married and this is his standard pickup line when he's out of town. There are men who have a girl in every port. You don't want to be one of them. But even if he's sincere, single, and really likes you, the answer is still no to a last-minute date. You think if you say no, he'll forget you. But *Rules* girls know that he'll remember you that much more if you turn him down.

So the next time you meet a man who asks you to dinner the same night because he's in town just a few days, say, "I'd love to, but I have other plans." Let him call you in advance the next time he plans to be in town or make a special trip to see you.

The only way to know if a man is really interested in you—instead of just filling up a few hours—is to not accept a last-minute date. When you make him wait several days to see you or you make him wait until he's in town again a month later, he gets to experience longing. If his feelings about you are just lukewarm, he won't bother to make a date beforehand—by following *The Rules,* you'll avoid wasting your time and having your hopes dashed later on. We know quite a few women who were full of hope, but then never heard from Mr. Bicoastal again.

Here's another common long-distance scenario. You meet Mr. Right on the first day of a seven-day vacation. Perhaps you're from different cities in the United States and you meet on a Club Med trip. He speaks to you first, asks you out for that night, and wants to be with you for all seven days and nights. You think, why not? He's cute. This is the whirlwind romance you always read about and dreamed about.

In this situation, you *must* force yourself not to see this man for the whole trip. See him once or twice for dinner and dancing over the seven-day period, but turn him down to be with other people so that he finds you mysterious and elusive and is forced to pursue you when he returns home. If he doesn't call you after the trip, at least you didn't waste seven days and nights on a man who's not that interested.

We know men who go on such trips, pursue one woman the whole time, sleep with her, and then never think about her (much less call her) again when they return home. Here, you're thinking this is true love, and he's thinking sex, sand, and fun for a week. If you don't want to be nothing more than the girl he slept with in Club Med, don't see him more than once or twice that week and don't sleep with him, otherwise you'll be crushed if you never hear from him again. It'll be a classic case of "I love you, honey, but the vacation's over."

So, by doing *The Rules,* you won't throw away a whole week on someone who may not have serious intentions, and you will be open to meeting other men. If he really likes you, he'll call you and visit you afterward.

_____

Chapter 7

Long-Distance Relationships. Part II: Making It Work

ASSUMING YOU'RE BEGINNING or already in a long-distance relationship, what are *The Rules*?

You don't call him. He calls you. He can call you often, but make sure you don't spend endless hours on the phone. Leave something to talk about when he visits you! Get off the phone in fifteen to twenty minutes—you can talk longer than the standard ten minutes since it is long-distance—whether or not he talks about making plans to see you. If he wants to visit you on the weekend, he must ask you by Wednesday.

Chances are if he approached you, he'll suggest coming to visit you first, which is *The Rules*. But if he says, "Why don't you visit me in Boston? I'll show you around Cambridge," or suggests that you meet him in some city halfway, simply say, "That sounds nice, but things are really hectic right now, I just couldn't get away." Don't spell out what's hectic or exactly why you can't get away. Just say no nicely and he'll realize that he has to visit you.

If he decides not to make the trip, he didn't like you that much. Remember that men drive for hours to go to football games and gambling casinos or to their college roommate's bachelor party, so it's not a big deal if they have to drive for hours to visit you.

Better that you never see him again than you visit him first or even meet him halfway. Meeting him halfway is the same as visiting him—it's not *The Rules* to do so in the early stages of a relationship. Wait until he's visited you *three times* to visit him or meet him halfway—and even then, not too often.

Of course, some women will rationalize visiting a man first (or sooner than they should) by saying that they wanted to get away anyway— they haven't taken a vacation in years! Some reason that they have the frequent-flier miles to make the trip for free, so why not? Yes, it would be fun or free, but it's not *The Rules*!

Others convince themselves that the trip would be a great opportunity to visit a friend or relative. Please make sure you're not finding excuses to be in his city. If you do have a legitimate reason for being there—a business trip or your friend's baby shower—don't tell him about it unless he specifically asks if you're planning to be in his area anytime soon. If he does ask and you tell him your plans, don't let him assume you'll see him. He has to ask you out and come to your hotel or sister's house if he wants to see you.

If you travel to see him before he's made at least three trips to see you, he won't think you're special, hard to see, and will not appreciate you or pursue you in the future. Even if he was initially drawn to you, he will expect you to travel to him all the time. He might start calling you at the last minute for the weekend and saying that he's too busy to leave town and suggesting that you visit him again. He might even say he's too busy to pick you up at the airport. Soon he might say he's too busy to see you at all, even though you offered to visit him. Once you start breaking *The Rules,* even promising relationships start to unravel quickly.

We've heard from women who've met multi-millionaires offering to send them plane tickets or even their private jets to bring them to their homes for the weekend as a first or second date. These women are naturally flattered and excited and think the offer is special and meaningful.

We tell them it may not be and to decline very sweetly. Even if he makes $3 million a year and you're a struggling secretary, you must say, "Thank you but I just can't get away this weekend."

The reason is, he has to visit you. He has to work to see you—pack a suitcase, be inconvenienced, possibly miss the ballgame he was going to watch on TV. For a man to have his secretary call and make the arrangements requires no sweat on his part. For very little effort, he gets to have companionship and perhaps sex for the weekend. *You* have to get someone to watch your dog, experience jet lag, you have to stop your life and be inconvenienced. *Rules* girls don't turn themselves upside down for a good deal or fun weekend. They hold out for love and marriage!

So don't be blown away by a private plane, Dom Pérignon, and a limo. You might be the first woman he's met who ever said no. Don't worry. If he likes you, he'll visit you!

Assuming he is visiting you, what are *The Rules*?

For the first three times he visits you, he should not stay with you. If he asks to, say, "I don't think so. We just met." It will be up to him to find a place to stay—at a hotel or with a friend or relative. That's not your problem. Remember, the first three visits are really nothing more than three dates ... and on the first three dates we don't have sex with a man or have him stay at our place overnight. You can invite him up on the third visit but he has to leave before the night is over. The fact that he's visiting from out-of-town doesn't change that.

Another reason not to let a man stay with you early on is to protect yourself from the type of guy who is more than happy to hop on a plane to see you, but not for the reason you think. He's just looking to have a good time in a new city with a fun girl (you!)—nothing serious. You're just part of the trip, not the main attraction. By asking him to stay in a hotel, you'll have avoided this noncommital, call-when-he's-coming-to-town type of relationship. You're not a hotel or a tourist attraction! Of course, there's nothing wrong with letting a man stay at your place as long as you can take it for what it is. But if you have dreams of love and romance, then you must do *The Rules*!

When he visits you the first three times, always see a little bit less of him than he would like. For example, if he suggests flying in Friday night and leaving Sunday evening, say Saturday morning would be better and end the weekend Sunday afternoon.

Don't cancel every single activity you normally do on the weekend so that you can be with him every minute. For example, if you have a Saturday afternoon exercise class, go to it. Let him keep himself busy and wait for you.

The point is, don't be a woman who drops everything when a man is in town. You're a *Rules* girl . . . you had a life before you met him and you still do! It's actually good for him if you have something—a previous commitment—other than him planned for that weekend. He should leave feeling that he didn't get enough of you instead of too much.

When he visits you, don't play social director. It's up to him to look into restaurants, museums, interesting places to take you or events going on that weekend. However, if he is not familiar with your town and asks you to suggest something to do, you can. But always err on the side of less. If he asks you to suggest a restaurant, do not pick out the romantic hot spot with the dim lighting and lovers' booths, but a decent place that you would take a friend or coworker. Don't try too hard to find things to do so that he's entertained and not bored.

Let him pick up the newspaper or an entertainment guide and figure something out, or make plans together when he arrives. Remember, he should think you were busy and just didn't have time to think about the weekend, even if that's all you thought about all week.

Women have a tendency to think too much about the man, the weekend, and act on every thought. They make reservations at a Cajun restaurant because they remember he likes spicy food. They get two tickets to the auto show because he mentioned he was a car buff.

Your efforts might be noticed—but they'll backfire. He'll know you are intrigued and like him, that you remembered everything he ever said, and that you've been thinking about him all week and planning the perfect weekend. He'll feel smothered and you'll wonder why he stopped calling.

After he has visited you three times, you can visit him once and stay at his place, if he invites you. Who pays for the trip? It depends. If he offers to pay the airfare, let him. If he doesn't, don't ask him for the money, but let him pay for everything when you're there. Don't worry. By doing *The Rules*—visiting him infrequently—you will automatically minimize your travel costs. On the other hand, do not fly out a lot to see him just because he offers to pick up the tab. *The Rules* is about letting him pursue you, not saving money.

If you have friends or relatives in that city, it would be a good idea to call them and meet them briefly while you're there so that you don't spend the entire weekend with this man and he doesn't tire of you. End the weekend first.

Being in a long-distance relationship does not give you license to send men letters and greeting cards. You are not pen pals. You can send him a birthday or holiday card if you are in a committed long-distance relationship, assuming he sent you the same. The cards should be warm but not mushy. No love poetry.

If the relationship progresses—he's calling you every week for the weekend, he's visiting you more than you're visiting him, he wants to be exclusive, and so on—you are in a long-distance *Rules* relationship. If this is not the case, be available to date others.

If things get serious, he might bring up the future and ask if you would ever consider relocating. Reply, "I haven't really thought about it." Until he actually proposes and gives you a ring, be vague. There is no reason to look into selling or renting your apartment or asking for a job transfer to his city or finding a job in his city if he hasn't formally proposed.

In fact, there's no reason to relocate until after you've set a wedding date. We do not live with a man before marriage, and we don't go away with him on seven-day vacations before the honeymoon. Try to see him only on the weekends until you have a wedding date.

If you are already in a long-distance relationship and did not know about *The Rules* until now, start doing *The Rules* very strictly today. Don't call him. Let him call you. Get off the phone in fifteen minutes. (Okay, twenty minutes if he's calling from Tokyo or Paris and you don't talk that often!) If he's used to you traveling to him most of the time, let him visit you more now. If he says he's too busy, simply say, "Things are so hectic . . . I just can't get away right now." This will get him to miss you, wonder about you, and figure out a way to visit you—if he's interested—and marry you!

You *Can* Ask Your Therapist to Help You Do *The Rules*

IN OUR FIRST BOOK, we told you not to discuss *The Rules* with your therapist. We felt that most therapists would not advise their patients to "play hard to get" or act contrary to their feelings. We were concerned that discussing *The Rules* in therapy would cause too much conflict. On the one hand, you have a book telling you, "Don't call him, don't tell him how you feel in the beginning of the relationship" and a therapist telling you to "Call him if you want to, tell him how you feel." We thought there would be some confusion.

We thought this because some of the women we originally helped with *The Rules* (long before it was a book) told us that it was the exact opposite of what their therapists were telling them to do with men. When they mentioned *The Rules* concept to their therapists, they were discouraged from doing them. However, when these women realized that it was *The Rules* that helped them date successfully and marry the man of their dreams, many either stopped going to therapy, or used *The Rules* for dating only and therapy for other issues.

So you can understand why we said "Don't discuss *The Rules* with your therapist." We were not trying to exclude therapists from their patients' dating process, we just didn't want women to feel torn. (After all, it's hard enough to do *The Rules* when you believe in them!)

We were pleasantly surprised to find out that a number of therapists saw our point of view. Since *The Rules* was published, we've received dozens of letters from psychotherapists and social workers saying that they agree with *The Rules* and that it gives women excellent and much needed dating guidelines and helps build their self-esteem. They are even recommending the book to their patients. Some therapists said they could never figure out why their own relationships were not working out until they read *The Rules*! Others have even started therapy groups based on *The Rules* to help women put *The Rules* into practice and overcome their resistances.

For example, one therapist told us that some of her patients feel that not returning a man's call is "rude," so she suggested they call his home number and leave a short message when he's at work. It's gratifying to know that therapists are trying to work with *The Rules*.

Therapists agree with us that such details matter. They admit that therapy has been "warm and fuzzy" about what to do and not to do, and that

The Rules fills a void. They have come to see that *The Rules* is not just a dating book with lots of do's and don'ts, but a way of building a full life and dating with self-esteem.

According to a therapist in the Midwest, "Before *The Rules,* many women were clueless. They gave too much too soon. They got involved too quickly and then were devastated. *The Rules* takes the guesswork out of dating. It gives women boundaries. Before *The Rules,* women were unsure how much to show or give a man. Now there are no more five-hour phone conversations or visiting a man often because you're a flight attendant and it's free. Now women have to take responsibility for their actions."

This therapist has found *The Rules* particularly helpful in guiding women in the early stages of a relationship to "control their impulse to be the aggressor, to say the first word." She advises them "to let things happen."

A New York therapist also praised *The Rules* for daring to tell the truth: "You are right. Men say that they want someone who lets her needs be known, who is honest, and up front. They like women like that, they make friends with women like that, but they fall in love with and marry women who do *The Rules.* Men may say they feel *The Rules* are manipulative but they are fascinated by a woman who does them. When they are attracted to a woman they operate on the animal level . . ."

A male psychotherapist wrote to us saying that he considers *The Rules* "the definitive text on how a woman can have power with a man. It speaks very well to boundary issues which so many women struggle with these days."

Yet another therapist praised *The Rules* for articulating "the behavioral version of managing deep feelings that can get stirred up early on in romantic relationships," noting that "women are sometimes so hungry for a relationship" that they get involved emotionally and sexually too quickly and "lose out on the experience of being sought after and cherished." Therapists agree that when you do *The Rules*, you let the man pursue you and that feels great!

In defense of psychotherapy, one therapist pointed out that what goes on in sessions—the degree of honesty and openness encouraged—was never meant to be practiced on dates. That was never the intention of therapy. Perhaps therapists assumed patients would *know* they should not tell all on a date. What therapists didn't realize was that their patients were in fact sharing very deep feelings on the second or third date. Before *The Rules*, some women just didn't realize how inappropriate that was, they simply were never told *not to*.

To make our point clear, pretend you are seeing a therapist who specializes in weight loss. In the session you talk about all the feelings, frustrations, and situations that make you want to overeat. Fine. As long as when you leave his office, you don't head for the donut shop. It's the same with *The Rules*. Talk to your therapist about how you want to marry a man that you've dated twice, just don't tell *him*.

Of course, there are therapists out there who don't believe in *The Rules*. We have no interest in changing anyone's mind. We tell women, try whatever approach you like, whatever works for you. *The Rules* has worked for us and countless other women.

Assuming you believe in *The Rules* and your therapist is *not against it,* there should be no conflict between *The Rules* and therapy—as long as you do *The Rules* after you leave the therapist's office. Use therapy to talk about your feelings and dating history, discuss how you get hurt too easily, and so forth, but use *The Rules* to help you with your *dating behavior.* That means that if you feel a strong desire to call a man you just started seeing after discussing the relationship in therapy for an hour, don't call him and don't tell him on your next date how your session went. Feel your feelings, but do *The Rules*.

So if you feel your therapist can help you do *The Rules,* by all means ask him or her to help you and incorporate them into therapy.

Be careful, though, if your therapist tells you to act contrary to *The Rules*. For example, if your therapist wants you to call a man who stopped calling you in order to find out what happened/ express your anger/keep the relationship going, don't. *The Rules* answer is not to call, but to tell yourself, "Good riddance, next!" If he stopped calling with no explanation, then you want nothing to do with him! You can express your anger in therapy or vent your rage on the StairMaster, but don't ask a man why he stopped calling and tell him you're angry or try to convince him to keep dating you. If he's not interested in you for whatever reason, it's nothing to be angry *at him* about. You are entitled to your anger, but calling him will seem desperate and will only make you feel worse. In addition, you don't want to *coerce* anyone to be with you!

In conclusion, the only way to know how your therapist feels about *The Rules* is to ask. So ask your therapist to help you do *The Rules*. But if he or she won't and you want to continue seeing him or her for their expertise with other issues, you probably don't need to even discuss *The Rules*. If you feel you need to discuss *The Rules* with someone, talk to *Rules*-minded women and/or join a *Rules* support group. They will provide *The Rules* help and support you need, and you won't have to do *The Rules* alone.

Chapter 9

If He Doesn't Call, He's Not That Interested. Period!

WE KNOW THIS IS hard to accept. We've heard it all—every rationalization imaginable used to avoid having to confront this unpleasant truth: he said he was going to call at the end of the last date, but didn't. Now you're sure it's because you didn't smile or talk enough, or you talked too much. You didn't thank him for dinner. You ordered the most expensive dish and now he thinks you're after his money.

Or he hasn't called because he's busy, or he's going through something with his father or ex-wife. Business is rough and that's why he hasn't called.

He thought you didn't have a good time on the last date, so he didn't call.

He hasn't called because he lost your number.

We can all come up with 100 reasons why a man didn't call. But the bottom line is, if he hasn't called, he's not that interested.

We're not saying he doesn't like you or that

you didn't have a great date or that you're not on his mind sometimes, but if he hasn't actually dialed your number, how interested can he be?

If you have to call him to remind him you exist, something is wrong. Then, if you pursue him and he ever marries you, you'll have to remind him it's your birthday or your wedding anniversary or call him at work to get his attention. You might have to initiate sex and vacations. You'll always have to be the one to call the travel agent because he may think about vacations, but he never gets around to calling. Things are the way they are! This is not the kind of relationship a *Rules* girl wants to get involved in.

So don't waste time analyzing what you may have done to discourage him from calling. Let it go. No matter what the reason, if he doesn't call, it's next!

Chapter 10 _____

25 Reasons Why Women Want to Call Men But Shouldn't!

1. He didn't call you.
2. You think he lost your number.
3. You think he thinks you're not interested.
4. You have two tickets to a show.
5. You need a date for a wedding.
6. Your mother told you to call him.
7. Your girlfriends said, "Call him, it's the nineties."
8. Your brother said he'd be flattered if a girl called him.
9. You can't sleep well since he stopped calling.
10. You want to ask him why he stopped calling.
11. You want to get his recipe for chili.
12. You left your umbrella in his apartment.
13. You can't live without him.
14. You want to ask him what it is about you he didn't like. "Was it my hair? the sex? what was it?" You'll change whatever it was.
15. You want to know how he's doing.

16. You want to wish him a Happy Birthday or Happy New Year.

17. Your phone number is unlisted now and you want to give him your new number.

18. You're thinking about joining a convent and wanted his opinion.

19. You want to know if the new woman is thinner, prettier, smarter, better in bed, or more successful than you are.

20. You're just calling to say "hi."

21. You're never home and you're hard to reach.

22. Your answering machine is broken.

23. You're going to Paris (his favorite city) on vacation and need some sight-seeing ideas.

24. You want to ask him one more time "Is it really over?"

25. He said "Call me."

Chapter 11

Show Up Even If You Don't Feel Like It

SOME WOMEN ARE LUCKY. They marry their high school or college sweetheart at twenty-two and never have to deal with dating again. But what if that's not your story and the only man in your life is your dry cleaner? You had some relationships in the past but they didn't work out because you didn't know about *The Rules*.

There are many women in your situation. They simply never meet men. Years go by without a Saturday night date. They spend New Year's Eve with girlfriends, Chinese takeout, or a rented video.

If this is you, realize that you may not meet Mr. Right naturally and that you therefore must take social actions immediately *even if you don't want to*.

Obviously, you can't do *The Rules* if there are no men in your life. Don't despair—instead, focus on doing something—anything—to increase your chances of meeting men so you can practice *The Rules* and get married.

A good rule to start is to carry out one social action per week, *no matter what!* Here are some suggestions:

Plan to go to a singles party this weekend, get involved in a church/synagogue social event, do charity work or work on a political campaign where you might meet men, book a trip to Club Med, place a personal ad, join a dating service, take a share in a ski house or summer beach house, play tennis, jog around the park in your neighborhood, anything! You don't have to dance well, campaign well, ski well, play tennis well, or jog very far. You just have to plan these activities, show up, do your best, and smile.

Perhaps you are thinking, "But I don't have anyone to go with." Then you *must go* alone! Of course, it would be great to have a friend (with similar interests) to go with, but if you don't have one, that's no excuse to sit at home. Many women we know actually pushed themselves to go alone to a party or social affair when they absolutely didn't want to go, and those were the very nights they met their husbands.

If you keep waiting for someone to go with, a convenient ride to the event, or perfect weather, you might never go. How serious are you about meeting someone if you won't go by yourself? Sometimes it's actually *better* to go alone because you're on your own time schedule and some men might find you easier to approach.

Besides, you must learn to accept that, as an adult, you can't always rely on a friend to do things with. There are many tasks in life that have to be done alone, such as going on job interviews or going to the dentist. Sometimes you have to think about social activities as work—you have to do them regardless of how you feel.

Motivating yourself to get off the couch, dress, put on makeup, and show up won't be easy, but it must be done. You may or may not have fun at the party, but at the very least, you'll practice *The Rules* for an hour or two and go home.

Don't think, "But I'm not comfortable" at this or that. Go anyway!

We know it's not always comfortable to be single in social gatherings, but then again, many things we tell you to do in *The Rules* are not always comfortable. You're also probably worrying that the kind of men you're attracted to won't come up to you, or that you'll be frustrated because you can't approach them since you're doing *The Rules*. You may not feel that you will have a good time and that you might have had more fun reading a good book in bed, but you'll never meet anyone that way, so you have to go!

Even if you don't meet Mr. Right, going out—whether it be to an "in" restaurant, museum, lecture, or party—is good for you. It's a chance to meet new people, broaden your horizons, learn to be at ease in crowds, and best of all, to practice *The Rules*.

Tell a friend that you're going to take one social action this week and make sure you stick to it!

Chapter 12

Keep Doing *The Rules* Even When Things Are Slow

A VERY IMPORTANT *RULES* credo is that it's better to date no one than to date or marry Mr. Wrong. Better to spend Saturday night baby-sitting for your nephews or curled up with a good book than with a man who's not in love with you.

Let's say you've been doing *The Rules* for six months or even a year, but have nothing to show for it. No husband, no steady boyfriend, and few Saturday night dates. You go to parties, museums, and singles events, you look good, and you don't pursue men. Men you're attracted to don't approach you and the ones you don't care about won't leave you alone! Meanwhile, your friends who aren't doing *The Rules* seem to be dating all the time. True, their relationships aren't good—sometimes downright bad!—and don't last, but at least they're busy and you're all alone. Even your mother is telling you to call men! What's wrong with this picture?

Unfortunately, nothing. You just haven't met

Mr. Right yet. The fact is, Mr. Right—the man you want to marry who wants and pursues you—only comes around a few times in a lifetime. So don't be surprised if you come home from parties with nothing good to report other than that you did *The Rules*. You didn't meet anyone. No man asked you for your number.

Many women we know went through the nothing-to-show-for-it period for a year or more, but now are happily married and glad they didn't weaken and stop doing *The Rules*.

Don't be surprised if you're tempted to break *The Rules* during these dead periods. You might long to initiate a conversation with the first cute guy you see or call an old boyfriend who didn't treat you well in an attempt to rekindle something dead and buried, just out of boredom and loneliness. We understand how you feel, but don't give in! You're just asking for heartache and wasting your time.

Realize that these dead periods are not dead at all. *The Rules* are actually working in your life because you are weeding out unsuitable men, which is just as important as holding out for Mr. Right.

When you feel that nothing is happening in the man area, take advantage of this downtime and pursue that MBA or law degree, finish the novel you started writing in college, redecorate, or find a hobby. Take up tennis or diving. Don't forget to call *Rules*-minded women or attend a *Rules* support group/seminar for reinforcement. Anything—but don't initiate a relationship with a man who isn't right for you. You never know—you might just meet your husband on the tennis court or at your adult education class.

Women who break *The Rules* when nothing is going on end up in relationships that don't work out and, even worse, get involved in relationships that prevent them from meeting Mr. Right. Five months or five years later, they're still single and older. *Rules* girls don't waste time!

Chapter 13

Don't Tell the Media About Your Love Life and Other *Rules* for Celebrities

IF YOU'RE BEAUTIFUL, rich, and successful, a celebrity or the owner of your own business, you may think that you don't have to do *The Rules*. You may believe that you can get and keep a man based on your looks, money, power, or persona.

But if being rich, beautiful, famous, or powerful were enough to catch and keep Mr. Right, why are so many models, actresses, and successful businesswomen single, divorced, or in unsatisfying relationships? The answer has nothing to do with money or fame. These women are just not doing *The Rules*. They either chase men outright or don't play hard to get with men who are initially interested in them.

Actresses, models, and socialites are sometimes the worst *Rules*-breakers because they're used to men falling all over them. So they think they can even win over men who never showed any initial interest in them. Needless to say, they're wrong.

The relationships they create invariably don't last, and some end up in messy public divorces.

Of course, it would help bolster our argument if we named names. However, that would hurt and embarrass the famous women involved and we would never do so. The most important lesson is to learn from these mistakes!

What's typical *Rule*-breaking behavior by an actress, model, or high-profile businesswoman? She spots a man at a party or a restaurant or a business function—if she's an actress, she may think an actor she just saw in a movie or TV commercial is really cute—and decides she wants to meet him. So she calls him up directly or has her assistant/business manager/publicist contact his assistant/business manager/publicist to make a date. If she's an actress, she may send him tickets or ask him to accompany her to a movie screening. If she's a tennis star, she may send him a VIP ticket to her next game. If she's a CEO, she may ask him to escort her to a black-tie dinner.

The man is usually flattered and agrees to go out with her. If he's attracted to her or in awe of her talent, he may date her for months or even years. He may even marry her. But in his heart he knows the relationship is not quite what he wanted. Because she wasn't someone he would have chosen on his own, there will always be something missing for him. She'll always be more interested in him than he is in her.

As time goes by, he may ignore her or even cheat on her. Eventually, he'll leave her for someone *he noticed first and had to chase, even some-one less attractive, less wealthy, or less famous.* The world may be surprised when this famous couple announces their breakup, but don't be. It was not *The Rules*.

Men want what they want. So even if you're beautiful, talented, and rich, you can't success-fully pursue a man!

Far from being exempt from *The Rules*, ac-tresses, models, high-powered, and famous women must follow *The Rules* more strictly than other women because their love life is public knowledge. If they pursue men, it will detract from their image, everyone will know about it, and they will be embarrassed.

For example, if a high-powered female execu-tive *actively* pursues a man and then talks about the relationship with her secretary or staff, the whole company could find out about it and it could get back to him. In addition to providing fodder for the company rumor mill, the man might lose interest in her when he finds out she's too obsessed with him and that she acted indis-creetly.

If you're a famous woman and you break *The Rules*, it's even worse because you are giving men ammunition to hurt you publicly. They could in-form the media and make your behavior a front-page story. They could sell love letters you wrote them to the *National Enquirer* or write a kiss-and-tell. On the other hand, when you do *The Rules*, men have nothing but good things to say about you because you left them alone. That's because the relationship—the calls, the letters, the attention, and so forth—was *their* idea. That's why we don't write men love letters or make anything happen. Why put ourselves in a position to be hurt?

In addition, by doing *The Rules,* rich and famous women can automatically weed out men who are only dating them for their fame or money. If you think nothing of inviting a man to your ski house because you have one and he doesn't, or taking a man on a vacation because you make more money than he does, remember that the trip is never as good when you invite him or pay for him. Instead, take a girlfriend, or go alone. A man might take advantage. We've heard about men who broke up with or never even called women right after these women took them on lavish vacations. Some men may accept your largesse, but then use you for it. When you do *The Rules,* you're silently letting him know that when he dates you, he gets only you—no extra perks. Unless he's interested in *you* for yourself, he drops out of the picture.

Do not use your social or business connections to help a man you are dating. If he's a lawyer and your company is looking for legal advice, don't bring him in. Think how awkward it would be if he were hired and then broke up with you! If you are wealthy, don't talk about your money or power or mention that your father is a millionaire. He should have no ulterior motives for wanting to be with you. Men should never get into the habit of expecting *anything* from you.

A wealthy woman we know who had a hard time meeting eligible men ran a personal ad in a magazine saying that she owned a large computer company, a sports car, and a ski house. She thought that her business savvy and wealth would attract interesting men—the same way some women think that giving men wild sex will keep them interested. But the men who responded to her ad showed more interest in getting a job at her company or free weekends at her ski house and country club than in dating her.

We told her to change her ad to play up her sexy smile, long hair, and great backhand. We advised her not to say anything about her business or assets in the ad or on dates until a man showed genuine interest in her. If asked about her career, we suggested she say, "I'm in management" or "I work for a computer company." We instructed her not to pick up the check on dates or invite men to her ski house. She followed our advice and is married to a man who fell for her smile and lively personality—long before he knew her net worth!

Trying to attract men with business smarts and money doesn't work. A man must feel a spark. He must like your looks and want to be with you, regardless of what you earn or own. In a *Rules* relationship, men fall in love with your essence, not your management skills.

Very wealthy women who marry men who have less money than they do should strongly consider asking them to sign prenuptial agreements. If a man gives you a hard time about it, think twice about marrying him. He may be after your money. If it's a *Rules* relationship, he won't mind a prenup. He wants nothing from you but to be with you.

By the way, there is nothing wrong with a movie star dating or marrying her personal trainer, bodyguard, gardener, or someone who works for her and makes less money—as long as he pursued her. She should not initiate a relationship by asking him to be her date at a film screening or shower him with expensive gifts if she wants him to desire her and treat her well down the road. Invariably, men who are pursued by famous and/or wealthy women and given a life vastly better than anything they would have had on their own still manage to hurt these women or take advantage of them.

Some actresses, models, and other high-profile women convince themselves that certain men are intimidated by their beauty, fame, or wealth and that's why these men don't ask them out, and that's why they had to make the first move.

Assuming a man is intimidated by your beauty or wealth or success, why would you want to be with him? If he's too threatened to initiate a relationship with you or walk across a room to talk to you and ask for your number, then he'll be too intimidated to *be* in a relationship with you. *Rules* girls only date men who pursue them and are not intimidated by them!

If you ignore *The Rules* and make the first move toward starting a relationship with such a man, he might be flattered and go out with you, but his initial reluctance to date you will resurface down the road. Sooner or later, you'll notice him being moody or withdrawn, rather than happy to be with you. He might get angry when fans recognize you in public, resent being called by your last name, or be unhappy because you make more money than he does. He will have problems with your fame and take it out on you in some way or even leave you for someone less famous or pretty.

You may find yourself trying to change him or turn yourself inside out to make the relationship work. Ask yourself, are you willing to stop being who you are, a model, actress, or successful businesswoman to please this man? Are you interested in taking him to couples therapy to deal with his "issues" about your fame? If you're not, then date only men who are not threatened by you, who like you, and are not unduly impressed by your wealth or fame.

The truth is, some men—even very good-looking men—are sometimes simply attracted to average-looking women, not great beauties. If you're a model, you should date only men who are not intimidated by models. If you're a gorgeous movie star, you should date only men who want a gorgeous movie star. Don't try to figure it out. Think of TV shows such as *Mary Tyler Moore*—some men like Mary, some like Rhoda, or *Friends*—some men like Monica, some like Rachel.

Movie stars, socialites, and other high-profile women must do *The Rules* on the media as well as on men.

If a reporter asks you if you ever want to get married (or why such a beautiful woman such as you isn't married), don't say anything like, "Actually I thought I'd be married by now. It's the only thing missing in my life," or "I'd trade all my success for a good relationship," or "I envy my sister who's not rich or famous, but has a husband and three kids. I haven't had a good date in years." Don't come across as depressed or cynical about love. Why reveal your personal anxieties? A press interview is not a therapy session. Don't be so open!

Instead, act confident and happy so that everyone thinks any man would be lucky to have you. Give the impression that you're not worried about your love life. Respond the same way you would to a man who asks why aren't you married. Count to five and say, "I never really thought about it" or "I'm just having fun right now!"

If you're in a relationship and reporters ask how it's going, just say "Great" and then talk about your movie, business, charity work, or whatever. Your love life is really none of their business, so be mysterious and vague, as if you were too busy to think about it. It's good for *The Rules* if you don't give away too much information.

Do not go into detail, as many famous people do, about how he's the man of your dreams, your soul mate, that you see each other all the time, or how great the sex is. Declaring your love on national television will not make him yours, scare other women away, or make him marry you. Talking openly about your relationship will only embarrass him and scare *him* away. Let *him* talk about you when he's interviewed. Better to do *The Rules* quietly and show up at the Oscars with an engagement ring than to talk for an hour about a man who hasn't proposed to you yet on a daytime talk show!

Another rule for the rich and famous: When the paparazzi snap photos of you and your boyfriend, you should not be all over him. Let him embrace *you*, pull *you* close to him, or hold *your* hand, whatever, just as long as it's all his doing. Otherwise the media and his friends will surely say, "Look who's a twosome now" and he'll get scared. And wouldn't you rather have a strong relationship that lasts a lifetime than just one more pretty picture?

Chapter 14 _____

Don't Be a Groupie and Other *Rules* for Dating Celebrities or High-Profile Men

IT'S NOT EVERYDAY that you meet a celebrity or CEO, but it can happen—at a party, on a plane, in the company cafeteria, or in a doctor's waiting room. And if you don't know *The Rules* and do them, you can easily ruin a once-in-a-lifetime opportunity.

For example, we know a woman who met a famous actor at a fund-raiser. He walked right up to her and said, "You're beautiful. When can we go out?"

Here was a perfect *Rules* beginning—he was obviously attracted to her and made the first move. But not knowing *The Rules,* she gushed, "Tonight."

Obviously, that was the wrong answer. When a famous actor says when can I see you, just smile and say, "Let me think, I don't know . . ." as if famous actors ask you out all the time. Even if he's ten times busier than you are, act as if you just don't know when you can see him. He must specifically ask you out for a particular night and it cannot be that night or the next night but several nights in advance.

The actor took our friend out to dinner, where she proceeded to tell him how much she admired his work and even asked him to autograph the menu. They spoke for hours (even closed the restaurant) and he hardly had to pressure her to go back to his hotel room. Although she did not have sex with him, she spent the night. He told her he would call her again when he was in town in a few weeks, but she never heard from him. By the time she found out about *The Rules*, it was too late.

What follows are *The Rules* for meeting and dating actors, athletes, famous authors, movie producers, directors, CEOs, and other powerful men. Assuming the celebrity or business VIP spoke to you first, here's what to do and not to do:

1. Take a deep breath. Stay composed.
2. Treat him as you would any other man—a coworker, your doorman—not the movie star or business tycoon he is.
3. Do not stare at him.
4. Do not light up or act giddy, as if you just won the lottery.
5. Do not carry on like a crazed fan. In other words, do not say anything like, "Oh my God, I can't believe it's—! I've seen all your movies!" (Even if you have seen all his

movies twice!) Act as if you've been out of the country for the last three years and you're not quite sure who he is, even if he was just on the cover of *People* magazine.

6. Don't ask for his autograph.

7. Don't compliment him, as in "You look much better in person than on TV."

8. Don't ask him about his next movie or show any interest in his career (or you'll sound like every other woman he's ever met).

9. If you're an aspiring actress, do not ask for an audition or a part in his movie. If you're looking for work, do not ask this high-powered executive for a job in his company. Do not ask for his business card or offer to send him your résumé or movie script.

10. Do not ask him to do you a favor, such as donate money to your favorite charity or give you tickets to his show or a free copy of his book.

11. Act interested, but not spellbound. Movie stars and CEOs are typically hounded and drooled over. So leave him alone. After five or ten minutes of conversation about whatever he wants to talk about, say, "Oh, look at the time. I must leave now. It was nice meeting you" and walk away. Do not spend the evening talking to this man. Do not agree to go out with him that night, even if he's leaving the country the next morning. (He can always call you—they have phones in other countries, too.)

12. Do not seem impressed by his Armani suit, limo, or entourage.

13. If you meet a performer and he offers you a ticket to see his concert or show as a first date, politely decline. Attending his show is not a date. If he wants to see you the night of the show, he must pick you up afterward and take you out.

14. If you're dating a sports star, don't run around the country wearing his jersey and attending all his games until you're in a committed relationship. Even then, he still must ask you out on dates to spend time with you.

15. Once you're actually dating a CEO or celebrity, don't see him whenever and wherever it's convenient for him because *he* has a busy schedule. He still has to ask you out in advance and you must turn him down politely if he expects to see you only on his terms—otherwise he will take you for granted. Celebrities are used to being spoiled, but you're a *Rules* girl!

16. Of course, it's tempting to drop your friends and family and revolve your whole life around this famous man. By following *The Rules*, you must still live your own life, see him only two to three times a week—until he proposes.

17. If he's handsome or widely popular, expect that other women might write him, call him, and throw themselves at him in public. Do not get angry or show jealousy or insecurity when this happens. Do not be possessive in

public. If he pursued you and you're doing *The Rules,* their advances won't matter. He'll still want you!

18. Be discreet. Do not call the tabloids and tell them you're dating a celebrity, as a way of announcing to other women or the world that he's yours—that doesn't work anyway—and don't talk to reporters if they call you. That would be self-serving, possibly hurtful or embarrassing to him, and might ruin any chances of his continuing to see you.

19. Don't try to become friendly with his secretary, publicist, or limo driver in an effort to keep tabs on him or so they put in a good word for you.

20. Don't seem overly interested in his fame, his wealth or the limelight. *Rules* girls are not groupies!

Keep in mind, sometimes a star is *not* your Mr. Right, and sometimes your Mr. Right is not a star. If you truly want things to work out between you, take things slowly, get to know him, and determine whether you love *him* or his image.

Chapter 15

Observe His Behavior on the Holidays

HOW HE TREATS YOU on the holidays is a good barometer of how he feels about you!

When a man is in love, he thinks about you and makes special plans with you *in advance* of Valentine's Day, New Year's Eve, your birthday, and Christmas or its equivalent. He'll circle the dates on his calendar and try to get the best table at a romantic restaurant—and that could mean calling a week or two ahead of time!

If it's Valentine's Day, he'll call the florist to buy you roses or your favorite flowers. If it's your birthday, he might buy you a piece of jewelry and a meaningful card. He might suggest you spend the holidays with his family, and make sure you ring in the New Year together in a romantic way. He'll make a thoughtful toast about the two of you. You're always on his mind and in his heart.

He looks forward to being with you on that special night and watching you read his card and open his present. What should you give him? A

Rules girl gives a man she is dating *a simple card* for Valentine's Day—something short and sweet; no poetry and no balloons—and maybe a scarf or sweater for his birthday or the holidays. (See Chapter 16: "Don't Go Overboard and Other *Rules* for Giving to Men.")

When a man is not in love, he sometimes doesn't even acknowledge the holidays. He may take you out on Saturday night as he usually does and not even mention the holiday—even if it falls the next day—hoping that you don't either. You may blame his lack of romantic interest in you at holiday time on his upbringing or past relationships, but a man in love with a woman acts differently with her than with anyone else.

If he's really not planning to marry you, he may not even call you the week of Valentine's Day or New Year's Eve. He may just skip the week to avoid the whole issue. If you ask him why he didn't call, he might say things were hectic at work or holidays are silly. But a man in love would not be too busy or cynical about the holidays. In fact, we've known a few men who even carved pumpkins for their girlfriends on Halloween, hardly an important occasion.

When a man is not in love, he may buy a silly card and just sign his name—with no "love." He finds the holidays stupid or commercial and gets irritable if you take it seriously or expect more from him.

If the man you are dating does little or nothing for your birthday, Valentine's Day, or New Year's Eve, what should you do?

Don't bring up the occasion either. Pretend you forgot or didn't care—and then cry to your girl-friends. Just don't let him know it bothered you!

Don't have a "talk" about how you thought your first Valentine's Day or birthday together would be more romantic and are really disappointed and hurt. You can't make a man feel romantic if he doesn't. If these special occasions are not important to him you must accept this.

Don't hint that it's Valentine's Day, or pressure him to take you out or buy you flowers. He either thought of it and wanted to or he didn't. Don't try to get something from the wrong source. Buy yourself flowers, if that's important to you.

If you demand that he take you out or buy you flowers, he may comply, but it won't be from his heart. He may do it just to avoid an argument or to continue to see you (until he meets someone else) or to have sex. It never works *long-term* if we force things.

If the man you are dating did not ask you out on New Year's Eve or Valentine's Day or did not suggest spending Christmas together, you cannot ask him to. Man must pursue woman! Do not offer to make him a candlelit dinner at your place (to make it easy for him or so that he doesn't have to plan or spend money). If he didn't initiate a romantic evening with you, then he didn't want to be romantic with you. Just put it in the back of your head that this man is not romantic or not in love with you and either accept that or move on. This is a good time to reevaluate the relationship and to determine if he is your Mr. Right.

On Valentine's Days and New Year's Eves in the past—before you discovered *The Rules*—you may have overlooked signs that a man wasn't in love with you. You may have rationalized his no card/silly card, and told yourself these gestures were not important. But in your heart, you knew the truth. You knew that a man in love would have bought you flowers or tried to do something special.

Now that you know *The Rules,* what do you do that night if the man you are dating did not ask you out at least several days—preferably a week—in advance for an important occasion?

Make plans with friends or go to a party where you might meet someone else. The holidays can be a very lonely and painful time for a single woman, so try not to be home by yourself.

But even if all you do is stay home, make sure to leave your answering machine on so, in case he calls, he doesn't know where you are. It really doesn't matter what you do that night as long as you don't—in a weak moment—call him and invite him over. Rent a video or invite a girlfriend over for dinner, and think seriously about breaking up with this guy. Resolve to do *The Rules* on every man you meet from this moment on so you don't spend your next birthday/Valentine's Day/New Year's Eve/Christmas, or holiday alone!

Chapter 16 —————————

Don't Go Overboard and Other *Rules* for Giving to Men

AS WE EXPLAINED IN *The Rules,* you should not offer to pay for anything on the first three dates. There's no need to. When a man is interested in you, he is not thinking about money (i.e., splitting the check), he's hoping to make a good impression and hoping that you'll see him again. Part of pursuing you is making plans and paying for everything.

Of course, if he *asks* you to split the check, cheerfully do so. You weren't trying to get a free meal. You want him to *want* to pay for you. We don't tell a man to pick up the check. We just notice he didn't and put it in the back of our mind. Maybe he's not Mr. Right.

We are not telling you to be a gold digger. It is not about how much he spends. Let him take you to an inexpensive restaurant or a movie, as long as he plans ahead and pays for the date. When a man is truly in love, he'll work extra hours or borrow from his parents or friends to come up with the money to impress you. Dutch treat is fine for friends and coworkers, not dates. You want a man who is crazy about you!

Women, especially those making good salaries, tend to get hung up on reciprocating. We tell them that in the first two to three months of dating they should be focusing instead on getting off the phone first and not asking a man out—not obsessing about buying him dinner or a tie. When you're married, you can buy him anything you want!

After three months, you can make or buy him dinner.

On his birthday and/or other gift-giving holidays, *The Rules* are:

Do not spend more than $50 to $100, even if you can well afford to. But more importantly, don't buy him anything romantic.

Good gift ideas include:

1. A book on a subject of interest to him, as long as it has nothing to do with astrology, therapy, love or relationships, such as business, politics, computers, or a novel (nonromantic) you know he'd love to read.
2. A winter scarf.
3. A T-shirt, sweatshirt, or cap of his favorite sports team.

Do not buy him:

1. Jewelry.
2. Anything monogrammed.

3. A picture frame or photo album.
4. Champagne glasses, or any houseware for that matter.
5. A book of poems.

Women are not only too generous to men in material ways—they tend to be too extending in social situations as well. They invite a man they just started dating to accompany them to a wedding, dinner party, business or family function, country club, summer house, or business trip/vacation. We strongly suggest you do not do so for at least three months. If you do, he will surely feel that you are more serious about the relationship than he is, get scared and pull back. In addition, if he is surrounded by married couples at these events, he will most surely feel pressured.

If you are in a business where you get free tickets to tennis matches, trips, or are regularly invited to business parties and shows as part of your job, do not take him for the first few months. Take a friend or go alone. Why?

1. You will not be mysterious if he knows your entire social calendar.
2. He should not think of you as a cash cow. Otherwise, how will you know if he really cares about *you* or your perks? He must fall in love with you *first!*
3. When a man is in love with you, he wants to be with *you*. If you are always giving him presents and taking him to places, he might believe you are trying to buy his love and af-

fection, that you are trying too hard, and care too much, which is never good.

One more way a woman may try to give too much to a man is by being overly involved in his life. Needless to say, you can listen and offer suggestions, but don't become wrapped up in his business problems, family affairs, or any other issues. You are not his therapist or his wife (yet).

Actually, the best gift you can give a man is to do *The Rules,* which gives him the thrill of pursuing you and the glory of getting you!

Chapter 17 ———————————

Buyer Beware (Weeding out Mr. Wrong)!

*T*HE RULES ARE NOT about marrying the first man you are attracted to who calls you by Wednesday for Saturday night and buys you flowers. It's about marrying your own personal Mr. Right—a man whom you love and whose character you admire and can live with.

Love may be blind, but *Rules* girls are not stupid! In addition to doing *The Rules*, you should be observing his behavior in various situations to decide if he's right for you. You may want to keep notes in *The Rules Dating Journal* to keep track of what he says and how he acts in his relationship with you. For example, is he a man of his word or does he promise and not deliver? Does he speak badly about people or tell horrible stories about ex-girlfriends? Is he cheap on dates? Is he critical of you? Does he drink or smoke too much? Is he rude to waiters? If either of you has been married before, how does he treat his children or your children?

It's easy to ignore certain behavior, but if it's written down in black and white, you will see a pattern emerge and not be able to lie to yourself or sweep it under the rug.

Don't marry thinking you will change this kind of behavior—people don't usually change that much. We believe that anything you don't like about the man you marry was there when you were dating him—you just didn't really think about it seriously or told yourself you didn't mind.

A woman we know who followed *The Rules* called us one day to say Mr. Right had proposed. We were thrilled, but we quickly got suspicious when she told us that six months had passed and he still hadn't committed to a wedding date. She, too, felt something was wrong, but she really wanted to marry this man. We advised her to try to pin him down to a date. When she did, he admitted that he was back with his ex-girlfriend.

If something doesn't feel right to you about a man, it probably isn't! If you don't want to be miserable and full of regrets later on, you have to pay attention now. *Rules* girls don't sleep at the wheel!

No, *Rules* girls take a very active role in choosing Mr. Right. At first glance, *The Rules* may seem like passive dating—let him call you, let him ask you out, let him pick you up, let him do all the work. In terms of the *chase,* that's certainly true. But we are also telling women to actively evaluate a man's character and behavior. Did he call when he said he'd call? Did he remember your birthday?

A *Rules* girl is always carefully observing his behavior and taking notes. This *is* active, not passive, dating.

When we told you to "be quiet and mysterious, act lady-like, and cross your legs and smile and don't talk so much" on the first few dates, we did not mean that you shouldn't *think!* We told you this for two reasons:

(a) so you don't tell him your whole life story too soon and live to regret it, and, equally important,

(b) so you *listen.* The less you talk, the more you can hear and pick up clues if he's right for you.

Sometimes a woman is so anxious to get married to a man she is attracted to—a man who is chasing her thanks to *The Rules*—that she blocks out traits she doesn't like about him. She hopes that love and marriage will change him in time. We say, maybe, maybe not. It's true that former playboy types lose interest in the club scene when they meet a *Rules* girl and become fond of changing diapers when they have a child. But we also say, what you see is what you get, so don't count on a man changing.

Let's look at some specific dilemmas you might be facing:

Dilemma #1: You're amazed—and impressed—by his sophistication with alcohol. He puts away countless gin and tonics without a problem, and you're charmed by the way he orders the best bottle of wine at romantic restaurants! But after reading this chapter, you remember that most of the time you had mineral water and *he* gladly drank the whole bottle.

Buyer beware: Love won't change an addiction and heavy drinking isn't charming when you have kids to support and he's throwing money away at bars, or you are the designated driver after every party. If you think he drinks too much, don't marry him unless he agrees to seek help and has stopped drinking for at least a year. It's good for him and it's good for you.

Dilemma #2: You think you've found Mr. Right, except that he'd rather read the newspaper or work on the computer than have sex with you most week nights and even Sunday mornings. Now that you're reading this chapter, you remember that he was always a little too intellectual for your taste. You wished he were more passionate, not so cerebral.

Buyer beware: This will be a problem in your marriage if sex and passion are important to you.

Dilemma #3: He's very good-looking, personable, and a ton of fun, but not as deep as you would like him to be. You are a serious reader— you tend to be analytical and you are into yoga and meditation. He likes action sports, such as tennis and basketball. You want to have soulful discussions; he's more pragmatic.

Buyer beware: This will be a problem if you like to have philosophical conversations with your mate. Just know that he may ask you to have breakfast with him or play tennis when you're in the middle of yoga or meditating.

Dilemma #4: He's into a whirlwind courtship. He calls you day and night and proposes after a month or two. You think he's a little impulsive, but you're also thrilled!

Buyer beware: If you allow yourself to get caught up in a whirlwind romance and move at his speed, you may live to regret it. You need to pace the relationship—to wait and allow yourself time to observe his behavior in many different situations—before you make such a serious commitment. Otherwise, you may find out *after* you're married that he's a womanizer, gambler, emotionally immature, in deep financial debt, or has a criminal past. By then it might be too late.

Dilemma #5: He's exciting and debonair, but he has a dark side. You've heard him scream at his family, his friends, and even business associates.

Buyer beware: He may yell or be violent toward you or your children.

Dilemma #6: He loves you, but is often a drop annoyed by your close girlfriends, your family, and any man who pays too much attention to you. He gets angry if you don't tell him everything or include him in everything.

Buyer beware: While it's flattering to be the center of a man's attention, as opposed to being ignored, know that you might have fights about his level of involvement in your day-to-day activities.

Sometimes the problem is not his character, but circumstances, such as:

Dilemma #7: You love him, but he's much older than you, divorced, and a devoted father to two teenagers. You never cared for children, much less stepchildren.

Buyer beware: You may resent his children and the time they take away from your relationship. You might also resent the amount of money he is paying to his ex-wife to support them.

Sometimes the problem is not him at all, but *you.* Your motives are not so good, such as:

Dilemma #8: You love him but, truth be told, you wouldn't be marrying him if he wasn't also rich.

Buyer beware: What are you going to do if his business sours and he no longer can buy you diamonds and fur coats? What if you actually have to go back to work?

In the above scenarios, we are not saying "don't marry him." We are simply saying go into the marriage with your eyes open. Be honest with yourself! Check your motives! *Rules* girls don't get married at any cost!

If you don't want to have problems later on, think twice about marrying for money or power, unless you can live with the downside. Think twice about marrying to get even with your ex-husband who left you for a younger woman or to escape a bad home life. Think twice about marrying anyone simply to have children.

And don't be lax about discussing major issues such as religion or whether to have children *before* you get married.

While making sure you are marrying Mr. Right is not always so easy, by doing *The Rules* you at least weed out Mr. Wrong.

For example, any man who is interested in you just for sex, money, or convenience automatically loses interest because you are not sleeping with him right away, you are not supporting him, and you are not meeting him when and where it's convenient for him.

A man has to *really care about you* to call you early in the week (every week), make plans, pick you up, and wait until you're ready to have sex! Mr. Wrongs simply won't put up with the rigors of *The Rules*—they move on to women without such standards.

So while you're doing *The Rules*, you should also be observing, writing, and thinking, *Is he the right one for me?* Take an active role—your long-term happiness is definitely worth the work.

Chapter 18 _____

Closing the Deal (Getting Him to the Altar)

WE'RE NOT TALKING about a business deal here, but getting the man you want to propose and then to turn that proposal into an actual wedding date—a feat some women would say can be tougher than any corporate transaction. Of course, it's made much easier by doing *The Rules*.

If you've been following *The Rules* from the moment you met Mr. Right and he says he loves you, he *will* propose—sometimes in a matter of a few months, but usually within fifteen months. (He may have his own "rules" about dating you for four seasons before proposing, and there's nothing wrong with that.)

By doing *The Rules* you will not only get a proposal, but you will know where the relationship is going long before he pops the question. You will sense a warm, open feeling emanating from him, a desire to include you in his world. Here are some of the key words and phrases he is likely to bring up in conversations with you:

1. The future—whether it be where he wants to live, his career goals, or the car he is planning to buy.
2. Marriage (the M-word)—for example, he'll *volunteer* that he's going to be the best man when his friend gets married.
3. Kids—he might mention his nephew's upcoming birthday.
4. Married friends—he might discuss his married friends or suggest doubling with them.
5. His family—he'll talk about his parents and ask you about yours or invite you to a family gathering for the holidays.

He'll also include you in the most minute details of his day—i.e., he'll tell you that he got a haircut or he washed the car. He's always bringing you closer to him.

Because you let him pursue you, didn't see him more than two or three times a week, refused to go away with him on week-long vacations, have not moved in or crowded him in any way, you've actually helped him to fall in love with you and *want* to marry you. He wants more of you, not less.

Within a year, if not sooner, he's figured out that he not only *wants* to marry you but *has* to marry you to see you more often, to really have you.

Your problem is not *if* he's going to marry you, but *when*. *Men can date for five years!* They are notorious for wanting to put off the actual engagement part until *later*. If he suggests living together first to see if you get along or to see you more often, tell him you're old-fashioned and want to wait until you're engaged or married.

A man can love you, but marriage . . . that's a little scary. Maybe he's just trying to hold on to his bachelorhood, maybe he's been married before and isn't in any rush to do it again, or maybe he's young (under twenty-five years old).

In general, the way to get a man to ask you to marry him in a reasonable amount of time is not to live with him before you're engaged or married and to continue to see him only three times a week, even though by this time you *want* to be inseparable.

If that doesn't work, you might have to shake things up a little bit—go away for a weekend with a girlfriend, cancel a Saturday night date, get very busy at work, mention that you are renewing your apartment lease, and be mysterious about your activities. All of the above should make him anxious to propose. As you already know, a man who is wary of commitment is made less wary by a woman moving *away* from, not *toward*, commitment. This isn't trickery. You're just giving him *space*.

On the other hand, if you have not done *The Rules* all along, getting a man to propose can be very difficult.

If you have been dating a man for two, three, or even five years and he has not proposed, you might be thinking that if you hang around long enough, he will eventually ask. You have probably accepted his excuses—financial problems, married before, not ready, and so on—as to why he can't marry you just yet. But now that you've read *The Rules*, you know that a *Rules* girl doesn't date a man forever and the way to get him to propose (if he's going to propose at all) is *not* to hang around.

Let's say you've been dating him for more than a year and he's somehow avoided the whole issue of marriage and the future, what should you do?

Ask him his intentions. If he says he has no plans to marry you, say "Okay" and then never see him again. Men don't lie about things like this. He's not scared of commitment—he doesn't want to marry you.

If he says he does plan to marry you some day, then it's up to you to *close the deal*. Ask him when and if it's more than a year, see less of him and think about dating others. You've already spent more than a year waiting for him to propose, do you have another year to wait?

If you are already living together (because you found out about *The Rules* after you moved in) and he says he doesn't want to get engaged, make plans to move out. But don't say, "I'm moving out because you won't commit." That would be too obvious. Just say you need more space and that you heard about a great apartment or your friend is renting hers. When a man doesn't want to commit, we leave him alone. If he doesn't try to stop you or get you back with a proposal, don't waste your time. If he asks what's going on, nonchalantly answer, "I don't know if this relationship is for me." If he can live without you, you don't want him. You move on.

Here are five things *not* to do, no matter how tempting:

1. Don't tell him you're hurt, mad, or reprimand him for wasting your time or leading you on. You lived with him—no one twisted your arm. Take responsibility for your actions. By not doing *The Rules,* you allowed him to be with you indefinitely. In a *Rules* relationship a man either proposes within a year—two years at the max!—or it's next!

2. Don't suggest going to couples therapy to discuss why *he* can't commit. Men can and do commit when they love you and you do *The Rules* on them. But they can become "commitment-phobic" when a woman has pursued them, is too available, or they're just not in love with her. They say things like, "I find marriage a difficult concept to swallow," or they conveniently cite the high divorce rate.

3. Don't let a man brainwash you into thinking that marriage isn't important—"just a piece of paper"—and that as long as you're together that's all that matters. If he doesn't want to marry you then he's not *that* in love with you, or it's not the brand of love you want. What it really means is he still wants the option of meeting someone else!

4. Don't let a man convince you that because he's been married before he can't marry you

or that you should give him time to recover from Wife No. 1 or 2.

5. Don't let a man you have been dating for years convince you to wait until "things slow down" at work or he's better off financially to make a commitment. This is the worst reason. There will always be work/money issues in life. They should have nothing to do with marrying you. When a man loves you and wants to marry you he hopes you *don't* notice these issues, or he includes you in their solutions and begs you to marry him anyway. He gets down on one bended knee and says something like, "Look, I know I'm not a millionaire, but I love you and I'd do anything for you." When a man says "You're too good for me," what he really means is "I don't want you."

In conclusion, the same man who won't commit because of issues with his ex-wife or his finances has no problem proposing to a woman who refused to date him longer than a year. Sometimes a man will date a woman for five years claiming he has commitment issues and after breaking up with her, easily marries someone else in six months.

If you are involved with a man for several years who isn't proposing, how much longer are you willing to wait? When a man knows that you will accept less than marriage he is not motivated to fully commit himself. You must be willing to walk away from a dead-end relationship.

Assuming you are engaged, how do you get him to walk down the aisle?

The truth is, if you're engaged as a result of *The Rules,* getting him to marry you should not be a problem. There's no "cold feet" in *Rules* engagements. In fact, just the opposite is the case. He's made his decision, he *wants* to get married, to be with you all the time, forever.

There's usually a wondrous, exciting planning of the wedding. He's calling caterers, videographers, and tuxedo places, and driving himself crazy trying to pick the most meaningful wedding song. He's intimately involved in every detail of the wedding. He's worried that you might not get your dress in time. The *only* time he is angry at you is when you're not making the wedding your top priority.

Of course, getting engaged is no *guarantee* of marriage, so don't get lax about *The Rules* when you're engaged. Don't think you can talk to him on the phone for hours, and it's still best not to move in together yet. Engagements can be broken and wedding dates postponed or never set. If you move in, he may change his mind and decide not to marry you so soon! Better that he miss you and move up the wedding date than feel claustrophobic as you take over his closet space.

Also, be on the alert for any special circumstances or excuses your fiancé might make, such as:

1. He thinks being engaged is great, but why rush marriage?
2. He's been married before, it was a disaster, and he's not anxious to tie the knot again. He

gave you the ring so he doesn't lose you (so you won't sleep with anyone else), but he's happy with the status quo.

3. He's young and still likes to go out with his friends, not be tied down. He likes the bachelor life and although you convinced him to get engaged, you can't pin him down for a wedding date. You have a ring, but you're not sure what the future looks like.

4. You were already living together when you got engaged, but you still don't have a wedding date set. What to do?

In general, we feel that when you get engaged you should set a wedding date. *Rules* engagements are usually a year or less. If you're young (under twenty-five), a two-year engagement is fine.

If the engagement is dragging on, you may want to think about giving him back the ring and moving on. Perhaps he's not Mr. Right. *Rules* girls don't waste time.

Not Closing the Deal (Being True to Yourself)

Perhaps you're the one having second thoughts. You did *The Rules,* he may or may not have proposed, but now you're having doubts about him and the relationship. Something just doesn't feel right, you're thinking about breaking it off. Perhaps you're finding out that he's not the man of your dreams after all, or there are just extenuating circumstances. What should you do?

If you've thought about it carefully and discussed your decision with a therapist, good friends, or family members, we suggest you *always* trust your instincts. *Do Not Close the Deal.*

Don't feel silly, embarrassed, or guilty. Don't hate yourself or feel like a failure or that you wasted a year or two of your life. You didn't. Ending a relationship that isn't right is a learning and growing experience. Besides, you're not the first woman to change her mind or cancel a wedding. It happens sometimes. You tried, it didn't work out, much better to find out and disentangle yourself now than later on. Don't stay with him because you're a couple, you've made future plans together, you like his parents, you're entrenched and it feels complicated to break it off at this stage of the game.

After you've made up your mind, give yourself time and permission to cry and grieve. Who wouldn't be upset? It's normal. But don't give up on love or throw yourself in front of a bus. Keep the faith. Always remember, there's another person out there—the real Mr. Right—for you and you're a winner for being honest with yourself! Pump yourself up by rereading *The Rules,* specifically **Rule #1:** *You are a Creature Unlike Any Other:* You trust in the abundance and goodness of the universe: if not him, someone better . . . Any man would be lucky to have you! Plan a social action, get back on track! Keep doing *The Rules.* Your *real* Mr. Right may be just around the corner and when you meet him, you won't regret past breakups!

Don't Be the Rebound Girl and Other *Rules* for Dating a Man Who Is Separated

IF YOU HAVE BEEN following *The Rules,* you are not dating a married man for all the obvious reasons. It's not honest, he's not yours, and you could waste a lot of time waiting for him to leave his wife, if he ever does.

Many women have called us to say they are dating a married man anyway. To these women, all we can suggest is that they find the courage—pray for it, do whatever it takes—to stop seeing him. Dating a married man is like driving down a dead-end street—it gets you nowhere. Better to date him when he's divorced and available. So don't call him, don't write him letters, don't initiate encounters, and don't meet him at a moment's notice.

Be sure the man you are dating is at the very least separated from his wife. But don't assume he is. How can you tell? If he doesn't give you his home number, tells you the best way to get in touch with him is by his beeper or gives you a phone number but he's never there when you call, doesn't introduce you to family or friends, and acts on the secretive side, then you must wonder! Something is off. Be on the alert. He might be trying to juggle two lives. You'll find out soon enough if you do *The Rules* and pay attention.

So now, hopefully, you are dating a man who is *really* separated. That can be messy enough! There's his ex-wife, money issues, lawyers, and sometimes complicated custody battles. It might feel like walking into the middle of a movie. Are you willing to deal with all these issues and a possibly lengthy courtship?

If you are, here are some rules:

In addition to following all the rules for dating a single man, you must *pay attention* to what he says about why his marriage didn't work out and how it might affect his chances of marrying and *staying* married to you. If he doesn't talk about the breakup, try to find out (without being too obvious) whether it was his idea or hers to get a divorce.

This information is important. If the divorce was his idea, it probably means he isn't hung up on his ex—a good sign. On the other hand, it also shows that he is capable of leaving a woman and that he could walk out on you one day. If you have been able to surmise that it wasn't a *Rules* marriage—in other words, she pursued him—and your relationship is, you have nothing to worry about. He just wanted out of a bad marriage.

But if you think he just picked up and left one

day for no good reason, keep your eye on him. He could be bad news. Fortunately, *The Rules* will help you screen out any disturbing behavior and inconsistencies—skipping a Saturday night date here and there, a few no-shows, forgetting your birthday—long before you walk down the aisle.

If it was his wife's idea to end the marriage, realize that he may still have feelings for her and there's a chance they could get back together. This is particularly true if he is newly separated—say, under six months. He may be dating you merely as a *distraction*—as a way of helping himself get over his ex. If he talks about *her* all the time when he's with you, then he's not crazy in love with you! Remember, you want to be his *Rules* girl, not his rebound girl!

So be on the lookout for signs that he finds excuses to contact her, still fights with her a lot and gets very emotional about the separation. That's not how he should behave when he's over her and in love with you! When a man is not interested in staying with an ex, he has little to do with her and does not try to prolong the divorce for any reason. He just wants it over.

Whatever the case is, don't play therapist to his marital problems. If he always wants to talk about the breakup, listen politely for a little while here and there, but don't give him advice and don't help him put down his ex-wife if he has a habit of doing so. He can put down his ex-wife, but you shouldn't. Don't show jealousy or seem too interested if he is in contact with her. The less you appear to care, the better.

Don't resolve to be the "nicer second wife" if and when he marries you. For example, if he complains that his ex-wife was too busy with her career and not there enough for him, you might think you shouldn't do *The Rules,* that you can't end dates first because he's so needy and you should put him before your career. You might decide to see him constantly, cook meals on the weekends for him to have during the week—literally, *take care of him.* This is a big mistake. We know women who played therapist/nurse, became the *woman who understands,* spent years on a man, only to see him remarry someone just like his ex! Whatever he may say about his ex-wife, remember, *he married her.* On some level, he likes that type. You can't always go by what a man says—it's what he does that counts. Just do *The Rules* and be true to yourself.

Remember, when you are dating a man who is separated, it is easy to get caught up in his problems, his schedule, his timetable, his needs. For example, he might say that he doesn't want to remarry "for a while" until things settle down or that he wants to wait until his children can handle all the changes, not to mention a stepmom.

Be understanding, but not *too* understanding. *Rules* girls don't wait forever. If he is serious about marrying you, there is no reason why he shouldn't be divorced within a year after meeting you or as soon as possible. You should be engaged within six months after his divorce comes through. You should have a wedding date *set* soon after you are engaged.

Keep in mind that these are general guidelines— don't be difficult or inflexible if there are children involved or extenuating circumstances. You should only be concerned if he avoids the whole subject of marriage or wants you to live with him first. In either case, you might have to reevaluate or stop seeing him for a while. *Rules* girls don't wait indefinitely for men to sort out their lives. Don't spoil him by waiting. If he needs more than two years to remarry, he may not be *your* Mr. Right.

The fact that he has children should not change this time structure too much, but it does mean that you need to be especially considerate of his relationship with his kids. Sometimes you really must take a backseat, sometimes you have to exhibit the patience of a saint.

Don't ask to meet his children. He must include you in that part of his life when he's ready and wants to. You never want to be in a situation where his kids resent you or blame you for his marital problems or feel that you are taking their father away from them. *He* should deal with their anger. He should explain to them that he loves you and that his marriage failed on its own, that it had nothing to do with you. You shouldn't get involved.

Don't be jealous if at times he puts his children before you—i.e., he can't have Sunday brunch with you because he must see his son play soccer. His desire to be a good father, his loyalty to his children are qualities to be proud of and admire—not to be resentful of. Bite your tongue, stay busy. Don't make him feel that he has to choose between you and his children. If you plan to be their stepmom one day, then you must also think of their needs, in addition to your own.

Although we are asking you to be considerate about his relationship with his kids—and divorce can be traumatic for any child—we are not telling you to be a doormat. We know men who ask their girlfriends to be baby-sitters, or take their daughter ice-skating, but they never propose. You are not a baby-sitter or the girlfriend who is there for him, who waits and waits forever.

Dating a man who is separated can be difficult. But by doing *The Rules*, you don't put your life on hold indefinitely. You don't make excuses to yourself about why he won't remarry or why he needs years to heal from his divorce. When you do *The Rules*, a man who is separated recovers pretty quickly and happily marries you!

Chapter 20

A *Rules* Refresher for Married Women

IF YOU'RE MARRIED, do you need to do *The Rules*? Married women who recently discovered *The Rules* often ask us this question. Although we touched upon this issue in **Rule #26** ("Even if You're Engaged or Married, You Still Need *The Rules*") in our first book, there has been a demand for more advice. In this chapter, we delve into the subject more deeply and offer tips for both *Rules* and non-*Rules* relationships.

If you did *The Rules* when you were dating your husband, you don't have to consciously play hard to get anymore. Your husband is *naturally* crazy about you. Because you did not see him all the time or talk to him for hours on the phone, he does not take you for granted and he is not bored with you. He still finds you interesting and exciting, even years later. He sees you as the prom queen and considers himself lucky to have won your affections . . . and that feeling never goes away. You have a wonderful sense of security.

Rules husbands are very involved. They're always calling, they initiate romance, and buy flowers or romantic gifts for your birthday, anniversary, and Valentine's Day. (And they remember all three without your help!)

Rules husbands like to do just about everything as a couple or a family. They take marriage very seriously. They don't complain about marriage or make jokes about you—calling you "the old ball and chain"—the way some of their unhappy friends do. Because you did *The Rules*, the way things are in the beginning can last forever—all the more reason to do *The Rules* strictly from the moment Mr. Right comes into your life.

In a *Rules* marriage, any work you have to do is on yourself—being happy or easy to be with, pursuing your career and interests, staying fit—not figuring out how to get your husband's attention.

What if you are in a non-*Rules* marriage and would like to improve your relationship? There are two kinds of non-*Rules* marriages: (1) he pursued you but you broke rules (i.e., saw him all the time, stayed on the phone for hours, or were too needy), and (2) you pursued him (called him, asked him out, initiated trips and so on).

The first situation is simple to remedy. Since he pursued you, if you start doing *The Rules* now, he'll be drawn to you all over again. Some suggestions: Don't ask him constantly if he loves you, don't remind him incessantly that it's Valentine's Day or demand flowers, don't suggest having talks, don't call him at work so often, get off the phone first when he calls, dress sexier, get involved in your own life, and work on being less needy and more independent.

Don't worry that it might feel strange to suddenly behave differently with him after a number of years. Just do *The Rules*. Men don't necessarily care or question *why* a woman is busy taking care of herself and is more positive, they just appreciate the difference and want her more.

But if *you* initiated the relationship with your husband and now find yourself unhappy because you wish he paid more attention to you, it may not be so easy. Start doing *The Rules*, first and foremost, for yourself and your self-esteem.

If you initiated sex, romance, weekend plans, or vacations when you were dating your husband and continue to in your marriage, then just stop being the pursuer, the planner, and the one who makes all romantic overtures. Do this for a week, two weeks, or even a month, and see what happens.

By doing *The Rules*—leaving your husband alone—he'll appreciate the space and you'll be clearer about how he really feels about you. He may miss your attention and start pursuing you, or not miss it at all. By doing *The Rules,* you'll find out. You'll let nature take its course.

Below are sixteen suggestions which, in addition to **Rule #26**, will improve your marriage:

1. *Start with your looks.*

If your husband is not paying attention to you, is it in any way warranted? Take a good look at yourself! Have you gained a lot of weight? (Is the treadmill in your bedroom being used just to hang clothes?) When was the last time you had a manicure or new hairstyle? Do you need some new stylish/sexy clothes?

Instead of demanding that your husband pay more attention to you or wishing his pretty secretary (who's only thin because *she's* never had kids) would quit or get fired, start on a self-improvement plan today. Don't tell yourself all this is superficial or that you have more important things to do. Appearance counts and there's no reason why your husband shouldn't find you hot and sexy. Pretend you're dating him all over again!

Starting this minute, go on a diet if you need to, exercise, grow your hair longer, get a makeover, and treat yourself to a manicure and pedicure. Looks aren't everything, but try not to scrimp on them or on your clothes. It never hurts to look the best you can. You will feel good and he will like it!

2. *Use your mind.*

Some women complain that their husbands aren't interested in them when the truth is they're doing little or nothing to make their own lives meaningful. Just as we told single women to "Fill up your time before the date" in *The Rules,* we encourage married women to get involved in *something* outside of their relationship with their husbands. It could be their work, their friends, volunteer work for a charity, furthering their education, taking up a hobby or sport, or simply reading the newspaper or a book.

3. *Don't analyze and reanalyze your relationship or force him to talk about it.*

It's no secret that women like to talk about their feelings and the "relationship" more than men do. If you feel the need to have a heart-to-heart talk with your husband, but suspect that he's not interested at that very moment, a good *Rules* credo is to wait. Talk to a friend instead. It's rarely a good conversation when he's not in the mood. Don't analyze why he doesn't want to talk. If you are relaxed and confident about your relationship, he'll be much more likely to want to discuss it with you.

Besides, unless a talk is absolutely necessary, sometimes the best way to get your husband's attention is to look extra good and be pleasant and enthusiastic with him about your life as it currently is.

4. *Leave him alone.*

If your husband wants to watch a football game or sit in his La-Z-Boy chair with the newspaper, try not to disturb him. Men like to go inward at times—and these are the worst times to try to get him to do something together. Accept that he's in his own world and get busy in yours!

If you interrupt him, he will feel annoyed and you might feel rejected and unloved. It's better to get involved in something of your own; he will seek you out when he's done with whatever he was doing. A marriage works better when husband pursues wife!

5. *Don't be a nag.*

Don't constantly complain about the lack of money, the size of your house, what needs to be done in the house, or tell him what your friends have and what you don't have. Hopefully, you married for love, not other reasons. Remember that, and don't let your relationship become adversarial. Instead of trying to make your husband feel inadequate, focus on the positive. Tell him how happy you are with him, your life, and your marriage.

Married women often complain that their husbands don't help around the house enough or don't really listen. Sometimes their gripes are valid, but nagging isn't the answer. If you constantly harp on his faults, he will simply learn to tune you out.

All you can do is ask him—once and nicely!—to make an effort to do this or that. But accept that he may or may not change. Remember, don't expect him to change to make you happy—work on accepting him as he is and focus on making yourself the best you can be.

6. *Let him initiate romance.*

Some married women wish their husbands came home with flowers more often. If your husband doesn't always act like a Hallmark relationship card, don't be angry and resentful. He married you! Don't expect him to prove his love to you everyday. Are you always romantic and loving when he comes home?

In *The Rules*, we told single women not to initiate romance because man must pursue woman and because you can easily get hurt if your advances are rejected. Now that you're married, of course you can initiate romance or sex, but only if you accept that he may or may not be in the mood. He could be preoccupied with problems at work. Can you take what appears to be rejection if he's not in the mood at the moment? Know your own limitations, and act accordingly.

7. *Don't be jealous.*

Instead of worrying about every woman he talks to at a party, put your energy into being confident and having fun at the party yourself. Don't cling to his side, but walk around and mingle. Jealousy is a chink in your armor. Your husband should not think that you'd be lost without him. *Rules* women actually think the opposite. They tell themselves, "Any man would be lucky to have me!"

Jealousy doesn't work anyway. *Rules* women don't waste time on behaviors that don't work. They're busy with their careers, kids, friends, hobbies, and learning new skills. So don't waste your time watching his every move at a social function, calling his office at 9:00 P.M. to be sure he's working, looking for lipstick stains, or going through his mail.

8. *Take the high road with friends and family.*

You may not get along with every one of his family members or friends. However, be careful not to criticize them in front of your husband. Always take the high road. Realize that he knows them in a special way that you may never understand. How would you like it if he found fault with your chatty but good friends or your meddling sister? Find an impartial friend to air your grudges with. Even if you're absolutely right, try not to complain to your husband. He shouldn't think of you as a grievance collector. Collecting grievances isn't healthy, so be careful not to fall into this bad habit.

9. *Try to compromise.*

You want to live in the city. He likes the suburbs. Your idea of a good meal is in a fancy French restaurant. He likes burgers and fries. You enjoy mushy movies, he likes horror movies with blood and gore. What to do?

Be open to new experiences. Broaden your horizons and see what you can learn from him. Maybe you'll learn to like scary movies. Failing that, remember why you married him and that being together is more important than anything in particular you do.

As hard as it may be, let him win sometimes. Why? Because your relationship is more important than always winning. Being a good sport will make you more desirable to him and he is more likely to feel that any man would be lucky to have you. He'll be more afraid of losing you because you're so wonderful to be around. He'll feel that you're easygoing, a summer breeze, not a tornado. It's a good spiritual exercise to com promise and the happiness it brings means you always end up winning in the end.

10. *Be quick to say you're sorry, preferably first.*
Fighting is a normal part of married life, but *Rules* women try not to yell all the time, nurse grudges, hang on to resentments, or turn a minor argument into a major ordeal. When you have a fight, try not to be mean or spiteful. Don't go to bed angry and try to make up first. You'll be glad you did.

11. *Be neat.*
This rule may sound trivial in the light of deep relationship issues, but practical ones do matter to men, even more than to women. Clutter, old newspapers piled around the house, stains on the carpet, runs in your stockings, dirty bathtub . . . all of this is not

sexy! You'll feel better when you're organized, neat and clean, and he'll respect you more because you respect yourself. After all, what can he think of you when you don't love yourself enough to wear pantyhose without runs or hang up your clothes?

Married women who are not naturally neat should consult those who are. Get tips on cleaning out closets and filing papers, or hire a cleaning lady. Cleanliness is sexy!

12. Be independent.

Don't talk constantly about your fear of being alone or that you could never make it on your own. Your husband should know that you feel you are desirable, a creature unlike any other, "a catch." Men really want women who can live without them, but have *chosen* not to. Don't flip out (in front of him) if you hear about a couple getting divorced. Don't say, "Oh my God. That's horrible. I just don't know what I'd do, I'd die without you!" Calmly say, "I feel so bad for them. I hope things work out," and then change the subject.

13. Have time out together.

If you have children, make it a point to hire a baby-sitter and go out for dinner with your husband on a regular basis—without feeling guilty! Of course your children deserve your attention, but they also need to grow up with parents who have a healthy established relationship. Strive to create a sound balance, bearing in mind that time apart from them is as important as time with them.

14. *Lock the bedroom door.*

Your children may initially feel left out and throw tantrums. But when they grow up, they'll remember that their parents had special times together. They'll be better equipped to create intimate marriages themselves.

15. *Say things nicely.*

Nothing dampens a loving relationship like yelling or finding fault. If you are annoyed, overwhelmed, or stressed, try to vent your feelings by taking a jog, talking to friends, or doing yoga so that you don't take it out on your husband. Even if you are frazzled, try not to pick on your husband or point out his weaknesses. For example, if you come home and he's put the baby's diaper on backward, don't make him feel bad. Say something positive like, "Wow! It's interesting how the diaper works no matter which way it's put on." Thank him for helping and gently show him the right way. He'll appreciate your gratitude—and he'll get it right the next time!

16. *Don't have exaggerated expectations.*

If he's working overtime on weekends or

didn't get you *exactly* what you wanted for your birthday, don't get all bent out of shape. Ask yourself, "How important is it?" When little problems bother you, try to be grateful that you are happily married!

Chapter 21 _____

Rules for the Bedroom (When You're Married)

IF YOU WANT to have a happy marriage, remember to make time for your sex life! You played hard to get, you got him, now make the effort to maintain a healthy sex life with him.

Make your sex life a priority, even if you had a long day at work or your kids were unusually demanding and sex is the last thing on your mind. Or, you may be having one of those superugly, bad hair days. You don't think you look very sexy and sure don't *feel* sexy. Okay, every woman has days like that. We say, try to make the time and be loving anyway!

In addition, be realistic about sex. You may want your time together to be just right—unhurried and romantic. That's not always possible—so try to be flexible. Sometimes sex is the culmination of a beautiful, enchanted evening. At other times, you just seize an opportunity—i.e., in the morning before the kids get up.

You may have a lot on your mind. You're

thinking about your sales presentation due the next morning, your kids, how the house needs straightening, and so on. *Let it go.* We all have thoughts whirling in our brains. You don't always have to have an uncluttered mind to have sex. Sometimes sex can unclutter it!

Some women use sex as a bargaining tool. This is a bad idea. If you are trying to make a point, use a different method to get your message across. Don't make his favorite pasta or go with him to the football game. It's not healthy for your relationship to use sex as a weapon, as a way to hurt him. Remember, he can go to the football game with one of his friends, but when it comes to sex, you're the only one!

Of course, if you *do* have the time and the energy, may we suggest you make sex extra special by creating a romantic evening? Take the silver candlestick holders you received as a wedding present out of the closet and cook his favorite dinner, play some soft music, wear his favorite outfit, and be loving. Once in a while, you could ask your parents or in-laws to watch the kids and plan a romantic weekend getaway.

You'll be happier—in the long run—if you have a healthy sex life! Here are seven reasons why:

1. It will help keep your commitment to each other strong!
2. He'll think about you more often during the day.
3. He'll appreciate your thoughtfulness.

4. He'll be less likely to stay late at the office.
5. He'll always want to be with you or call you.
6. He won't be so grouchy. (Big smile.)
7. You won't be so grouchy. (Even bigger smile.)

Always be pleased and flattered because your husband *wants* to have sex with you. In a *Rules* marriage, your husband comes to *you* for sex and you're both happy.

Starting Over—*Rules* for the Mature Woman

IF YOU ARE AN older woman, *The Rules* may come as no surprise to you. You probably agree with our ideas more than your twenty-five- or thirty-five-year-old daughters. After all, when you were dating thirty or forty years ago—before the full advent of feminism, dutch treat, and the sexual revolution—*The Rules* was the accepted way to date. It was the *only* way. Back then, you didn't call men, ask them out, sleep with them on the first date, or live together before marriage. You didn't think twice about it either, it just wasn't done!

But that doesn't mean you did *The Rules* in their entirety, and it doesn't mean you don't have things to learn, especially if your first marriage was a disaster.

Your mother may have told you not to chase men, but did she tell you to pursue a career and/or interests, to develop boundaries and self-esteem, and not to make a man the center of your life or accept his bad behavior? Did she tell you to marry for love (not just to get out of the house or to be taken care of financially)? If she didn't, you need *The Rules*.

We have heard from older women who said that their first marriages ended in divorce—not necessarily because they pursued their husbands, but for other reasons that simply would not have occurred if they had done *The Rules*.

For example, they married a good friend— someone whom they felt affection for, but not passion—and their marriage and sex life reflected it. They married for financial security and were miserable emotionally. They married because of social pressures to do so—they didn't want to be spinsters. They did not recognize the signs, or they chose to ignore them. They thought, "My love will change him," and married an alcoholic, a gambler, or a womanizer and lived to regret it. Love was not enough. They didn't create an interesting life of their own and became completely dependent on their husbands, which drove them away.

These women did not necessarily chase these men, but they did not do *The Rules* either. *The Rules* are not just about getting married, but about marrying Mr. Right and having a fulfilling life of your own.

So if you find yourself in the dating market again because you are divorced or a widow, use what your mother taught you—don't chase men—but also do *The Rules*—create a life of your own and only date and marry men you truly care for who treat you well. Don't marry believing you will change him. If he is a little abusive or puts you down in any way before marriage, it will only get worse.

If you are from the old school, not calling a man or sleeping with him on the first date is probably easy for you. So you must work on other changes that could prevent you from catching Mr. Right.

For example, have you stopped caring about your appearance—gained weight, stopped wearing makeup, cut down on salon visits?

If you're divorced, are you bitter about men because of your failed marriage? Or too eager and available (not challenging and mysterious) when men do show interest?

If you're a widow, do you feel hopeless about finding a love as great as your first husband? Have you stopped socializing? Or when you do go out occasionally, are you unenthusiastic?

If some or all of the above is the case, here are some rules for you to work on:

Don't let yourself go. Remember, you are a creature unlike any other. This rule applies to older women as much as twenty-five-year-olds. It has nothing to do with age. It's mental. Think you're beautiful and worthwhile . . . and you will be! Think positive. Keep your mind occupied with interesting ideas, activities, people, and reading material and you will be interesting. You'll have something to talk about on dates other than your doctors' visits and grandchildren.

Whatever you do, don't neglect your appearance. There is no reason you shouldn't do everything you can to look attractive. Don't console yourself with excess food or alcohol or painkillers. Eat right, exercise daily, and wear pretty clothes. Read books by Helen Gurley Brown *(The Late Show)* and Joan Rivers *(Bouncing Back)* that focus on being positive and exercising to fight off aging. Try to emulate them or anyone else you know who is your age and in good shape. Be old-fashioned about dating, but youthful about your attitude and looks.

Socialize. You must. If you are recently divorced or widowed, your feelings probably range from lonely and lost to bitter and confused, especially if your husband died or left you for a younger woman. You might be suffering from grief, fear, and panic. Perhaps you haven't dated in thirty years and don't know where to begin. Of course, you must allow yourself time to grieve—grieving is natural and healthy—but don't let it go on too long.

If you want to remarry or at least have a loving companion, you must make every effort to meet men. Instead of believing that your life is over and all you have to look forward to is grandchildren, tell yourself that there are plenty of divorced men and widowers out there, and go where you can meet them.

We understand that this is not always easy or pleasant. You would much rather stay at home and watch TV, call your children, knit, cook, or read a book, but don't become a recluse, or spend every free evening going to the movies and dinner with other women. Don't bury yourself in canasta, card games, or mah-jongg with your single friends. These are all pleasant ways to pass time and you should do them sometimes, but they are no way to meet men!

Motivate yourself to take social actions by thinking of spending your old age with a loving man, not only as a companion to your married couple friends and your children. Think of how a romance will brighten up your life, and the benefits of spending nights, weekends, and vacations with a man.

Where to meet men? Try everything. Go to museums, church/synagogue, vacations/cruises for your age group, or get involved in a charity or a sport such as golf where men are sure to be found. You must force yourself!

Be on the lookout for men who are newly single. Keep in mind that men who have been married for most of their adult lives are often lost and searching for someone to fill that void. Show up wherever they may be found, but remember, they must approach you!

If you can't find a woman to go to social events with, go alone. In fact, you might be better off alone! Older men who are themselves not so confident socially may feel uncomfortable invading a group of women. So if you do attend a party or lecture with a group, at least stand a little apart from the other women you came with so you look approachable. Take care to appear relaxed no matter how you really feel. For example, don't clutch your pocketbook tightly against your chest as if you are trying to ward off a mugger.

Be happy and carefree on dates. You probably have had your share of life's difficulties and maybe even some physical ailments. Possibly you're worried because your daughter is getting divorced, your back bothers you, your husband died and left you with big bills, you have high blood pressure, or had a brush with cancer. You may have plenty to complain about, but try to complain to your women friends, not to a man you are dating. Be cheerful and light. Don't let him think that you are desperate to remarry, concerned about money, or feel lost without a man. It's not good to seem desperate.

Once you start dating someone you like, almost all *The Rules* apply:

Don't call him—of course, you already knew that!—but you *can* return his calls. While older men enjoy the chase, it's a different kind of hunt. It's no longer a bungee jump! They're not looking for that kind of a thrill. They're not trying to have children with you. They're older, they're tired, they've been through many things, so you can call them back . . . the next day. (Try to use the twenty-four-hour rule; wait twenty-four hours before returning the call.)

Don't accept a last-minute date and don't see him unless it's for the weekend. If he's always asking you out for tea on Tuesday, he doesn't think you're that special or he has a girlfriend. Let him pick you up and take you to dinner.

Don't mention your children or grandchildren and show pictures of them or ask him to meet them unless he suggests it, and don't ask about his children or ex-wife unless he brings them up. Don't volunteer information about your ex-husband. If he asks about your divorce, just say the relationship didn't work out. If you are a widow, don't get too emotional or show how much you are suffering. This will be hard, but you must!

Keep it casual in the beginning and end the date first. Wait until you are in a committed relationship—he is calling you regularly and asking you out for Saturday nights for several months—to become very involved or go away with him.

Don't buy him expensive gifts or pamper him, even if you are a wealthy woman and can afford to do so. Also, if you have more money than he does and he wants to marry you, don't be shy about asking him to sign a prenuptial agreement. (Of course, if he asks you to sign a prenup, go ahead. You are not marrying for money.)

Older women might not necessarily want to remarry. The reasons are usually children and money. But if you do want to get married and he doesn't, then you must pull back a little—stop seeing him for a few weeks, go on a separate vacation, give him an ultimatum, whatever shakes him up a little—and see how he responds.

If getting remarried is not that important to you—if it's love and companionship you want, not a wedding and lifestyle that you crave—then it's fine to live with him or go steady forever! You can act married—go away on vacations together and split the expenses. You can even spend a whole winter with him in your condo in Florida.

So long as he is calling you, making you feel special—weekend dinners and flowers on holidays—and is civil to your children, you don't have to walk down the aisle again. For you, the second time around is about having someone you love who loves you to spend your golden years with.

Rules for Same-Sex Relationships

DO *THE RULES* APPLY to same-sex relationships? If so, how? Do both people do *The Rules*? Or one? Which one?

Confused? Don't be. It's really quite simple. It's a self-diagnosable problem. If you are reading this book or this chapter right now, you probably can apply *The Rules* to your life!

If you read *The Rules* and identified with the feelings of hurt and abandonment that come when a relationship ends and thought to yourself, "I wish they would put in a same-sex chapter because if they substituted a few words I could really relate!", then you do need *The Rules*!

Everyone who is gay or lesbian knows whether or not they are the kind of person who needs structure, some sort of self-protection, in a relationship. If you are this type of person, you're probably very sensitive. You think a lot—obsessively may be more accurate—about the other person and the relationship. You get down—really down—when overlooked or rejected. You're not the type who *naturally* moves on. You don't think breakups are for the best. You think they are downright devastating!

Perhaps you've been hurt before, or experienced a lifetime of hurts, not to mention the social pressures that go along with being gay. You *want* to be in a loving relationship, but you can't bear getting hurt again. Then *The Rules* are for you.

Much of the focus on gay issues has been on coming to recognize and accept one's individual sexual identity, not on how to *behave* in same-sex relationships. This chapter attempts to fill that void with some sound advice.

The Rules can work like a charm when used by individuals who want to know the "how to" of dating when they are completely at ease with their sexuality but at an emotional roadblock as to how to proceed. Do you ask someone out or wait to be asked? Should you play hard to get?

Don't think there aren't any rules. There are, it's just that there's a little more camaraderie and mutuality in same-sex relationships than in male-female relationships. You can show some interest, you can return some phone calls. It's not so one-sided. There's more balance.

When you go out to places alone or with friends, you're open to meeting someone, you're just not desperate. You don't aggressively approach anyone at a party. You smile back if someone smiles at you, and if someone moves a little closer to you, you give an "It's okay to move in closer" smile. You want to let the person know you're approachable, that you are open to the idea of meeting someone. But that's all.

Eventually a conversation begins. It's going well. You're both animated. You laugh, at the room, at the night, at the jokes, but you don't bare your soul, your feelings. You're lighthearted. You come on slow, not like gangbusters. You're not *too much, too soon.*

Being gay or lesbian, perhaps you've felt a little isolated or separate your whole life. You've been waiting to meet someone who "understands." But when you do actually meet someone special, don't reveal too much—find a good friend or therapist to share your intimate problems with. Don't unload all of your past history on a new person for they will probably be overwhelmed by your intensity. Worse, they may be very happy to have you depend so much on them, but it will create the kind of codependent, needy relationship you *don't* want.

It is very hard to keep from sharing too much when you find someone who is receptive. After all, there aren't a lot of people who understand what you have had to go through. But motivate yourself to use restraint with the knowledge that you are building a solid relationship and sparing yourself the pain that accompanies the inevitable end of an overly dependent one.

So, be casual. The person must give you signs that they would like to get together again. You will get a *feeling*. It's different from a male-female relationship because if the man doesn't ask the woman out, that's it, it's over. In same-sex relationships, the lines are a little more blurry, but rules still exist, and following them is not as hard as you think.

Pace the relationship. Get to know the person you're interested in slowly—don't spill all the beans during a three-hour coffee date. You are drawn to the person, but you don't bare all. Wait as long as you can, knowing that the more mysterious you are, the better.

The idea is to bring the *spirit* of *The Rules* into your dating life. You should *never* pursue anyone relentlessly. If there's no mutual interest, no give and take, then there's nothing. If the person you're involved with seems to enjoy being the pursuer, that's great and actually makes things easier. You enjoy being pursued and you're sure of their feelings for you so you're less anxious.

Regardless, don't stay on the phone for hours and don't see the person at a moment's notice. You have a life, you have other plans, you are not waiting to be rescued.

Don't feel pressured to have sex right away. Don't see this person all the time or live together until you're exclusive.

Maintain your self-esteem and self-respect. If the other person has a wandering eye, neglects you, or constantly makes sexual comments about other people when you're around, move on to new possibilities.

You know that a relationship without boundaries, without give and take, is not a relationship that is worth having. Perhaps you've settled before. Now, armed with *The Rules,* you don't want anything less than lasting, secure love. You want the best. You *deserve* the best, and by following *The Rules,* you will get the best!

Rules for Personal Ads and Dating Services

IF YOU ARE PLANNING to use personal ads, voice-mail ads, video dating, or matchmaking services to meet men, we recommend that *you* place the ad and let men respond to *you*.

Why? It goes back to the basic premise of *The Rules*: man pursues woman. He must search through a sea of print ads, voice mails, or video images and pick *yours* out. He has to like *your* hair color, *your* distinctive voice, the way you wrote *your* ad, *your* height and profession, and so on. Remember, he's the hunter! Every man has a type, a voice, or a look he likes. There has to be a spark for him that attracts him to you, something that makes him find you unexplainably special.

We have found that responding to a man's ad doesn't seem to work as well. Answering his ad, liking his type, liking his voice or looks, or what he does for a living puts you in the unwanted position of being the pursuer. In addition, he'll know you are interested in him or his type and the challenge will be over.

Of course, even if he picks you out and likes you, there's no guarantee that you'll like him. But this would also be true at a bar or a party. You wouldn't go up to the guy who's "your type"; but you would wait for a man to approach you. The same pretty much applies to dating services and ads, although it's not quite as black and white.

You just need to keep going on dates until a man who responds to your ad is someone who appeals to you. Hopefully, you are getting lots of responses from men—see tips below for placing an ad that draws the most letters—and have many choices. Having many men to choose from is always good—the more dates you have, the more practice you will get, and you will be less inclined to get hung up on any particular man.

What should your ad say?

To get the most and best responses, your ad should be short, light, flirtatious, and focused on your physical attributes, not your feelings.

Any man responding to your ad wants to know, first and foremost, what you look like. If you are placing a print or voice-mail ad, you must give him a mental picture of you.

You may find it difficult to describe your appearance. If so, one method we've found to be effective is to say which model or actress or well-known personality you resemble. Don't lie, but don't be modest either. Hasn't anyone ever told you you look like someone famous? If you're tall, blonde, and slim, try to think of a well-known model with those attributes. If you are short with dark hair and big eyes, perhaps there's a movie star or TV sitcom character you resemble. Ask your friends to help you come up with someone who you could honestly say you look like. Put it in your ad. Men love this stuff!

Limit your ad to about four lines and stick to the facts—age, height, profession, hobbies. Don't say you're looking for true love or romance. He should think you're just dating.

Here's a good voice-mail ad:

"I'm twenty-eight years old, five feet seven inches with long brown straight hair and green eyes. People tell me I look like (model/movie star). I'm a dental hygienist. I like tennis and swimming. Well, that's me! [Giggle] Have a great day."

Here's an ad you would *not* want to use, even if this is exactly how you feel:

"At the end of my rope. It's really hard to meet men so I decided to try this. I'm thirty-five, a financial analyst, looking for someone to spend the rest of my life with. I'm not into playing games."

Aside from the fact that a man seeing or hearing this has no idea what she looks like, the ad is much too serious, too revealing, and quite depressing.

When you receive responses, call the men you are interested in meeting when you think they will not be home and leave your name and phone number on their answering machine. Of course, if he answers, only stay on the phone for ten minutes.

Assuming you get his machine and he calls you

back, still don't stay on the phone for more than ten minutes. Hopefully he will set up a date to meet you within that period of time. If not, hang up after ten minutes anyway. Staying on the phone longer to give him more time to ask you out is not *The Rules*. Don't become best friends on the phone. We know women who stayed on the phone for hours getting to know men who answered their ads. These men never even asked to meet them, or they made tentative plans and then didn't follow through. They proved to be complicated or unreliable. In cases where a relationship did start, it usually fizzled within a few months. There was no mystery, no buildup—it was simply too much too soon. This won't happen if you're getting off the phone in ten minutes. Get to know him on dates.

So if you don't have many blind dates and you haven't connected recently with any men at singles events, work, or the gym, you should most definitely try personal ads and dating services. The men who respond to ads and sign up with services are usually serious about meeting someone and often marriage-minded—otherwise, why would they spend the time or money? In fact, we know several women who met and married men through ads and dating services.

In conclusion, our advice is to try *everything* until you meet Mr. Right! Remember, placing an ad or joining a dating service does not mean you should stop going to parties, bars, resorts, singles weekends, or take up a social sport like tennis. The bottom line is: *Never give up and never stop trying!*

_____

Chapter 25

Rules for On-line Dating

DATING ON THE Internet has become so popular in recent years and we have received so many requests for "*The Rules* way" to go about it, that we felt the subject deserved its own chapter.

So what do we think of on-line dating? To be perfectly honest, while we encourage you to try it if you haven't been able to meet men any other way, we have found that these relationships usually don't pan out. At best, women end up with male friends or pen pals, not husbands.

The main problem with on-line dating is that the relationships are based on chatting—not physical attraction, the spark so necessary for a *Rules* relationship.

In addition, on-line dating can be downright *dangerous*. You have probably read articles about women raped or killed by men they met through the Internet. The truth is, no matter how nice, interesting or sincere the person seems to be on-line, all you know about him is what he tells you. He could be a lunatic, a rapist, a killer, a teenager having fun, or a married man—you just don't know!

Of course, we understand why some women prefer dating on the Internet to the singles scene. They are fed up with finding Mr. Right at bars and parties. If they don't feel attractive, they think they are at a disadvantage in social situations. They believe that they have a better chance of attracting a man with their mind, great personality, or witty way of writing, than their looks. The Internet allows them to date with no makeup on and in sweatpants.

We understand how they feel, but we just don't think this method works as well as face-to-face meetings. The best romantic relationships start out with physical chemistry. Internet relationships are based on chatting. We know several women who spent months talking to men on the Internet before meeting them. Few of these relationships worked out. He calls you his "soul mate," the one who knows his innermost thoughts and dreams, and then marries someone else he's really attracted to!

But if you are determined to meet men on-line, we suggest that you do *The Rules* the best you can so you don't waste time conversing with men who will never marry you or putting yourself in danger. Here are some suggestions:

1. Once he's shown interest in you—responded to your personal ad or approached you in a chat room—tell him you'd like to exchange photos by E-mail right away. There's no point in continuing an on-line romance if he's not attracted to you.

2. Once he's seen your photo, it's up to him to suggest meeting you. (If he doesn't, then he's not crazy about your looks and it's next!) If he lives in another city, he should visit your city. You don't visit him. (See Chapters 6 & 7: *Rules* for long-distance relationships.) We've heard about women who "hop on a plane" to meet a man they've been chatting with for weeks or months. *Rules* girls let men visit them! When he hops on a plane or drives to visit you, you must meet at a public place. *He should not know where you live!*

   We cannot stress the safety factor enough. We've heard about women who risked their lives because they invited men they met on-line to their apartment on the first or second date. This is dangerous. In addition, make sure to give a friend or relative any information about the date—who, what, where, when—so he or she can keep track of your whereabouts.

3. Don't use the Internet to have heart-to-heart conversations or to bond with a man. Many women think that *The Rules*—i.e., don't open up too fast, be honest but mysterious—don't apply to on-line dating. They wonder how they can get to know this stranger if they don't tell him their whole life story right away. They think nothing of baring their souls or discussing their past relationships and their desire to meet and marry Mr. Right. And if he lives in another city and they

don't see him that often, they feel that justifies frequent E-mails.

Don't kid yourself. E-mails are no different from phone calls, letters, and greeting cards. We don't call men, we don't write them letters or cards, and we don't overdo E-mail.

Whether you are dating on-line or face-to-face, men are still men. They do not fall in love with and marry the women who send them the most revealing and most frequent E-mails, even if they say that's what they want. They might tell you that they like women who are honest and open, who say they want a commitment if they want a commitment, who don't play games. But they actually *chase and/or marry* women they are physically attracted to who are elusive and challenging and whose E-mails are as well. Short and sweet is always the best.

If you're on the computer chatting with him so much, how challenging are you? How interesting can your life be if you are glued to your terminal and have time to chat with him ten times a day?

Let him get into the habit of E-mailing you interesting tidbits about his day without necessarily receiving a response every time. Remember, on-line or in person, you are a creature unlike any other and worth pursuing, so let him.

Chapter 26

Use a *Rules* Support Group

LET'S FACE IT, doing *The Rules* is not easy! Holding back from calling a man you like, resisting the urge to sleep with him on the first or second date, keeping from telling him everything about yourself right away, and all the other rules require tremendous self-control, patience, and faith in this process. The *Rules* may feel like a very strict diet or giving up smoking. If you are used to doing things your way, we encourage you not to do *The Rules* alone!

We strongly suggest you form or join a local *Rules* support group—much like a weight-loss group or Smokenders—that meets regularly to reinforce *The Rules,* or at the very least, get phone numbers you can call. It's easy to rationalize breaking rules—calling a man who hasn't called you or living with a man who won't marry you—when you're doing it alone. But having *Rules*-minded women to call or a group to discuss your dates with and report to every week makes *The Rules* harder to break. It helps you be true to yourself and *The Rules.*

Besides, you will experience tremendous comfort, hope, and relief when you meet and share your experiences with other women who have gone through what you have gone through with men and are now committed to dating a better way. Being part of a group or simply calling like-minded women will be especially important if your friends, coworkers, or family members don't understand *The Rules*. Talking to other women who do understand will make you feel better and not so alone. Helping other women not break rules—i.e., literally staying on the phone for ten minutes explaining to someone why they can't call him until the urge to passes—will make you stronger and reinforce your own commitment. It's putting money in the bank for a big withdrawal one day!

It has been gratifying for us to watch *Rules* groups form in cities around the country, to hear about women (perfect strangers!) calling each other and networking to do *The Rules*—their only bond being their desire to stop dating in a manner that doesn't get results. They are united in their common goal: to be in loving relationships and marry Mr. Right. Of course, the group fosters close female friendships as well. Some of these women have become good friends who go on singles trips together to meet men, and eventually attend each other's weddings. Being part of a *Rules* support group is an experience you don't want to miss!

How do you start a support group?

If you have friends, acquaintances, or coworkers who believe in *The Rules,* invite them to your apartment for a meeting. If you do not know any *Rules* followers, you can write to us (see back of book) and we will be happy to provide you with the names and phone numbers of *Rules* girls in your area.

Other ways to find women for a *Rules* support group:

1. Make up a flier. For example, one leader of a *Rules* support group photocopied the following message and posted it on kiosks, bookstore bulletin boards, and other prominent spots around her neighborhood:

   "Many women today grew up in the '60s and later, where 'free love' and nonexistent boundaries were the fad. '*The Rules*' show women how to set up good boundaries and build a full life for themselves. Living a joyous and fulfilling life makes women radiant, very attractive, and feel great. So if you want to be a *Rules* woman, contact____."

2. Try to get free publicity by sending fliers to your local newspaper to run an item in its singles/personal ads section or local radio station. You may find a female deejay at a radio station who thinks your group is interesting, worth promoting, and will be helpful to you!

3. Post fliers at health clubs, bookstores, churches/synagogues, and wherever else single women might see them.

4. Contact singles organizations and dating services and ask them to tell their clients.
5. Ask your therapist to start a group.
6. If you are in high school or college and want to start a group, ask your guidance counselor/ psychology teacher if you could use a classroom where the group can meet. Explain that there are rules for high school and college students and how students could benefit from a *Rules* group.

Once a group has been formed, we suggest that you try to meet at the same time every week or every month. It's up to you where you meet. If you know one another, meet in someone's apartment. If you're strangers, you're better off meeting in a public place, such as a coffee shop. Some groups meet for lunch or dinner and then go to the movies. Saturday afternoon for an hour or two is a popular meeting time since most people have the day off and it's a great way to prepare for a Saturday night date. Other groups meet on Sunday afternoon and analyze the previous night's dates.

You'll find the group works best if you pick someone to be in charge—to call on people and field their questions. Bring copies of *The Rules* and *The Rules II* to the meeting in case you need to refer to them to answer questions. If the group cannot figure out the answer to a question, suggest the person call or write to us. Some groups have actually booked a group consultation by phone with us during their meeting, with each woman asking a question or two.

The format of the group is entirely up to you. But keep in mind that *Rules* support groups should not be group therapy sessions for discussing one's childhood, money, career, or body image issues, unless these issues are blocks to doing *The Rules*. Some groups are in fact led by therapists or social workers, but the meeting should still focus on *The Rules,* your dating history, and how you are doing them today. It is the leader's job to make sure attendees stick to *The Rules*.

One way to get the group going is to have everyone take turns sharing which rules they did and didn't do that week.

You can raise questions, such as:

What rules are you having a hard time with?

Is anyone thinking of asking a man out?

Or, you can ask hypothetical questions, such as:

If a man leaves his umbrella in your apartment after the third date, what should you do? (*The Rules* answer: Don't use it as an excuse to call him. Wait until he calls *you* and then mention it.)

Encourage women to keep a diary of how they are doing *The Rules*. You could use *The Rules Dating Journal* that asks you to write about your dating history and to keep track of how you are doing *The Rules* day by day (i.e., Who talked to whom first when you met? Has he ever said "I love you"?).

Group members should exchange phone numbers so you are able to call one another in between meetings. These phone numbers will come in handy when you feel compelled to call a man! If a woman is married or living with a man, it might be better to call her at work. Be sure to ask if it's okay to call her at home. You don't want her husband or boyfriend to get upset when he hears messages about playing hard to get!

Rules support groups are intended to be free of charge so that those who can't afford private consultations can get help. However, sometimes an organizer will charge participants a nominal fee to cover costs such as postage, phone calls, meeting rooms, and coffee.

Even if it's nothing organized or planned—no fliers, no leader, no format—just a person whose *Rules* knowledge you trust or you and five of your favorite gal pals meeting on Sunday for brunch and talking about *The Rules*, it's still a *Rules* support group . . . and it can really help, so use it!

Chapter 27 _____

Rules for Girlfriends, Bosses/Coworkers, and Children

BECAUSE *THE RULES* work so well with men, many women have asked us if there is a way to apply *The Rules* to platonic relationships with other people, such as girlfriends, bosses, coworkers, and even children. Absolutely. *The Rules* can be applied to other people so that you have good, healthy relationships, arc well-liked, and not taken for granted. Here are our rules for other people:

Girlfriends

1. Do *The Rules* with men. By doing *The Rules* with men, you automatically become a good girlfriend. Think about it. You're not canceling plans at the last minute to accept a date with a man. You take your plans with your girlfriends seriously—you don't break them for a better offer. You're loyal. Of course,

you're not sleeping with, chasing, or flirting with your girlfriend's boyfriend or husband. You're trustworthy.

2. Figure out who your friends are. You don't want to become a doormat. For example, if you're the one giving all the time, calling, lending your clothes, books, money, and makeup, and getting little or nothing in return, pull back a little and see what happens. It's not good for you or her if the relationship is one-sided. Maybe she's not that interested in the friendship. On the other hand, if *you* are the one always taking, try to give more or not accept as much.

3. Don't be a burden. If you're going through a particularly hellish time—man, health, work issues—don't dump it all on one friend, day and night. Try to complain to several friends so that no one takes the brunt of it and you don't lose friends. Try to give back an hour for every hour they give of their time. Always remember to ask how they're doing, even if you *know* they're doing better than you. Everyone gets their fair share of good and bad in life. It all evens out in the end. To compare is to despair!

4. Be happy for your friends. If your girlfriend is getting married and you don't even have a boyfriend or she lands a great job and you hate yours, it may be hard to feel genuinely

pleased by her good fortune, but you must work on summoning up these feelings. Maybe she was lucky. On the other hand, maybe she worked hard for her success—took more social actions and sent more résumés than you did. It doesn't matter. Whatever the reason, she is your friend and she deserves to feel that you are happy for her, not jealous. Rather than seethe with envy, see what you can do about meeting a man and finding a better job of your own. Send her a congratulations card and smile at her wedding. Wishing others happiness is the best way to ensure our own.

Bosses and Coworkers

1. Don't act too casual or talk about your private life at the office. You might think talking about personal matters or your feelings at work will make you feel more at home. But your boss and coworkers will respect and trust you more if they sense that you are professional and not the gossipy type.

2. Work for the good of the company, not for your own personal gain. Every day think, "How can I contribute to my company or help customers?" Don't think we're being corny or naive here. We know that business can be cut-throat. But when you think of the company, you automatically succeed.

3. Don't focus solely on how to get a raise or a promotion or how to do the least amount of

work without getting found out. Think about doing quality work and being a good worker, or you won't feel good about yourself.

4. Don't be over-eager or volunteer to do too much too quickly in an effort to make your boss notice you. He'll find you if he needs you; be available when he does!

5. Don't be a self-centered, short-term thinker. Everyone around you will smell self-interest and think less of you.

6. Be a team player.

7. Don't work round the clock. Have a social life. Remember that work isn't everything; you will be a much better worker if you are happy in other areas of your life.

Children

Children are a lot like men. They'll take advantage of you if you let them! One of the benefits of having a *Rules* marriage is that your kids tend to treat you as nicely as your husband does. They copy his behavior, making him their role model for how to treat you.

For example, if your son observes his father being loving and attentive and buying you cards and flowers, he will try to do the same in his own way (i.e., break his piggy bank for a bracelet or bouquet of flowers).

In *The Rules,* we said, "when he loves you, he loves your kids." We would like to add, "when he loves and respects you, your kids learn to love and respect you."

In addition, here are some rules to make sure your children treat you well:

1. Don't let your children treat you as their equal. For example, if they call you by your first name, don't answer. Instead ask, "Did someone say something? I respond to the name Mom." That way they know you're the boss.

   Similarly, don't *ask* them if they want to go to school, brush their teeth or go to bed. Tell them what they must do. Children respond well to discipline and orderliness. You are doing them a disservice when you let them run the show.

2. Don't spoil your kids. You might be tempted to overdo, particularly if you waited until later in life to have children or had to adopt or overcome infertility problems. You might want to jump every time the baby cries. Assuming the baby is fed, dry, and not sick, you do not have to spend endless hours pampering him or her, or you will become trapped in a pattern that's almost impossible to break. Encourage your child to be self-sufficient. As your children get older, encourage them to help with household chores. If you let your children have some responsibility, instead of constantly doing everything for them, you

will help to foster independence and competence.

3. Don't make an issue out of food. Don't force them to finish every meal; you may unknowingly begin a lifetime of weight problems for them. Unlike adults, children eat when they're hungry and stop when they're full. They won't starve to death. Save your energy for more important matters like teaching them good manners and values.

4. Have a life! Don't feel guilty for working, talking on the phone about business or with friends. You are entitled to some time to yourself, and you'll be a better mother for having a full life. Mothers who spend too much time with or overindulge their children and neglect themselves are often frustrated and resentful. It's not necessarily the quantity of time you spend with your child, but the quality.

   In the same vein, let your child know it's not okay to interrupt you when you have company or are on the phone. Unless it's an emergency or your child is hurt or sick, tell him or her that you are busy and will talk to him or her later—and make sure you stick to your word. This way your child learns to respect your private life and learns patience. He or she will get mommy time, just later.

5. Don't buy out the toy store. You might be able to afford the best of everything, but should you buy it? We think not, unless you want your child to turn into a monster, the kind of kid who throws tantrums in a department store. So even if you can afford the whole store, restrain yourself. The same goes for pushing your child to participate in every hobby and sport. Check your motives. Are these really your child's interests or your ego at work?

6. Let your children take responsibility for their actions. If your children don't want to do their homework, try to find out why; perhaps they didn't understand the assignment. Help them, but don't do it for them. If it's just a case of being lazy or willful, tell them they are responsible and they will have to face the consequences. If you want you can explain that you did your homework when you were growing up and that's how you got to where you are today.

7. Stick to your word. Explain to your child if he/she engages in bad behavior—i.e., curses, hits someone, or acts out—he/she has to suffer the consequences. You decide what the punishment is—i.e., no TV—and stick to it. If you make idle threats, you will lose credibility and your children will get away with murder.

8. Encourage your child to confide in you. Lay down the law about good and bad behavior, but *always* leave the door open for your child to tell you something you may not approve of. In other words, be strict, but not judgmental. That way if there's something your child doesn't want to tell you, he/she can at least tell you that much, i.e., "I have a secret I don't want to tell you." If you don't want to find out about your child's problems too late or from someone else, make sure your child knows that he or she can always confide in you and count on you *no matter what.*

A general tip: Good mothers are observant mothers. If you sense that your child is anxious or edgy, perhaps you want to cancel your social plans or leave work early to spend "a kid day" or "kid's night out," something as simple as pizza and a movie may get him or her to open up and tell you what's going on.

Don't Worry, Even Men Like *The Rules*

IN CASE YOU FORGOT, you're doing *The Rules* because it's good for *you* and your self-esteem. Whether men like or dislike *The Rules* is irrelevant. The truth is, men can talk about wanting to date in an open, up-front, rational way, but what they *respond* to is altogether different—they respond to challenge, mystery, and intrigue. If a man likes a woman, he'll call her again. If he likes her and she doesn't let the first date become a marathon, he'll want to see her again that much sooner. He'll lose interest if she breaks rules, regardless of *what he says!*

But you are probably curious what men think and say about *The Rules* anyway. We have found that, if presented correctly, most men don't find *The Rules* objectionable at all. They actually like the results *The Rules* produce.

Here is what men have told us in their own words:

"If I met a woman and thought she was The One, I wouldn't let any book she was studying get in the way [of pursuing her]," says an executive at a university in New York.

He believes that men feel "cheated" of the chase and "refuse to commit" or demand "space" when women break rules.

He is not alone. We have received dozens of letters and calls from men thanking us for writing *The Rules* and letting us know that they are buying copies for their daughters, sisters, female friends, and ex-girlfriends.

A teacher from Lexington, Kentucky, wrote to say that he loved our description of a *Rules* girl— "busy, with high self-esteem, not sleeping around or chasing married men, having values and ethics, and loving with her head and her heart. That is a very attractive woman to any sane man . . ."

An M.D. from Chicago, Illinois, wrote to say that he was "always getting into relationships with codependent women who had no lives of their own. These women were unusually clingy and bordering on being fatal attractions. Now, I have a renewed sense of hope in finding a woman who possesses the qualities of a *Rules* girl."

Yet another male *Rules* fan from Los Angeles wrote, "You are right—it is more exciting for us men when the girl is hard to get. I have never been interested in any girl who chased me. Flattered yes, but not interested."

An Illinois medical student who is planning a career in psychiatry wrote, "In my opinion, any young woman who knows and uses *The Rules* correctly will have a tremendous advantage in finding and keeping successful long-term relationships."

Of course, there are men who think *The Rules* are just silly—not offensive, just silly! These men simply cannot believe that women read such books. But they don't realize the extent to which women can obsess about relationships. If a man actually *knew* how much a woman thought about him, a relationship gone wrong, or lost herself over a breakup with a man, he would really encourage her to do *The Rules*. He'd say, "Well, go ahead then, read that book if it helps!"

So even if your boyfriend suspects you're doing *The Rules,* even if you think he'd be mad if he found out about it—so that's why you don't call me!—still do *The Rules*. Don't talk about it. Deep down, a man would rather you do *The Rules* than not, *no matter what he says*. Deep down, every man would rather marry a girl who gives him space and lets him breathe. So don't worry about what men think about *The Rules,* just do them. Men *do* like *Rules* girls—in fact, they do more than like them—they love and marry them!

Chapter 29

Rules Tips for Men

WE WROTE *THE RULES* to help women enjoy dating, not to confuse men. But since *The Rules* was published, quite a few men have contacted us. Some have called, some have written us letters, and some have even attended *Rules* seminars.

Why? Well, some men simply wanted to thank us for telling women what they knew to be true about relationships. Others expressed confusion about *The Rules* and what "dating in the nineties" should be like.

Some men wanted to know how they should behave in relationships and exactly how to tell if a woman they were dating was interested in them. This was not really news to us. We had heard that men were actually asking women who wouldn't call them or wouldn't go out with them, "Are you doing *The Rules* on me?"

Some men suggested that we write a book or a chapter called "*Rules* for Men." They wanted answers, insights, clues, anything really—most of all, they wanted to be included! This was not entirely news to us either. We had heard about and witnessed men poring over *The Rules* in bookstores or borrowing the book from female friends to pick up pointers, to understand women—and themselves—a little better. We had also heard that some men were blaming *The Rules* when a woman refused to go out with them.

Therefore, we have written this chapter to address men's concerns, to include them, to dispel any tensions between the sexes, and to explain why they should not blame *The Rules* for a woman's lack of interest. We never meant to create any conflict between men and women. We don't think relationships should be adversarial. We want men and women to make happy couples.

Hopefully you will find the following useful!

How To Tell If She Is Interested

She's interested in you if:

1. She gives you her phone number *if you ask for it.*
2. She declines to take your phone number or business card, but is willing to give you hers *if you ask for it.*
3. She says "yes" to a Saturday night date if you ask by Wednesday.
4. She says "I'd love to, but I can't," if you call too late in the week or she is truly busy.
5. She seems to have fun on the date, laughs, lets you kiss her good night. Maybe you're not sure if she'll marry you one day, but you

definitely get the sense that she'll probably see you again.
6. She doesn't call you back all the time, but when you get her in, she's happy to hear from you.
7. She doesn't stay on the phone for too long—but when she gets off she is always nice about it.

She's *not* interested in you if:
1. She says "no" when you ask for her number or offer her yours.
2. She says "no" when you ask her to dance at a party.
3. She says "no" or "I don't think so" when you ask her out *early* in the week for Saturday night—several weeks in a row.
4. She *never* returns your calls, *ever!*
5. She says "I don't feel a spark" or "I'm not interested" or "please don't call me again."

Chapter 30 _____

The Rules Are a Healthy Way of Life

AT FIRST GLANCE, you might think that *The Rules* are just a practical guide to dating—no more, no less. But if you take the time to think about it, you'll see that *The Rules* help you with more than dating—they assist you in establishing a healthy, balanced lifestyle.

By not pursuing men or allowing yourself to rationalize staying in a dependent or destructive relationship, you automatically become a healthier, more grounded and self-empowered person. You're not a nervous wreck, trying to get a man who isn't interested in you to love you or begging the man you are dating to make a commitment.

If you have ever chased after a man you were in love with but who did not share your feelings and who eventually rejected you, you will know what we're talking about. If you're like most women, you took a long time to recover. The relationship took its toll on your work, your sleep, your appetite, your friends, and your nervous system.

A *Rules* girl does not initiate or stay in a bad relationship out of fear of being alone and low self-esteem. She has enough self-confidence to trust that the right man will appear in her life, and she knows if she walks away from a relationship that is going nowhere, something better will take its place. Being optimistic, growing, changing, striving for the best are all wonderful by-products of *The Rules*. Believing in the abundance of the universe—that there are plenty of other fish in the sea!—is a sane and healthy attitude to take.

Of course, even in good relationships, women can become quite obsessive, wanting to call their boyfriends or husbands all the time or act overly dependent and needy. By sticking to *The Rules*, these women learn not to call so often and are encouraged to pursue independent interests, form friendships, and become more self-sufficient so that they don't end up believing that they are "nothing without a man." Depending too much on any person is not good for you.

By doing *The Rules*, you learn the value of leaving men alone sometimes. Everyone benefits. The man is grateful to be left alone to watch the ballgame or whatever else interests him, and you have more time to read a book or cultivate your own interests. *The Rules* trains women to practice self-control, to concentrate on matters other than "the relationship." Perhaps by not seeing him all the time or getting too wrapped up in his life, you will find your energy going into something useful. Maybe you will find yourself calling a girlfriend or a charity that really needs your help—and that's a much more productive use of your time than fixating on whether or not to call a handsome stranger or the man you are involved with.

When you do *The Rules, you live and let live*—and you yourself will reap the benefits of your forgiving behavior. *The Rules* also encourage you to cultivate healthy coping skills. Take this example: You've had a fight with your boyfriend. You think it's life and death. You want to resolve it immediately by spending hours analyzing your relationship with him. He doesn't want to. He'd rather shoot hoops with the guys to get the anger out of his system and then discuss it with you quietly over dinner and a movie.

Let him play ball. Let him handle the fight in a way that is comfortable for him. Don't try to make it happen your way all the time. If you need to talk about it, call a good friend or your mother. He'll work through it in his way; you'll talk it out in yours. Little fights stay little this way, and don't escalate into big ones.

Sometimes the best way to resolve disputes is *not* to talk about them, especially if *he* really doesn't want to. Many women love to talk about the relationship, but big discussions can give most men a headache. Trying to get him to talk every time won't necessarily bring him closer, but might drive him away. Demanding that he read relationship books or attend relationship workshops may be what *you* like and good for *you,* but it might be boring for him, so *focus on yourself.*

Sometimes the best way to mend a fight is to do something thoughtful. Be loving, wear a nice outfit, give him a backrub, have a romantic evening together. Paradoxically, you might learn that when you don't nag him to talk about the fight when *you* want to, he is more likely to bring it up or say something loving when *he's* ready.

When you do have a disagreement, as we say in Chapter 20: "A *Rules* Refresher for Married Women," if at all possible, try to be the first to say you're sorry. You'll feel better in the long run if you apologize, take the high road, and forgive and forget. Your boyfriend or husband will appreciate your willingness to patch things up. Don't stand on ceremony, waiting for him to do it. Why ruin your serenity with resentment and sleepless nights? Don't think we are being naive here. We know that men are not always right and that it's sometimes hard to forgive and forget. But try—you'll be amazed at how much better you feel when you don't hold on to your anger!

We have also shared our philosophy with women who, because they did not know about *The Rules,* have had bad experiences with men— men who stopped calling suddenly after a long-term relationship, cheated on them, or treated them disrespectfully. Understandably, these women feel bitter, which is certainly not a serene way to live.

Of course, we acknowledge their pain—there is nothing more devastating than being hurt by a man we love. But we try to discourage these women from acting on their feelings. We tell them that *The Rules* are never about hurting others or getting even—i.e., sending men hate mail or harassing them with phone calls. Instead, we focus on ourselves, we evaluate our part in the breakup, we see where we broke rules, and how we tolerated bad behavior. *We change.* That's why we encourage women to get their anger out in therapy or a *Rules* support group.

It is important to realize that you can't *make* a man treat you well or marry you, you just have to do *The Rules.* We help these women see that by not doing *The Rules* in these relationships, they helped place themselves in a position to be hurt. For example, one woman simply ignored the fact that her boyfriend of fifteen months only asked her out every *other* Saturday night and had never told her he loved her or mentioned marriage or the future. She thought he had "trouble expressing his feelings." She was devastated when she found out that he was actually seeing other women. If she had known about *The Rules,* she would have seen the warning signs.

We tell these women that the best action they can take is to do *The Rules* on the next man they meet! Living well is the best revenge! To let go of the past and move on are empowering! Or as we say in *The Rules, Next!*

However, even though we know *The Rules* work, we don't force them on our friends or anyone else for that matter. *The Rules* is all about leaving men and other people alone. We're tolerant, not judgmental. If someone is having trouble with men, we're happy to share our method, but that's it. We don't preach.

Perhaps you know of a woman—a friend or a coworker—who is suffering in a relationship because she is not doing *The Rules*. You keep telling her to do *The Rules* but she thinks it's silly or just not for her. You bought her the book, you invited her to a *Rules* support group, you've even said "I told you so" when her boyfriend forgot her birthday. What should you do?

The next time your friend complains that her boyfriend of three years still hasn't proposed, be sympathetic, as if she had called you to say she's in pain from spraining her ankle while in-line skating. Say, "Gee, that's too bad." Don't say, "Well, if you just did *The Rules* . . ."

She is more likely to do *The Rules* if you don't preach. She is more likely to do *The Rules* if she sees them work in your life. So leave her alone and invite her to your wedding. By just doing *The Rules*, chances are you will become a healthy influence in her life.

Chapter 31 ——————————————

Answers to Frequently Asked Questions About *The Rules*

Q: If I do *The Rules*, how will he know the real me?

A: On dates you *are* yourself. There's a big difference between being mysterious and being deceptive. You don't lie, you just don't open up too fast. You don't say you went to an Ivy League school if you went to a community college. But you don't bring up subjects that would tip your hand, such as marriage, the future, children, or feel you have to answer questions that would reveal too much too soon or make you uncomfortable.

For example, if he asks why "a nice girl like you is not married," you can casually say, "I really haven't thought about it" and then change the subject. Don't say anything depressing like, "I haven't been on a date in six years" or "It's really hard to meet men." Don't say anything cynical like, "I guess I'm just lucky."

The point is, you don't have to answer every question he asks you. Your dating history is none of his business on the first, second, or third dates. Realize that if he really presses the issue, he probably is either not that nice, or not that interested in you. When a man is interested in you, he doesn't want to make you uncomfortable.

Don't worry, "the real you" will definitely shine through. Your conversation, your appearance, your laugh—all of these are uniquely yours, and will help him to discover the creature unlike any other that is you.

Q: If I do *The Rules*, how will he know I like him?

A: You say "yes" when he asks you out by Wednesday for Saturday night. You show up on the date—you smile, you're warm and pleasant, fun to be with, you thank him for a nice evening. That's how he knows you like him.

Contrary to popular belief, you do not have to call men or send them thank-you notes or buy them presents for them to see that you are interested.

If you like him, but he calls too late in the week for you to accept the date, you say, "I'd love to, but I have plans." By saying "I'd love to," and declining nicely, with genuine regret, he'll know you would actually like to spend time with him, you're just busy. If he likes you, he'll call again. But next time it will be earlier in the week.

Q: What do I do when a man gives me his business card and says "Call me?"

A: Look at the card as if no man has ever given you one before, smile, and sweetly say, "No thanks. I don't think so."

Rules girls don't call men and have no use for their business cards or phone numbers. If a man is really interested in you, he will then ask for your number. Don't say, "I don't call men. It's better if you call me." That's telling him what to do. He either asks for your number on his own or he doesn't. You only want men who *want* your number.

Q: What if a man leaves a message on your answering machine on Wednesday? Can you call him back to secure a weekend date?

A: In the first month of dating, it's best not to call him back at all. This way he'll have to call again (at the beginning of the following week) if he really wants to see you. Better to lose one Saturday night date than show too much interest and risk destroying a potentially long-term relationship.

The first month should establish a pattern: he is the hunter—calling you and calling you, if only to just find you in! Better that he keep trying to pin you down and not actually reach you in time for a Saturday night date than your calling him back right away and being readily available. By not calling back, some women we know didn't actually have dates with men for a month or so, but now they're married to them. They set the chase in motion and created longing.

Of course, if he calls you two to three times in one week and still gets your machine, a quick call back can be okay. Use your common sense. Remember, we said you should *rarely* return his calls, not *never!*

After the first month, you can return his calls a day or two later or call him occasionally (say, once for every four of his calls), preferably when he's not home. If he absolutely insists that you call him, call once in a while so that he doesn't think you're not interested.

Q: If a friend sets you up on a blind date and the date goes very well, do you call the friend to thank her and to tell her you like him?

A: No, don't call the friend to thank her or express interest in the person she introduced you to. This may sound harsh or rude, but *The Rules* answer is to make a mental note to do something nice for the friend in the future. To call and tell is to kiss and tell. She'll either inadvertently mention to him that you called or possibly call him to tell him so, and he'll definitely interpret it as a sign of interest. Let *him* call her to find out what you thought of him. If your friend does ask, you should keep your answer as evasive as possible. For example, you can say, "He seemed nice! We had fun." This is noncommittal but positive—just the tone you want to take.

Q: Do *The Rules* work on *all* men?

A: Fortunately, yes. *The Rules* work on all men from all countries and from all walks of life. And that's actually a good thing. It means we don't have to rewrite *The Rules* for every nationality, or every time we meet a man or figure out how the man we're dating is the exception to *The Rules*.

We do not have to initiate relationships with "shy men" and only play hard to get with corporate titans. We believe all men like a challenge and that men are not shy when they see a woman they are attracted to. If they don't make the first move, it's because there may be no spark and they are simply not that interested! The same man you think is shy will jump on a plane to be with the woman he's crazy about. The same man you've chased for five years and called "commitment-phobic" will marry another girl in six months.

Women try to tell us otherwise. We've been told some men are withdrawn and that's why women have to approach them. We've been told some men are talkative, so how can one get off the phone in ten minutes? We've been told some men need women to mother them because they didn't get enough attention or nurturing as children. Yet these men do not necessarily marry their "nurturing" girlfriends, but the women who were slightly aloof, laughed, and didn't play savior, the girls who didn't care too much too soon.

That's why you should do *The Rules even* if you meet a man in a relationship workshop or a program where feelings are freely discussed and defenses are down. A man is still a man and still likes a challenge *even* if he attends weekend seminars on self-improvement or goes to Tibet for spiritual healing. That means that even if he "opens up too fast" and talks about his feelings right away, you should still be "honest but mysterious." *The Rules* supercede any philosophy, therapy, or religion he may be involved in because he's a man before he's anything else!

So rather than trying to figure out every man's ethnicity, character, or upbringing, simply do *The Rules* on every man you meet. You will have plenty of time down the road to be his salt of the earth, his Rock of Gibraltar, and his soul mate when you're married!

Q: My problem is not *The Rules,* but finding men to do them on. Any suggestions?

A: *The Rules* is not a guide to finding eligible men, but how to behave once you've met them. But since so many women have asked for help in meeting men, we'd like to offer some suggestions.

Two thoughts to get you going: Your chances of meeting a man greatly improve when you leave your apartment, so get off the couch! And remember, you only have to find one!

Also keep in mind that you shouldn't go out blindly, but try to go to places that singles frequent, not married couples and/or kids.

So why don't you try?

1. Club Med or any singles vacation.

2. Church or synagogue or other place of worship.
3. Jogging in the park.
4. Joining a gym.
5. Taking up a male-dominated sport such as golf, scuba diving, tennis, or skiing.
6. Putting a personal ad in a newspaper or magazine.
7. Signing up with a dating service.
8. Joining a ski house.
9. Meeting friends for dinner at a trendy restaurant (where men hang out at the bar), instead of a diner.
10. Going to a lecture or book signing that would draw men.
11. Taking a summer share.
12. Asking friends to fix you up (but don't be too aggressive about it).

However, wherever you go, whatever you do, don't talk to any man first, *sit or stand next to him* hoping he'll notice you.

Q: If I can't talk about my feelings or my past relationships on dates, what can I talk about?

A: Sports, politics, your favorite books and movies, museums, the Internet, work, weather, and dining (the restaurant, the meal, the ambiance). Dating is not a therapy session—talk about subjects outside yourself. There's a whole world out there!

Q: The book is so popular, what if a man asks you point blank, "Are you doing *The Rules* on me? Is that why you don't call me?"

A: You could say, "What rules?" and hope he thinks you've never heard of the book and drops the subject. Also remember, just because a man asks a question doesn't mean you have to answer it. But if you feel compelled to say something, you can say, "Actually, I'm just not a big caller." Before reading *The Rules,* you called men more often, now you don't. We've all read advice books that have deeply influenced us and incorporated some of their ideas into our lives until it *became* who we are. Now it's *part of your personality* to rarely call men! (Besides, no one can *prove* you're doing *The Rules*!)

Q: How do I know if he's The One?

A: If you are feeling ambivalent, we suggest you ask yourself these questions: "Do I like to kiss him? Can I wake up with him for the rest of my life? Do I like his voice, talking to him, the way he dances, the way he treats people? Do I like the way he treats me? Do I like him as a person?" The answers to these questions really matter on a day-to-day basis. *You have to really like just being with him!*

Of course, we cannot tell you how to feel about a man, but it's best if you feel something like, "Wow, I've got to marry this man! I must be with him." If you are tortured, confused, or have to make a list of his pros and cons, it's not a good sign. If you're forcing yourself to like him because he *appears* to be the proper match (your mother loves him, your friends say he's perfect for you, and he makes a good living) but he's not your type, you may be settling. Trust your gut feelings!

Q: I went out with a man who at the end of the date said he had a great time and would call again. He never called. Why? It's been a month. I thought I did *The Rules*. May I call him to find out what went wrong?

A: Don't be surprised. We hear from many women who have this happen to them. Some men are just being polite when they say it. Some had a good time, but didn't *really* want to go out with you again. A *Rules* girl doesn't spend a whole lot of time trying to figure it out. She moves on . . .

We don't recommend calling him for an explanation. It's simply not *The Rules* to chase a man or put him on the spot. And what could he possibly say without hurting your feelings? But if you absolutely must call, wait a considerable amount of time until you're sure he's not going to call you, then go ahead. Better to break *The Rules* with this (dead) man than with a real candidate.

Q: How can I meet his parents and friends before he meets mine if he moved from L.A. to New York and everyone he knows is on the West Coast?

A: Hold off for as long as possible from introducing him to your family and friends before you meet his. If he's truly in love, he'll probably tell his parents about you and they may book a trip to New York to meet you. Or, since he's living in New York he has probably established his own "New York family"—close friends, his boss, coworkers—so at least wait until after he introduces you to them.

Q: You have a date for Saturday night, but it's Saturday afternoon and he still hasn't called to confirm. Do you call him and ask, "What's up? Do we still have plans?"

A: No, you *act as if you knew* you had a date, and be dressed and ready to go when he does call or shows up at your door. In other words, he should never know that you wondered all day (and possibly all week!) if you'd ever hear from him again. If he doesn't call and forgot the date, don't call him. Just know that one day he could forget your wedding date. *Next!*

Q: At a party, is it okay to make eye contact or smile at a man?

A: You can look at him if he looks at you. By all means, smile back if he smiles at you. You just don't initiate anything, from flirting to standing in front of him to make him notice you. On the other hand, you don't have to look down to avoid his gaze if he stares at you, or turn your back to him. You're polite, you just don't pursue men!

Q: I don't like to give out my home number to a man I just met. Is it okay to take his number and call him?

A: While we understand the safety reasons for not giving a stranger your home number, we're not fond of this approach. It throws off *The Rules*. How do you know he was really going to call you? Sometimes a man doesn't know how to say, "It was nice meeting you. Have a nice life." Instead, out of politeness, he says, "Can I have your number? Maybe we can get together sometime." You say, "Well, actually, I don't give out my number. Why don't you give me yours?" You call him and feel justified in doing so. After all, he did *ask* for your number. And then you wonder why the relationship doesn't work out.

We suggest you try to figure out a way for men to get in touch with you first—whether it's by giving them your work number or getting a personal voice-mail number—so that they can make the first move. That way you keep your privacy, but you can still do *The Rules*. Of course, if there is no other way, try to wait a week before you call him. But keep in mind, even if you call him, he must still be the one to ask you out. If he hasn't done so within ten minutes, end the conversation and move on. If you *do* go on a date, and after spending several hours with him you still feel uncomfortable giving him your number, you probably have reservations about him and might want to move on to someone you do feel comfortable giving your number to.

Chapter 32

A Final Bonus—
20 Extra Hints

1. You just found out about *The Rules* but you're already in a relationship. What can you do? Start doing *The Rules* today! Yes, you can do *The Rules* midstream. Starting right now, don't call him, don't beep him, and don't stay on the phone for more than ten minutes when he calls you. If you are seeing him every night, see him only once or twice a week. If he asks why, you're busy, busy, busy! If he asked you to go away for a week, tell him you can only go away for a three-day weekend—your job is hectic, that kind of thing. If you're living with him but you don't have an engagement ring or a wedding date, start looking in the real-estate section of the newspaper for an apartment. Get the idea? Whatever you're doing, cut back. If you're giving too much or losing yourself, pull away and see what happens!

2. On dates or in phone conversations, don't use the words "nurturing," "relationship," "bonding," or talk about getting your needs met. You don't want to sound like a walking relationship book. In the early stages of dating, staying light is essential.

3. Make sure whatever message you record on your answering machine is sensible and in good taste, not outlandish. In the course of returning hundreds of women's phone calls, we have heard pretty crazy stuff—everything from wild cowboy music to the lyrics of very sensual songs to special holiday greetings. Outrageous messages show that you are trying too hard and that can easily alarm or turn off some men. You don't have to express your creativity on your answering machine. Err on the conservative side. A pleasant message is usually the best, something like: "Hi. You've reached Karen. I can't come to the phone right now. Please leave a message."

4. Don't be jealous if your boyfriend or husband's ex-girlfriend calls him or sends him letters. As long as *he's* not initiating the calls and letters, you have nothing to worry about. No one can take away what's yours!

5. If you're on the phone and he calls on the other line, do not get off the phone every time for him. You don't want to seem too interested or the kind of woman that will cut

short an important call with a friend or business associate the second a man calls. Just tell him, "Oh, I'm on the other line. Can you call me back in ten minutes [or whatever time is convenient for you]?" That way *you* don't have to call him and he calls *you* again, but make sure to be available when he calls back.

6. Don't send a man letters, brochures, or newspaper/magazine clippings that you think they'd be interested in. Tell a friend or *Rules* support group member that you were going to send them these items and then throw them away. Men can find this kind of attention too intense. Sometimes they don't even acknowledge it or bother to thank you. You might think they're rude or didn't receive the material. The real reason is you overwhelmed them!

7. If you think a man is doing *The Rules* on you because he's pulling back, ending the calls and dates first—he probably isn't. He may just not be that crazy about you. When a man loves you, he just wants to be with you. If he doesn't seem to be pursuing you, he probably isn't really interested.

8. If you are doing *The Rules,* but aren't getting any dates, the problem may not be *The Rules.* (In other words, don't use this as an excuse to ask men out.) You must either go out more often—try personal ads and dating

services—or consider improving your appearance, if necessary. Try wearing contact lenses instead of glasses, try working out more often or eating less if you're not in great shape, or updating your wardrobe. Keep working on yourself, look your best, and the men will come!

9. Now that *The Rules* is a bestseller, a man might have heard of it and think you are doing *The Rules* on him. Not to worry. Even if he does suspect you're doing *The Rules*, it won't reverse its effectiveness.

10. How to compete with all the *Rules* girls out there? You don't, except to keep doing *The Rules*. When a man likes you, he likes *you*.

11. Remember to say "please" and "thank you" on dates as well as to friends, family members, and business associates. *Rules* girls are a refreshing breed—they're polite! They value themselves and the people they come in contact with.

12. The first or second date can be a Thursday or any week night. But the third date *should* be a Saturday night.

13. Remember, if he's attracted to you and you're quiet on the date, he thinks you're not a big talker. If you're not his type, he thinks you're

boring. This just goes to show you, you don't have to try too hard.

14. If he's dating others, you should date others as well. We're not exclusive until *he* wants to be exclusive and *he* brings it up.

15. Try not to speak to him every day. If you're following *The Rules,* you're seeing him once or twice a week for the first month or two. But what if he's *calling* every day, or several times a day, just to chat? What if he beeps you every day? Should you speak to him every time? No, you shouldn't be that accessible. Leave your answering machine on at home sometimes and say it's hard to talk at work. You don't have to return his beeps—let him get into the habit of beeping you to let you know he's thinking about you without necessarily getting a response. You should be busy and mysterious. If you've been talking daily, talk every other day (when he calls). The rest of the time, he should get your machine. Let him miss you. If he wants to talk to you several times a day, let him marry you!

16. Don't tell men you're doing *The Rules.* Do not explain or discuss *The Rules* with men, and don't tell them how to date. We've heard stories of women who actually tell men, "You have to call me by Wednesday if you want to see me Saturday." That's not *The*

Rules. That's revealing your hand; it's like wearing a slip without a dress. *The Rules* answer is to tell a man who calls late in the week, "Thanks, but I have plans."

He must figure out that if he wants to see you on Saturday, he'll have to call you earlier in the week. We can't make a man really interested in us by telling him when to call. He either is or isn't. You'll find out fast by doing *The Rules*.

17. Don't go away with a man for a week. Save it for your honeymoon! What if, after dating Mr. Right for a month or two, he invites you on a cruise or to an exotic island for a week? *The Rules* answer? You're busy and can't get away.

    Cruises and weeklong vacations make men go backward! Things can get hot and heavy when you see each other seven days a week, twenty-four hours a day. You might act too wifey—telling him to watch his fat intake or giving him advice about a family or business problem. He might be romantic on the trip, but pull back when you return, saying he needs his "space." You may not hear from him for a week or two. The only big trip you should take is your honeymoon. He can take you for an overnight or weekend trip occasionally after dating you for three or four months, but that's it!

18. How to end a relationship or stop seeing someone who you like but aren't crazy about? As soon as you're sure he's not for you, just say, "I think you're great, but I just don't feel a spark" or "I don't think this is working out for me." It's not good for you to tie yourself up with someone you don't love—and it's not good for him either. If he really cares about you, you could end up leading him on and preventing him from meeting someone else. That's not fair. Remember, following *The Rules* saves you both a lot of heartache.

19. Don't have more than one drink on dates so that you do *The Rules,* end the dates first, and, most important, remember what happened!

20. Remember, Cinderella ended the date first!

Success Stories: Women Who Followed *The Rules* and Changed Their Lives!

*S*INCE THE RULES *came out in February 1995, thousands of women have contacted us to ask for help with this successful dating method and to share their experiences. Around the world, women are buying* The Rules *for themselves as well as for their single friends and forming support groups to help one another follow* The Rules. *Mothers are sending* The Rules *to their daughters and grandmothers are sending it to their granddaughters. The word has gotten out.* The Rules *work! Here are some true success stories that may inspire you to do* The Rules *better—or for the first time!*

Jennifer T.'s story, Los Angeles, California

When she stopped sending a doctor greeting cards and gave him space, he decided she was The One.

Jennifer T., thirty-three, called us from Los Angeles to ask for our advice. A friend sent her *The Rules* and she was anxiously trying to practice them on Mark, a thirty-one-year-old doctor, divorced for two years. She said that after four months of dating Mark, he started pulling away. She wanted to know what she was doing wrong. She was crying when she called us—she really wanted to marry this man!

We went over all the important facts—how they met, who pursued whom, what rules were broken—to pinpoint the problem.

They met on a blind date. It was instant attraction. Mark called her *early in the week* for Saturday nights for the first two months. A good sign. They started seeing each other once or twice a week. They had sex after three months. So far, so good. But one evening over dinner, Mark told her he wasn't sure how he felt and what the future would bring. What went wrong?

After some close investigation, we discovered Jennifer had strayed in several key areas. Her major slip was actually after the second date. She sent him a romantic card saying that she was glad they met and signed off with, "XO, Jennifer." Mark didn't acknowledge the card. After spending a weekend in Aspen a month later, she sent him a second card thanking him for the trip. Again, he never called to thank her for the card.

Of course, *Rules* girls know not to send men thank-you cards. They simply thank a man in person after the date or the weekend. Putting it in writing is not necessary, shows too much interest and effort and possibly low self-esteem. He got to spend time with you! Who needs a thank-you card for that?

A romantic thank-you card tells a man exactly how you feel and destroys the mystery and challenge of pursuing you. *Rules* girls *receive* cards, they don't send them. Mark never sent her a card, much less said, "I love you."

Jennifer's other mistakes: After seeing Mark for two months, she started to accept last-minute dates on Monday nights. And when Mark told her he wasn't sure how he felt, she asked him a lot of questions to get him to pinpoint the problem. What wasn't he sure about? Was there something he didn't like that she could change? Did he still have feelings for his ex-wife?

Mark said it wasn't anything in particular. He suggested they "take a break" for a week or two so he could sort out his feelings. Jennifer was devastated.

This is what we told her:

When a man says he's "not sure how he feels" and wants to "take a break" after dating you for four months, what that usually means is he feels overwhelmed by your interest and intensity. It also means that, because he knows exactly how you feel, he doesn't find you intriguing or challenging. He feels slightly bored or too comfortable, not excited about you. He may even be annoyed that you made the pursuit too easy.

We advised Jennifer not to call or write Mark—she was thinking about sending him an "I'm here for you when you're ready" card. We suggested that she go away with a friend on a singles vacation and take other actions to meet men, so she was busy and not waiting by the phone for Mark to call, or too eager when he did call.

We told her that if and when Mark called that she sound light and breezy and not bring up their last serious talk, but to turn him down for a date if he asked by nicely saying, "Gosh, I'd love to, but the next couple of weeks are no good." We suggested she end the call in ten minutes, and simply say she was on her way out, if necessary.

The reason is, the only way Jennifer would ever know if Mark loved her and couldn't live without her was to let him miss her. Mark had to feel that she was slipping away and only a declaration of love could win her back. Jennifer agreed, since being with a man who was "not sure how he felt" after four months was just too painful.

Since following this plan of action—dating others, booking a trip to Club Med, turning Mark down for a couple of dates—Jennifer called recently to report that Mark was aggressively pursuing her. For the first time, he sent her flowers and a romantic card that said, "Miss you terribly! Love, Mark." He asked her in advance for Saturday nights as he did when they first met. On the first date since their breakup, Mark apologized by saying, "You know I wasn't sure how I felt before. I guess I needed some time to think. Now I know, you're the one!"

Rather than ask him to elaborate or turn that remark into a serious talk, Jennifer simply smiled. She sent him only one card since they reconciled—a simple birthday card, nothing scenic or too sweet. Three months later, Mark proposed. Jennifer is sold on *The Rules* and telling all her single friends to try them.

Barbara N.'s story, Athens, Ohio
When she stopped being "friends" with men, she got a friend for life, a husband!

After reading *The Rules,* Barbara, a twenty-nine-year-old social worker, called us to seek advice. She confessed that her big downfall is becoming close friends with men on the rebound or men who want to talk about their girlfriends and get her advice, and then falling in love with them and getting hurt. Barbara was always caught up in some three-way relationship—waiting for a man to be dumped by the girl he really liked, or playing second fiddle to another girl. In other words, she was constantly accepting crumbs (Thursday night dates and Monday lunches). It was always the same story: These men thought Barbara was nice and sweet, but they never thought about marrying her.

When we told Barbara to stop being friends with men and to quit playing therapist to their relationship woes, she argued that she valued male friendships because she liked to know how men think to help her date better. We told her that all the dating help she needed was contained in *The*

Rules and that her future husband would be her best friend. But until then, men should not be her bosom buddies.

We put Barbara on a plan of not getting into any deep conversations with men about relationships—theirs, hers, or anyone else's. We knew this would be difficult. Being a social worker, Barbara loves to talk about this kind of stuff.

We also told her not to call men and rarely return their calls, and not to be so serious. This has been very hard for Barbara who feels it's "rude" not to return calls and "superficial" not to talk about one's feelings. But she agreed to take our advice because her way hasn't worked. She hadn't been in a satisfying relationship in five years and was tired of being alone.

Six months ago, Barbara started doing *The Rules* on Barry, whom she met at a singles bar. He approached her. After about fifteen minutes of light conversation, she forced herself to mingle (even though she would have liked to talk to him the entire night), which prompted him to ask for her phone number. She did not offer him her business card as she usually did, so he flagged down the bartender for a pen to write it down. She couldn't believe it. *The Rules* were really working!

Like clockwork, Barry called her the following Tuesday for a Saturday night date and they have been dating ever since. For the first time, Barbara is not trying to be best friends with an eligible bachelor. She doesn't accept last-minute dates to hang out in his apartment. She ends dates first. If he talks about his problems, she doesn't play therapist. She listens, she sympathizes, she's sweet, but she ends the conversation first.

Barbara used to think that a man would lose interest in her unless she solved his problems. Now she realizes that she doesn't have to be this or that or do anything really, except *The Rules*, to keep a man interested. Now she sees that a man falls in love with a woman's essence. She also didn't bring Barry into her world too soon by introducing him to family and friends before he introduced her to his.

By following *The Rules*, she let Barry simply fall in love with her—and it's working. Barry recently took Barbara as his date to his best friend's wedding. As the bride and groom walked down the aisle, he whispered, "I want the next wedding we go to to be ours."

Susan G.'s story, Boca Raton, Florida
After years of dating Mr. Wrong, The Rules helped this divorcee catch Mr. Nice and eventually Mr. Right.

Susan, forty, a divorced interior designer, has a history of dating men who are moody, sarcastic, and difficult. Her ex-husband, Brian, constantly found fault with her and her last boyfriend, Steven, withheld affection and complained that she wasn't "there enough for him." Susan's response was to drop her friends and hobbies to make him dinner, type his résumé when he suddenly decided to change careers; she even decorated his apartment for free. The more she tried, the more he criticized. He eventually broke up with her.

Susan went to a therapist who concluded that she's attracted to men who remind her of her critical father. But after thirty sessions, Susan's therapist could not stop her from dating such men nor did she offer her specific instructions on how to attract and keep desirable men. She was just good at helping Susan see her destructive patterns.

At the suggestion of a girlfriend, Susan read *The Rules,* called us, and decided to give them a try. We advised her that in addition to following *The Rules,* she should be on the alert for men who are moody, critical, or difficult even if she was physically attracted to them. This worked. For the first time in her life, she began to date men who treated her well, complimented her, and pursued her without much effort on her part. For the first time, she wasn't jumping through hoops to please a man, but dating with self-esteem.

Susan finally met a really considerate guy, Alan. But she wasn't sure if she liked Alan because he was nice or because she really liked him. Susan was also not sure she even wanted to get married again, but she did want a *Rules* relationship. We encouraged her to write down her feelings so she could see them in black and white and analyze them more honestly.

Susan soon realized she was not really in love with Alan, but simply forcing herself to love "a good guy" because he was treating her well, thanks to *The Rules*! Susan concluded that she did not find Alan particularly exciting, merely kind and considerate. She was just so happy not to be mistreated that she tried to love him. Sometimes when you do *The Rules*, you don't fall in love, but you certainly don't get treated badly either!

Susan agreed with our assessment. And although it was painful to break up with "a good guy," she did it anyway and started dating again. If you're anything like Susan, it bears repeating that *The Rules* are not about settling—that is, forcing ourselves to love a man simply because he loves us or does all the right things, like calling often and buying us flowers and so on. The purpose of *The Rules* is to get the guy you are truly crazy about to marry you.

We assured Susan that by doing *The Rules* on men she truly liked, she would get the big payoff. She would catch Mr. Right. We were right. Susan has since met Robert, who she thinks is really, really sexy, not *just nice*. She thinks about him a lot and doesn't have to ask anyone if he's Mr. Right. He calls her almost every day and makes her feel special.

Susan credits *The Rules* for changing her life. She feels that following *The Rules* forced her to think more highly of herself, to not accept just any treatment from a man.

Susan joined a *Rules* support group—about a dozen women who meet every week in her neighborhood to discuss their particular dating situations and to support one another. Susan recently announced to the group that, after ten months, Robert proposed. He wanted to live together as soon as they had gotten engaged, but she refused, saying she was an old-fashioned girl, so he moved up the wedding date!

Stacey G.'s story, Houston, Texas
She discovered The Rules *four years after she got married. Better late than never!*

Stacey, a thirty-three-year-old secretary, found out about *The Rules* a little late—four years after she got married! After reading the book, she craved a real *Rules* marriage. If anyone tells you they got married without doing *The Rules*, keep in mind that *The Rules* are not just about getting married, but having a great marriage and a husband who is attentive and really crazy about you!

Indeed, *The Rules* would have saved Stacey much heartache over the years! She met Neil, a cute stockbroker, at a health club. Both are avid exercisers. He approached her at the bicep machine, offered to show her a couple of moves, and then asked her to go for coffee after the workout.

So here we have a good *Rules* beginning—he thought she was beautiful and made the first move. But dazzled by his good looks, Stacey readily said yes and that was her first mistake. She was too eager, too available. She should have said, "Oh, I would love to, but I can't." Remember, we don't go for coffee on a moment's notice! This is not a game, it's because you value yourself and your time. A man has to wait to spend time with you!

That started a year's worth of last-minute dates because Neil realized he could see Stacey without giving her advance notice. Quite often, Neil would ask Stacey for a Saturday night date on a Friday afternoon. She would cancel plans with her girlfriends, only to run into Neil at the gym that Saturday afternoon and be told, "I'm not in the mood. I think I'll hang out with the guys tonight." She'd be crushed, but he was really cute and she thought this was the best way to "get him." If she wasn't always available, maybe he would think she didn't like him, or worse, ask another girl who was available! She'd cry to herself and her friends, but hoped this would lead to marriage anyway.

This went on for about two years. Neil rarely treated her well. After a romantic weekend away together—her idea—he said to her rather matter-of-factly, "You know, Stacey, I like you, but I'm not sure I'm ever going to settle down. I like my freedom." One Sunday afternoon she came over and offered to make dinner. He said "great" and then left her in the kitchen while he played basketball with his friends. She cooked and cried while he shot hoops.

Not knowing what to do about this going-nowhere relationship, Stacey finally threatened to quit her well-paying job and share an apartment with her older sister in another city. She didn't know she was doing *The Rules*—she wasn't even aware of the concept. She simply had

had enough and her sister suggested she give him an ultimatum: either marry me or good-bye. She took the advice. Afraid of losing her and feeling that she had been such a good sport, Neil proposed.

Four years later, Stacey wished she had some of the payoffs of a *Rules* marriage. For example, when they went to a party, Neil was always leaving her side to talk to strangers. At home, he was sometimes affectionate, but didn't try to initiate intimacy. In general, he treated her like good, old dependable Stacey—the girl who cooked while he played basketball—rather than a creature unlike any other.

We advised Stacey to study Rule #26 ("Even if You're Engaged or Married, You Still Need *The Rules*") and apply them from this day forward. For example, we told her to wear more flattering clothes (she tends to dress conservatively), to join a gym (she stopped exercising after they got married), to leave *his* side and mingle when they go to parties, not to initiate intimacy or hand-holding, not to call him at work so often, or leave love notes on the refrigerator door. We suggested she act a little more elusive—like the girl who threatened to leave town. After all, it was not the "good girl" Stacey who cooked his dinner that made Neil propose, but the *Rules* part of Stacey that finally won him over.

Already Stacey has noticed a difference since applying *The Rules*. Neil calls her more often from work and is more attentive both at home and in public. He recently surprised her by taking her to a romantic inn for her thirty-fifth birthday.

Once hopeless about changing the course of her marriage, Stacey is now a big believer in *The Rules*.

Amy D.'s story, San Diego, California
  This chronic Rule-breaker learned the hard way: moving to be closer to a man makes him run the other way!

Amy, forty-three and divorced, felt she finally hit the jackpot. After seven years of being single since her husband left her and in relationships that didn't wind up at the altar, she met Jack on a business trip. Amy and Jack worked at the same computer company but in different offices—she in San Diego, he in Minneapolis. All employees were invited to corporate headquarters in Chicago to learn a new software system.

Amy noticed Jack right away and sat next to him at the seminar. Big mistake! *Rules* girls don't make things happen. A man either notices us or he doesn't, sits near us or he doesn't. Having more software experience than Jack, she offered to give him a few pointers. That's a common ploy smart women use to get a man to notice them. Unfortunately, it never works! Trying to be a gentleman, Jack took Amy out to dinner to say, "Thank you." One thing led to another, a few drinks, and they ended up sleeping together in his hotel room.

The fast and furious courtship continued after the seminar was over. They E-mailed and called each other constantly. He suggested she move in with him and try to get a job in the Minneapolis office. The company didn't have an opening in

Minneapolis, but Amy quit her San Diego job anyway to be with Jack. (How many women have thrown away their careers and apartments for a man? Of course, they always live to regret it. *Rules* girls know better!)

The first month or so of living together was pure bliss—he worked hard and she decorated and cooked while looking for work, unsuccessfully. But by the second month, the fun faded. Jack was annoyed that he was supporting Amy. He stayed at the office later and later and called at the last minute to say he wasn't coming home for dinner. On weekends, he left her alone to play golf.

Amy had no real friends in Minneapolis and became increasingly depressed and lonely. She worked up the courage to ask Jack what was going on. He told her "things weren't working out as he expected" and to move out as soon as possible. (When you don't do *The Rules*, men can be pretty cruel. They just want you gone, yesterday!)

Devastated, Amy called a friend in San Diego who offered her a couch to sleep on and a copy of *The Rules*. Amy read it in one sitting and wept, realizing all the mistakes she had made with Jack (and with many other men, including her exhusband). She spoke to Jack first and sat next to him; she used her computer smarts as an excuse to strike up a conversation; he wasn't really interested in her, just her expertise; she slept with him on the first date, which wasn't really a date, but simply his way of thanking her for computer help. And worst of all, she quit her job and left her family and friends to move in with him.

After reading *The Rules,* Amy started attending *Rules* support group meetings, practiced not initiating conversations with men or helping them with business. She recently met Bruce at a computer trade show in New York City, where he lived. He approached her. After talking for fifteen minutes, Amy told him she had to get going, so he asked for her number. This was radically new behavior for Amy, who pre-*Rules* typically told a man her whole life story right away. After the show, Bruce called her, made a special trip to San Diego to visit her, and sent her postcards in between visits for the first few months. After dating for eight months, he proposed and said he would move to San Diego.

Amy just can't believe it. This is the first time she didn't have to make things happen with a man, the first time she let a man do all the work . . . and it worked! They're planning a June wedding and she's keeping her apartment and her job. For a savvy businesswoman who first thought *The Rules* were for "other women," Amy is now leading a *Rules* support group and loving it!

For more information about *The Rules*, including:

- *The Rules* **Newsletter** (available only online at <u>www.therulesbook.com</u>)
- **Private phone and e-mail consultations with the authors.** One-hour consultations include evaluation of dating history, analysis of childhood issues that may affect the men you date, advice on where to meet men, how to do TR in person and online, how to write and post an ad online, how act on dates for the first three months, how to get a man to propose and how to move on if he doesn't, how to do TR if you are engaged, married, separated or divorced, plus personal shopping, makeover, and diet and exercise advice.
- *Rules* **Facilitator Program.** Our intensive 12-week online training course teaches you TR so that you can coach other women to do TR.
- *Rules* **seminar**
- *Rules* **audiotapes and videotapes**
- *Rules* **Dating Journal**
- *Rules* **Gift Certificates**
- *Rules* **contacts and support groups worldwide**

please contact *The Rules* authors at
<u>www.therulesbook.com</u>
(212) 388-7910 (phone)
(973) 422-0048 (fax)

TOP 10
CHICAGO

ELAINE GLUSAC
ELISA KRONISH
ROBERTA SOTONOFF

D0037102

EYEWITNESS TRAVEL

Left *Nighthawks*, The Art Institute of Chicago Right View from Willis Tower

LONDON, NEW YORK,
MELBOURNE, MUNICH AND DELHI
www.dk.com

Produced by Departure Lounge, London
Reproduced by Colourscan, Singapore
Printed and bound by South China Printing Co. Ltd., China

First American Edition, 2004
12 13 14 15 10 9 8 7 6 5 4 3 2

Published in the United States by
DK Publishing,
375 Hudson Street,
New York, New York 10014

Reprinted with revisions 2006, 2008, 2010, 2012

Copyright 2004, 2012 © Dorling Kindersley Limited,
London, a Penguin Company

Published in Great Britain by
Dorling Kindersley Limited.

A catalog record for this book is available from the Library
of Congress.
ISSN 1479-344X
ISBN 978-0-75668-454-9

Within each Top 10 list in this book, no hierarchy of quality
or popularity is implied. All 10 are, in the editor's opinion, of
roughly equal merit.

Floors are referred to throughout in accordance with
British usage; ie the "first floor" is the floor
above ground level.

MIX
Paper from
responsible sources
FSC
www.fsc.org   FSC™ C018179

Contents

Chicago's Top 10

The information in this DK Eyewitness Top 10 Travel Guide is checked regularly.
Every effort has been made to ensure that this book is as up-to-date as possible at the time of
going to press. Some details, however, such as telephone numbers, opening hours, prices,
gallery hanging arrangements and travel information are liable to change. The publishers
cannot accept responsibility for any consequences arising from the use of this book, nor for
any material on third party websites, and cannot guarantee that any website address in this
book will be a suitable source of travel information. We value the views and suggestions of
our readers very highly. Please write to: Publisher, DK Eyewitness Travel Guides, Dorling
Kindersley, 80 Strand, London WC2R 0RL, Great Britain, or email: travelguides@dk.com.

Left **Frontera Grill** Center **Buddy Guy's Legends** Right **Chicago Blues Festival**

Left **Wave Swinger, Navy Pier** Right **Baha'i Temple, Wilmette**

 Key to abbreviations
Adm *admission charge payable* **Free** *no admission charge* **DA** *disabled access*

3

CHICAGO'S TOP 10

CHICAGO'S TOP 10

Chicago Highlights

Big-city sophistication combined with small-town hospitality create the perfect blend in this, the Midwest's largest city. Chicago's influential architecture, cuisine for every budget and taste, great shopping, diverse ethnic neighborhoods, and outstanding museums are reason enough for a visit. And the icing on the cake? The city boasts a lakefront and park system that are as beautiful as they are recreational.

1 The Art Institute of Chicago

This grande dame of Chicago's art scene features world-renowned collections. The ever-popular Impressionist section *(see pp8–11)* includes outstanding exhibits such as Renoir's *Acrobats at the Cirque Fernando*.

2 Willis Tower & its Views

The city's skyscraping superlative is actually made up of nine tube-like sections. The views *(left)* are absolutely awesome: on a clear day, you can see up to 40 miles (64 km) from the 103rd-floor Skydeck *(see pp12–13)*.

3 Field Museum

Delve into cultures and environments from ancient Egypt to modern Africa, via Midwestern wildlife, and the underground life of bugs. The Field also offers a closeup of the world's largest and most complete *Tyrannosaurus rex* skeleton, as well as many other fossils *(see pp14–15)*.

4 Museum of Science & Industry

An enduring family favorite, this museum is the only building left from the 1893 World's Columbian Exposition. Exhibits emphasizing interactivity cover everything from space exploration to coal-mining, including the Walk-Through Heart and Silver Streak train, which visitors can climb aboard *(see pp16–19)*.

5 Navy Pier

Once dilapidated, this Lake Michigan pier is now a bustling year-round playground for kids and adults alike, complete with a Ferris Wheel and carousel. In warm weather, take a boat tour or join the throngs that stroll along the pier and get some amazing city views *(see pp20–21)*.

400 — yards — 0 — meters — 400

6 John G. Shedd Aquarium

Chicago's amazing aquarium is located on the lakefront and is home to thousands of marine animals from big beluga whales to tiny seahorses. Get a fun, fish-eye view at the Oceanarium's underwater viewing galleries *(see pp22–3)*.

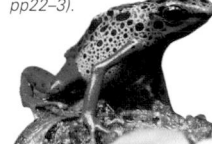

7 Lincoln Park Zoo

It might not be the biggest but it's one of the oldest zoos in the country and, after more than 100 years, still free. Kids love the hands-on Pritzker Family Children's Zoo and Endangered Species Carousel *(see pp24–5)*.

8 Magnificent Mile

Chicago's premier shopping destination is a four-lane stretch of North Michigan Avenue. It also has historic significance, claiming two of only a few structures to survive the 1871 Great Chicago Fire *(see pp26–7)*.

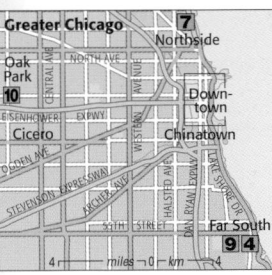

Greater Chicago

Streeterville

Near North

Navy Pier Park

Gateway Park

Chicago River

Millennium Park

Monroe Harbor

Chicago Harbor

Grant Park

9 The University of Chicago

Opened in 1892, this private university is an important part of the southside Hyde Park neighborhood. Its public attractions include museums and galleries, and a Frank Lloyd Wright home *(see pp28–9)*.

10 Frank Lloyd Wright's Oak Park

Frank Lloyd Wright, creator of Prairie Style architecture, was based in this Chicago suburb for 20 years. His legacy is an "outdoor museum" of 25 buildings. Take a self-guided or guided tour of his creations and those of other Prairie Style architects *(see pp30–31)*.

The Art Institute of Chicago

Guarded by iconic lions, and up a flight of grand stone steps (a favorite local meeting place) is the Midwest's largest, and one of the USA's best art museums. Housed in a massive Beaux Arts edifice with an impressive Modern Wing by Renzo Piano, the Institute has some 260,000 works from around the globe, and is famous for its Impressionist and Post-Impressionist works and touring shows.

Main museum entrance

🍽 **Terzo Piano, in the Modern Wing, is a must-stop for a fine-dining lunch with stunning city views, or cross over to Cosi (116 S. Michigan Ave.) for great sandwiches.**

🕐 **Join a free, hour-long introductory tour. Meet in gallery 100 (noon daily, plus 2pm Tue, Wed, and Fri).**

Don't miss the reconstruction of the 1893 Stock Exchange Trading Room.

• 111 S. Michigan Ave. • Map L4 • "L" Station: Adams (Green, Orange, Purple, Brown & Pink lines), Monroe (Blue & Red lines) • 312-443-3600 • www.artic.edu • Open 10:30am–5pm Mon–Fri (to 8pm Thu); 10:30am–5pm Sat & Sun • Adm: adults $18; students, seniors and children 14 yrs and older $12; under 14 yrs free; free adm 1st and 2nd Wed of month, 5–8pm Thu, 5–9pm summer, and Feb • DA

Top 10 Paintings

1. A Sunday on La Grande Jatte–1884
2. Acrobats at the Cirque Fernando
3. At the Moulin Rouge
4. Stacks of Wheat series
5. America Windows
6. Nighthawks
7. The Child's Bath
8. The Old Guitarist
9. The Herring Net
10. American Gothic

1 A Sunday on La Grande Jatte–1884
Massive and mesmerizing, this painting took Georges Seurat two years to complete. The scene *(below)* is created from dots of color, based on his study of optical theory, later known as pointillism.

2 Acrobats at the Cirque Fernando
Children were often the subjects of Renoir's sunny paintings: this luminous 1879 work shows a circus owner's daughters taking a bow after their act.

3 At the Moulin Rouge
Unlike many of his fellow Impressionists who painted serene, often natural scenes, Toulouse-Lautrec was drawn to the exuberant night- and lowlife of Paris. This dramatic composition (1892) celebrates the famous Moulin Rouge cabaret *(above)*.

4 Stacks of Wheat series
From 1890–91, Monet painted 30 views of the haystacks that stood outside his house at Giverny in France. This museum has six of them, which illustrate the basic Impressionist doctrine of capturing fleeting moments in nature.

5 America Windows
Unveiled at the Art Institute in 1977, Marc Chagall's stunning stained-glass windows were a gift to the city he loved. The six vibrant panels depict the US as a place of cultural and religious freedom.

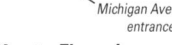
Michigan Ave. entrance

Nighthawks
6 One of the best-known images in 20th-century American Art, this 1942 painting by Realist Edward Hopper has a melancholy quality. It cleverly depicts fluorescent lighting, at the time a recent introduction to US cities.

Key to Floorplan
▢ Lower Level
▢ Ground Level
▢ First Floor
▢ Second Floor

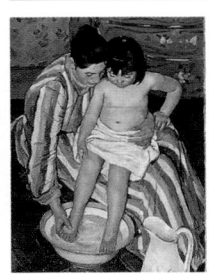

The Child's Bath
7 The only American to exhibit in Paris with the Impressionists, Mary Cassatt is known for using then-unconventional techniques such as elevated vantage points. She often portrayed women and children as in this, her most famous painting (1892).

The Old Guitarist
8 A 22-year-old, struggling Picasso painted this tortured 1903 portrait during his Blue Period. This reflected his grief over a friend's suicide and was a precursor to his own style of Cubism.

The Herring Net
9 Winslow Homer honed his realist skills as an illustrator for magazines and later for the Union during the Civil War. After moving to Maine, he created a series of images, including this one (1885), depicting man's complex relationship with the sea.

American Gothic
10 Grant Wood borrowed from the detailed style of Flemish Renaissance art to create this much-parodied painting (1930). Though perceived by many as satirical, the painting (left) celebrates rural American values.

Museum Guide
Including its stunning Modern Wing, the Art Institute is now the second-largest art museum in the US. The locations of works and the accessibility of specific galleries are subject to change, so if there is a particular work you would like to see, please check in advance of your visit to ensure it is on view.

For more Chicago art galleries and museums See pp38–9

  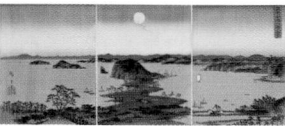

Left **Ritual figure, Amerindian Art** Center **Thorne Miniature Rooms** Right **Exhibit, Asian Art**

10 Collections

1 European Paintings

Arranged chronologically, and spanning the Middle Age through 1950, this prodigious collection includes a significant array of Renaissance and Baroque art. However, its main draw is a body of nearly 400 Impressionist and Post-Impressionist paintings. Instrumental in its creation was Bertha Honoré Palmer who acquired over 40 Impressionist works (largely ignored in France at the time) for the 1893 World's Columbian Exposition.

2 American Arts

This impressive holding contains some 5,500 paintings and sculptures dating from the colonial period to 1950. In addition, paintings and works on paper are on loan from the Terra collection, and there is a range of decorative arts, including furniture, glass, and ceramics

Vincent Van Gogh, *Self-portrait (1886–7)*, European Paintings

Floorplan

Michigan Ave. entrance

from the 18th century through to the present. The silver collection is especially noteworthy.

3 Architecture

Given the city's strong architectural heritage and focus, it is not surprising that Chicago's Art Institute boasts an architecture and design department, one of only a few in the US. Sketches and drawings are accessible by appointment, and changing public displays feature models, drawings, and architectural pieces, such as a stained-glass window by Frank Lloyd Wright.

4 Modern & Contemporary Art

This important collection represents the significant arts movements in Europe and the US from 1950 to the present day, including a strong body of Surrealist works, and notable paintings by Picasso, Matisse, and Kandinsky, as well as showing how American artists, such as Georgia O'Keeffe, interpreted European Modernism.

For more on modern art in Chicago **See pp79, 94–5, 101**

Photography
5 Spanning the history of the medium, from its origins in 1839 to the present, this eminent collection was started by Georgia O'Keeffe in 1949 with the donation of works by Alfred Stieglitz. Many modern masters, including, Julien Levy, Edward Weston, Paul Strand, and Eugène Atget, are represented.

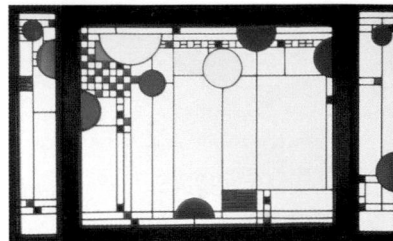

Frank Lloyd Wright art glass, Architecture

Asian Art
6 This sizeable collection covers 5,000 years and features Chinese ceramics and jades, Japanese screens, and Southeast Asian sculpture. The museum's assemblage of Japanese woodblock prints, such as *Courtesan* (c. 1710) by Kaigetsudo Anchi, is one of the finest outside Japan. Look out, too, for the rare early 14th-century scroll painting, *Legends of the Yuzu Nembutsu*.

African & Amerindian Art
7 A variety of artifacts, including sculptures, masks, ceramics, furniture, textiles, bead-, gold-, and metalwork, make up this relatively small, but interesting collection. Exhibits from both continents are arranged by region and culture: ceremonial and ritual objects are particularly intriguing.

Clematis, Arthur Rubloff paperweight

Arms & Armor
8 The Harding Collection of Arms and Armor is one of the largest in America. On permanent display are over 200 items related to the art of war including weapons, and complete and partial suits of armor for men –

as well as horses. The items displayed originate from Europe, the United States, and the Middle East, and date from the 15th through the 19th centuries.

Arthur Rubloff Paperweight Collection
9 This fabulous and unusual assemblage numbers in excess of 1,400 paperweights, making it one of the largest of its kind in the world. It showcases colorful and exquisite examples from all periods, designs, and techniques. The paperweights mostly originate from 19th-century France, though some were made in America and the United Kingdom. Displays also reveal the secrets of how paperweights are made.

Thorne Miniature Rooms
10 Narcissa Ward Thorne, a Chicago art patron, combined her love of miniatures with her interest in interiors and decorative arts to create the 68 rooms in this unique Lilliputian installation. Some of the 1 inch:1 foot scale rooms are replicas of specific historic interiors, while others are period recreations, combining features copied from a variety of sites or based on illustrations and other records of period furniture.

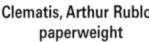

🔟 Willis Tower & its Views

It might have lost the world's tallest building slot to Taipei 101 Tower in Taiwan, thanks to its enormous spire, but Willis Tower (center, left), formerly known as Sears Tower, is still the tallest in the United States, at 1,450 ft (442 m). Designed by Chicago firm Skidmore, Owings & Merrill, the tower uses nine exterior frame tubes, avoiding the need for interior supports. For awesome 360-degree views of the city, head to the 103rd-floor Skydeck. From here you will also be able to access The Ledge, a series of enclosed glass boxes jutting out from the Skydeck and providing a fascinating view straight down to the ground.

Willis Tower

🍴 The tower has eight restaurants to choose from (open Mon–Fri).

Take an audio Sky Tour to get "inside" information on Chicago at the Skydeck's 16 viewing points.

✔ Check visibility levels at the security desk before you wait in line for the Skydeck.

• 233 S. Wacker Dr. (note: entrance is on Jackson Blvd.)
• 312-875-9696
• Map J4
• www.theskydeck.com
• "L" Station: Quincy/ Wells
• Open Apr–Sep: 9am– 10pm daily; Oct–Mar: 10am–8pm daily
• Skydeck adm: $17; children (3–11): $11 • DA
• Marina City: 300 N. State St. • Soldier Field: 425 E. McFetridge Dr.
• United Center: 1901 W. Madison St.
• McCormick Place: 2301 S. Lake Shore Dr.

Top 10 Views

1. John Hancock Center
2. Grant Park
3. Soldier Field
4. Navy Pier
5. United Center
6. Marina Towers
7. Merchandise Mart
8. McCormick Place
9. Lake Michigan
10. Chicago River

John Hancock Center
The Willis Tower's North Side counterpart is this 100-story skyscraper *(right, center)*. It houses a retail area, offices, and apartments – as well as an open-air observatory on the 94th floor *(see p79)*.

Grant Park
Built entirely on land-fill following the Great Chicago Fire *(see p34)* this 200-acre (81-ha) park *(right)* is the city's largest and the site of summer music festivals *(see p62)*.

Soldier Field
Home to the Chicago Bears football team *(see p51)* for over 30 years, the 1924-built lakeside stadium *(below)* saw the addition of a controversial 63,000-seat structure in 2003. Critics have likened it to a padded toilet seat.

United Center
5 This vast indoor sports arena and concert venue *(left)* is also known as 'the house that Michael built,' as it was Michael Jordan's fame that attracted the money to fund it. Outside the center there's a statue of the now-retired, but ever-popular, basketball player.

Navy Pier
4 A former naval base turned fun-filled mecca, this is Chicago's leading attraction *(see pp20–21)*.

Marina City
6 When built in 1964, these distinctive 60-story buildings (nicknamed the corncobs), were both the tallest residential and the tallest concrete structures in the world *(see p36)*.

Merchandise Mart
7 The largest (in floor area) commercial building in the world, this 1930-built structure covers two blocks and was run by *the* Kennedy family until the late 1990s *(see p79)*.

McCormick Place
8 The first convention center opened here in 1960 but burned down seven years later. Helmut Jahn built the second in 1971 at twice the size with 40,000 sprinkler heads. Three buildings now make up this complex, and are connected by a shop-lined promenade.

Chicago River
10 Chicago's 156 mile- (251 km-) long river *(above)* tops world records with its 52 opening bridges. An extraordinary engineering feat resulted in the reversal of the river flow in 1900 *(see p34)*. Every St. Patrick's Day the main branch is dyed green.

Lake Michigan
9 This is the third largest of the five Great Lakes. Water temperatures struggle to hit tepid during summer, but many beach-goers swim nevertheless. On a clear day, you can often see across to the shores of Indiana and Michigan.

Top 10 Tower Facts

1 It is 110 stories high
2 It weighs 222,500 tonnes
3 The tower took three years to construct
4 Building costs topped $150 million
5 It contains 2,000 miles (3,220 km) of electric cables…
6 … And 25,000 miles (40,233 km) of piping
7 25,000 people enter and exit each day
8 1.5 million people visit the Skydeck each year
9 The elevators travel at 1,600 ft (490 m) per minute
10 Six automatic machines wash its 16,100 windows

Field Museum

Founded in 1893 to display items from the World's Columbian Exposition, and renamed in 1905 to honor its first major benefactor, Marshall Field, this vast museum offers fascinating insights into global cultures and environments past and present. Home to all sorts of cultural treasures, fossils, and artifacts, as well as to myriad interactive exhibits, make no bones about it: this natural history museum is one of the best in the country.

Museum façade

○ Grab a bite to eat under the watchful gaze of dinosaur Sue at the Corner Bakery on the main level.

◐ Two free trolley services link the Field, the Shedd *(see pp22–3)*, and the Art Institute *(see pp10–11)* with the nearest Metra and CTA stations and Downtown.

Have a museum-related question? Look out for attendants carrying a big "Ask Me" sign.

- 1400 S Lake Shore Dr.
- Map L5
- 312-922-9410
- www.fieldmuseum.org
- Metra station: Roosevelt Rd.
- Open 9am–5pm daily
- Adm: adults $15, children (3–11) $10, seniors and students with ID $12
- DA

Top 10 Exhibits

1. Sue
2. Pacific Spirits
3. Underground Adventure
4. Lions of Tsavo
5. Inside Ancient Egypt
6. Grainger Hall of Gems
7. Evolving Planet
8. Africa
9. Crown Family Play Lab
10. Ancient Americas

Pacific Spirits
A real celebration of vibrant Pacific islander culture: visitors can see dramatic masks *(above)*, listen to recorded sounds from the swamps of New Guinea, and bang on an impressive 9-ft (3-m) drum.

Underground Adventure
Enter this larger-than-life "subterranean" ecosystem to get a bug's-eye view of life. Wander through a jungle of roots *(right)*, and listen to the chatter of a busy ant colony. Extra admission charged.

Sue
A *Tyrannosaurus rex*, 13-ft (4-m) high by 42-ft (12.8-m) long – the largest, most complete, and best preserved ever found. Her real 600-lb (272-kg) skull, too heavy for the skeleton, is on view nearby.

Lions of Tsavo
In 1898, these two partners in crime killed and ate 140 men constructing a bridge in Kenya, before they in turn were hunted and killed. The skins were first used as rugs, before being mounted as you see today.

Inside Ancient Egypt

This part-original, part-replica Egyptian ruin leads you up and down stairs, into Egyptian bedrooms and tombs, and even through a marketplace. Discover how Cleopatra lived and how mummies were wrapped.

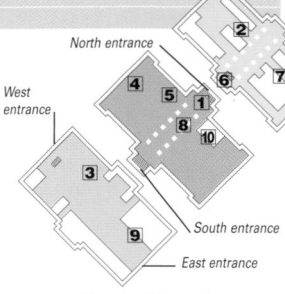

North entrance

West entrance

South entrance

East entrance

Key to Floorplan

☐	Ground Level
☐	Main Level
☐	Upper Level

Grainger Hall of Gems

Fiber-optic lighting illuminates over 500 glittering gems, precious stones, and minerals. Even though it's a replica, the star of the show is the breathtaking Hope Diamond.

Evolving Planet

Journey through four billion years of life on Earth as a wide range of displays tell the story of evolution. Interact with single-celled organisms, giant dinosaurs, and our first human ancestors.

Africa

Browse the wares of a Saharan market, experience life on a slave ship, and see a pair of fighting elephants *(left)*: this exhibit offers an amazing journey through ancient and modern Africa.

Crown Family Play Lab

Six themed areas, from a scientist's lab to a dinosaur dig, are full of things for kids to try out and discover.

Ancient Americas

Step into the world of Ice Age mammoth-hunters, wander through an 800-year-old pueblo, and explore the Aztec Empire, as artifacts and reconstructions uncover 13,000 years of human history in the Americas.

Museum Guide

The main entrance is located on the museum's north side, though visitors typically enter on the south, where buses, trolleys, and cabs drop off. A third (ground level) west entrance is suitable for wheelchair access. If you visit on a weekday, it's worth asking staff about the museum's Free Highlights Tours, which take place twice daily. And don't forget to look for information on the day's special events, tours, and activities, posted throughout the building.

Chicago's Top 10

🔟 Museum of Science & Industry

The cultural star of the city's Far South, this museum was the first in North America to introduce interactive exhibits, with a record of innovative, hands-on displays dating back to the 1930s. More than one million visitors flock annually to this vast neoclassical building, which houses more than 800 exhibits and is a Chicago must-see, especially for families. Make sure you arrive rested, since it takes a whole day to hit just the top attractions.

Great Hall entrance

🍴 The Brain Food Court serves above-average fare, including wood-fired pizzas, and has a kids' dining zone.

🎫 Advance tickets reserved on the Internet or telephone cost an extra $3.75 each but are worth it on busy weekends.

Additional Omnimax tickets are sold at all museum entrances: adults $8, children (3–11) $6, seniors $7.

• 57th St. & Lake Shore Dr.
• Map F6
• 1-773-684-1414
• www.msichicago.org
• Metra station: 55th/56th/57th Sts.
• Open 9:30am–4pm Mon–Sat, 11am–4pm Sun
• Adm: adults $15, children (3–11) $10, seniors $14; including one Omnimax show: adults $23, children $16, seniors $21 • DA

Top 10 Features

1. Apollo 8 Command Module
2. The Great Train Story
3. Walk-Through Heart
4. The Coal Mine
5. Colleen Moore's Fairy Castle
6. All Aboard the Silver Streak
7. Science Storms
8. Omnimax Theater
9. Toy Maker 3000
10. U-505 Submarine

2 The Great Train Story

Thirty-four miniature trains (below) race past skyscrapers, through prairies, and over the Rockies to the Pacific Docks on 1,425 ft (437 m) of track that replicates the 2,200-mile (3540 km) train trip from Chicago to Seattle.

4 The Coal Mine

Venture down a simulated 600 ft (184 m) in an authentic shaft elevator to discover how coal was extracted in the 1930s compared to today. The mini train ride enhances the underground illusion.

1 Apollo 8 Command Module

This, the first manned spacecraft to orbit the moon, offers a genuine peek into the 1960s space race. The historic photos, space suits, and training module on display all help set the scene.

3 Walk-Through Heart

A museum favorite since the 1940s, this 20-ft (6-m) tall model of the human heart would fit inside the chest of a 28-story person. Enter its chambers to see the marvel of human engineering.

5 Colleen Moore's Fairy Castle

Star of the silent screen, Colleen Moore commissioned the design of this lavish 9-sq-ft (0.8 sq-m) castle *(left)* and lovingly filled it with over 2,000 one-twelfth-scaled objects, including the world's smallest Bible.

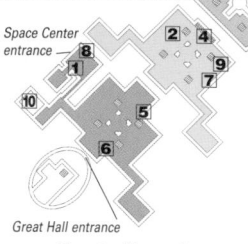

Space Center entrance

Great Hall entrance

Key to Floorplan

	Ground Level
	Main Level
	Upper Level

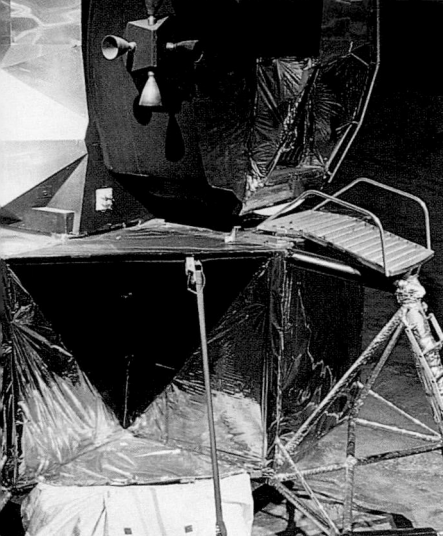

6 All Aboard the Silver Streak

Both Art Deco design afficionados and rail buffs alike are drawn to this streamlined, vintage Zephyr train with its ground-breaking diesel-electric engine. Onboard visits are by tour only.

7 Science Storms

This two-story exhibit illustrates basic principles of physics and chemistry using recreations of natural phenomena, including a 40-ft (12-m) tornado, a giant Tesla coil that produces lighting, and a 30-ft (9-m) wave tank.

8 Omnimax Theater

Films shown in this five-story theater make the viewers feel like they are right in the thick of the on-screen adventures. Films on a rotating program are screened about every 50 minutes.

9 ToyMaker 3000

Twelve robotic arms work the assembly line to produce toy top after colorful top in this display of computer integrated manufacturing technology. You can race a robot to see who can trace letters faster, and souvenir tops come gratis.

10 U-505 Submarine

Take a tour around this 1941 German U-boat: captured during World War II, it looks much as it did then, complete with an Enigma codebreaking machine.

Museum Guide

The museum has two main entrances – the Great Hall (ground level) and the Henry Crown Space Center entrance (for the Omnimax Theater). Head first to tour-only displays – the Silver Streak, U-505, and the Coal Mine – as later in the day waits for these can be more than an hour. If purchasing Omnimax tickets, choose a later time, when you'll truly appreciate sitting down. Strollers can be rented for $2 in the Great Hall.

Left **Communications Zone** Right **Boeing 727, Transportation Zone**

Exhibits

1 Transportation Zone

A full-size Boeing 727 and a British World War II fighter plane dangle dramatically above a steam locomotive and the world's fastest land vehicle, while visitors explore the forces of flight via computer games and videos.

2 U-505

Artifacts, archival footage, and interactive challenges bring to life this restored U-505 German submarine. Optional on-board tours of the boat are available.

3 Genetics: Decoding Life

Explore the complex and controversial world of genetics and genetic engineering and learn how cloning is possible, while viewing real cloned mice.

4 The Farm

Learn about life on today's farms and the modern technologies that get food from the field to your table. Children can ride in a real combine and take part in a cow-milking challenge.

5 Networld

The binary world of cyberspace comes alive here via educational yet fun hands-on displays.

6 Smart Home

This three-story model home demonstrates how to make eco-friendliness part of your daily life.

Museum Floorplan

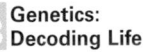

Main Level

Ground Level

Upper Level

Entrance

7 Ships Through the Ages

Here, model ships chart marine transportation from Egyptian sailboats through to modern ocean liners. Highlights include scale versions of Christopher Columbus' three ships.

Boiler Clock

8 Petroleum Planet

The journey from pipeline to polymers is told from an oil molecule's perspective, ending in a huge display of by-products, from running shoes to chewing gum.

9 Communications Zone

The Whispering Gallery illustrates how sound-waves make even the faintest whisper audible at the other end of a room, while the World Live Theater lets visitors witness TV broadcasts being beamed in from around the world.

10 Poop Happens

In this one-of-a-kind science theater show, viewers follow food right the way through the digestive process, from the mouth to the stomach – and beyond.

Top 10 Features of the 1893 Exposition

1 First ever Ferris Wheel

2 Palace of Fine Arts

3 Midway Plaisance, first separate amusement area at a world's fair

4 Jackson Park, land-scaped by designer Frederick Law Olmsted

5 Exotic Dancer "Little Egypt" in the "Streets of Cairo" exhibit

6 Nickname "Windy City" introduced (see p106)

7 A 1,500 lb (680 kg) chocolate Venus de Milo

8 A 70 ft- (21 m-) high tower of light bulbs

9 Floodlights used on buildings for the first time

10 250,000 separate displays on show.

The Museum's Origins

Built as the Palace of Fine Arts in 1893, the Museum of Science and Industry is now the only building left from Daniel Burnham's vast "White City." This was constructed for the World's Columbian Exposition, which marked the 400th anniversary (albeit one year late) of Christopher Columbus' arrival in the New World. Burnham, the Director of Works for the fair (see p37), commissioned architects like Charles Atwood to create structures that would showcase the best in design, culture, and technology. The Field Museum (see pp14–15) inhabited the building until the 1920s when it moved to its present-day Museum Campus home. Sears Roebuck retail chief Julius Rosenwald then decided that a fortified palace, stripped to its steel frame and rebuilt in limestone, would be the perfect home for a new museum devoted to "industrial enlightenment" and US technological achievements. Appropriately, the Museum debuted in 1933 when Chicago hosted its next World's Fair, the Century of Progress Exposition.

A stone figure on the Museum

The Restoration

Although built to withstand fire, due to the value of its contents, the Palace of Fine Arts was originally intended as a post-Fair tear-down, so it needed massive reconstruction when Rosenwald decided to restore it to its former glory in the 1920s. The financial support of many local businessmen and the city of Chicago helped him to fulfill this dream.

The Museum as it stands today

Navy Pier

As recently as 1995 Chicago's Navy Pier was a drab slab of concrete projecting into Lake Michigan, formerly used as a military and freight terminal. But a huge effort to funnel locals and tourists onto the Pier has seen the installation of a variety of attractions on the waterfront – for kids as well as adults – that draw over eight million people annually, making this Chicago's most visited attraction. An added bonus of spending time at the Pier: the breathtaking city views.

Navy Pier

🍽 Skip the chain eateries in favor of ribs and live jazz at Joe's Be-Bop Café.

In summer the beer garden at the far end of the Pier offers stellar city views as well as free bands.

⛵ Join a 90-minute lake tour *(see p111)* on a four-masted schooner, or take a ride on a Seadog speedboat.

Save money and time spent in line with a combination ticket for the Musical Carousel, Ferris Wheel, and Wave Swinger.

- 600 E. Grand Ave.
- Map M3
- 1-800-595-7437
- www.navypier.com
- CTA Bus: 29; 65; 56; 66; 120; 121 • Open summer: 10am–10pm daily (to midnight Fri & Sat); Sep & Oct: 10am–8pm Mon–Sat (to 10pm Fri & Sat); winter: 10am–8pm Mon–Sat (to 10pm Fri & Sat), 10am–7pm Sun
- Free entrance but many attractions charge • DA

Top 10 Exhibits

1. Wave Swinger
2. Chicago Children's Museum
3. Skyline Stage
4. Smith Museum of Stained-Glass Windows
5. Musical Carousel
6. Ferris Wheel
7. Chicago Shakespeare Theater
8. IMAX® Theatre
9. Amazing Chicago's Funhouse Maze
10. Miniature Golf Course

Chicago Children's Museum
Kids love this hands-on museum that educates through play. Under-twos get dedicated spaces, including a water room, with clothing protection provided *(see p56)*.

Wave Swinger
Each of the 48 chain-suspended chairs on this colorful, old-fashioned thrill ride lifts riders 14 ft (5 m) in the air, and spins them until the skyline blurs *(below)*.

Pepsi Skyline Stage
During the summer this unique 1500-seat theater, with its state-of-the-art acoustics, hosts ticketed pop, rock, folk, and jazz concerts against a stunning backdrop. Children's theater, dance performances, and other live events are also staged in this intimate setting.

Smith Museum of Stained-Glass Windows
The first museum of its kind in the USA, the Smith displays 150 artworks made of colored glass *(above)* along 800 ft (240 m) of the Pier's interior corridors. Highlights include 13 pieces from Louis Comfort Tiffany's workshop.

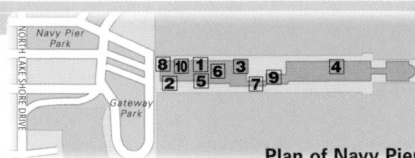

Musical Carousel
A quaint merry-go-round of 36 hand-painted horses and chariots located next to the Ferris Wheel replicates a similar ride installed on the Pier in the 1920s.

Ferris Wheel
It's hard to miss the Pier's 15-story Ferris Wheel. The slowly and continually revolving ride seats six passengers in each of its 40 enclosed cars. Daytime rides offer fine lake views, while evening rides show off the magical city lights.

Chicago Shakespeare Theater
This highly renowned theater aims to make the Bard accessible to the pleasure-seeking masses visiting Navy Pier. As well as Shakespearean standards, productions also include the "Short Shakespeare" series for younger audiences.

IMAX® Theatre
The six-story, 80-ft-(24-m) wide flatscreen movie theater offers celluloid fare ranging from scientific documentaries to Disney features. Sound and vision headsets aid 3D movie enjoyment.

Amazing Chicago's Funhouse Maze
This mirror-filled, Chicago-themed walking maze leads you on a disorienting, 15-minute trip. Expect spinning lights, startling sound effects, and new perspectives on city sights.

Miniature Golf Course
Putt your way around Pier Park via the 18 holes of this mini-golf course, situated at the base of the Pier's Ferris Wheel. Each hole has a Chicago theme and the course is suitable for all ages.

Orientation

Take public transit, a taxi, or walk to Navy Pier. If driving, there are over 1600 parking spaces right on the Pier. Once there, be sure to stop off at the Guest Services desk, just inside the main entrance, to pick up a schedule for details of the day's events, including performance times and locations for the resident comedy troupe, brass band, and a capella singing group.

John G. Shedd Aquarium

The eponymous John G. Shedd, president of Marshall Field's department store (see p74), donated this Beaux Arts aquarium to Chicago in 1929. One of the city's top attractions ever since, it houses some 25,500 marine animals representing 2,100 different species that include amphibians, fish, and aquatic mammals. The latter romp in the saltwater of the glass-walled Oceanarium, which places an infinity pool in front of Lake Michigan to transporting effect.

The Oceanarium

Choose one of three dining options at the Shedd: the sit-down Soundings serves upscale fare with stellar lake views; the Bubble Net Food Court offers pizzas, sandwiches, and burgers; or you can brown bag it at one of the picnic tables.

Don't miss the Shedd's underwater viewing galleries.

Check out Jazzin' at the Shedd on Thursdays (5–10pm, adm $10) from June through August.

• 1200 S. Lake Shore Dr.
• Map M6
• 312-939-2438 • www.sheddaquarium.org
• "L" station: Roosevelt (Green, Orange, & Red lines)
• Open summer (Memorial Day to Labor Day): 9am–6pm daily, (to 10pm Thu Jun–Aug); winter: 9am–5pm Mon–Fri, 9am–6pm Sat & Sun
• Adm: adults $26.95; children (3–11) & seniors $19.95; aquatic show an additional $2 • DA

Top 10 Exhibits

1. Caribbean Coral Reef
2. Oceanarium
3. Wild Reef
4. Habitat Chats
5. Waters of the World
6. Special Exhibit Gallery
7. Amazon Rising
8. Animal Encounters
9. 4-D Special FX Theater
10. Oceanarium Shows

1 Caribbean Coral Reef

This vibrant tropical tank contains glinting tarpon, bonnethead sharks, fluttering rays, and many other fish. A scuba diver hand-feeds them six times daily *(right)*, narrating his task via an underwater microphone.

2 Oceanarium

Underwater galleries afford incredible views of the likes of dolphins and beluga whales swimming through the Oceanarium's vast pools. It is bordered by rocky outcrops and towering pines in an amazing re-creation of the Pacific Northwest coast.

3 Wild Reef

Gain a daring diver's perspective of whitetip reef, blacktip reef, sandbar, and zebra sharks. The Sawfish and fearsome Lionfish *(left)* happily hold their own amid the predator school.

4 Habitat Chats

Oceanarium staffers hold daily discussions about the beluga whales, sea otters, and gentoo and rockhopper penguins in their charge. Twice daily there are also chats covering a changing roster of fish from the aquarium.

5 Waters of the World

Themed tanks hold over 90 re-created aquatic habitats, including Ocean Coasts, Tropical Waters, and Africa, Asia, and Australia. An Australian lungfish, known as "Grandad", has been a resident since 1933.

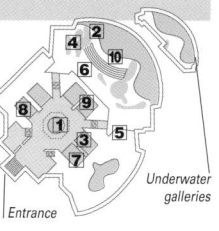

Entrance | Underwater galleries

Aquarium Plan

6 Special Exhibit Gallery

This 3,600 sq ft (334 sq m) special exhibit gallery is located on the mezzanine level of the Oceanarium and features changing exhibits focused on aquatic animals.

7 Amazon Rising

Demonstrating the huge seasonal tides of the world's longest river, this exhibit presents a year in the life of the Amazon flood plain. Look out for the ferocious red-bellied piranha *(above)*.

8 Animal Enounters

Get up close and personal with Chilean rose tarantulas, African bullfrogs, and red-tailed boas in handler-controlled encounters, held hourly.

9 4-D Special FX Theater

The whole family will enjoy this hi-tech theater experience. The "special FX seats" bombard the spectator with bubbles, wind, smells, sounds, and all manner of surprises.

10 Oceanarium Shows

Four or five times a day trainers put the belugas *(left)* and dolphins through their paces. Children are chosen from the audience to reward the animals' intrepid feats (such as tail-walking, and vocalizing) with tasty treats.

Aquarium Guide

Consult the day's event schedule – which is printed on the map you're given – to get the most out of your visit. Try to arrive 10–15 minutes early for an Oceanarium Show to get the best seats, and remember that the 20–30-minute Habitat Chats often follow the shows. There are special events for the little ones on Tuesdays – call the Aquarium for more information.

Lincoln Park Zoo

Chicago's second most popular attraction after Navy Pier, this menagerie is not only one of the oldest zoos in the country but also one of the last not to charge admission. Established in 1868 with just a pair of swans, its age helps to account for how well integrated it is with the surrounding North Side community. While small compared to lots of top US zoos, it is a leading light for ape research, and its park setting, duck ponds, historic café, and landmark red barn endear it to all who visit.

Entrance, Lincoln Park Zoo

🍴 **Check out the Mexican fare year round at the Park Place Café.** In summer, grab a fresh-grilled burger at the historic Café Brauer, which also has a beer garden – rare in the usually alcohol-free Chicago parks.

❓ **Have any animal-related questions?** If so, ask staffers at the "Discovery Carts" located all around the zoo.

• 2200 N. Cannon Drive
• Map F3
• 312-742-2000
• www.lpzoo.org
• CTA bus 151; 156
• Grounds open: 9am–6pm daily.
• Buildings open summer & fall: 10am–5pm daily (summer: to 6:30pm Sat, Sun & hols); winter: 10am–4:30pm daily • Adm: free but $2 charge for Endangered Species Carousel
• Parking: $17 • DA

Top 10 Exhibits

1. Polar Bear Pool
2. Small Mammal-Reptile House
3. Regenstein African Journey
4. Endangered Species Carousel
5. Regenstein Center for African Apes
6. Bird House
7. Pritzker Family Children's Zoo
8. Lion House
9. Sea Lion Pool
10. Farm-in-the-Zoo

2 Small Mammal-Reptile House

Replicating the warm climes of South America, Asia, Africa, and Australia, this exhibit introduces the exotic worlds of animals such as snakes *(below)*.

1 Polar Bear Pool

The highlight of this pool is the underwater viewing window through which zoo-goers can spy the beautiful sibling bears pawing their way through the water *(below)*.

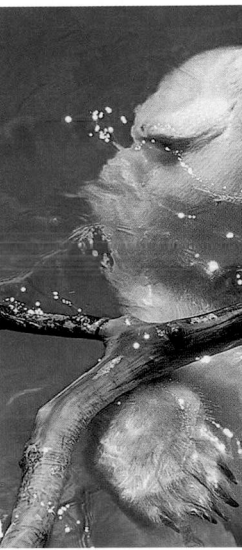

3 Regenstein African Journey

Elephants, rhinos, hippos, giraffes, and wild dogs are among the many animals to roam this expansive exhibit. Begin your walking adventure and experience total immersion in the sights and sounds of the varied African landscape around you.

4 Endangered Species Carousel

Ride a wooden tiger or a bamboo-munching panda on this tent-topped merry-go-round devoted to almost 50 endangered species, many of which are represented in the zoo itself. Admission is charged for this attraction.

For information on the neighboring Lincoln Park Conservatory See p86

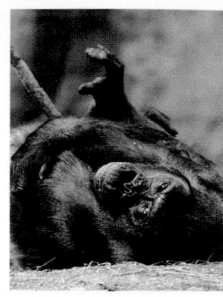

5 Regenstein Center for African Apes
Simulating the natural habitat of chimps and gorillas, this exhibit offers huge indoor, tri-level spaces rigged with lifelike trees and vines, as well as an outdoor yard for use in summer.

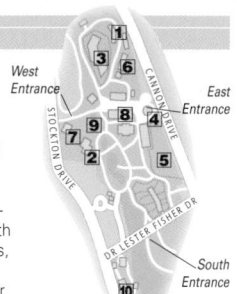

West Entrance
East Entrance
STOCKTON DRIVE
CANNON DRIVE
DR LESTER FISHER DR
South Entrance

Lincoln Park Zoo Plan

6 Bird House
Here, a series of habitats showcase their native bird species. And a walk-through tropical aviary allows you to have a close encounter with 20 exotic and endangered species, such as the African fairy bluebird.

7 Pritzker Family Children's Zoo
Children of all ages can feel "at home in the woods" while visiting animals native to North America, including Black Bears and Spotted Turtles.

8 Lion House
This 1912 structure stands out not only for its grand architecture but also the grand inhabitants. Many kinds of big cats, including Siberian Tigers, prowl – and roar – both inside the hall and in outdoor enclosures.

9 Sea Lion Pool
Despite the name, harbor and gray seals inhabit this pool. Watch them play at the pool's edge or through an underground viewing window. Try to catch the 2pm feeding session *(above)*.

10 Farm-in-the-Zoo Presented by John Deere
Keeping city kids in touch with their Midwestern roots, this exhibit offers a daily roster of activities such as goat-milking, cow-feeding, and butter-churning, and the chance to see chicks being born.

Visitor Guide

Stop by the Gateway Pavilion, just inside the east gate, when you arrive at the zoo. There, you can pick up a free visitor guide to find out about feeding times and special events. Staff are on hand here to provide extra information about any new animal arrivals or exhibits. Parking facilities, lockers, strollers, and wheelchairs are also available there.

Magnificent Mile

This glitzy strip of stores and striking buildings runs for, you guessed it, about a mile (1.6 km), along North Michigan Avenue. A sharp developer came up with the "magnificent" moniker in 1947, and it has stuck ever since. Often known as the Mag Mile, it is home to big-guns department stores like Neiman Marcus, as well as high-end boutiques such as Tiffany & Co, and popular chain stores (Gap et al). The strip is at its best around Christmas when twinkling trimmings provide welcome relief from the often gray days.

North Michigan Ave. Bridge

Choose from a wide range of high-end, global, fast food at Foodlife food court in Water Tower Place.

The Pumping Station houses the main Chicago Visitor Center and a Hot Tix booth (open 10am–6pm Tue–Sat, 11am–4pm Sun) for reduced same-day theater tickets *(see p80)*.

• Map L2–3
• Visitor Information 312-409-5560, www.the magnificentmile.com
• "L" Station: Grand/State; Chicago/State
• Water Tower Place Mall: 835 N. Michigan Ave., 312-440-3166, open 10am–9pm Mon–Sat 11am–6pm Sun
• Ghirardelli Ice Cream & Chocolate Shop: 830 N. Michigan Ave., 312-337-9330, open 10am–10pm daily (to midnight Fri, Sat)

Top 10 Features

1. The Drake Hotel
2. John Hancock Center
3. Water Tower Place
4. Historic Water Tower & Pumping Station
5. American Girl Place
6. Hershey's Chicago
7. Ghirardelli Ice Cream & Chocolate Shop
8. Hotel Intercontinental
9. Tribune Tower
10. Wrigley Building

The Drake Hotel
This elegant hotel became an instant glamor hot-spot when it opened on New Year's Eve in 1920. Marilyn Monroe was among the many stars who have graced it with their presence. High tea in the lobby café is a real treat *(see p115)*.

John Hancock Center
When this sleek 100-story building was built in 1970, it was the world's tallest. Exhilarating views of Chicago and beyond are afforded by the 94th-floor observatory and adjoining open-air area, the Skywalk *(see pp76–7)*.

Water Tower Place
Housing one of the city's busiest shopping malls, this multi-use complex is one of the world's tallest reinforced concrete buildings. Its 100-plus shops and venues include a branch of Macy's and a Broadway-style playhouse.

Chicago Water Works & Pumping Station
Dwarfed by the surrounding skyscrapers, these structures are among the few that survived the Great Fire of 1871. The water tower *(left)* now contains an art gallery, while the pumping station still functions and also houses a visitor center *(see p80)*.

Chicago's Top 10

American Girl Place
Eager girls and their moms swarm to this palace of little-girliness *(see p82)*, which stocks all kinds of merchandise from the American Girl doll range. Try the store café *(see p57)* or attend the acclaimed musical performances.

Magnificent Mile Map

Hershey's Chicago
North America's largest chocolate manufacturer offers a themed retail experience in its Chicago store. Old favorites such as *Hershey's Reese's* and *Kit Kat* are on sale alongside the latest new products *(see p81)*.

Ghirardelli Ice Cream & Chocolate Shop
One of only two Midwestern locations for this San Francisco company is situated just across from Water Tower Place. It is the perfect spot for a sinfully rich dessert.

Hotel Inter-Continental
Built in 1929 as a luxury club for the all-male Shrine association, this amazing hotel *(see p115)* reveals a range of flamboyant architectural styles in its public spaces. Take a self-guided tour to see the highlights, including the stunning swimming pool *(above)*.

Tribune Tower
The result of a design competition organized by the *Chicago Tribune* newspaper, this Gothic tower *(above, right)* is either adored or abhorred by locals. Either way, it's a dramatic Mag Mile landmark *(see p80)*.

Wrigley Building
The two towers of the former Wrigley headquarters add to Michigan Avenue's exciting skyline *(above left)*. At night, colored lights illuminate them, as they have done since the building opened in 1921 *(see p61)*.

Bridge to Success

The North Michigan Avenue bascule bridge, built in 1920, was the first of its kind in the world. Instrumental in Chicago's northward expansion, it provides a fitting gateway to the city's main retail artery – the Mag Mile. The southwest tower houses the McCormick Tribune Bridgehouse and River Museum, which details the history of Chicago River and displays the interworkings of this landmark drawbridge.

ᴛᴏᴘ10 The University of Chicago

With Chicago's expansion in the late 19th century, a major university was the perfect addition to an array of new cultural institutions. Funded by oil magnate John D. Rockefeller, (who deemed it his best ever investment) the forward-thinking institution opened in 1892. Today, the university is one of the USA's most respected, boasting 82 Nobel prize winners as students, faculty, or researchers, as well as several on-campus attractions that are destinations in their own right.

Cobb Gate

🍴 Go for a deep-dish pizza at a Chicago favorite, Giordano's (5309 S. Blackstone Ave.).

🎵 Rockefeller memorial chapel's carillon is played Oct–Jun 6pm Mon–Fri, noon Sun, Jun–Sep, every Sun.

• 5801 S. Ellis Ave.
• 1-773-702-1234
• www.uchicago.edu
• Map E6
• Metra Station: 55th/56th/57th Sts.; 59th St.
• Bond Chapel: open 8am–4:45pm daily, Free
• Smart Museum of Art: open 10am–4pm Tue–Fri (to 8pm Thu); 11am–5pm Sat & Sun, Free
• Cobb Hall: Renaissance society open 10am–5pm Tue–Fri, noon–5pm Sat & Sun, Free
• Rockefeller Memorial Chapel: open 8am–4pm daily (except during services), Free
• Regenstein Library: special collections exhibits open to the public 8:30am–4:45pm Mon–Fri, Sat 9am–12.45pm term-time, Free

Top 10 Features

1. Oriental Institute
2. Bond Chapel
3. Smart Museum of Art
4. Main Quadrangle
5. Robie House
6. Cobb Gate
7. *Nuclear Energy*
8. Rockefeller Memorial Chapel
9. Cobb Hall
10. Regenstein Library

1 Oriental Institute

The institute's amazing museum *(see p99)* has five galleries that showcase the history, art, and archaeology of the ancient Near East. Don't miss the Egyptian Gallery's towering 17-ft (5.2-m) statue of King Tutankhamun *(right)*.

2 Bond Chapel

Built in 1926, this small, ivy-covered chapel features exterior stone carvings of angels, imps, and Adam and Eve. Inside, stained-glass windows illustrate scenes from the New Testament *(below)*.

3 Smart Museum of Art

Magazine moguls David and Alfred Smart founded this museum in 1974. It might be small, but its contents (ranging from ancient ceramics to 20th-century sculpture) pack an impressive punch.

4 Main Quadrangle

Rejecting post-Civil War modernity, Henry Ives Cobb's 1891 campus plan mimics England's Gothic Oxford University, with this main unifying quad surrounded by smaller ones.

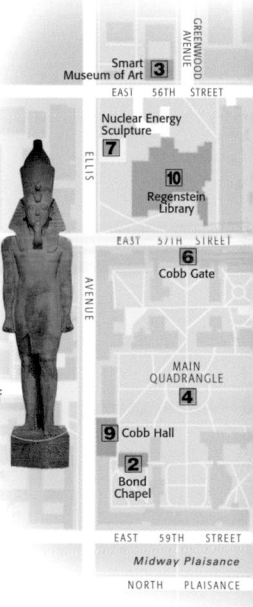

GREENWOOD AVENUE

Smart Museum of Art **3**

EAST 56TH STREET

Nuclear Energy Sculpture **7**

ELLIS

10 Regenstein Library

EAST 57TH STREET

6 Cobb Gate

AVENUE

MAIN QUADRANGLE **4**

9 Cobb Hall

2 Bond Chapel

EAST 59TH STREET

Midway Plaisance

NORTH PLAISANCE

Unless otherwise stated, all attractions have Disabled Access.

Robie House
5 Frank Lloyd Wright described his striking low-rise, Prairie-style masterpiece as "the cornerstone of modern architecture." The not-so-humble architect built it in 1909 for bicycle manufacturer Frederick C. Robie (see p100).

Cobb Gate
6 This ornate northern entrance to the Main Quad is adorned with gargoyles. University lore says they represent students' four years of college life: from struggling freshman at the base to graduation at the apex.

Nuclear Energy
7 This 12-ft (3.65-m) bulbous bronze sculpture by Henry Moore marks the general area where Enrico Fermi and his team of scientists achieved the first controlled self-sustaining nuclear chain reaction in 1942.

Rockefeller Memorial Chapel
8 The tallest building on campus is this mini-cathedral named for university patron John D. Rockefeller. It boasts magnificent stained glass, a 72-bell carillon (the world's second largest), and a 10,000-pipe organ.

Cobb Hall
9 Confusingly, the oldest building on campus is not named for its architect, Henry Cobb, but for an unrelated donor, Silas Cobb. Built in 1882, the beautiful Gothic structure houses classrooms, offices, and the Renaissance Society, a contemporary art gallery.

UNIVERSITY

WOODLAWN

Robie House **5**

EAST 58TH STREET

1 Oriental Institute

AVENUE · AVENUE

8 Rockefeller Memorial Chapel

100 ⌐ yards ¬0 ⌐ meters ⌐ 100

Top 10 Alumni

1 Milton Friedman (1912–2006), economist

2 James D. Watson, (1928–), scientist

3 Philip Glass (1937–), composer/musician

4 Edwin Hubble (1889–1953), astronomer

5 Susan Sontag (1933–2004), critic/author

6 Eliot Ness (1903–57), author/law enforcer

7 John Ashcroft (1942–), US Attorney General

8 Philip Roth (1933–), author

9 Carl Sagan (1934–96), astronomer/author

10 Studs Terkel (1912–2008), oral historian

Regenstein Library
10 The 1970-built limestone "Reg," *(above)* honors Chicago industrialist Joseph Regenstein. Exceptional jazz archives, map collections, and children's books feature among its seven million plus volumes.

Frank Lloyd Wright's Oak Park

This quiet suburb, seven miles (11 km) west of downtown Chicago, contains the world's largest collection of Frank Lloyd Wright-designed buildings. It was here that Wright developed his Prairie style, (inspired by the flat lines of the Midwestern plains), influencing other architects such as George Maher. His work was first considered radical, even ugly, compared to the typical styles of the day. Walking through Oak Park's quaint, tree-lined streets, it's evident that Wright's unique architecture does stand out from the norm – but in all the right ways.

Detail of house in Oak Park designed by Wright

🍝 Dine Italian at family-run La Bella Pasteria (1103 South Blvd. 1-708-524-0044)

🎫 The Visitors' Center sells maps, books, and tickets for area tours (1010 Lake St., 1-888-625-7275)

- Map A5
- "L" Station: Oak Park
- Frank Lloyd Wright Home & Studio, 951 Chicago Avenue, 312-994-4000, www.gowright.org, open 10am 5pm daily, tour times vary, no DA
- Unity Temple, 875 West Lake Street
- Pleasant Home, 217 South Home Avenue
- Arthur Heurtley House, 318 Forest Avenue
- The Bootleg Houses, 1019/1027/1031 Chicago Avenue
- Charles Matthews House, 432 North Kenilworth Avenue
- Edwin Cheney House, 520 North East Avenue
- Beachy House, 238 Forest Avenue
- Nathan Moore House, 333 Forest Avenue
- Harry Adams House, 710 Augusta Boulevard

Top 10 Buildings

1. Unity Temple
2. Frank Lloyd Wright Home & Studio
3. Pleasant Home
4. Arthur Heurtley House
5. Beachy House
6. Charles Matthews House
7. Edwin Cheney House
8. The Bootleg Houses
9. Nathan Moore House
10. Harry Adams House

1 Unity Temple

This compact church (1908) wonderfully demonstrates Wright's use of poured concrete for both structural and decorative purposes *(right)*.

2 Frank Lloyd Wright Home & Studio

Built when Wright moved to Oak Park (1889), this is where he designed over 150 structures *(above)*. The children's playroom is luminous with signature art-glass windows.

3 Pleasant Home

This 30-room Prairie-style 1897 home built by George Maher, was Oak Park's first to have electricity. It holds a small history museum, including exhibits relating to Tarzan creator and former local resident, Edgar Rice Burroughs.

4 Arthur Heurtley House

Wright's beautiful 1902 house *(above)* is absolute Prairie, with its low, wide chimney, and band of art-glass windows that makes the over-hanging roof appear to float.

For detailed information on opening hours call the Visitors' Center. Most buildings open to the public are visited by tour only.

5 Beachy House

An impressive 1906 home that contradicts many of Wright's trademarks. Instead of just stucco and wood or brick and concrete, he used them all: it also has a seven-gabled, rather than a hipped, roof.

Oak Park Street Map

6 Charles Matthews House

Architects Thomas Eddy Tallmadge and Vernon S. Watson designed this elegant 1909 Prairie-style residence for a wealthy druggist. Among the interior details are Prairie-inspired light fixtures and folding art-glass doors.

7 Edwin Cheney House

Now a B&B, this home sparked a tragic love affair between Wright and Mrs. Cheney, leading him to abandon his family and practice. Mamah Cheney and her children were murdered at Wright's Wisconsin home by an insane servant in 1914.

9 Nathan Moore House

Out of financial desperation, Wright built this charming Tudor-style home *(above)* for his neighbor. After a fire destroyed the top floors in 1922, Wright's modifications echoed his West Coast concrete block houses.

8 The Bootleg Houses

Wright lost his job over these three private commissions, built while he was actually employed by Louis Sullivan *(see p37)*. Though Queen Anne-like in style, they hint at the design elements that were to be his hallmarks.

10 Harry Adams House

This striking 1913 home marks the last of Wright's Oak Park houses and features several of the elements that made him famous, such as exquisite stained glass, and a low overhanging roof.

Frank Lloyd Wright

After moving to Oak Park in 1889, Wright (1867–1959) appeared to lead the perfect suburban life. But in the early 20th century he created scandals by galavanting with married women, and wearing flamboyant clothes and long hair. During the Depression, however, he transformed into a respected social visionary, and later redefined himself as a quick-witted sage. Ultimately, though, he became a master of self-promotion, establishing himself as the first celebrity architect.

Literary buffs take note: Ernest Hemingway's Oak Park birthplace is open to the public (339 N.Oak Park Ave., 1-708-848-2222)

Great Chicago Fire of 1871

Moments in Chicago History

1871: Great Chicago Fire
Over 250 people died and 17,000 buildings were destroyed in this fire, allegedly started by a cow kicking over a lantern. Just a few buildings survived, including the Historic Water Tower and Pumping Station (see p80).

1885: First Skyscraper
Though just a measly – by today's standards – nine stories, the Home Insurance Building (now demolished) was the tallest of its time. William LeBarron Jenney achieved this architectural feat by designing the first weight-bearing steel frame. From then on, the only way was up.

1886: Haymarket Riot
Wealthy industrialists funded amazing Chicago arts institutions, but their workers toiled long hours in abominable conditions. In May 1886, a labor protest ended in an explosion at Haymarket Square that killed eight policemen and two bystanders. Eight anarchists were convicted of murder, though three were later pardoned for lack of evidence.

1892: First Elevated Train
The first train traveled just 3.6 miles (5.8 km) along tracks built above city-owned alleys (avoiding the need to negotiate with private property owners). By 1893, the line was extended to

Jackson Park (see p62) to transport visitors to the World's Columbian Exposition (see p19).

1900: Reversal of the Chicago River
With sewage flowing downriver to Lake Michigan, the source of the city's drinking water, thousands of Chicagoans were dying from the contamination. To solve the problem, engineers created a canal that forced the river to flow away from the lake: an extraordinary feat of modern engineering.

1919: Chicago Black Sox Scandal
The Chicago White Sox was a winning baseball team but poorly paid, so players sometimes fixed games, pocketing money from gamblers. After a group of players conspired to lose the 1919 World Series, eight of them were indicted, acquitted for insufficient evidence, but banned for life from baseball – and forever nicknamed the "Black Sox."

Al Capone

1929: Valentine's Day Massacre
This brutal murder of seven of Al Capone's rival gangsters is one of history's most notorious massacres. Capone set up a sting that sent George "Bugsy" Moran's main men to a nearby garage. There, Capone's henchmen, dressed as police officers, lined them up and riddled them

The Chicago White Sox in 1919

Top 10 Residents

1 Jean Baptiste Point du Sable
Chicago's first non-native settler was an African-American trader who set up camp around 1779.

2 Jane Addams
This social activist (1860–1935) founded Hull House social center *(see p95)* and won a Nobel Peace Prize.

3 Carl Sandburg
One of Chicago's nicknames "City of big shoulders," was penned by this author/poet (1878–1967).

4 Al Capone
America's best-known mobster (1899–1947) was Chicago's "Public Enemy Number One" until jailed in 1931 for tax evasion.

5 Ernest Hemingway
Born in Oak Park, this hard-living author (1899–1947) left the suburb of "wide lawns and narrow minds" at age 19.

6 Richard J. Daley
This effective, if corrupt, Chicago mayor (1902–76) served longer than any other.

7 Benny Goodman
Born to poor Russian-Jewish immigrants, jazz great Goodman (1909–86) earned the title "King of Swing."

8 Hugh Hefner
Lothario and founder of *Playboy* (1926–), whose first issue sold over 50,000 copies.

9 Curtis Mayfield
Soul musician and social activist (1942–99), Mayfield had his first hit *For Your Precious Love* at age 17.

10 Oprah Winfrey
TV's talk-show darling (1954–) filmed in Chicago from 1984 to 2011 and has become an honorary native of the city.

with bullets. Seven bushes now mark the spot (at Clark Street and Dickens Avenue).

8 1942: First atom split
Under the football stands on the campus of the University of Chicago *(see pp28–9)* Enrico Fermi made history. He supervised the creation of a primitive nuclear reactor and took the first major step in understanding how to build an atomic bomb.

9 1955: First McDonald's franchise opens
Ray Kroc, a milkshake mixer salesman, changed diets world-wide by convincing Dick and Mac McDonald's to franchise their San Bernadino, California burger stand. The original restaurant in Des Plaines – 15 miles (24 km) west of Chicago – is now a museum.

10 1983: Harold Washington elected Mayor
Chicago's first African-American Mayor, Washington tragically died of a heart attack shortly into his second term. His accomplishments included the creation of a new central library *(see p69)*. Barack Obama moved to Chicago in 1985 and was eventually elected president of the US in 2008.

Left **333 W. Wacker Drive** Center **Art glass, Auditorium Theatre** Right **860–80 N. Lakeshore Drive**

🔟 Skyscrapers

1 The Rookery
One of the earliest remaining skyscrapers, this 1888 Chicago landmark *(see p70)* combines traditional wall-bearing and newer steel frame construction. The latter made it possible for its architects, Burnham and Root, to design an open interior, with office spaces set around a central light well.

2 Auditorium Theatre
Built by Adler and Sullivan in 1889, the ornate Auditorium also originally contained a hotel and office building and had one of the first public air-conditioning systems. The revamped 4,000-seat theater boasts near-perfect acoustics. 🕲 *50 E.Congress Pkwy.* • *Map K5* • *For tours call 312-431-2354*

3 Monadnock Building
Constructed in two stages, this Loop edifice represents the evolution of skyscraper architecture. The northern half was built in 1891 using solely wall-

Detail of staircase, Monadnock Building

bearing construction, while the southern half was built two years later and incorporated the then-emerging steel-frame technology that is still used today *(see p72)*.

4 Reliance Building
The steel skeleton on this 1895-built skyscraper allowed it to be wrapped in glass. It offers an excellent example of the Chicago window, which is characterized by a bay window placed between two narrow, double-hung windows – a signature feature of the Chicago school of architecture. Occupied by the Hotel Burnham *(see p116)* the interior sports replicas of original features *(see p72)*.

5 860–80 N. Lakeshore Drive
You might think these two high-rise apartment buildings (1949–51) look like many others along this classy strip. Actually, the others look like these. German architect Mies van der Rohe perfected the "less is more" approach which so many other architects went on to copy.

6 Marina City
With its twin cylindrical structures (1959–64) on the Chicago River, Marina City is a "city within a city," containing offices, residences, a theater, a grocery store, and more. The apartments start on the 21st floor, affording spectacular views, but their slice-of-pie shape creates some interior decorating challenges.

The Rookery

7 Willis Tower

This soaring tower, built in 1974 as the headquarters of retailer Sears Roebuck and Co. (who have since moved out), can be seen from almost anywhere in the city. Its Skydeck affords sensational views *(see pp12–13)*.

8 333 W. Wacker Drive

The graceful curve of this triangular, tinted-glass office building (1983) hugs the Chicago River. The water, together with the changing light and clouds create dynamic reflections: the green and silver lobby continues the shimmering show. ⊗ *Map K3*

9 James R. Thompson Center

From inside the circular atrium of this magnificent 17-story building (1985), a quick glance up is almost dizzying. Take the elevator to the top for an impressive view of the stunning marble rosette on the concourse level *(see p70)*.

10 Ogilvie Transportation Center

Rising 40 stories in waves of glass and steel is this striking 1996-rebuilt commuter train station (aka the Northwestern Station). Its streamlined façade mimics a vintage luxury train. ⊗ *500 W. Madison St. • Map J4*

Top 10 Architects

1 William Le Baron Jenney
The "father of the skyscraper" (1832–1907) who designed the first all-metal-framed structure in 1885 *(see p34)*.

2 Daniel Burnham
Visionary city planner and architect, Burnham (1846–1912) was the man behind the White City *(see p19)*.

3 William Holabird & Martin Roche
This influential team (Holabird 1854–1923; Roche 1855–1927) developed early Chicago-style skyscrapers including the Marquette Building *(see p72)*.

4 Louis H. Sullivan
The creator (1856–1924) of the "form follows function" doctrine designed according to a building's intended use.

5 Frank Lloyd Wright
Inspired by the wide open spaces of the Midwest, Wright *(see pp30–31)* was the originator of the Prairie style.

6 George Maher
A Prairie School architect (1864–1926) who favored Arts and Crafts motifs.

7 Walter Burley Griffin
Another Prairie–style architect (1876–1937) with a namesake historic district on Chicago's Southside.

8 Ludwig Mies van der Rohe
Minimalist architect (1886–1969) and creator of the modern glass-and-steel box.

9 Bertrand Goldberg
Goldberg (1913–97) designed Marina City, typical of his curvilinear concrete shapes.

10 Harry Weese
A Modernist (1915–98), but one sympathetic to existing buildings of merit.

For other examples of notable Chicago architecture See pp72–3

Left **Exhibit, National Vietnam Veterans Art Museum** Right **Jane Addams Hull House**

TOP 10 Niche Museums

1 National Museum of Mexican Art

The largest Latino museum in the US explores the culture *sin fronteras* (without boundaries), showcasing works from both Mexico and Mexican-American communities. Pre-Columbian ceramics, Day of the Dead candelabras, and prints by such luminaries as Diego Rivera are highlights of the permanent collection. ✆ *1852 W. 19th St. • Map B5 • 10am–5pm Tue–Sun • Free • DA*

2 Spertus Museum

From cartoons to ancient Torah scrolls, this museum offers a lively, multifaceted retelling of Jewish history and culture. The museum's Zell Holocaust Memorial was the first such permanent installation in the US. The Gray Children's Center gets kids involved in unearthing the past in a hands-on "archeological dig," although this is not currently open to the public. ✆ *610 S. Michigan Ave. • Map L6 • 10am–5pm Sun–Thu • Adm free • DA*

Work by Jesus Helguera, National Museum of Mexican Art

3 Swedish–American Museum Center

Located in Andersonville, the historic neighborhood of Scandinavian immigrants, this tiny museum's permanent collection of personal items brought over by early settlers is supplemented by temporary exhibitions on Swedish culture. An interactive children's museum on the third floor brings the immigrant journey to life. ✆ *5211 N. Clark St. • Map K2 • 10am–4pm Tue–Fri, 11am–4pm Sat & Sun • Adm: $4; children, seniors, students $3 • DA*

4 Hellenic Museum and Cultural Center

Located in the city's Greektown, this museum is dedicated to celebrating Hellenic culture and the Greek immigrant experience in America. ✆ *801 W. Adams St. 4th floor. • Map J4 • 10am–4pm Tue–Fri, 11am–4pm Sat • Adm: $5; children under 12 free • www.hellenicmuseum.org*

5 Ukrainian Institute of Modern Art

Housed in three converted storefronts, this tiny institute in the colorful Ukrainian Village neighborhood hosts rotating cultural programs, exhibitions, literary events, film screenings, and concerts. The permanent collection includes works by Chicago artists, as well as by painters and sculptors of Ukrainian descent. ✆ *2320 W. Chicago Ave. • Map J2 • noon–4pm Wed, Thu, Sat & Sun • Free*

Chicago's Top 10

Hope and Help, International Museum of Surgical Science

6 Mary & Leigh Block Museum of Art

This well-edited collection of paintings, drawings, and sculpture is housed in a striking glass and limestone building designed by local architect Dirk Lohan. The Block Museum offers rotating exhibitions, as well as numerous timely lectures and workshops.
🔖 *40 Arts Circle Dr., Evanston • Map B2 • 10am–5pm Tue, 10am–8pm Wed–Fri, 10am–5pm Sat & Sun • Free*

7 DuSable Museum of African-American History

Named for Jean Baptiste Point du Sable, Chicago's first settler (who was of African descent), this museum chronicles the African-American experience. There is a powerful exhibit on slavery, complete with shackles, while temporary displays cover topics such as early black millionaires, African hair art, and the *Kwanzaa* holiday celebration *(see p99).*

8 International Museum of Surgical Science

Medicine meets the macabre at this museum, with four floors displaying historic instruments that span 4,000 years of surgery.

Murals and sculptures pay tribute to the profession. Stronger stomachs may appreciate the ancient Peruvian skulls showing evidence of early surgical attempts. 🔖 *1524 N. Lake Shore Dr. • Map F4 • 10am–5pm Tue–Thu, 10am–9pm Fri & Sat, 10am–5pm Sun • Adm: $10; students and seniors $6 • DA*

9 National Vietnam Veterans Art Museum

Veterans of the Vietnam War, both US and Vietnamese, have contributed to the vast and moving collection of artworks cataloged by this thought-provoking museum. Some 130 artists created 1,000 works in pen, paint, clay, and word testifying to war's horrors *(see pp94–5).*

10 Jane Addams Hull House

Nobel Peace Prize-winning social reformer Jane Addams worked her good on Chicago's immigrant population from these two Victorian houses. In addition to her original art and furniture, Hull House stages temporary exhibits relating to the social settlement that brought day care, counseling, and education to the working class *(see p95).*

Left **Lou Mitchell's** Right **Blackbird**

Places to Eat

1 Charlie Trotter's

One of Chicago's top gourmet eateries, and one of the nation's best, Charlie Trotter's serves the exquisite and rarefied fare of its eponymous chef. The menu changes daily but expect creations such as venison loin with semolina cake, braised kale, and Niçoise olive *boudin*. Reservations must be made many weeks in advance though a last-minute call often turns up a table due to cancellations *(see p91)*.

2 Alinea

In the space of a few years, Alinea has established itself as one of the world's foremost restaurants. The decor is simple so as not to detract from the textures, aromas, and sensations of its multi-course offerings. Everything is uniquely presented on specially designed dinnerware – for example, the bourbon sweet-potato tempura is served with a stick of cinnamon inside a wire basket *(see p91)*.

Deep Dish Pizza, Pizzeria Uno

3 Gibson's Steakhouse

Boisterous and convivial, Gibson's exudes a good time. A regular crowd of politicians, sports figures, and conventioneers packs the place nightly. The steakhouse fare is in every way a match to the atmosphere – big and bold. Huge lobster tails vie for attention with large slabs of beef. A reservation is critical, but for a more casual, walk-in experience try the burgers next door at Hugo's Frog Bar. ◈ *1028 N. Rush St.* • *Map L2* • *312-266-8999* • *$$$$*

4 Blackbird

Foodies and the fashion set both agree on Blackbird, an eatery that sports minimalist decor and shoves the tables so close together that eavesdropping becomes part of the experience. Chef Paul Kahan generates the buzz, preparing sophisticated American dishes with French leanings. Menus change seasonally, but reservations are perennially a must. ◈ *619 W. Randolph St.* • *Map J4* • *312-715-0708* • *Dinner 5–10:30pm (to 11:30pm Fri & Sat), closed Sun* • *$$$$*

5 North Pond Café

Hidden from the road in leafy Lincoln Park, North Pond is a treasure – once you find it. Lodged in an Arts-and-Crafts-style building, the café offers a seasonal menu with an emphasis on produce sourced in the Midwest. Though dinner is the star, lunches of sandwiches, soups, and salads are equally creative and well presented *(see p91)*.

6 MK

Located in a former paint factory, MK's contemporary cuisine shines in its comfortable yet elegant River North setting. Choose the tasting menu,

Chicago's Top 10

which highlights locally sourced ingredients. Be sure to save enough room for dessert – some of the country's best pastry chefs have called MK home. ⓢ *868 N. Franklin St. • Map L2 • 312-482-9179 • Dinner only • $$$$$*

TRU
Two award-winning chefs, Anthony Martin and Gale Gand, create unique offerings such as truffle freeform lobster with lobster mushrooms and sumptuous chocolate desserts. Everything is served on Austrian crystal and Versace-designed china. Reservations are recommended. ⓢ *676 N. Saint Clair St. • Map L2 • 312-202-0001 • Closed lunch and Sun • $$$$$*

Frontera Grill
Signature restaurant of chef Rick Bayless, Frontera Grill is credited with bringing authentic regional Mexican food – rather than Tex-Mex taco fare – stateside. Chili-roasted salsas and rich *moles* accompany grilled meats and delicious seafood. Since reservations are only available for parties of more than six, seats in the colorful, folk art-filled room go early as smaller groups try to avoid disappointment *(see p83)*.

Pizzeria Uno
Uno's has been baking deep-dish pizza since 1943 – about as long as Chicagoans have debated whose pie is best. Its version comes several inches deep, filled with cheese and toppings of your choice, truly a meal in one slice. The smallish Victorian brownstone strains under demand, sending the overflow up the street to its spin-off Pizzeria Due. Uno's individual pizza served at lunchtime is a bargain. ⓢ *29 E. Ohio St. • Map L3 • 312-321-1000 • $*

Gibson's Steakhouse

Lou Mitchell's
A classic diner in the Loop where the waitresses call you "Honey" and the coffee is bottomless, Lou Mitchell's has been around since 1923. Its trek-worthy meal is breakfast, highlighted by double-yolk eggs and homemade hash browns served in a skillet. Tables turn quickly and the staff doles out free donuts and candy to those waiting in line with good cheer. ⓢ *565 W. Jackson Blvd. • Map J4 • 312-939-3111 • No credit cards • No dinner • $*

Unless otherwise stated, all restaurants accept credit cards, recommend reservations, and are open for lunch and dinner.

Left **Dim Sum at Phoenix** Right **Sushi Bar at Mirai**

🔟 Ethnic Eats

1 Arun's
Distinct from other Thai restaurants in the city, Arun's serves a gourmet version of the spice-and-vegetable driven Asian fare with high quality ingredients and careful presentation. Multi-course fixed-price menus change nightly, and dietary restrictions can be taken into consideration with advance notice. The quiet Thai art-trimmed rooms are conducive to conversation.
◈ 4156 N. Kedzie Ave. • Map B4 • 1-773-539-1909 • Closed Mon, lunch • $$$$$

2 Fogo de Chão
This authentic Brazilian steakhouse, or *churrascaria*, offers more than 15 different cuts of meat, sliced at your table by a gaucho chef – and it keeps coming until you signal "stop". Choose from the gourmet salad bar, *pao de qeijo* (puffed cheese rolls), crispy polenta, or garlic mash for your sides. All you can eat for $50.
◈ 661 N. LaSalle Blvd. • Map K3 • 312-932-9330 • Closed lunch Sat & Sun • $$$$

¡Salpicón!

3 Phoenix
Superior Chinese dim sum, served with a panoramic view of downtown Chicago, garner out-the-door lines for this Chinatown gem. There are more than 50 varieties of dim sum to choose from. ◈ 2131 S. Archer Ave. • Map A6 • 312-328-0848 • $$

4 Mirai Sushi
This hip, two-story eatery carves some of the city's best Japanese sushi. Options include the usual suspects such as tuna and salmon but for the most creative fare sit at the sushi bar, make a special request, and put yourself in the chef's hands. An upstairs lounge serves up sake martinis. ◈ 2020 W. Division St. • Map J1 • 1-773-862-8500 • Closed Sun, lunch • $$$

5 ¡Salpicón!
Colorful decor and a wide-ranging array of wines and tequilas complement the classic and contemporary Mexican fare on offer here. Enjoy dishes such as *pescado al carbón*, a charcoal-grilled fillet of seasonal fish served with a tomato, onion, cilantro, and chile sauce and white rice. ◈ 1252 N. Wells St. • Map K1 • 312-988-7811 • Closed lunch (except for weekend brunch) • $$$

6 Reza's
Mouthwatering Persian cuisine is the star of the show at this Andersonville restaurant that serves top-notch Middle Eastern

food. Kabobs, hummus, *baba ganoush*, and an excellent selection of vegetarian appetizers are all full of flavor. One of the menu highlights is *fessenjan*, chicken simmered in a piquant sauce of crushed walnuts and pomegranate, served with Persian bread. ⊗ *5255 N. Clark St. • Map K2 • 312-664-4500 • $$*

Ann Sather

7 Locals line up on Sunday mornings at the original Belmont Avenue Ann Sather for plates of oversized, sticky cinnamon rolls. But the Swedish diner makes a more ethnic appeal at lunch and dinner with *limpa* (Swedish rye bread), zesty duck with lingonberries, and hearty Swedish meatballs *(see p91)*.

Marigold

8 This Indian restaurant has a modern vibe and the menu reflects multiple regions of India, with vegetarian, seafood and meaty options such as *samosas*, South Indian seafood curry, coriander-crusted halibut with *pakora*-style vegetables, and lamb shank vindaloo. Knowledgeable waiters are on hand to help curry-challenged diners navigate the menu. ⊗ *4832 N. Broadway • Map B3 • 773-293-4653 • Dinner only, closed Mon • $$*

Red Apple

9 In the heart of Polish Avondale, Red Apple offers budget priced, all-you-can-eat buffets, including dessert and coffee. This diner draws a cross-section of immigrants, artists, students, and the just plain thrifty for authentic dishes such as *pierogi*, borscht, goulash, and stuffed cabbage. ⊗ *3121 N. Milwaukee Ave. • Map B4 • 1-773-588-5781 • $*

Ann Sather

Mr. Beef on Orleans

10 Lean over the Formica counter so you don't drip on yourself while savoring spicy Italian beef or Italian sausage on a crunchy roll. Mr. Beef serves the best Italian beef sandwiches in Chicago. Be aware that there are no vegetarian options on offer. A Chicago tradition, Mr. Beef is decorated with photographs of famous customers. ⊗ *666 N. Orleans St. • Map E4 • 312-337-8500 • Closed Sun • No credit cards • $*

Unless otherwise stated, all restaurants accept credit cards, recommend reservations, and are open for lunch and dinner.

Left **Funky Buddha Lounge** Right **Bin 36**

🔟 Bars & Clubs

1 Roof on the Wit
Nestled amid the skyscrapers of the Loop, with spectacular views of the bustling city, the winding "L", the Chicago river, and Lake Michigan, the Wit is a chic complex of lounge-bars. Snuggle by an open fire and take in the ultra-hip ambience and stunning vistas, with a cocktail in hand. 🟡 *201 N. State St. • Map K2 • 312-239-9501 • Closed Sun*

2 Whiskey Sky
Nightlife goes sky-high at this intimate club on the 33rd floor of the W. Chicago Lakeshore hotel *(see p117)*. Locals and guests mingle among '70s retro furnishings while soul and light house music provide the beat (though there's no dancing) to a backdrop of stunning views. 🟡 *644 N. Lake Shore Dr. • Map M3 • 312-255-4463 • Free*

3 Zebra Lounge
An illegal speakeasy during Prohibition, this tiny piano bar has stood the test of time and

Zebra Lounge

competition, packing in loyal revelers nightly. Zebra prints dominate the decor, and martinis are the drink of choice. Singing along with the pianist to show tunes, torch songs, and oldies is expected *(see p83)*.

4 Funky Buddha Lounge
This favorite is easily identified by the fat, happy Buddha statue outside. Inside, a mixed crowd of urban hipsters and young professionals sip everything from beer to bubbly in the low-ceilinged lounge. As the evening unfolds, the dance floor heats up with clubbers grooving to soul, salsa, hip-hop, R&B, house, rap, and reggae. 🟡 *728 W. Grand Ave. • Map K3 • 312-666-1695*

5 Evil Olive
This fashionable bar places a heavy emphasis on interesting drinks, with hand-stuffed olives served in martinis or by the plateful. A DJ spins rock and hip-hop tunes, while pool tables, an old-fashioned jukebox, and a photo booth all add to the ambience. 🟡 *1551 W. Division St. • Map J1 • 1-773-235-9100 • Open 9pm–4am (to 5am Sat), closed Tue & Sun*

6 Privét
Tucked along an alley and down a flight of stairs is the exclusive Privét nightclub. The luxe room is divided by gold-wrapped columns. Velvet chairs are free for lounging early on,

Unless otherwise stated, bars and clubs are open daily, have a cover charge after 9/10pm, and have DA.

Le Bar

9 Beauty Bar

A late-1960s New Jersey beauty parlor was dismantled and transported here to form what the owners call "a luxurious, swanky time capsule of big hair, pink nails and dry martinis." Their specialty Martini & Manicure does exactly what it says, for just $10. There's also everything from edgy DJ sets to burlesque shows and pin-up model classes on offer at this deliciously quirky and original venue. ◈ 1444 W. Chicago Ave. • Map J2 • 312-226-8825 • Free

but later they're reserved for big spenders. The dance floor fills up late, with DJs playing pop remixes. Would-be guests need to dress – and look – the part to get through the door. ◈ 937 N. Rush St. • Map L2 • 312-255-0022 • Closed Sun & Mon

7 Bin 36

This lofty space is a triple pleasure, with its high-end restaurant, casual café, and sociable wine bar. The large, zinc-topped oval bar is a lively setting for couples to share conversation and a cocktail, or for singles to mingle. "Wine flights" are a must-try, offering four half-glasses of different, but related, wines (see p83).

8 Le Bar

In the beautiful Sofitel Hotel (see p115), a fashionable, over-30, mixed crowd fills this lobby lounge after work, lingering until the wee hours. Black-clad servers dispense martinis with scrumptious flavors such as chocolate and raspberry. ◈ 20 E. Chestnut St. • Map K2 • 312-324-4000 • Free

10 J Bar

This sleek, luxurious lounge in The James Hotel offers signature deconstructed cocktails, such as a Ketel One martini with a vermouth and olive lollipop, or the James – made with Stoli Raz, elderflower and lime juice, served in a martini glass coated in a hard, raspberry candy shell. Modern design, low-slung lounge seating, candlelit cocktail tables, and plasma screens with video art all go to set the swanky scene. ◈ 610 N Rush St. • Map L2 • 312-660-7200 • Closed Sun & Mon

Left **Kingston Mines** Right **Green Mill Cocktail Lounge**

🔟 Blues & Jazz Joints

1 Kingston Mines

The largest of Chicago's blues joints, Kingston Mines packs its Lincoln Park locale with students, young professionals, and a broader spectrum of tourists. Two stages provide non-stop musical entertainment from 8pm to near 4am (5am on Saturdays). Acts range from homegrown house bands to national touring headliners. The kitchen serves up beer-sopping barbecue. ⬙ *2548 N. Halsted St. • Map E2 • 1-773-477-4646*

2 Buddy Guy's Legends

A legend himself, bluesman Buddy Guy operates perhaps the best blues club in the city. The South Loop destination draws a mix of students, tourists, and local fans, particularly when Guy himself headlines. The place gets so packed that aisles are marked on the flooring and monitored by bouncers who make sure standing-room-only patrons keep them clear *(see p96).* ⬙ *700 S. Wabash Ave. • Map L5 • 312-427-1190*

3 B.L.U.E.S.

Among Chicago's many blues clubs, B.L.U.E.S feels the most like a Southern juke joint. Chalk it up to the narrow confines, loud sounds, and sweaty dancers. The club is across the street from the popular Kingston Mines, but it's a better choice for older, more musically versed blues fans. Better yet, why not stop into both! ⬙ *2519 N. Halsted St. • Map E2 • 1-773-528-1012*

4 Green Mill Cocktail Lounge

A former Prohibition era speakeasy, Uptown's landmark Green Mill is a vintage treasure with a sweeping curved bar, vinyl booths, fading murals, and an authentic air of Chicago's gangster past. The city's premier jazz talents like Kurt Elling and Patricia Barber regularly play gigs here and Uptown Poetry Slam feature every Sunday. It's out of the way but every cabbie knows how to get there. ⬙ *4802 N. Broadway • Map E2 • 1-773-878-5552 • Limited DA*

5 House of Blues

Folk art and exotic architectural remnants festoon the funky House of Blues. The vast 1500-seat concert hall presents a variety of national touring acts from hard rock to hip-hop in addition to blues. The Sunday gospel brunch with seatings

Andy's Jazz Club

Unless otherwise stated, all venues are open daily, charge admission, and have DA.

from 9:30am to noon is a must.
🔊 329 N. Dearborn St. • Map K3
• 312-923-2000

California Clipper

Home of the Purple Martini, this restored, retro club, with a 40-ft (12-m) wooden bar and red-leather booths, bills itself as "the only bar with grape soda on its gun." Catch local, live country, dance, jazz, and blues from Thursday through Sunday. Monday night is bingo night. See if you can spot "The Woman in White", the Clipper's elegant 1940s ghost. 🔊 1002 N. California Ave. • 1-773-384-2547 • www.californiaclipper.com

Rosa's

Though off the beaten club path, the family-owned Rosa's is beloved citywide for its support of local artists such as blues harpist Sugar Blue and the genuine welcome by its owners, Tony Mangiullo and his mother Rosa. The latter sometimes cooks for the patrons of this simple tavern. 🔊 3420 W. Armitage Ave. • Map E4 • 1-773-342-0452 • Closed Sun & Mon • www.rosaslounge.com

Green Dolphin St.

This slick Northside jazz club offers some of the city's best sightlines. Named for a jazz standard, Green Dolphin encompasses both a separate fine dining restaurant and an equally spacious showroom that also serves casual café fare. On the musical bill expect the sorts of ensembles that can audibly fill the space, such as big bands and Latin groups. 🔊 2200 N. Ashland Ave. • Map D2 • 1-773-395-0066 • Closed Mon • www.jazzitup.com

Blue Chicago

Popular with tourists, Blue Chicago in River North operates two clubs located two blocks

Buddy Guy's Legends

apart. Seats at both venues are few and far between, so come early if you need one, or be prepared to dance. The admission charge covers both clubs, which encourages bar hopping. 🔊 536 N. Clark St. & 736 N. Clark St. • Map K2 • 312-661-0100 • Closed Mon & Sun respectively • www.blueschicago.com

Andy's Jazz Club

With its musical programming that begins at lunchtime and continues into the evening, Andy's fills a void for those jazz fans who can't hold out for the late-night headliners. Prime perches are much sought after at the horseshoe-shaped bar in the no-fuss River North club. 🔊 11 E. Hubbard St. • Map K3 • 312-642-6805

Left **Steppenwolf Theatre Co.** Right **Gene Siskel Film Center**

🔟 Arts Venues

1 Civic Opera House

This imposing Art Deco building is largely devoted to performances by the Lyric Opera. Each year (September through March), the company stages work by everyone from Wagner to Gilbert and Sullivan. Touring classical dance troops and musicals fill the off-season bill.
🅢 *20 N. Wacker Dr.* • *Map I4*
• *www.civicoperahouse.com*

2 Symphony Center

While visiting orchestras, lecturers, and jazz artists feature on its program, this center is first and foremost the home of the Chicago Symphony Orchestra. The complex holds a main stage, recital hall, and a bar-restaurant named Rhapsody *(see p75)*.
🅢 *220 S. Michigan Ave.* • *Map I6*
• *www.cso.org*

3 Steppenwolf Theatre Co.

Founded in 1974 in a church basement, Steppenwolf has gained acclaim based on the fame of its ensemble, which includes actor John Malkovich. Though the company has moved upscale to a specially built theater in Lincoln Park, it is still distinguished by raw emotion and edgy productions. 🅢 *1650 N. Halsted St.* • *Map E2* • *www.steppenwolf.org*

4 Goodman Theatre

One of Chicago's leading theater companies, the Goodman frequently spins off

Court Theatre

productions to Broadway in New York and has earned a Tony award, the theater community's highest, for its efforts. Noted productions include dramas by Eugene O'Neill and August Wilson and an annual version of Charles Dickens' *A Christmas Carol.* 🅢 *170 N. Dearborn St.* • *Map K3*
• *www.goodman-theatre.org*

5 Chicago Shakespeare Theater

This Navy Pier venue presents a dynamic space for Shakespeare's repertory. The 510-seat courtyard design is inspired by the original layout in traditional playhouses of the Bard's day. Visiting non-Shakespeare productions take over after the company's September-to-April season.
🅢 *800 E. Grand Ave.* • *Map L3*
• *www.chicagoshakes.com*

Second City

Since 1959, Chicago's famed Second City comedy troupe has launched such comic lights as John Belushi, Mike Myers, and Bill Murray. Actors improvize their lines in a series of skits connected by a current events theme on the cabaret-style main stage. Reservations are a must.
Ⓢ 1616 N. Wells St. • Map K2
• www.secondcity.com

Court Theatre

This theater traces its roots to three Molière productions performed at the University of Chicago in 1955. The Court still mounts many classics, but it varies its seasons with musicals like Guys and Dolls and literary adaptations such as James Joyce's The Dead. Ⓢ 5535 S. Ellis Ave. • Map E5 • www.courttheatre.org

Old Town School of Folk Music

Since the 1950s the Old Town School has brought world and homegrown folk music performers to Chicago. Its new home in Lincoln Square opened in 1998 with a concert by Joni Mitchell, though you're more likely to catch a women's ensemble from Mali and contemporary folkies such as Patty Larkin. Ⓢ 4544 N. Lincoln Ave. • Map E3
• www.oldtownschool.org

Lookingglass Theatre

In 1988, eight Northwestern University students founded Lookingglass, a bold company incorporating dance, circus arts, and live music in its original theatrical productions. Celebrity

Old Town School of Folk Music

membership (including Friends actor David Schwimmer) and Broadway bound, award-winning shows have furthered this company's stardom. Ⓢ 821 N. Michigan Ave. • Map L2
• www.lookingglasstheatre.org

Gene Siskel Film Center

Tiny by cineplex standards, the Gene Siskel Film Center screens films from the silent era onwards. Cineastes will rave about the cushy rocking chairs, excellent sightlines, and art gallery as well as foreign, independent and experimental films rarely shown elsewhere.
Ⓢ 164 N. State St. • Map K2
• www.siskelfilmcenter.com

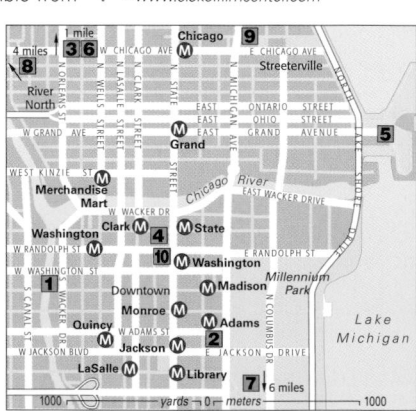

Left **Taste of Chicago** Center **Chicago Jazz Festival** Right **Chicago Gospel Music Festival**

Festivals & Events

Chicago Blues Festival
The raucous weekend-long Blues Festival kicks off summer in Chicago. An estimated 750,000 listeners converge on Grant Park for the world's largest free blues event. The main stage hosts traditional bluesmen like Honey Boy Edwards, jazz interpreters such as Mose Allison, and blues-inflected popsters like Bonnie Raitt. Smaller side stages offer a more intimate experience.
⊗ Map L6 • 312-744-3315 • www.chicago bluesfestival.org • Late May–early Jun

Chicago Summer Neighborhood Festivals
Chicago is a city of neighborhoods with upwards of 100 neighborhood festivals to prove it. Virtually every summer weekend features an event or three ranging from the gay oriented North Halsted Market Days to the ethnic Korean Street Festival. ⊗ 312-744-3315
• www.explorechicago.org • May–Sep

Neighborhood festival in Chinatown

Chicago Gospel Music Festival
For three days Grant Park resounds with stirring choirs and impassioned soloists. Headliners have included R&B-star-turned-Memphis-preacher Al Green.
⊗ Map L6 • 312-744-3315 • www. explorechicago.org • Early Jun

Old Town Art Fair
This 50-year-old fair installs 250 artist booths along Old Town's historic and leafy lanes. There are also food vendors, kids' entertainment, and garden tours. ⊗ 1763 N. Park Ave. • Off Map • 312-337-1938
• www.oldtownartfair.org • Jun • Adm

Ravinia Festival
The summer home of the Chicago Symphony Orchestra, Ravinia stages concerts (classical, jazz, and pop) in suburban Highland Park. Sheltered seats are available but it's more fun to pack a picnic and join the crowds on the lawn. ⊗ Off Map • 1-847-266-5100 • www.ravinia.org • Jun–Sep • Adm

Taste of Chicago
Chicago's signature foods including deep dish pizza star during the nearly two week-long Taste. Musical entertainers, a carnival with rides, and cooking demonstrations entertain at the sprawling Grant Park event. ⊗ Map L6 • 312-744-3315 • Late Jun–early Jul

World Music Festival
This city-wide, multi-venue, week-long festival showcases

Unless otherwise indicated all festivals and events are free and have DA.

Chicago Air & Water Show

the very best of traditional and contemporary international music. Concerts are low-cost or even free. ◎ *312-744-3315* • *www.world musicfestivalchicago.org* • *mid-Sep*

Chicago Air & Water Show
This massive display of military power features historic aircraft flybys, a staged amphibious attack, and precision flying teams. Prime beachfront viewing spots are from Oak Street to Montrose Beach. ◎ *312-744-3315* • *Mid-Aug*

Chicago Jazz Festival
Just as the Blues Fest ushers in summer, the smaller Jazz Fest caps it. Music fans are drawn to Grant Park for free concerts by greats like Branford Marsalis and Roy Hargrove. ◎ *Map L6* • *312-744-3315* • *www.explorechicago.org* • *Late Aug/early Sep (inc. Labor Day weekend)*

Magnificent Mile Holiday Lights Festival
Merchants mark the start of the holiday season by lighting the shops, lampposts, and trees along Michigan Avenue. The parade and fireworks above the Chicago River on the Saturday night before Thanksgiving warrant braving the inevitable chill.
◎ *Map L2* • *Mid-Nov–end Dec*

Top 10 Sports Teams & Events

Chicago Cubs
Despite the Cubbies' losing streak, their baseball games are often sell-outs *(see p85)*.

Chicago White Sox
The White Sox are renowned for their top-quality baseball. ◎ *312-674-1000* • *www.whitesox.com* • *Apr–Sep*

Chicago Bears
A football team generating rabid fans and tailgate picnics on Soldier Field *(see p12)*. ◎ Ticketmaster *800-745-3000* • *www.chicagobears.com* • *Sep–Dec*

Chicago Bulls
Their basketball just hasn't been the same since superstar Michael Jordan left. ◎ *312-455-4000* • *www.bulls.com* • *Oct–Apr*

Chicago Blackhawks
NHL ice hockey team sharing the United Center *(see p13)* with the Bulls. ◎ *312-455-7000* • *www.chicagoblackhawks.com* • *Oct–Apr*

Arlington Park
Thoroughbreds race just north of Chicago. ◎ *1-847-385-7500* • *www.arlingtonpark.com* • *May–Sep*

Chicago Fire
Many local Latino soccer fans support the Fire. ◎ *1-888-657-3473* • *www.chicago-fire.com* • *Apr–Oct*

Chicago Wolves
Four-time league champions offer a great evening of hockey. ◎ *1-800-843-9658* • *www.chicagowolves.com* • *Oct–May*

Chicago Marathon
40,000 entrants run through the city. ◎ *312-904-9800* • *www.chicagomarathon.com* • *Oct*

Chicago Triathlon
Over 6,000 run, bike, and swim in this one-dayer. ◎ *www.chicagotriathlon.com* • *Aug*

Left **Mi Barrio Taqueria, Pilsen** Right **Mural, Lincoln Square**

Ethnic Neighborhoods

Pilsen

Named after a city in the former Czech Republic, whose immigrants settled here in the mid-1800s, this neighborhood now claims the Midwest's largest Mexican community. It's anchored by the National Museum of Mexican Art *(see p38)* and animated by street vendors, mariachi music, and Mexican restaurants. Vibrant outdoor murals and mosaics portray Mexican culture and history. ✪ *Map B5*

Avondale

In the early 20th century, menial jobs at Avondale's local factories and brickyards attracted many hard-working Polish immigrants. Today, the area also has many Hispanics, but it's still known as Little Warsaw because Chicago holds the largest concentration of Poles outside the Polish capital. Milwaukee Avenue and the neighboring streets also abound with bakeries, bookstores, delis, and a Polish Museum. ✪ *Map B4*

Building detail in Chinatown

Devon Avenue

Chicagoans who crave cheap, authentic Indian food head north to Devon Avenue in Rogers Park. Nineteenth-century English settlers named it after Devonshire, but since the 1960s, it's been a thriving Indian community, mingled with Russian, Greek, Syrian, and Jewish enclaves. From colorful saris to Indian videos to savory curried meats, it's almost like being in Delhi. ✪ *Map B3*

Andersonville

Amid a mix of Middle-Eastern and Asian cultures, the late-19th century Swedish heritage here still makes its presence felt with billowing yellow and blue flags, Swedish bakeries and shops, and the Swedish-American Museum *(see p38)*. Adding to the minority mix is an increasing gay population – more laid-back than Boys Town *(see p85)* – evident in a number of trendy, gay-owned restaurants. ✪ *Map B3*

Little Italy, Taylor Street

The rich smells of garlic, basil, and baking bread waft from restaurants that line one of Chicago's oldest southern Italian neighborhoods. Though the streets have fewer Italians than when immigrants arrived in the late 19th century, you'll still see Italians chatting on street corners and toting groceries from Italian markets. ✪ *Map G6*

Heart of Italy

Northern Italians settled here in the 1920s, and some Chicagoans argue that this west side neighborhood is actually

For Ethnic Eats **See pp42–3**

Little Italy

Lincoln Square

Beer, bratwursts, and grainy rye breads are order of the day in this bustling German enclave, where a 96-ft (29-m) outdoor mural depicts a rural German village. The hub of activity is a relatively small strip of Lincoln Avenue, between Lawrence and Western Avenues. The area maintains Old World charm with its German shops, delicatessens, bakeries, and an old-fashioned apothecary. ◎ *Map B3*

the real Little Italy. It has a handful of authentic Italian restaurants and delis, as well as the "Festa Pasta Vino" festival, held over Father's Day weekend every June. ◎ *Map B5*

Chinatown

An ornate arched gateway at Wentworth Avenue signals your entrance to this distinctly Chinese neighborhood. Asians and non-Asians alike flock to aroma-filled dim-sum restaurants that serve a mouthwatering selection of dumplings, duck, egg rolls, and other delicacies. Shops sell everything from lanterns to delicate tea sets and mysterious Chinese herbs *(see p94)*.

Uptown

The eclectic Uptown neighborhood is nicknamed the United Nations for its ethnic diversity. Along Argyle Street, it's called Little Saigon for its predominantly Vietnamese flavor. Inexpensive restaurants serve thinly sliced beef, tangy soups, and shrimp crêpes. Though it can sometimes feel rather seedy, Uptown is always a fascinating area to explore. ◎ *Map B3*

Bridgeport

First called Hardscrabble, this South Side neighborhood is one of the city's oldest, being settled in the 1830s by Irish laborers who came to help build the Illinois-Michigan Canal. Bridgeport still has a mostly Irish population, and has bred five Chicago mayors, including Richard J. Daley *(see p35)* and his son, Richard M. Daley. The area centerpiece is US Cellular Field (formerly Comiskey Park), home ground of the Chicago White Sox *(see p51)*. ◎ *Map B5*

Next Pages **Mexican Mural, Pilsen**

Left **Museum of Science & Industry** Right **Visitors viewing animals, Lincoln Park Zoo**

Kids' Chicago

Chicago Children's Museum

The engrossing, imaginative exhibits here emphasize doing – be it digging up a dinosaur bone or designing a water channel. A central, three-story rope tunnel immediately snares the attention of older visitors, though there are age-appropriate attractions for infants to pre-teens. If this place can't exhaust the younger set's energies, nowhere can. 🅢 *700 E. Grand Ave. • Map L3 • 312-527-1000 • Open 10am–5pm Tue–Sun (to 8pm Thu, Sat) • www.chichildrensmuseum.org • Adm*

Lincoln Park Zoo

Free admission encourages repeat visits to the Lincoln Park Zoo *(see pp24–5)*. Many exhibits, including the working Farm in the Zoo and the Children's Zoo, allow kids to pet the animals. In summer a motorized "train" makes a scenic loop around the park, while on the pond, swan-shaped paddleboats float among the ducks.

Navy Pier

Kids make a beeline for Navy Pier's old-fashioned carnival rides including a 10-story Ferris Wheel and musical carousel. The ships that line the docks, from sleek, tall-masted schooners to powerful motor boats will also grab their attention. All the restaurants here are family friendly, and even the sculptures

that line the Pier in summer are designed to withstand climbers *(see pp20–21)*.

Elevated Trains

Chicago's elevated trains (the "L") provide an inexpensive roofline tour of the city. The Brown Line in particular warrants riding en famille from Chicago Station south over the Chicago River and around the Loop, threading between the massive buildings of the financial district. Sit in the first row of the front car for an exciting view of the city ahead of you *(see p108)*.

Shedd Aquarium

Upon arrival, head straight for the Oceanarium to watch the thrilling dolphin and beluga whale show. Staff trainers frequently choose children in the audience to help them reward the marine mammals with a snack after each trick. At the daily Tide Pool Touch and reptilian Animal Encounters kids can indulge their urge to lay hands on the critters *(see pp22–3)*.

Shedd Aquarium

Westfield North Bridge Mall

Level 3 of this tony Michigan Avenue mall is primarily devoted to children's retailers including funky kids' designerwear boutique Kooky Kidstuff, the LEGO store, and Hello Kitty! specialist, Sanrio.

Unless otherwise stated, all attractions have Disabled Access.

Across the hall from the LEGO store, the LEGO Construction Zone sets out bricks for play. The fourth floor food court sells kid-favored foods like hot dogs and pizza.
⊗ 520 N. Michigan Ave. • Map L2 • Open 10am–8pm Mon–Sat, 11am–7pm Sun • www.the shopsatnorthbridge.com

Navy Pier

7 Emerald City Theatre Company

In Chicago there's a theater company for every demographic and Emerald City is its troupe devoted to young audiences. Expect lively productions such as *Where the Wild Things Are* as well as holiday season shows in weekend-only midday matinees at Lincoln Park's Apollo Theater.
⊗ 2540 N. Lincoln Ave. • Map E3 • 773-935-6100 • Open Oct–May • www.emeraldcitytheatre.com • Adm

8 Museum Of Science & Industry

Though this museum dazzles kids and adults alike with its submarine ship and replica coal mine, it's The Idea Factory that's designed just for Junior. With the pulling of gears and shifting of knobs, kids experiment through play with balance, construction, magnetism, and more. A current-fed waterway encourages boat building. Arrive early on weekends or expect to have to wait for access *(see pp16–19)*.

9 Wrigley Field

A baseball lover's park, Wrigley is a small and intimate stadium that's far less intimidating for children than many larger stadia *(see p85)*. A ticket to anywhere in the grandstand allows you to walk around and get to the rooftop terrace with its great views: the outfield stands can get rowdy, but a neighboring family section bans the beer that fuels the "bleacher bums."

10 The Café at American Girl Place

Vendor of dolls with educational aims, American Girl Place feeds its fantasy world, literally, in a café where dolls are welcome in clip-to-the-table chairs. Lunch leans to simple crowd-pleasers like tomato soup, while dinner supplies standards like chicken potpie. In between, the imaginative tea proffers chocolate pudding in a flowerpot or heart-shaped sandwiches. Reservations recommended *(see p82)*.

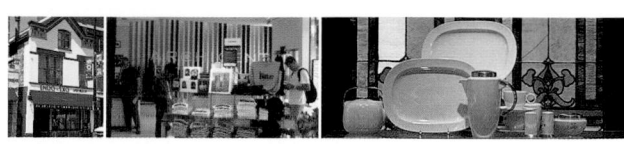

Left **Endo Exo, Armitage Avenue** Center **CAF Shop** Right **Bloomingdale's Home Store**

🔟 Shopping Destinations

1 State Street
A slew of chain stores line this legendary street *(see p70)*, but it's the two old-time department stores that make it unique. The former Marshall Field's, now Macy's *(see p74)*, here since 1907, has merchandise to satisfy every wealthy woman's needs. At Filene's Basement the prices are lower, but the variety is still extensive *(see p74)*.

2 Magnificent Mile
Some 450 stores make this stretch of North Michigan Avenue one of the world's retail meccas. Besides sophisticated designer boutiques, there are malls (each with high-end department stores); and big-name chain and flagship stores *(see pp26–7)*.

3 Oak Street
If you have to ask how much it costs, you should probably plan on just window-shopping along

Magnificent Mile

this stretch of Chicago's upper-crust Gold Coast. Boutiques here sell designer wear, accessories, and shoes fit for a Paris runway – and include some shops exclusive to Chicago such as Tessuti (menswear) and Designs by Ming (custom clothing design). ◈ *Borders: N. Michigan Ave. & Rush St.* • *Map L1*

4 Jeweler's Row
This small strip in the Loop boasts a large number of jewelers that sell everything from discount diamonds to top-of-the-range gems. The Jeweler's Center at the beautiful 1912 Mallers Building *(see p74)* packs about 50 wholesale and retail jewelers and appraisers into 13 floors.

5 Bucktown Neighborhood
Once a hot-spot for starving artists, Bucktown and adjacent Wicker Park are now gentrified locales brimming with vintage clothes stores, edgy music shops, high-style designer boutiques, and antiques importers. ◈ *Borders: Fullerton Ave. to Division Ave. & Kennedy Expressway to Western Ave.* • *Map B4*

6 Broadway Antique Market
An old-time movie palace marquee indicates the 1939 building that houses this market. With 85 dealers stocking artwork, jewelry, clothing, and more in styles such as Arts and Crafts, Art Deco, and Victorian, you're sure to find something that pleases. ◈ *6130 N. Broadway* • *Map E2* • *Open 11am–7pm, Mon–Sat, 11am–6pm Sun* • *DA*

7 Shop at the Cultural Center

This eclectic shop specializes in merchandise that celebrates Chicago's diverse arts and cultural scene. Just outside is the Art-O-Matic, a recycled cigarette vending machine that now sells original artworks for $5 a pull. ⚜ *78 E. Washington St. • Map L4 • Open 10am–5pm Mon–Sat • DA*

8 CAF Shop

The CAF (Chicago Architecture Foundation) Shop, located in the historic Santa Fe Center *(see p72)*, is part of the CAF's ArchiCenter, which also puts on exhibitions and runs city tours. Browse the shop for architecture and design-related books; art-glass panels and lamps in Frank Lloyd Wright designs; desk gadgets; and desirable kitchen gizmos. ⚜ *224 S. Michigan Ave. • Map L6 • Open 9:30am–6pm daily • DA*

9 Bloomingdale's Home & Furniture Store

This store's lovingly restored 1913 Moorish-style building is an attraction in its own right. Inside there's a sleek, four-level atrium with home decor departments that sell everything from high-thread-count bedding to chic cookware and top-quality furniture. ⚜ *600 N. Wabash Ave. • Map K3 • Opening times vary • DA*

10 Armitage Avenue

This tree-lined street in Lincoln Park *(see p85)* is a favorite for those who are seeking out-of-the-ordinary clothing, home decor, bath and body products – and don't mind spending more to get it. Have patience finding a parking spot on weekends; once you're in, just shop-hop from one adorable boutique to the next.

Top 10 Souvenirs

1 Frango Mints
Marshall Field's/Macy's *(see p74)* doesn't make these melt-away mint chocolates anymore, but still sells them by the box-full.

2 Blues & Jazz CDs
CDs by Chicago music legends are on sale at the Water Tower Visitor Information Center *(see p109)*.

3 Cows on Parade
Mini versions of the highly decorated cows from 1999s "Cows on Parade" display are sold at the CAF Shop.

4 Art poster
See the real thing, then buy a copy at the extensive Art Institute gift shop *(see p8)*.

5 Michael Jordan Jersey
No longer a Bull, but he's still a star. Buy Jordan's merchandise at United Center's *(see p13)* Fandemonium store.

6 Cubs baseball cap
Head to the Tribune Tower *(see p27)* gift shop for caps of the Major League team owned by the *Chicago Tribune*.

7 Art glass
Get a little Prairie style with a replica Frank Lloyd Wright art-glass panel from the Chicago Architecture Foundation store.

8 Chicago mugs
The Chicago History Museum *(see p86)* sells mugs depicting the faces of famous local residents like Al Capone.

9 Sue skeleton
Sue, the world's largest *T. rex* skeleton is far less menacing in mini model form from the Field Museum *(see p14)*.

10 Chicago snowglobe
Recall Chicago winters with a city skyline snowglobe from Accent Chicago in the Water Tower Place mall *(see p26)*.

Left **Scene from *The Relic*, set at the Field Museum** Right **Andy Garcia in *Hero*, Drake Hotel**

Film Locations

1 Daley Center & Plaza

Daley Plaza *(see p73)* with its famed Picasso sculpture was the setting for a sensational chase scene in cult movie classic *The Blues Brothers* (1980). Stars John Belushi and Dan Aykroyd, playing ex-criminal brothers, dramatically crash their car through the center's plate-glass windows, specially installed for the filming, as the authorities hopelessly attempt to stop them.

2 James R. Thompson Center

In *Running Scared* (1986) Billy Crystal and Gregory Hines are Chicago police pals planning early retirement, but first they must thwart a drug kingpin and stay alive. The final chase scene takes place in the Thompson Center *(see p37)* where the two swap wisecracks while swinging on ropes through the airy atrium, shooting out glass elevators, and ultimately triumphing.

3 The Art Institute of Chicago

The consummate high school comedy *Ferris Bueller's Day Off* (1986) stars Matthew Broderick,

While You Were Sleeping at the Randolph "L" Station

Exterior of State of Illinois Center as featured in *Running Scared*

who skips school and takes his girlfriend (Mia Sara) and best friend (Paul Ruck) on an action-packed Chicago day. At the Art Institute, Broderick and Sara kiss in front of a window designed by Chagall, while Ruck stares intensely at *A Sunday on La Grande Jatte –1884 (see p8)*.

4 Union Station

Elliott Ness (Kevin Costner) brings down Chicago gangster Al Capone (Robert DeNiro) in the true story *The Untouchables* (1987). In one unforgettable scene, a shoot-out on a Union Station staircase causes a mother to lose her grip on her baby carriage, which bounces in slow motion down the stairs, saved at the last moment by Ness's partner.
⟨⟩ *210 S. Canal St. • Map J5*

5 Drake Hotel

In feel-good film *Hero* (1992) John Bubber (Andy Garcia) dupes the public into thinking he's a hero. Feeling

Chicago's Top 10

guilty, he resolves to jump off a window ledge at The Drake *(see p115)*. Reality interrupted the filming when guests arrived for a party at the hotel. Director Stephen Frears protested so violently, he almost got arrested.

A scene from *Chain Reaction* on Michigan Avenue Bridge

The Hilton Chicago

Wrongly accused and convicted of murder, Dr. Richard Kimble (Harrison Ford) dodges the authorities led by Tommy Lee Jones to prove his innocence in *The Fugitive* (1993). He winds up in a pulse-pounding chase through this grand hotel *(see p116)* onto its roof, down its elevator shaft, and into the hotel's laundry room.

Randolph "L" Station

The "L" tracks are an apt symbol of hard-working Chicago, and they feature significantly in the romantic comedy *While You Were Sleeping* (1995). Sandra Bullock plays an "L" station clerk who falls in love with a handsome commuter. He tumbles off the platform, Bullock saves his life, and comedy and romance ensue. ◈ *Map L4*

Field Museum

Scare-fest *The Relic* (1997) starred Penelope Ann Miller and Tom Sizemore as researchers trying to stop a murderous monster before it killed again. Many interior scenes were shot on replica sets but were near-perfect matches to the real museum *(see pp14–15)*.

Michigan Avenue Bridge

Chain Reaction (1996) sees Keanu Reeves as a science student at the University of Chicago *(see pp28–9)* who is framed for murder. In a nail-biting chase scene, he tries to escape by running up the Michigan Avenue Bridge *(see p27)* as it's raised.

Wrigley Building

In *Road to Perdition* (2002) Tom Hanks is Michael Sullivan, an Irish gangster living in 1930s Chicago. After his wife and young son are murdered, he flees town with his older son. In seeking a safe refuge, they enter a hotel, the exterior of which is the beautiful Wrigley Building *(see p27)*. However, the interior scenes were actually filmed at The Hilton Chicago.

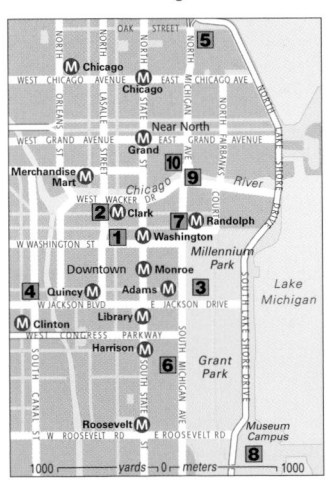

Left **Blues Festival, Grant Park** Right **Gold Coast seen from Oak Street Beach**

Parks & Beaches

Millennium & Grant parks

As well as a center for world-class art, music, architecture and landscape design, the 24-acre (10-ha) Millennium Park offers winter ice skating, interactive public art, al fresco dining and free classical music concerts. Together with the adjoining 19th century Grant Park, which hosts many of the city's varied and vibrant festivals *(see pp50–51)*, it constitutes one of the finest, user-friendly green spaces in Chicago *(see p71)*.

Lincoln Park

The greenway Lincoln Park stretches from North Avenue up to Hollywood Avenue, a recreational apron between lakefront and housing. In Chicago's infancy, the southern portion of the park was a cemetery for Civil War dead, later exhumed and interred elsewhere to make way for the park. Now it's the North Side's counterpart to Grant Park. Popular attractions such as Lincoln Park Zoo *(see pp24–5)*, the Lincoln Park Conservatory *(see p86)*, and Peggy Notebaert Nature Museum *(see p85)* supplement the beaches, harbors, playing fields, and bike paths. ⊛ Map F3

The Republic, Jackson Park

North Avenue Beach

Chicago's most populist beach, North Avenue Beach attracts a broad range of urban-dwellers. Its lively ocean-liner-shaped bathhouse (which includes umbrella rentals, shower rooms, snack vendors, and a rooftop restaurant) makes it particularly family friendly. Rows of beach volleyball courts draw teams often made up of impromptu players, and a seasonal outdoor gym welcomes day use *(see p86)*.

Oak Street Beach

At the foot of the tony Gold Coast shopping lane, Oak Street Beach reflects its environs. Though just next to North Avenue Beach, you won't see many children here. With its emphasis on flesh and flash, Oak Street is usually filled with toned bodies and tiny bikinis. Still, the crescent-shaped strand is the closest beach to the Magnificent Mile *(see pp26–7)* and makes a great place to stop and dip your toes after some serious shopping. ⊛ Map L1

Jackson Park

Laid out by the famed landscape designer Frederick Law Olmsted for the 1893 World's Columbian Exposition, Jackson Park, along with its Museum of Science & Industry *(see pp16–19)*, is among the few developments still remaining from that World's Fair. The Southside park includes a Japanese garden with waterfalls,

 All city beaches have lifeguards on patrol 9am–9:30pm, Memorial Day–Labor Day.

Bathhouse, North Avenue Beach

colorful lanterns, and a bird sanctuary on an island in a peaceful lagoon. ◈ *Map F6*

Burnham Park

Designed by and named for city planner Daniel Burnham, Burnham Park is the city's green lawn rolling south from Museum Campus *(see p92)* to Hyde Park. Like Lincoln and Grant parks, it is charted by the lakefront bike path, but unlike its northern counterparts Burnham Park's section isn't overrun, making this south-leg journey far more enjoyable. Along the way you'll find basketball courts and beaches. The return trip north provides city skyline panoramas. ◈ *Map C6*

Montrose Beach

Stretching nearly to Wilson Avenue, Montrose is spacious where downtown beaches are jammed. Convenient for swimmers, this North Side spot includes a changing house and shower facilities. The vast playing fields wedged between the sand and Lake Shore Drive are the domain of Hispanic soccer clubs: on weekends their numbers draw Latin food and balloon vendors. Look for kayak rentals that launch here in summer. ◈ *Map C3*

Foster Beach

Near the northern end of the lakefront bike path, Foster Beach proves a timely spot to cool off. There's a snack bar, and the nearby picnic tables and grills draw family crowds. A beachside basketball court hosts lively free-for-all games to which only the talented should apply. ◈ *Map B3*

Olive Park

A pocket-sized park just beside Navy Pier *(see pp20–21)*, Olive Park makes great strolling grounds. Jutting into Lake Michigan just off Ohio Street, it provides skyline views similar to Navy Pier's though without the tourist mobs. Quiet and out of the way, this is one of the city's most romantic parks. ◈ *Map M2*

Washington Square

Opposite the historic Newberry Library, Washington Square is a prime plot of Gold Coast for resting tired feet and gazing at the handsome 1892 building. The park's ample benches tend to draw bookish sorts and picnicking office workers at lunchtime. ◈ *Map K2*

For information on bike rental **See p108**

Chicago's Top 10

Left **Chicago Botanic Garden** Center **Church window, Historic Pullman District** Right **IIT**

🔟 Sights off the Beaten Track

1 Garfield Park Conservatory

Beneath glass-domed roofs, flora from around the world thrives in spacious greenhouses. Information panels give the lowdown as you stroll through six indoor areas that include a Children's Garden and the Sweet House (containing plants such as cacao and sugar cane). ⊛ *300 N. Central Park Ave.* • *Map B5* • *312-746-5100* • *www.garfield-conservatory.org* • *"L" station: Conservatory-Central Park Dr. (green line)* • *Open 9am–5pm daily (to 8pm Thu)* • *Free* • *DA*

2 Chicago Botanic Garden

About 25 miles (40 km) north of Chicago, you can find 385 acres (155 ha) of natural habitats and beautifully landscaped gardens. Some of the most popular are the romantic Rose Garden, the tranquil Japanese Garden, and the charming English Walled Garden. ⊛ *1000 Lake Cook Rd., Glencoe* • *Map A1* • *1-847-835-5440* • *www.chicago-botanic.org* • *Metra station: Glencoe* • *Open 8am–sunset daily* • *Adm* • *DA*

Grosse Point Lighthouse, Evanston

3 Historic Pullman District

This industrial town was conceived in the 1880s by railroad magnate George Pullman for his workers. The planned utopia had apartments, shops, a hospital, and a hotel, but failed after a strike in 1894, when a decrease in wages made rents unaffordable. ⊛ *Map C6* • *Metra Station: Pullman/111th St.* • *Visitor Center: 11141 S. Cottage Grove Ave., open 11am–3pm Tue–Sun* • *1-773-785-8901* • *DA*

4 Illinois Institute of Technology (IIT)

In 1940, Ludwig Mies van der Rohe planned the campus of this new university. He also designed around 20 of the buildings, which demonstrate his design philosophies. Stop by the on-campus visitor center for information and docent- or iPod-guided tours. ⊛ *3201 S. State St. (Visitor Center)* • *Map C5* • *312-567-7146* • *"L" station: 35th-Bronzeville-IIT (green line)* • *Tours $10* • *DA*

5 Sheridan Road

This lakefront road's low speed limit is perfect for gawping at the palatial, architecturally diverse homes that line it as you drive north to Evanston and beyond. Art buffs might like to stop at the Evanston Art Center at Harley Clarke House – one of the oldest and largest community visual art centers in Illinois. ⊛ *From Rogers Park to Lake Bluff* • *Map B2* • *Evanston Art Center, 2603 N. Sheridan Rd., 847-475-5300, open 10am–10pm Mon–Thu, 10am–4pm Fri & Sat, 1–4pm Sun, Free*

Bronzeville

A bronze memorial at Martin Luther King, Jr. Drive and 35th Street honors the journey many African-Americans made to this neighborhood as they fled the oppression of the South in the early 20th century. Nearby, sidewalk plaques celebrate local luminaries. Chicago's answer to Harlem offers jazz and blues in its clubs, graceful mansions aplenty, and lots of fine soul food. ◎ *Map C5* • *"L" station: 35th-Bronzeville-IIT (green line)*

Baha'i Temple

This exquisite white structure is one of eight temples of the Baha'i faith worldwide. Its nine doors symbolize how people can come to God from any direction. At night, spotlights enhance its ethereal beauty. ◎ *100 Linden Ave., Wilmette* • *Map A1* • *"L" station: Linden Ave.* • *Visitors' Center open 10am–5pm daily; Temple open 6am–10pm daily* • *1-847-853-2300* • *Free* • *DA*

Historic Long Grove

Thanks to strict regulations, the 19th-century heritage of this quaint town 30 miles (48 km) northwest of Chicago has been preserved. The candy-filled Long Grove Confectionery store is a local institution. Annual events include the popular Chocolate Festival. ◎ *Off Map* • *At Route 83 & Old Route 53* • *Visitor Center: 1-847-634-0888* • *Open Mon–Sat 10am–5pm, 11am–5pm Sun*

Brookfield Zoo

Over 5,900 animals live together in themed, naturalistic environments at this popular zoo. Zones include Tropic World, where thunderstorms occur regularly (you stay dry) and Habitat Africa, whose Forest exhibit has shy okapi and a re-created African village. In Be A Bird House, see

Baha'i Temple

what kind of bird you'd be on a machine that measures your flapping ability. ◎ *3300 Golf Rd., Brookfield* • *Map A5* • *Metra station: Hollywood* • *Open 10am–5pm daily* • *1-708-688-8000* • *Adm (2 and under, free)* • *DA*

Evanston

Just north of Chicago, this dynamic suburb brims with acclaimed restaurants, galleries, and independent shops. Northwestern University's Mary and Leigh Block Museum of Art and Sculpture Garden is well worth a visit, as is the historic Grosse Point Lighthouse and Maritime Museum. ◎ *Map B2* • *Visitors Bureau 1-847-866-6319* • *"L" station: Davis*

AROUND TOWN

CHICAGO'S TOP 10

Left **Harold Washington Library Center** Right **Elevated train, The Loop**

The Loop

NAMED AFTER THE RING OF ELEVATED TRAIN TRACKS *that encircle it, this is downtown Chicago's core, and the city's financial and governmental hub. Abuzz with laptop-toting business folk during the week, the Loop is transformed on weekends when a veritable shopping frenzy erupts along its famous State Street. Those thirsty for culture also come flocking to view the area's many architecturally significant buildings and notable public art. An infusion of corporate dollars has given the Loop a real boost: the resulting restoration of old theaters and the promotion of the theater district has lured in more visitors, and the many great bars and restaurants that have sprung up mean that the area now offers a burgeoning nightlife.*

Lion, Art Institute of Chicago

🔟 Sights

1. Art Institute of Chicago
2. Willis Tower
3. Chicago Cultural Center
4. The "L"
5. Harold Washington Library Center
6. Chicago Board of Trade
7. State Street
8. State of Illinois Center
9. The Rookery
10. Millennium & Grant parks

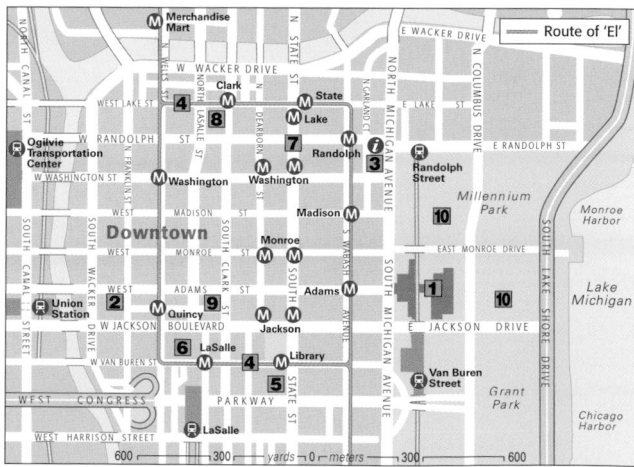

The Art Institute of Chicago
1 This extraordinary collection of exhibits spans over 4,000 years of international art, much of it donated by wealthy Chicago collectors *(see pp8–11)*.

Willis Tower
2 An architectural superlative, the tower offers breathtaking bird's-eye views from its 103rd floor Skydeck, where you'll find yourself standing on top of 76,000 tons of steel *(see pp12–13)*.

Chicago Cultural Center
3 Built in 1897 as the city's first main library, this magnificent Beaux Arts building was described at the time as the "people's palace." In 1991, the library moved out, allowing several galleries, performance spaces and a visitor information center to move in. Guided tours offer a historical overview of the building, which occupies an entire block and features one of the world's largest domes, designed by L. C. Tiffany, and rooms modeled after the Doge's Palace in Venice and the Acropolis in Athens. ◈ *78 E. Washington St. • Map L4 • 312-744-2400 • Open 8am–7pm Mon–Thu, 8am–6pm Fri, 9am–6pm Sat, 10am–6pm Sun • Tours 1:15pm Wed, Fri & Sat • Free • DA • www.chicagoculturalcenter.org*

The "L"
4 Originally called the Union Loop, this system of elevated trains came about after the 1871 Great Chicago Fire *(see p34)* when the city was rebuilt with such unexpected success that, within 20 years, its streets could no longer handle the influx of people, streetcars, and horses filling them. Today, four lines ring the business district – the

Tiffany Dome, Chicago Cultural Center

Orange, Purple, Pink, and Brown lines – with three others connecting it to destinations farther afield *(see p56)*.

Harold Washington Library Center
5 Named after former city Mayor Harold Washington, Chicago's first Afro-American mayor *(see p35)*, this is the largest public library building in the country. Its collections, which include a superlative Blues Archive and a vast children's library, fill an incredible 70 miles (110 km) of shelving. Architects Hammond, Beeby, and Babka incorporated architectural elements of several Chicago landmarks, such as The Rookery *(see p70)* and The Art Institute *(see pp8–9)* in the building's design: don't miss the ninth-floor Winter Garden atrium, which soars two stories to a spectacular glass dome. ◈ *400 S. State St. • Map K5 • Open 9am–9pm Mon–Thu, 9am–5pm Fri & Sat, 1–5pm Sun • Free • DA*

Willis Tower

  Borrow piano sheet music at the Harold Washington Library and tickle the ivories in one of the six free-to-use practice rooms.

Chicago Board of Trade

6 The Chicago Board of Trade (CBOT) was founded in 1848 to create a central marketplace in the fast-developing city, and moved to its current 45-story home in 1930. Designed by Holabird and Root, this landmark building is a stunning example of Art Deco. Capping the majestic limestone building is a huge statue of Ceres, the Roman goddess of grain and harvest. A glittering 23-story glass-and-steel addition designed by Helmut Jahn was completed in 1980. ◎ *141 W. Jackson Blvd. • Map K4 • Closed to the public until further notice*

State Street

7 This "great street" got its nickname from the 1922 hit song Chicago. Although it didn't always live up to this catchy moniker, it has won back many fans since its multi-million-dollar face-lift in 1996. It now sports replica Art Deco lampposts and subway entrances, and was listed on the National Register of Historic Places in 1998. This dynamic stretch has it all: shopping, history, education, architecture, theater, and dining. The atmosphere is especially merry during the run up to Christmas, when the Thanksgiving parade brings Santa to town, and department stores like Macy's

(see p74) fill their windows with elaborate and imaginative decorations. ◎ *From Wacker Dr. to Congress Parkway • Map K4*

The Loop's Sculpture

Setting a trend for public artwork Downtown, Pablo Picasso's untitled sculpture, simply known as "the Picasso," was donated to Chicago in 1967. The Loop's street corners now accommodate more than 100 sculptures, mosaics, and murals by both established and upcoming artists. A guide to the open-air artworks – the *Loop Sculpture Guide* – is available from the Chicago Cultural Center *(see p68)*.

James R. Thompson Center

8 Also known as the State of Illinois Center, this striking 17-story, steel and granite structure shimmers with 24,600 curved glass panels. Helmut Jahn designed the controversial 1985 building to be a democratic fusion of government offices and public spaces, such as shops, restaurants, and art galleries. The soaring skylit atrium is sliced by internal glass elevator shafts and contains unusual, see-through escalators. Outside, the plaza features the intriguing 1984 sculpture *Monument with Standing Beast* by Jean Dubuffet. ◎ *100 W. Randolph St. • Map K4 • Atrium, shops, & food court open to public: 8:30am–6pm Mon–Fri • Free • DA*

The Rookery

9 This 11-story building, with its rusticated red granite base, was the country's largest office building and a precursor to modern skyscrapers when it was completed in 1888 by Burnham and Root *(see p37)*. Its stunning skylit lobby was

Buckingham Fountain, Grant Park

State of Illinois Center

redesigned in 1907 by Frank Lloyd Wright *(see pp30–31)*, who added a grand staircase and hanging light fixtures, both of which carry his signature circle-in-square motif. The building's unusual name refers to the rooks that once roosted at the site. ⊛ *209 S. LaSalle St. • Map K4 • Open 9am–5pm Mon–Fri • Free • no DA*

🔟 Millennium & Grant parks
The modern Millennium Park *(see p62)* is Chicago's superb adaptation of its "front yard". The park is home to a dynamic Frank Gehry-designed music pavilion and pedestrian bridge, and a vast sculpture by British artist Anish Kapoor. It also boasts lush gardens, restaurants, a winter ice rink, peristyle, and an interactive fountain by Spanish artist Jaume Plensa. The adjoining Grant Park *(see p62)* hosts many summer festivals including the Taste of Chicago *(see p50)*. It is also home to Museum Campus *(see p92)*, the Art Institute of Chicago *(see pp8–11)*, and the ornate 1927 Buckingham Fountain. ⊛ *Map L6 & L4 • Open daily • Free • DA*

A Day in The Loop

Morning

🕐 Start early with breakfast at the charming Atwood Café in the lobby of the historic **Hotel Burnham** *(see p116)*, with its beautifully reconstructed interior. Then stroll a block west to Daley Plaza to see the giant unnamed **Picasso sculpture**, stopping off at the Hot Tix booth at 72 E. Randolph Street, to get half-price, same-day tickets to a Loop theater performance. Continue along Michigan Avenue, past the **Chicago Cultural Center** *(see p68)*, and south to **The Art Institute of Chicago**. A whirlwind tour of the highlights *(see pp10–11)*, all conveniently located on the upper level, can be done in a couple of hours, though you may want to come back for a second helping.

Afternoon

Either have lunch in The Art Institute's outdoor café or head west along **State Street** to eat at **Macy's** *(see p74)* legendary seventh-floor Walnut Room, a Chicago fixture since 1907. Then burn off the calories by shopping your way around the vast store and along the famous street that it's situated on. For pre-theater dining, try the sophisticated **Rhapsody** *(see p75)*, convenient for the **Symphony Center** *(see p48)*. Or, on weekdays, try the all-you-can-eat buffet at **Trattoria No. 10** *(see p75)*.

Evening

After the show, hop a quick cab ride to stylish **Nine** *(see p75)* for a cocktail or some dancing late into the night in the slick second-floor Ghost Bar.

Left **Chicago Theater** Center **Fisher Building** Right **One North LaSalle**

🔟 Architectural Sites

1 Monadnock Building
At 16 stories, this Holabird and Roche designed building (1891) is one of the world's tallest all-masonry high-rises. Inside, there's a magnificent wrought-iron staircase *(see p36)*.
Ⓢ *53 W. Jackson Blvd. • Map K4*

2 Marquette Building
Holabird and Roche also built this 1895 Chicago School structure with a steel skeleton and decorative ornamentation.
Ⓢ *140 S. Dearborn St. • Map K4*

3 Reliance Building
Daniel H. Burnham's stunning glass-and-white-glazed-terra-cotta building (1895) is now the Hotel Burnham *(see p116)*.

4 Fisher Building
Another Chicago School edifice with a steel structure, this 1896 neo-Gothic building is also by Daniel H. Burnham. Aquatic motifs on the façade honor the building's first owner, L. G. Fisher.
Ⓢ *343 S. Dearborn St. • Map K5*

5 Carson Pirie Scott Building
Eye-catching cast-iron swirls on part of the exterior of this building (1899 & 1903) express architect Louis H. Sullivan's love of elaborate detail.

6 Santa Fe Center
Daniel H. Burnham designed this elegant high-rise in 1904: its carved building signs are from Chicago's days as a railroad hub. The ground level houses the Chicago Architecture Foundation *(see p59)*.

7 Chicago Theater
The red marquee of this Beaux Arts-style theater is a symbol of Chicago. Built in 1921, today it is a performance venue.
Ⓢ *175 N. State St. • Map K4*

8 One North LaSalle
This 1930-built, 49-story building was Chicago's tallest for 35 years, and is one of the city's best surviving examples of Art Deco architecture. Ⓢ *Map K4*

9 Inland Steel Building
One of the first skyscrapers to be built (in 1957) on steel, not concrete, pilings. It predated the John Hancock building *(see p12)* in using external supports. Ⓢ *30 W. Monroe St. • Map K4*

10 Federal Center
Flanked by Ludwig Mies van der Rohe's federal buildings, this plaza (1959–74) contains Alexander Calder's striking statue Flamingo (1974).
Ⓢ *219 S. Dearborn St. • Map K4*

Left **Civic Opera Building** Center **Old St. Patrick's Church** Right **Palmer House Hilton**

🔟 Best of the Rest

Around Town – The Loop

1 Loop Theater District
A sidewalk plaque at Randolph and State Streets denotes Chicago's Theater District, a cluster of old and new theaters. *Map K4*

2 Civic Opera House
This 1929 structure was inspired by Paris's Opera Garnier. Inside, there are gleaming marble floors, crystal chandeliers, and a grand staircase *(see p48)*.

3 Symphony Center
At the heart of this center is Orchestra Hall (1904), the home of the Chicago Symphony Orchestra. A major 1997 extension added offices and the Rhapsody restaurant *(see p48)*.

4 Old St. Patrick's Church
Chicago's oldest church (1856) is crowned by two towers – one Romanesque, one Byzantine – symbolizing East and West. *700 W. Adams St. • Map J4*

5 Fine Arts Building
This historic landmark was designed by Solon S. Beman and completed in 1885. It was used as a carriage showroom by the Studebaker Company. *410 S. Michigan Ave. • Map L5*

6 Chicago Temple
A Gothic-inspired structure that was designed by Holabird and Roche in 1923. Under the majestic spire is a 35-seat chapel. *77 W. Washington St. • Map J4*

7 Federal Reserve Bank
This impressive structure is one of 12 regional Reserve banks. When it was first built in 1922, it had the largest bank vaults ever constructed. *230 S. LaSalle St. • Map K4*

8 Palmer House Hilton
The first Palmer House was destroyed in the Great Chicago Fire *(see p34)*. The current grand hotel is the third version and is lavishly decorated with frescos, Tiffany light fixtures, and marble floors *(see p116)*.

9 Daley Plaza
The location of the county court headquarters, Daley Plaza is best known for its giant steel unnamed Picasso sculpture (1967), donated by the artist. It was mocked when unveiled, but is now a city icon. *Map K4*

10 Four Seasons
Chagall's glittering 70-ft (21-m) long, rectangular slab (1974) is covered in thousands of tiles that depict the cycle of the seasons. *First National Plaza, at Dearborn and Monroe • Map K4*

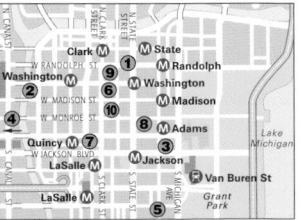

73

Left **Artwork for sale in Gallery 37** Center **Clock at Macy's** Right **Poster Plus**

10 Shops

1 Macy's
Once Marshall Field's, Chicago's oldest and best-known department store continues to be famous for its elaborate Christmas displays, dazzling Tiffany dome, and iconic clock. Established more than 100 years ago, it offers top styles for home and body *(see p58)*. ◈ *111 N. State St. • Map K2 • DA*

2 Filene's Basement
Here you'll find some fantastic budget-friendly buys and once-in-a-lifetime bargains on bridge, designer, and even couture goods. ◈ *1 N. State St. • Map K4 • DA*

3 Sears on State
After 18 years away, a hipper Sears returned to State Street in 2000 offering five levels of everything from tools to toddler outfits. ◈ *2 N. State St. • Map K2 • DA*

4 Pendleton Products Store
American-made fine woolens for men and women are the highlight of this small store located within the Palmer House Hilton *(see p116)*. Cozy wool blankets are also on sale. ◈ *120 S. Wabash Ave. • Map L4 • DA*

5 Jeweler's Center
On the strip commonly known as "Jeweler's Row" this one-stop-shop is a friendly place to source gold, pearls, watches, diamonds, and gems at relatively low prices. ◈ *5 S. Wabash Ave. • Map K4 • Closed Sun • DA*

6 Nordstrom Rack
High style on sale at a fraction of the original prices lure bargain hunters to this charming little sister of the upscale and pricey Nordstrom. ◈ *24 N. State St. • Map K4*

7 Poster Plus
This enormous store opposite The Art Institute of Chicago *(see pp8–11)* sells contemporary, vintage, and collectors' posters, as well as artsy gifts. ◈ *200 S. Michigan Ave. • Map L6 • DA*

8 Gallery 37 Store
Teenage artists involved in an arts training program create the incredible paintings, sculptures, and other artwork sold here. All proceeds from sales are returned to the program. ◈ *66 E. Randolph St. • Map L4 • DA*

9 Old Navy
This regional flagship store offers the ultimate Old Navy shopping experience, with two floors of discount jeans and T-shirts, and other casual comfort clothes at bargain prices. ◈ *35 N. State St. • Map K2 • DA*

10 Iwan Ries Tobacco
A smoker's paradise since 1897, this store now sells around 100 cigar brands, 15,000 pipes, and countless smoking accessories. It also contains a small tobacco museum. ◈ *19 S. Wabash Ave. • Map K2 • Closed Sun • DA*

Store opening hours are at least 10am–5pm (Chains & Department Stores to 8pm) Mon–Sat & 11am–6pm Sun.

Russian Tea Time

Price Categories		
Price categories in-	**$**	under $20
clude a three-course	**$$**	$20–30
meal for one, a glass	**$$$**	$30–45
of house wine, tax,	**$$$$**	$45–60
and a 15–20% tip.	**$$$$$**	over $60

🔟 Places to Eat & Drink

1 Nine
This hip restaurant specializes in steaks and seafood. There's also a champagne bar and the Ghost Bar for drinks and dancing. ◈ 440 W. Randolph St. • Map J4 • 312-575-9900 • Closed Sat lunch & all day Sun • $$$$$

2 Everest
The restaurant on the top floor of the Chicago Stock Exchange has dazzling views and to-die-for chocolate soufflé. ◈ 440 S. LaSalle St. • Map K5 • 312-663-8920 • Closed lunch, Sun & Mon • $$$$$

3 Rhapsody
A perfect choice for modern American food (like the signature onion-crusted sturgeon) before or after a concert. ◈ Symphony Center, 65 E. Adams St. • Map L4 • 312-786-9911 • Closed Sat lunch & Sun, except on concert days • $$$$

4 Rivers
In the summer the deck of this elegant riverside restaurant offers some of the best views of the city. ◈ 30 S. Wacker Dr. • Map J4 • 312-559-1515 • Closed Sat lunch & Sun • $$$$

5 Trattoria No. 10
Ravioli and risotto are the specialties here. A $12 buffet (plus $6 drink minimum) is available Monday through Friday evenings. ◈ 10 N. Dearborn St. • Map K3 • 312-984-1718 • Closed Sat lunch & Sun • $$$$

6 Catch 35
This sophisticated seafood restaurant has live piano jazz in the evenings. Don't miss the key lime pie. ◈ 35 W. Wacker Dr. • Map K3 • 312-346-3500 • Closed Sat & Sun lunch • $$$$

7 Ada's Famous Deli
Walk right in for generous portions of deli favorites such as matzo ball soup and stuffed cabbage. ◈ 14 S. Wabash Ave. • Map K4 • 312-214-4282 • $

8 Atwood Café
Expect top-notch hotel dining, where creative American cuisine leans toward comfort food. ◈ Hotel Burnham, 1 W. Washington St. • Map J4 • 312-368-1900 • $$$$

9 Italian Village Restaurants
Choose between upscale Vivere, The Village with its extensive menu, or mid-priced La Cantina – all under one roof. ◈ 71 W. Monroe St. • Map K4 • 312-332-4040 (Vivere), 312-332-7005 (The Village & La Cantina) • Days closed vary • $$$–$$$$ • No DA

10 Russian Tea Time
A spirited taste of Russia, where the vodka flows freely and the beef stroganoff is a crowd-pleaser. ◈ 77 E. Adams St. • Map L4 • 312-360-0000 • $$$$

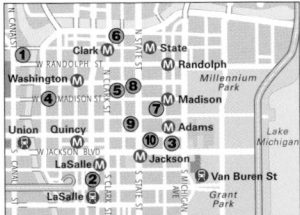

Unless otherwise stated, all restaurants recommend reservations, accept credit cards, have DA, and are open for lunch and dinner.

75

Left **Merchandise Mart** Center **Tiffany vases** Right **Carl Hammer Gallery, River North Gallery District**

Near North

HISTORY, CULTURE, AND COMMERCE *collide on Chicago's densely-packed Near North side. This area is a pleasure to explore on foot, whether motivated by a penchant for shopping or an appreciation of fine art and architecture. The city's classiest shopping boulevard – the Magnificent Mile, a.k.a. the Mag Mile – bridges the posh 19th-century mansions of the lakeside Gold Coast (which has its own clutch of upscale boutiques) and the former industrial warehouses of River North, now mostly converted into art galleries. In addition to these, two local art museums prove that "exhibitionism" in Chicago isn't just about the Art Institute (see pp10–11). But ultimately, it's the Magnificent Mile on a Saturday that says more about Midwestern vitality and giddy American consumerism than any other Chicago experience.*

Observation Deck, John Hancock Center

🔟 Sights

1. **Magnificent Mile**
2. **John Hancock Center**
3. **Merchandise Mart**
4. **Museum of Contemporary Art**
5. **River North Gallery District**
6. **Gold Coast Area**
7. **Chicago Water Works & Pumping Station**
8. **Tribune Tower**
9. **Fourth Presbyterian Church**
10. **Hershey's Chicago**

Previous Pages **James R. Thompson Center**

Magnificent Mile

Magnificent Mile

Whether you're a shopper or not, this store-lined strip warrants a visit if only to get a feel for the commercial pulse that seems to keep Chicago humming (see pp26–7).

John Hancock Center

Skidmore, Owings & Merrill designed this 1970 landmark using the signature X's on the façade as cross-braces to help the 1,100-ft (335-m) building withstand the winds coming off Lake Michigan. Soak up the view from the 94th-floor observatory or drink it in from the Signature Room restaurant and lounge directly above. Many say you get a better view from here than from the South Side's Sears Tower – and the lines are usually shorter too. ® 875 N. Michigan Ave. • Map L2 • Observatory open 9am–11pm daily, Adm., DA • Signature Room open 11am–2:30pm Mon–Sat, 10am–2pm Sun, 5–10pm Sun–Thu, 5–11pm Fri & Sat, DA • www.johnhancockcenterchicago.com

Merchandise Mart

This massive two-square-block edifice houses Chicago's premier interior design trade showrooms. When completed in 1930, the four million-sq-ft (390,000-sq-m) building was the largest in the world. Today, it is second only to the Pentagon in size, and is still the world's largest commercial building. A 90-minute guided tour includes a visit to several showrooms. ® 300 N. Wells St. • Map K3 • Free • DA • Tours 1pm Mon & Fri, call 312-527-7762, Adm (cash only)

Museum of Contemporary Art

One of the country's largest collections of international contemporary art, the MCA displays over 6,000 objects, from painting and sculpture to photography and video installations. Trendy Spago chef Wolfgang Puck runs the airy café, which draws museum-goers and Mag Mile shoppers alike. In summer, the terraced sculpture garden enhances the MCA experience, while the front lawn often plays host to displays of performance art. ® 220 E. Chicago Ave. • Map L2 • Open Tue–Sun 10am–5pm (to 8pm Tue) • Adm (free on Tue) • DA • www.mcachicago.org

Sculpture, Museum of Contemporary Art

River North Gallery District

Said to be the most concentrated art hub in the US outside of Manhattan, this district is jammed with great galleries. Most are to be found in the handsome, 19th-century, converted brick warehouses found along either side of the "L" brown line. Huron and Superior Streets are particularly worth a visit. ® Bounded by Merchandise Mart (south), Chicago Ave. (north), Orleans Ave. (west), Dearborn St. (east) • Map K3 • Chicago Gallery News 312-649-0064 • www.chicagogallerynews.com

Stained glass, Fourth Presbyterian Church

Gold Coast Area

Chicago boasts many upscale neighborhoods, but none more historic and prestigious than the Gold Coast. Railroad, retail, and lumber tycoons built this elegant district in the decades following the Great Fire of 1871 *(see p34)*, and its leafy streets are lined with 19th-century mansions interspersed with early 20th-century apartment buildings. There are no less than 300 designated historic landmarks in the Astor Street District alone, including buildings by Stanford White (such as 20 E. Burton Place), and Charnley House, designed by Louis Sullivan (assisted at the time by Frank Lloyd Wright). (1365 N. Astor Street). ✆ *Map K1*

Chicago Water Works & Pumping Station

When the Great Fire of 1871 swept north, only the 1869 Water Works and Pumping Station escaped ruin. Built by William W. Botington, the castellated

Gothic-Revival Water Works, modeled after a medieval castle, was once called a "monstrosity" by Irish playwright Oscar Wilde. It now houses the City Gallery (specializing in photography), and the fountain and chairs outside make it a focal point for downtown street life. The Water Pumping station across the street still functions, and also houses the Chicago Visitor Center and the Lookingglass Theatre, co-founded by *Friends* star David Schwimmer. ✆ *Map K2*
• *Water Pumping Station & Works 163 E. Pearson St., Visitor Center open 7:30am–7pm Mon–Thu, 312-744-8783, www. explorechicago.org • City Gallery open 10am–6:30pm Mon–Sat, 10am–5pm Sun, Free, 312-742-0808, DA*

Chicago Water Works

Tribune Tower

Topped by flying buttresses, this Gothic-style building was completed in 1925. Its faux-historic design had won a competition organized by Colonel Robert McCormick, publisher of the *Chicago Tribune*, the newspaper whose offices still occupy the building. Look closely at the façade, which is embedded with over 120 stones collected by correspondents from famed sights. There's a rock hailing from each of the 50 states, as well as fragments from international monuments such as Greece's Parthenon, India's Taj Mahal, and The Great Wall of China. ✆ *435 N Michigan Ave.*
• *Map L3*

Fourth Presbyterian Church

The first Fourth Presbyterian church, dedicated in 1871, celebrated its first sermon just hours before it was incinerated in the Great Fire. Rebuilt in 1914 when

Magnificent Mile was the little-used Pine Street, today's church offers a peaceful respite from the now highly commercial boulevard. Designed by Ralph Adams Cram, one of the architects behind New York's Cathedral of St. John the Divine, it's not surprising that this church boasts a cathedral-like interior, with an impressive stained-glass west window. A tranquil courtyard is often the place for classical concerts in summer. ◎ *126 E. Chestnut St. • Map K2 • Open 9am–6pm daily • Free • DA*

10 Hershey's Chicago

When candy-manufacturer Milton Hershey visited the city of Chicago in 1893, he purchased the equipment that he would use to revolutionize the chocolate industry. With mass production, he was able to lower the cost of manufacturing milk chocolate, once a luxury item, making it affordable to all. Today, the Hershey Foods Corporation is the largest North American producer of chocolate and non-chocolate confectionery. Hershey's Chicago, a themed store on Magnificent Mile, stocks all the well-known brands such as *Hershey's, Reese's,* and *Kit Kat,* as well as the latest products and goods unique to the Chicago store. Sugar-free versions of the most popular products are also available. A hit with children is the store's interactive "bake shoppe" where visitors can customize cookies, cupcakes, and brownies. ◎ *822 N Michigan Ave. • Map L2 • 312-337-7711*

Store sign for Hershey's Chicago

A Day in the Near North

Morning

Line up early with the locals for a fortifying stack at The Original Pancake House (22 E. Bellevue Pl.). Afterward, stroll south on Rush Street to Oak Street. Take a left and walk the most exclusive shopping block in the city, where you can pop into stores such as Barneys New York. Once you hit Michigan Avenue, it's a short jaunt to the **John Hancock Center** *(see p79)* and its sky-high views. Back on terra firma, cross the street to the **Chicago Water Works** for a close-up look at a piece of Chicago's history. Lovers of modern art should cross Michigan again and head to the **Museum of Contemporary Art** *(see p79)* with its spacious galleries and sculpture garden.

Afternoon

Everyone will get what they want for lunch at Foodlife, a gourmet food court on the second level of the mall in **Water Tower Place** *(see p26).* You can shop the seven floors of Chicago's first ever vertical mall, and then shop some more – and sightsee – along the **Magnificent Mile** *(see pp26–7).* If you've worked up an appetite, stroll over to the **Drake Hotel** *(see p115)* for high tea, which serves until 5pm.

Evening

Alternatively, NoMI in the **Park Hyatt Chicago** *(see p115)* serves stylish contemporary fare (reservations needed), as befits the neighborhood. Or just join the smart set over cocktails at the Bar at the **Peninsula Chicago** *(see p115).*

Left **American Girl Place** Right **Paper Source**

Shopping

Burton
1 You don't have to be a snow-boarder to shop at this flagship store, known for its range of funky boards and bold cold-weather gear. ◈ *56 E. Walton St. • Map K2*

Barneys New York
2 This branch of the Big Apple's downtown department store draws together the latest cosmetics, shoes, jewelry, accessories, and men's and women's apparel in a minimalist, open-plan, tri-level space. ◈ *15 E. Oak St. • Map L1*

Bloomingdale's
3 An outpost of New York's hometown department store that features in-store designer boutiques and a well-stocked shoe department. ◈ *900 N. Michigan Ave. • Map L2*

Ikram
4 Launched by a former Ultimo buyer, Ikram specializes in high-end women's fashion sold at top dollar. Chic wares and lines change seasonally, but shop assistance is uniformly personal. ◈ *873 N. Rush St. • Map L2*

Polo/Ralph Lauren
5 This massive four-story shop so thoroughly transforms itself from a store to a swell den devoted to Lauren's to-the-manor-born lifestyle – note the horse and hound paintings throughout – that it warrants a visit from even the less well-heeled among us. ◈ *750 N. Michigan Ave. • Map L2*

American Girl Place
6 Parents of girls age four to twelve make a beeline to this store, the only retail outlet of the American Girl line of dolls. A theater and café *(see p57)* supplement three floors devoted to dolls, books, and accessories. ◈ *835 N. Michigan Ave. • 877-247-5223 • Map L2*

Anthropologie
7 Women's apparel with a bohemian bent and housewares gathered from around the world sell briskly at this loft-like store. ◈ *1120 N. State St. • Map K2*

P.O.S.H.
8 Recalling the days of elegant steamships and grand hotels, this store uses old-fashioned suitcases and steamer trunks to lovingly display vintage china and silverware engraved with hotel and ship logos. ◈ *613 N. State St. • Map K2*

Paper Source
9 This arty River North shop is part art supply store, part stationer. The creative selection of cards and small gifts includes handmade stationery, cloth-covered sketchbooks, and novel desktop accessories. ◈ *232 W. Chicago Ave. • Map J2*

Original Penguin
10 Famous for outfitting classic American icons such as Bing Crosby, this 1950s golf brand offers a full range of men's and women's clothing. ◈ *901 N. Rush St. • Map L2*

 Most Near North shops are open 10am–7pm Mon–Sat & 11am–6pm Sun and have DA.

Frontera Grill

Price Categories

Price categories include a three-course meal for one, a glass of house wine, tax, and a 15–20% tip.

$	under $20
$$	$20–30
$$$	$30–45
$$$$	$45–60
$$$$$	over $60

🔟 Places to Eat & Drink

1 Frontera Grill
Chef Rick Bayless' regional Mexican cuisine warrants the two-margarita waits that inevitably face diners here. ⊗ *445 N. Clark St. • Map K2 • 312-661-1434 • Closed Sun & Mon • Reservations only for groups of 5+ • $$$*

2 Keefer's
A steakhouse that goes beyond the men's club stereotype, also serving French specials and ample fish selections. ⊗ *20 W. Kinzie St. • Map K3 • 312-467-9525 • Closed Sun & lunch Sat • $$$$$*

3 Bin 36
A wine bar of warehouse proportions, Bin 36 engenders an infectious enthusiasm for wine and food. The many small dishes encourage sampling. ⊗ *333 N. Dearborn St. • Map K3 • 312-755-9463 • $$$*

4 RL
This in-store steakhouse and power-eatery is furnished in upper crust style by the Ralph Lauren Home shop while elegantly attired hostesses sport Polo. ⊗ *115 E. Chicago Ave. • Map L2 • 312-475-1100 • $$$$*

5 Pierrot Gourmet
Run by the elegant Peninsula hotel, this café serves inventive salads, open sandwiches and pastries. ⊗ *108 E. Superior St. • Map L2 • 312-573-6749 • No reservations • $$*

6 Coco Pazzo
In the gallery district Coco Pazzo prepares dramatic, earthy Italian cuisine in an impressive loft space. ⊗ *300 W. Hubbard St. • Map K3 • 312-836-0900 • Closed Sat & Sun lunch • $$$$$*

7 Graham Elliot
This hip restaurant serves classic down-home fare with tongue-in-cheek twists: kung pao chicken with peanut brittle, Scottish salmon with tater tots, and so on. ⊗ *217 W. Huron St. • Map K2 • 312-624-9975 • Closed lunch • $$*

8 Pump Room
A jazz trio, opulent decor, and a forward-leaning continental menu serve diners here. Celebrities love its famed "booth 1." ⊗ *1301 N. State Pkwy. • Map K1 • 312-266-0360 • $$$$*

9 Whiskey Bar & Grill
Run by Rande Gerber, husband of supermodel Cindy Crawford, this sophisticated, sleek bar attracts a trendy crowd. ⊗ *1015 N. Rush St. • Map L2 • 312-475-0300*

10 Zebra Lounge
A classic piano lounge, the Zebra is intimate, friendly, and decorated wall to wall in animal prints. It's a funky place to drink cocktails in the Gold Coast. ⊗ *1220 N. State St. • Map K2 • 312-642-5140*

Unless otherwise stated, all restaurants recommend reservations, accept credit cards, have DA, and are open for lunch and dinner.

Left **Armitage/Halsted Shopping District** Right **Butterfly, Peggy Notebaert Nature Museum**

Northside

ENCOMPASSING PARTS OF OLD TOWN, *Lincoln Park, Lakeview, and Wrigleyville*, Chicago's Northside boasts upscale restaurants and chi-chi boutiques galore, as well as some of the city's best bars and one of its most progressive theater companies, the Steppenwolf (see p48). Older buildings have been transformed into beautiful condominiums, while stylish new apartments are springing up on empty lots. In season, nearby Wrigley Field fans bolster the lively Wrigleyville atmosphere by swarming the surrounding streets and bars – whether or not the Cubs win. The vibrant gay hub of "Boystown" is also in this area, while running along Northside's eastern border is the incredible lakefront, with sand volleyball and a beach bar heating up as soon as the temperature allows.

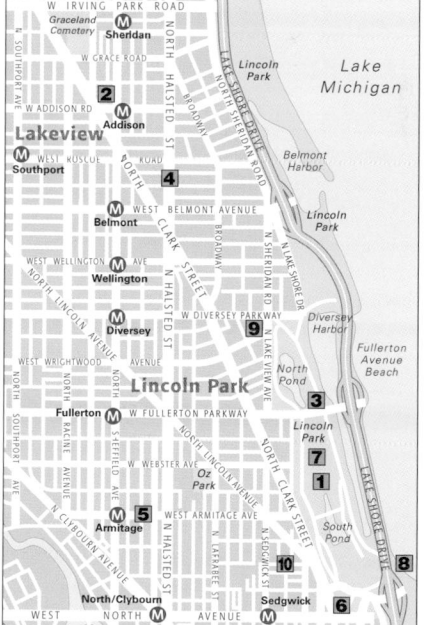

Tiger, Lincoln Park Zoo

Sights

1. Lincoln Park Zoo
2. Wrigley Field
3. Peggy Notebaert Nature Museum
4. Boystown
5. Armitage/Halsted Shopping District
6. Chicago History Museum
7. Lincoln Park Conservatory
8. North Avenue Beach
9. Elks National Memorial Building
10. Menomonee Street

1 Lincoln Park Zoo
Who's watching who at this beloved city zoo, which attracts more than three million visitors annually *(see pp24–5)*.

2 Wrigley Field
Built in 1914, this is the USA's oldest National League baseball park. Home team, the Chicago Cubs, haven't won a World Series championship since 1908 (before the field even existed), but that doesn't stop Northsiders from being behind them every step of the way. In season (March–September), spending an afternoon cheering on the "Cubbies" in this marvelous stadium, with its ivy-clad walls, is a quintessential Chicago experience.
Ⓢ *1060 W. Addison St. • Map D1 • 1-773-404-2827 • Tours daily, $25 • Adm • DA • www.cubs.com*

3 Peggy Notebaert Nature Museum
This museum's sloping, beige exterior was inspired by the sand dunes that once occupied its site. Inside are a host of engrossing interactive exhibits, the highlight being the walk-through Butterfly Haven, a light-filled space, constantly aflutter. The outdoor grounds, with their native

Wrigley Field

Boystown

wildflowers and prairie grasses, are perfect for a peaceful walk or rest. Ⓢ *2430 N. Cannon Dr. • Map F3 • 773-755-5100 • Open 9am–4:30pm Mon–Fri, 10am–5pm Sat & Sun • Adm • DA*

4 Boystown
Strolling down North Halsted Street, it's fairly evident you're in Chicago's gay neighborhood when you hit shops called Gay Mart, Cupid's Treasures, and a club named Manhole. Just 30 years ago, this area – officially East Lakeview – was pretty shabby, the bars were without signs, and parking was a cinch. But now buzzing Boystown is gay central – by day and by night.
Ⓢ *N. Halsted St. (& much of Broadway) from Belmont Ave.–Grace St., & Clark St. from Belmont–Addison Aves. • Map E1–2*

5 Armitage/Halsted Shopping District
This area of unique boutiques is a boon for fashionistas. Dozens of shops here sell everything from sophisticated evening wear to high-end accessories. Many of the stores occupy renovated Victorian town homes, set along pretty, tree-lined streets.
Ⓢ *Armitage Ave. from Halsted St.–Racine Ave., & Halsted St. from Webster–Armitage Aves. • Map E4*

For more Chicago shopping See pp58–9

Lincoln Park Conservatory

Chicago History Museum

Focusing on Illinois and Chicago history since settler days, this museum was established in 1856 and is the city's oldest cultural institution. One of the society's first donors bequeathed his collection of Lincoln memorabilia: the ex-president's deathbed is one of the items displayed. Visitors can climb aboard the Pioneer locomotive, while events such as the World's Columbian Exposition and the Great Chicago Fire *(see p34)*, are brought to life by photographs, decorative arts, and other exhibits. There are also costumes belonging to famous figures, from George Washington to sportsman Michael Jordan. ⓢ *1601 N. Clark St. • Map K2 • Open 9:30am–4:30pm Mon–Sat (8pm Thu), 12–5pm Sun • Adm (free Mon) • DA*

Chicago History Museum

Lincoln Park Conservatory

Take a free trip to the tropics at this spacious conservatory, just next to Lincoln Park Zoo. Opened in 1893, the glass structure is a year-round, 80° F (40° C) sanctuary from the Chicago's bustle, and offers a welcome respite from the city's long winters. Paths meander past lush palms, flourishing ferns, and exquisite 100-year-old orchids. Avoid the crowds by coming on a weekday when, unless a seasonal show is taking place, it's a quiet space, with the sound of trickling water as background music. ⓢ *2400 N. Stockton Dr. • Map F3 • Open 9am–5pm daily • Free • DA*

North Avenue Beach

When summer finally graces Chicago with its presence, locals of all ages and nationalities converge on this short, but inviting stretch of beach. Running along its edge is the lakefront path, where cyclists, in-line skaters, runners, and walkers stream by. An outdoor gym gives confident folks a place to strut their stuff, sand volleyball courts allow the energetic to let off steam, and the rooftop bar of the steamship-shaped beach house is perfect for downing a cool drink while lazily watching the activity below. ⓢ *Lakeshore Dr. & North Ave. • Map F4 • Open dawn to dusk • Lifeguards on duty from Memorial Day–Labor Day*

For more on Chicago parks and beaches See pp 62–3

9 Elks National Memorial Building

The Benevolent and Protective Order of Elks, an American fraternity (founded in 1868 and still going strong), built this magnificent structure in 1926 to honor its World War I veterans. It's since been re-dedicated to pay homage to World War II, Korean and Vietnam war veterans. Two larger-than-life elk statues flank the wide entrance steps, while inside, every inch is richly decorated. The 100-ft (30-m) marble rotunda, murals depicting the Sermon on the Mount, intricate windows, and allegorical bronze sculptures are awe-inspiring. ◈ *2750 N. Lakeview Ave. • Map E2 • Open 9am–5pm Mon–Fri; mid-Apr–mid-Nov also open 10am–5pm Sat & Sun • Free • DA*

10 Menomonee Street

This street lies in the heart of a delightful area of vintage cottages and Queen Anne-style row houses. Most of the original buildings were destroyed in the Great Fire of 1871 *(see p34)*. The clapboard house at No. 350 is a rare example of the relief shanties built for people made homeless by the fire. Today, the area's narrow tree-lined streets are home to picturesque houses and some interesting shops and restaurants. ◈ *From N. Sedgwick St. to Lincoln Park W. • Map B1*

Elks National Memorial Building

Exploring Northside

Morning

Fuel up for the day at one of Lincoln Park's favorite breakfast joints, **Frances'** (2552 N. Clark St.), where they serve a wonderfully fluffy French toast. Afterwards, take a leisurely stroll east down Wrightwood Avenue and keep walking until you come to the **Lincoln Park Zoo** *(see pp24–5)*, where you can take a ride on the wild side on the African Safari motion simulator, complete with 3D visuals. Then see all the animals in person, before breaking for lunch with a view at **Café Brauer**, built in 1908 by Prairie School architect Dwight Perkins.

Afternoon

During warm weather, head to the lakefront along Fullerton Avenue where you can stroll, rent bikes, sunbathe, or even brave the ever-chilly Lake Michigan waters. In colder months, catch a bus (nos. 22 or 151) and immerse yourself in the exhibits at the **Chicago History Museum**, or take a five-minute cab ride to **Armitage/Halsted Shopping District** *(see p85)* for some classy retail therapy.

Evening

This part of town has an abundance of good eateries: hop the "L" four stops or cab it to try **Mia Francesca's** *(see p91)*, a lively Italian trattoria where the pasta dishes are big enough for two, and there's an excellent wine list. Still going strong? Round off your day with a visit to **Kingston Mines** *(see p46)* – just a short cab-ride away – to hear some of best blues that the city has to offer.

Left **Barker & Meowsky** Right **Cynthia Rowley**

Shops

Isabella Fine Lingerie
1 This charming boutique has something silky, soft, and sexy for women whose sizes range from barely there to 44JJ. You'll also find teddies, bustiers, pajamas, and nightgowns.
Ⓢ *840 W. Armitage Ave. • Map E3*

Cynthia Rowley
2 Internationally acclaimed clothing designer Cynthia Rowley grew up in Chicago, so it's fitting that one of her upscale boutiques is here. Her collection of dresses, accessories, and separates is trendy and feminine.
Ⓢ *808 W. Armitage Ave. • Map E4*

Lori's Designer Shoes
3 Devoted shoe hounds flock to this Lincoln Park store for its hot styles at discounted prices. The floors and walls are stacked high with boxes for handy self-serve try-on access. Ⓢ *824 W. Armitage Ave. • Map E4*

Beatnix
4 This store boasts the best supply of costumes and vintage gear in the city, including wigs, distinctive mod jewelry, and make-up, as well as day-to-day items. Ⓢ *3400 N. Halsted St. • Map E2*

Unabridged Bookstore
5 Known for its large gay and lesbian section, this Boystown *(see p85)* bookstore also stocks books of all types, particularly kids' and Spanish language books. Ⓢ *3521 N. Broadway. • Map E2*

Hubba-Hubba
6 Women appreciate this boutique for its romantic and flirty vintage fashions and jewelry. It also sells modern items with a retro feel. Ⓢ *3309 N. Clark St. • Map F4*

The Leigh Gallery
7 Set in the heart of Lakeview, this gallery provides an inviting setting for art suited to all tastes, from modern to old-school classic, watercolor to sculpture.
Ⓢ *3306 N. Halsted St. • Map E2*

Barker & Meowsky
8 Four-legged friends are the focus at this store. From ceramic dog bowls to catnip-filled toys, rhinestone-studded collars to cookie-shaped dog biscuits, this store is a pet's best friend.
Ⓢ *1003 W. Armitage Ave. • Map E4*

Uncle Fun
9 This toy store is especially fun for grownups who yearn to feel like a kid. You'll find retro items like Mr. T coloring books, silly accessories like oversized sunglasses, and gag gifts like the tried-and-true whoopie cushion.
Ⓢ *1338 W. Belmont Ave. • Map E2*

Art Effect
10 An institution on trendy Armitage Avenue since 1984, this eclectic, funky boutique offers a little bit of everything, from off-beat fashions, accessories and statement jewelry to retro kids' toys and quirky homewares.
Ⓢ *934 W. Armitage Ave. • Map E4*

Most of these stores are open at least 11am–7pm Mon–Sat & noon–5pm Sun, unless otherwise stated, and they all have DA.

Left **Kit Kat Lounge & Supper Club** Right **Bucks Saloon**

TOP 10 Gay & Lesbian Bars & Clubs

1 Circuit/Rehab
At Circuit, men often dance shirtless to grinding house music. In contrast, the Rehab lounge bar is a sophisticated chill-out spot. ◈ *3641 N. Halsted St. • Map E2 • Circuit: open Thu–Sun, Adm.*

2 The Closet
This dance club attracts a mostly lesbian crowd, but gay men and straight couples also groove to R&B, rap, dance, and diva videos. ◈ *3325 N. Broadway • Map E2*

3 Roscoe's Tavern
A young, preppy set packs this neighborhood bar for its antique decor, cozy fireplace, poppy dance tunes, pool table, and, in summer, backyard beer garden. ◈ *3356 N. Halsted St. • Map E2*

4 Sidetrack
Find some of the best cruising at this vast, four-room bar with more than two dozen video monitors that highlight a different theme (like show tunes or 1980s music) every night. ◈ *3349 N. Halsted St. • Map E2*

5 Spin
One of Boystown's most diverse clubs: gay, lesbian, bi, and straight crowds mingle at this dance club and lounge. ◈ *800 W. Belmont Ave. • Map E2*

6 Kit Kat Lounge & Supper Club
Martinis come in 52 flavors at this swanky spot, where female impersonators divert attention from significant others with their lip-synching talent. ◈ *3700 N. Halsted St. • Map E2 • Closed Mon*

7 Berlin
For 20 years, this edgy club has attracted every type from straight girls to drag queens. After midnight, the dance floor hits its peak, rocking with a stellar sound system and light show. ◈ *954 W. Belmont Ave. • Map E2*

8 Cocktail
This laid-back club is ideal for sipping must-try martinis, while Boystown people-watching through wall-to-wall windows. ◈ *3359 N. Halsted St. • Map E2*

9 Crew Bar and Grill
With 20 enormous HDTVs, you'll always find a good spot to catch a game at this premier gay sports bar. ◈ *4804 N. Broadway • Map E2*

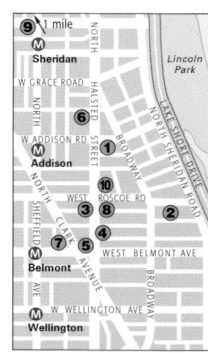

10 Bucks Saloon
A friendly, local bar (for boys and girls) where deer, elk, moose, and buck heads adorn the walls. The outdoor beer garden is wild in summer. ◈ *3439 N. Halsted St. • Map E2*

Left **Guthrie's Tavern** Right **Decorative Brickwork at Schubas Tavern & Harmony Grill**

Neighborhood Bars

1 Schubas Tavern & Harmony Grill
Twenty-somethings dress down for beer, live music, and a great restaurant that packs in crowds, especially on the patio during warm-weather weekends. ⊗ *3159 N. Southport Ave. • Map D1*

2 Four Farthings Tavern
This casual, family-owned bar is a perfect spot to kick back with one of 18 beers on tap, a single-malt whiskey, or a glass of wine. ⊗ *2060 N. Cleveland Ave. • Map E3*

3 Delilah's
Declared one of "the great whiskey bars in the world" by *Whiskey Magazine*, Delilah's has been a neighborhood watering hole for years. It has some 400 different whiskeys on offer, not to mention many beers on tap. ⊗ *2771 N. Lincoln Ave. • Map D2*

4 The Duke of Perth
This Scottish pub hits the mark, with nearly 90 varieties of single-malt whiskey and plenty of Celtic paraphernalia and music. ⊗ *2913 N. Clark St. • Map F4*

5 Guthrie's Tavern
Amid chitchat and free pretzels, boisterous patrons play board games. Come early for the best choice. ⊗ *1300 W. Addison St. • Map D1*

6 John Barleycorn Memorial Pub
Disguised as a laundry during Prohibition, this cozy pub has been dispensing beer and spirits for over a hundred years. ⊗ *658 W. Belden Ave. • Map E3*

7 Tilli's
This open-air bar is the perfect spot for people-watching in the summertime, with a cocktail in hand. Cozy up to the large stone fireplace in the winter. ⊗ *1952 N. Halsted St. • Map E2*

8 Southport Lanes & Billiards
During the day, this is a laid-back bar: at night, a rowdy young crowd covets turns at the four hand-set bowling lanes. ⊗ *3325 N. Southport Ave. • Map D1*

9 Wrightwood Tap
The centrally positioned bar promotes an open, *Cheers*-type feel, with conversation flowing among patrons. TVs typically air

college sports, while dart boards provide participatory entertainment. ⊗ *1059 W. Wrightwood Ave. • Map E3*

10 The Tin Lizzie
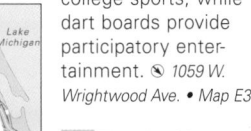
A sports bar-and-dance club, Tin Lizzie is wall-to-wall with twenty- to thirty-somethings most weekend nights, when DJs spin a variety of tunes. ⊗ *2483 N. Clark St. • Map F4*

Unless otherwise stated, all bars and clubs are open daily and have DA. At weekends many stay open until 2/3am.

Price Categories	
Price categories include a three-course meal for one, a glass of house wine, tax, and a 15–20% tip.	**$** under $20 **$$** $20–30 **$$$** $30–45 **$$$$** $45–60 **$$$$$** over $60

North Pond

⑩ Restaurants

1 North Pond
This pond-side restaurant (a former skaters' "warming house") serves up American gourmet cuisine. ◎ 2610 N. Cannon Dr. • Map F3 • 1-773-477-5845 • Closed Mon (and Tue, Jan–Apr), lunch (except Mon–Fri and Sun brunch, Jun–Sep) • $$$$

2 Alinea
This smart restaurant serves delicious unique food pairings in a minimalist setting. ◎ 1723 N. Halsted St. • Map E2 • 312-867-0110 • Closed lunch, Mon & Tue • DA (mention in advance) • $$$$$

3 Charlie Trotter's
Light French food is artfully designed by master chef Charlie Trotter at this restaurant. ◎ 816 W. Armitage Ave. • Map E4 • 1-773-248-6228 • Closed Mon & Sun, lunch • $$$$$

4 Geja's Café
The ultimate fondue in a romantic setting. Choose cheese or hot oil, or just opt for the divine chocolate fondue. ◎ 340 W. Armitage Ave. • Map E4 • 1-773-281-9101 • Closed lunch • No DA • $$$

5 erwin
Erwin Drechsler serves "melting-pot" cuisine, complemented by a superb wine list. Sunday brunch is a real treat. ◎ 2925 N. Halsted St. • Map E2 • 1-773-528-7200 • Closed Mon, lunch (except Sun) • $$

6 Tarascas
Mexican food gets a fancy touch at this colorful restaurant. Nights get spirited as diners down huge margaritas. ◎ 2585 N. Clark St. • Map F4 • 1-773-549-2595 • Closed lunch (except Sat & Sun) • $$

7 Robinson's No. 1 Ribs
The perfect, low-key spot for getting messy with thick, saucy barbecue ribs. A back patio opens during warm weather. ◎ 655 W. Armitage Ave. • Map E4 • 312-337-1399 • Closed Mon, Sat lunch • No DA • $$

8 Stanley's Kitchen & Tap
Comfort food, like macaroni cheese and apple pie, is the draw at this family-friendly spot. The all-you-can-eat brunch gets packed. ◎ 1970 N. Lincoln Ave. • Map E3 • 312-642-0007 • Closed Mon lunch • $$

9 Ann Sather
Known for its scrumptious breakfasts, this Swedish restaurant also serves lunchtime specialties such as meatballs. ◎ 909 W. Belmont Ave. • Map E2 • 1-773-348-2378 • $

10 Mia Francesca
The wait for the generous portions of flavorful pastas, seafood, and chicken at this lively eatery is definitely worth it. ◎ 3311 N. Clark St. • Map F4 • 1-773-281-3310 • Closed Mon–Fri lunch • $$$

Unless otherwise stated, all restaurants recommend reservations, accept credit cards, have DA, and are open for lunch and dinner.

Left **Adler Planetarium** Right **Shedd Aquarium (left) & Field Museum (right), Museum Campus**

South Loop

JUST SOUTH OF THE *business-centric Loop, this sprawling area mixes ethnic enclaves such as Chinatown (founded in the 1870s by migrant transcontinental railroad workers) with upper crust addresses, built after the Great Chicago Fire of 1871 (see p34). The region has many Chicago "must-sees," but the jewel in the crown is undisputedly the impressive Museum Campus: here, the Field Museum, John G. Shedd Aquarium, and Adler Planetarium celebrate the wonders of the earth, sea, and sky respectively, collectively drawing over four million visitors each year. The highway that once separated the Field from its neighbors has been replaced by an inviting green campus, where cyclists and skaters join museum-goers on the plant-bordered paths in fair weather.*

🔟 Sights

1. Field Museum
2. John G. Shedd Aquarium
3. Adler Planetarium
4. Prairie Avenue District
5. Blues Heaven Foundation
6. Maxwell Street Market
7. Museum of Contemporary Photography
8. Chinatown
9. National Vietnam Veterans Art Museum
10. Jane Addams' Hull House

Seals, Shedd Aquarium

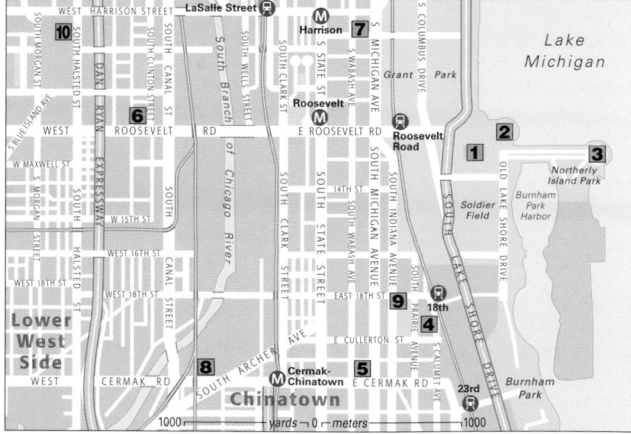

Field Museum

One of the three lakefront institutions to occupy the 57-acre (23-ha) Museum Campus, this vast museum boasts a collection of more than 20 million fascinating natural history and anthropological artifacts (see pp14–15).

John G. Shedd Aquarium

The second of the three Museum Campus sights, the Shedd is also one of the oldest public aquariums in the world. Dive in to discover the many treasures of the aquatic world (see pp22–3).

Blues Heaven Foundation

Adler Planetarium

The first planetarium in the Western Hemisphere completes the Museum Campus trio. Visit its numerous galleries to walk among the stars, explore the worlds that orbit the Sun, and be enlightened by 1,000 years of astronomical discovery. Don't miss the Sky Theater show, which is projected on the 68-ft (21-m) dome of the historic Zeiss planetarium. The virtual reality events in the StarRider Theater are also awe-inspiring, launching you into the outer reaches of space and even give you the chance to interact with the show via a panel in the armrest. ✪ 1300 S. Lake Shore Dr. • Map M6 • Open summer (Jun–Sep) 9:30am–6pm daily; winter 10am–4pm daily; third Thu of month 6–10pm for "Adler After Dark" (over 21s only); for showtimes call 312-922-7827 • Adm • DA

Figurine, Field Museum

Prairie Avenue District

Of the wealthy enclaves both north and south of the Chicago River that grew up following the Great Fire of 1871, Prairie Avenue was the most

fashionable – and Chicago's ritziest. Only a few of its mansions remain today, of which two are open to the public (by tour only): the imposing, Romanesque-Revival 1887 Glessner House, and Chicago's oldest remaining building – Clarke House – built in 1836 in the Greek-Revival style by New York emigré Henry B. Clarke. ✪ Map C5 • For info on walking-tours (Jul–Sep, on alternating weekends) call 312-326-1480 • Clarke House, 1827 S. Indiana Ave., tours noon & 2pm Wed–Sun, adm, DA • Glessner House, 1800 S. Prairie Ave., tours 1 & 3pm Wed–Sun, adm, no DA

Blues Heaven Foundation

Located in the former studios of Chess Records, where blues greats from Muddy Waters to Willie Dixon once recorded, Blues Heaven has an interesting collection of records, photos, and stage costumes dedicated to Chicago's blues style and its performers. Chess music plays on the PA, and there are occasional live performances. Rock aficionados will note the address is the namesake of a Rolling Stones song. ✪ 2120 S. Michigan Ave. • Map C5 • For tours call 312-808-1286 • Closed Sun • Adm • Limited DA

Feel like playing the blues? At Blues Heaven Foundation, staff say they can teach visitors the harmonica in 10 minutes.

93

Fresh produce, Maxwell Street Market

Maxwell Street Market

Both 19th-century European immigrants and 20th-century African-American settlers fleeing the Deep South got their entrepreneurial start selling from pushcarts around Maxwell Street. In 1994 the market was relocated to make way for the new University of Illinois at Chicago and, while a shadow of its former self, it still makes for a vibrant Sunday morning. Don't expect valuable finds; do expect plenty of Mexican housewares and used tools. But the occasional treasure, such as a vintage fur coat, does show up. Perhaps the best reason to visit is to try the homemade tacos from the Mexican food stalls that line the street. ✆ 548 W. Roosevelt Rd. • Map J6 • Open 7am–3pm Sun • Free

Architectural detail, Chinatown

Museum of Contemporary Photography

Run by and located in Columbia College Chicago, this museum is one of a kind in the Midwest. It exhibits the portfolios of international modern masters, with shows (including student shows) tending toward the experimental rather than the traditional

documentary. Changing exhibitions also present a mixture of local talents and well-established ones, such as Gary Winogrand and William Eggleston. Frequent gallery talks give curators and artists the chance to discuss the shows with museum-goers. ✆ 600 S. Michigan Ave. • Map L5 • Open 10am–5pm, Mon–Sat (to 8pm Thu), noon–5pm Sun • Free • DA • www.mocp.org

Chinatown

Crowned by the landmark Chinatown Gate spanning Wentworth Avenue, Chicago's Chinatown isn't that large – running roughly eight blocks – but it is colorful. Home to Chicago's oldest Asian community, Chinatown was founded in the 19th century by transcontinental railroad workers fleeing West Coast prejudice. It continues to be a place where Cantonese and Mandarin are spoken far more widely than English. Stroll Wentworth to see the ornate On Leong Tong Building, buy fresh almond cookies from Chinese bakeries, peruse the many import and herbal shops, or chow down in one of the dozens of local restaurants. ✆ Around Wentworth Ave. & Cermak Rd. • Map B5

National Vietnam Veterans Art Museum

A moving tribute to the horrors of war, this museum, started in the late 1970s, now showcases over 1,000 works by more than 130 artists once involved in the conflict. Most of the artworks, which include paintings, sculptures, and drawings, as well as prose and poetry, come from former US soldiers, doctors and

R. R. Yonkha's *This Is How You Died*, National Vietnam Veterans Art Museum

POWs, though powerful entries by former Viet Cong and native Cambodians attest to the universal effects of the conflict. ⊛ *1801 S. Indiana Ave. • Map C5 • 312-326-0270 • Open 10am–5pm Tue–Sat • Adm • DA*

10 Jane Addams' Hull House
When European immigrants were flooding Chicago to work in its rail and stock yards during the late 19th and early 20th centuries, Jane Addams bought Hull House for a specific purpose. From here, she offered social services and facilities to this immigrant working class, including day care, employment counselling, and art classes. A great social reformer and winner of the 1931 Nobel Peace Prize, Addams also championed the rights of women and helped usher in child labor laws. Her original office, furnishings, and artwork are still in place for visitors to see, supplemented by temporary exhibits that tell the story of the settlement at Hull House and the invaluable work of its residents. ⊛ *800 S. Halsted St. • Map H5 • 312-413-5353 • Open 10am–4pm Tue–Fri, noon–4pm Sun • Free • DA*

Exploring South Loop

Morning

🕐 Start by grabbing coffee and an oreo cookie flapjack at **The Bongo Room** (1152 S. Wabash Ave., 312-291-0100). From there, walk through Grant Park to Museum Campus. Here you can choose between the **Field Museum** *(see pp14–15)*, **Adler Planetarium** *(see p93)*, and **Shedd Aquarium** *(see pp22–3)* all within walking distance of each other. If you plan to visit other museums on your trip, it makes sense to purchase a City Pass *(see p108)*. If you opt to see the highlights of each, end up at the Shedd, where the **Soundings** restaurant offers good food and great views overlooking the lake.

Afternoon

Hail a cab (plenty wait outside the museums) or walk to the nearby pedestrian bridge at 18th Street to get to the **Prairie Avenue District** *(see p93)*, where you can stroll the historic streets and maybe even catch the 3pm tour of the **Glessner House** *(see p93)*. If you've still got the energy, walk one block west to the fascinating **National Vietnam Veterans Art Museum**.

Evening

Head over to Wabash Avenue for an early supper at one of the trendy eateries on what is now a burgeoning strip. Mayor Richard Daley has been known to frequent **Gioco** *(see p97)* for its stellar Italian fare (reservations are recommended). Ready for more? Then stay up late to hear the blues at **Buddy Guy's Legends** *(see p96)*.

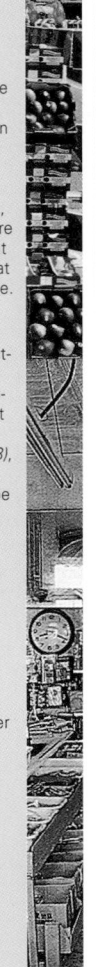

Left **Diners, Hawkeye's Bar & Grill** Right **Reggie's Rock Club**

🔟 Bars & Clubs

1 Buddy Guy's Legends
Run by bluesman Buddy Guy, this club is arguably the city's best. To get a table, come early and dine on decent barbecue. 🚫 *700 S. Wabash Ave. • Map K4*

2 Reggie's Rock Club
This rock venue and grill-pub offers nightly musical entertainment and surprisingly good bar fare. Next door, Record Breakers sells rare vinyl and CDs. 🚫 *2109 S. State St. • Map K6*

3 M Lounge
Listen to traditional and modern jazz in style on comfy couches and low-slung seating in cranberry, chocolate, and sage. Stop by for live jazz on Wednesdays. 🚫 *1520 S. Wabash Ave. • Map K6*

4 Vintage Lounge
The mahogany bar, classic cocktails, and chandeliers at Vintage Lounge will take you back to Old Chicago. Pizzas and homemade donuts are on the menu. 🚫 *1449 W. Taylor St. • Map H6 • Free*

5 M/X
A popular gathering place, M/X airs news and sports on an array of TVs. 🚫 *Hyatt Regency McCormick Pl., 2233 S. Martin Luther King Dr. • Map D5 • Free*

6 South Loop Club
This sports bar boasts a 70-inch TV screen, 10 different draft beers, and twice as many bottles. 🚫 *701 S. State St. • Map K5*

7 The Drum and Monkey
Popular with the university crowd, this old-world pub also offers entertainment, ranging from karaoke to Guitar Hero competitions. 🚫 *1435 W. Taylor St. • Map H6 • Free*

8 Beviamo Wine Bar
This dark, intimate Little Italy hideaway is a great place to cozy as a couple before or after dinner with one of forty by-the-glass wines, or a "sampling flight" of three wines. 🚫 *1358 W. Taylor St. • Map H6 • Free • Closed Sun*

9 Vernon Park Tap
Also known as Tufano's, this popular bar counts legions of local and celebrity fans who pile in for house wine and generous, inexpensive pastas. 🚫 *1073 W. Vernon Park Pl. • Map H5 • Free • Closed Mon*

10 Hawkeye's Bar & Grill
Try this sports bar for beer-fueled camaraderie and a genuine slice of Chicago fan zeal. A shuttle bus even delivers patrons to the United Center and US Cellular Field. 🚫 *1458 W. Taylor St. • Map H6 • Free • No DA*

Unless otherwise specified, bars and clubs charge admission, are open nightly, and have DA.

Price Categories

Price categories include a three-course meal for one, a glass of house wine, tax, and a 15–20% tip.	$ under $20
	$$ $20–30
	$$$ $30–45
	$$$$ $45–60
	$$$$$ over $60

Phoenix

TOP 10 Places to Eat

1 Phoenix
Phoenix attracts dim sum diners from near and far. Go early on weekends or prepare for long waits. ◎ *2131 S. Archer Ave. • Map A6 • 312-328-0848 • $$*

2 Joy Yee's Noodles
Specializing in bubble tea and smoothies, plus an enormous selection of noodle dishes, Joy Yee's is a bright spot to stop in for lunch or dinner while exploring Chinatown. ◎ *2129 S. China Place • Map C5 • 312-842-8928 • $$*

3 Gioco
Rustic Italian food is the draw at this stylish restaurant and one-time speakeasy. ◎ *1312 S. Wabash Ave. • Map K6 • 312-939-3870 • Closed lunch Sat & Sun • $$$$*

4 Lao Sze Chuan
Located in the Chinatown Square shopping mall, this simple eatery serves authentic Chinese Szechuan cuisine. ◎ *2172 S. Archer Ave. • Map C5 • 312-326-5040 • $*

5 Chez Joel
A quaint French bistro in the heart of Little Italy charms fans with its sunny decor and fine classics like steak au poivre. ◎ *1119 W. Taylor St. • Map H6 • 312-226-6479 • Closed lunch Sat, Sun & Mon • $$$$*

6 Pompei Bakery
A top Little Italy lunch pick, Pompeii showcases a dozen varieties of square, by-the-slice pizzas. Hot sandwiches and stuffed pastas round out the offerings. ◎ *1531 W. Taylor St. • Map H6 • 312-421-5179 • No reservations • $*

7 Francesca's on Taylor
The Little Italy branch of Wrigleyville's Mia Francesca offers generous portions of refined Italian cuisine at reasonable prices. ◎ *1400 W. Taylor St. • Map H6 • 312-829-2828 • Closed lunch Sat & Sun • $$$*

8 Rosebud Cafe
Its Italian cooking isn't daring but Rosebud's convivial vibe is hard to resist. Long waits for tables are common. ◎ *1500 W. Taylor St. • Map H6 • 312-942-1117 • $$$*

9 Chicago Firehouse
The menu at this former fire station is best at its most basic, including burgers and sandwiches. ◎ *1401 S. Michigan Ave. • Map L6 • 312-786-1401 • Closed lunch Sat & Sun • $$$$*

10 Evergreen Restaurant
Szechwan and Hunan specialties are served in this authentic restaurant. Try the black pepper short ribs or hot and sour shrimp. ◎ *2411 S. Wentworth Ave. • Map C5 • 312-225-8898 • $$$*

Unless otherwise stated, all restaurants recommend reservations, accept credit cards, have DA, and are open for lunch and dinner.

97

Left **South Shore Cultural Center** Right **University of Chicago Campus**

Far South

WITH MAGNIFICENT ARCHITECTURE, *interesting ethnic enclaves, and standout museums, Chicago's Far South encompasses districts such as Hyde Park and Kenwood that merit a journey off the beaten tourist track – despite being bordered to the south by some less-than-welcoming neighborhoods. Hyde Park and Kenwood began life as suburbs for the wealthy escaping the dirty city; today, this part of town is a fascinating melting pot of University of Chicago students and Mexican, Asian, African-American, and Indian residents. Recreation and leisure opportunities abound on spectacular tracts of green space, including the University of Chicago's Midway Plaisance and Jackson Park, site of the 1893 World's Columbian Exposition (see p19).*

🔟 Sights

1. Museum of Science and Industry
2. University of Chicago
3. DuSable Museum of African-American History
4. South Shore Cultural Center
5. Oriental Institute
6. Robie House
7. Kenwood Historic District
8. Washington Park
9. Osaka Japanese Gardens
10. University of Chicago Sculptures

Giant Heart, Museum of Science and Industry

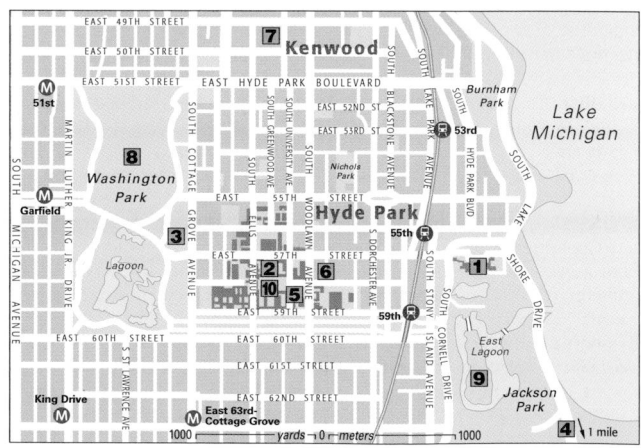

1 Museum of Science and Industry

The largest science museum within in a single building in the Western Hemisphere, this museum attracts an amazing two million people a year *(see pp16–19)*.

2 University of Chicago

Noted for its research and high educational standards, this remarkable private university has produced over 80 Nobel Prize winners *(see pp28–9)*.

Annie Malone exhibit, Dusable Museum

3 DuSable Museum of African-American History

Located on the eastern edge of the beautiful Washington Park, this museum is named after Chicago's first non-native settler, Jean Baptiste Point du Sable. The permanent exhibits here celebrate other firsts, such as the first black US astronaut, Major Robert Lawrence, and Chicago's first and only African-American mayor, Harold Washington. Thought-provoking exhibits include rusted slave shackles and the "Freedom Now" mural, depicting 400 years of African-American history from the early days of slavery to Civil Rights marches. ✆ *740 E. 56th Pl. • Map D5 • Open 10am–5pm Tue–Sat, noon–5pm Sun • Adm (free Sun) • DA*

Bust (c. 1840 BC), Oriental Institute

4 South Shore Cultural Center

How ironic that this bustling arts and community center, which serves a largely African-American demographic, began in 1905 as an exclusive country club that barred minority members. Designed by the team who later worked on the elegant Drake Hotel *(see p115)*, this grand Mediterranean-style structure was bought and lovingly restored by the Chicago Park District when the country club fizzled out in the 1970s. Extravagant landscaping and flower beds complete the pretty picture, making it a popular spot for weddings and festivals, as well as for all kinds of performances and classes. Its golf course, nature park, and the public beach behind it add to its many draws. ✆ *7059 S. Shore Dr. • Map F6 • Open 9am–6pm Mon–Fri, 9am–5pm Sat • Free (except classes) • DA*

5 Oriental Institute

Learn about the origins of agriculture, the invention of writing, the birth of civilization, and the beginning of the study of arts, science, politics, and religion at this University of Chicago departmental museum. Its five galleries showcase ancient Near Eastern civilizations from about 3500 BC to AD 100, and the exhibits were largely unearthed during the department's own excavations. ✆ *1155 E. 58th St. • Map E6 • 10am–6pm Tue–Sat (to 8:30pm Wed), noon–6pm Sun • Free • DA*

6 Robie House

This splendid 1910 residence by Frank Lloyd Wright is easily spotted by its steel-beam roof, which overhangs the building by 20 ft (6 m) at each end. Take a tour through its low-ceilinged interior,

Frank Lloyd Wright tables and chairs in Robie House

past more than 170 art-glass windows and doors, to gain insight into the extensive ten-year restoration program. The building was a private home until 1926, when it became a dormitory for the Chicago Theological Seminary. It was later bought by a development firm, who donated it to the University of Chicago in 1963, the same year it was designated a National Historic Landmark. ☉ 5757 S. Woodlawn Ave. • Map E6 • Tour times and prices vary; for information and to buy tickets, call 1-800-514-3849 or visit www. gowright.org • Adm: adults $12, children and seniors $10 • No DA

7 Kenwood Historic District

A world apart from some of the Far South's dicier areas, this wealthy enclave within Kenwood, founded by John A. Kennicott in 1856, has mansions that must be seen to be believed. In the late 19th century this area was an upscale Chicago suburb, where wealthy residents built majestic homes on spacious lots, a rarity in the quickly booming city. A stroll around the district uncovers architectural styles ranging from Italianate and Colonial Revival to Prairie style, by influential figures such as Howard Van Doren Shaw and Frank Lloyd Wright *(see pp30–31)*. ☉ Boundaries: E. 43rd St. (north), E. 51st St. (south), S. Blackstone Ave. (east), and S. Drexel Blvd. (west) • Map E5

Detail of Taft's *Fountain of Time*, Washington Park

8 Washington Park

Frederick Law Olmsted and Calvert Vaux, the designers of New York's Central Park, also created this 371-acre (150-ha) green space for Chicago residents in the early 1870s. It originally attracted mainly wealthy city dwellers who enjoyed parading around the scenic space. Today, it's a beautiful and widely used park with recreational programs, the DuSable Museum of African-American History, and Lorado Taft's striking 110-ft (34-m) long sculpture, *Fountain of Time*, which took him 14 years to build. It is unwise to venture into the park after dark. ☉ Map D5 • Open dawn–11pm (approx) • Free • DA

9 Osaka Japanese Gardens

At the north end of Jackson Park's serene Wooded Island (which is excellent for bird-watching) lies this hushed retreat, complete with meandering paths, lagoons, and fountains. The extraordinary garden is a partial re-creation of the one formed in 1934 around the beautiful Japanese Pavilion that had been built for the 1893 Expo, but which sadly burned down in 1946. The gardens were renamed in 1993 for one of

For more on Frank Lloyd Wright architecture **See pp30–31**

Chicago's sister cities, Osaka, which donated the Japanese gate seen here. ⊙ *Jackson Park, 58th St. & Lake Shore Dr. • Map F6 • Open dawn–dusk • Free • DA*

10 University of Chicago Sculptures

Strolling around the University of Chicago campus, there's more of visual interest than its buildings alone. Over the years, the university has acquired around 12 outdoor sculptures, including Wolf Vostell's whimsical 1970 *Concrete Traffic*, a car embedded in concrete at the southwest end of the Midway Plaisance and the sobering *Nuclear Energy*, a bronze by Henry Moore that resembles a mushroom cloud. Set within a reflecting pool at 60th Street and University Avenue is *Construction in Space in the Third and Fourth Dimension*, a soaring abstract piece created in the 1950s by Constructivist Antoine Pevsner, which visually depicts the space-time continuum *(see pp28–9)*.

Osaka Japanese Gardens

Exploring Far South

Morning

🕐 Mingle with University of Chicago students over good coffee and great pancakes at the **Original Pancake House** *(see p103)*, where the sweet, baked Apple Dutch Baby is a must-try. From there, walk about a mile (1.6 km) south or hop on the no. 28 bus at the corner of Hyde Park Boulevard and Lake Park Avenue to visit the **Museum of Science & Industry** *(see pp16–19)*, where you can easily spend an engrossing few hours exploring the hands-on exhibits. For lunch, skip the museum food and head west about a mile (1.6 km) to **Medici** *(see p103)*, a great student and faculty hangout, known for its delicious pizzas. The extravagant Garbage Pizza is a favorite.

Afternoon

Stroll about four blocks southwest to the **Oriental Institute** *(see p99)* at the **University of Chicago** *(see pp28–9)* whose museum will transport you back to ancient times. Its Suq gift shop offers unique souvenirs, such as a replica of an ancient board game. Just east of the institute is Frank Lloyd Wright's masterpiece of Prairie-style architecture, **Robie House**. Take a tour of this to really gain some insight into the great man's vision. Then stroll around the university's leafy quadrangles if it's good weather, or backtrack a little to the **Smart Museum of Art** *(see p28)* if you'd rather be inside. Either way, round off your day with cool vibes, spicy flavors, and classy cocktails at Asian-American fusion **Chant** *(see p103)*.

Left **Little Black Pearl Workshop** Right **House of Africa**

10 Shops

1 Powell's Bookstore
Here, used books in top condition are stacked floor to ceiling on painted wood shelves, with antique editions protected behind glass. ⊘ *1501 E. 57th St. • Map E6*

2 Seminary Co-op Bookstore
Housed in the basement of the Chicago Theological Seminary on the University of Chicago campus, it's fitting that this bookstore has a well-respected academic section, especially humanities and social sciences. ⊘ *5757 S. University Ave. • Map E5*

3 57th Street Books
This basement-level shop carries new fiction, children's books, and African-American interest titles. Low ceilings, brick walls, and a painted cement floor all create a cozy atmosphere, conducive to browsing. ⊘ *1301 E. 57th St. • Map E6 • No DA*

4 Treasure Island
The Treasure Island chain of grocery stores is a niche, specialty company selling everything from rabbit to ramen to this otherwise supermarket-starved community. ⊘ *1526 E. 55th St. • Map E5*

5 House of Africa
The scent of sandlewood incense fills this small boutique that sells African artifacts, carved wooden sculptures, and CDs of music from all over the continent. ⊘ *1510 E. 63rd St. • Map E5 • Closed Sun*

6 Alise's Designer Shoes
Shop for the latest men's and women's designer shoe fashions from Italy, France, Brazil, and the Far East, as well as ladies' bags, fine jewelry, and men's belts. ⊘ *5210C S. Harper Ave. • Map F5*

7 Toys, Etc.
This inviting store focuses on non-violent toys galore. Good-old standbys include kites, face-painting kits, balls, and dress-up clothes. ⊘ *5211 S. Harper Ave. • Map F5*

8 Little Black Pearl Workshop
The gift shop at this children's arts program and cultural arts center sells the students' amazing creations, such as one-of-a-kind painted furniture and vibrant mosaics. ⊘ *1060 F 47th St. • Map E5 • Closed Sun*

9 Hyde Park Records
This is the place to start up or fill the gaps in your record collection, with reasonable prices and friendly, knowledgable staff. New and used vinyl and cds cover a wide range of genres, and there are bargains galore. ⊘ *1377 E. 53rd St. • Map E5*

10 Artisans 21
This gallery showcases locally made art. You can purchase designs both to wear and to show, from whimsical ceramics to fringed silk scarves and handpainted jackets. ⊘ *5225 S. Harper • Map F5 • No DA*

Most of these shops are usually open at least 10am–6pm Mon–Sat and noon–5pm Sun and, unless otherwise specified, have DA.

Price Categories

Price categories include a three-course meal for one, a glass of house wine, tax, and a 15–20% tip.

$	under $20
$$	$20–30
$$$	$30–45
$$$$	$45–60
$$$$$	over 60

Chant

📷10 Places to Eat

1 La Petite Folie
An upscale French restaurant offering a fixed-price menu, as well as entrées featuring ingredients such as rabbit and quail. ⊗ 1504 E. 55th St. • Map E5 • 1-773-493-1394 • Closed Mon, Sat & Sun lunch • $$$

2 Snail Thai
Delicious Thai food, including regional specialties such as northern Thai sausages and duck spring rolls, plus a great range of "Veggie Lovers" dishes. ⊗ 1649 E. 55th St. • Map E5 • 1-773-667-5423 • $

3 Chant
With its funky vibe, unique cocktails, and global fusion cuisine Chant is great at any time, but its Sunday brunch with live music is a real bargain. ⊗ 1509 E. 53rd St. • Map E5 • 1-773-955-2200 • $$

4 Harold's Chicken Shack
Enjoy fast soul food, including catfish and fried chicken at this casual, authentic café. ⊗ 2109 S. Wabash Ave. • Map K6 • 1-773-752-9260 • $

5 Medici on 57th
Great pizza draws the crowds, but sandwiches on home-baked bread and rich milkshakes are also offered. ⊗ 1327 E. 57th St. • Map E6 • 1-773-667-7394 • $$

6 Cedars Mediterranean Kitchen
Delicious falafel, lamb kabobs, hummus, and dozens of other Middle Eastern dishes will fill you up for next to nothing at this bring-your-own-bottle eatery. ⊗ Kimbark Plaza, 1206 E. 53rd St. • Map E5 • 1-773-324-6227 • $

7 Nile Restaurant
The extensive menu at this Middle Eastern diner makes decisions difficult, but combination plates let you try an assortment. ⊗ 1611 E. 55th St. • Map E5 • 1-773-324-9499 • $ • No DA

8 Woodlawn Tap
A casual dress code, good food, and cheap beer attract all types to this bar especially for burgers and hearty soup. ⊗ 1172 E. 55th St. • Map E5 • 1-773-643-5516 • $$

9 Mellow Yellow
This laid-back eatery offers specialties of rotisserie chicken and sweet or savory crepes. There's also a separate bar. ⊗ 1508 E. 53rd St. • Map E5 • 1-773-667-2000 • $

10 Original Pancake House
This homey breakfast haven does everything well, but its signature dish is the apple pancake. ⊗ 1517 E. Hyde Park Ave. • Map E5 • 1-773-288-2322 • Closed dinner • $

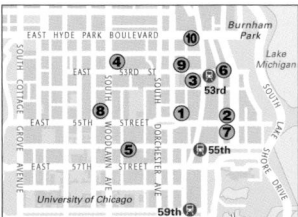

Unless otherwise stated, all restaurants recommend reservations, accept credit cards, have DA, and are open for lunch and dinner.

103

STREETSMART

CHICAGO'S TOP 10

Left **Christmas lights** Center **Wrapping up warmly** Right **Spring tulips, Magnificent Mile**

🔟 Planning Your Trip

1 When to Go
For a moderate climate, the best time to visit is spring or fall. But if you can bear the bitter cold of the festive season you'll see Chicago sparkle with Christmas lights – and you'll have a lot fewer tourists to contend with. Summer sees street festivals and live music in the parks. Avoid visiting in November, when hotels are full of conventioneers.

2 Weather
Chicago winters are usually intemperate with heavy snow and temperatures ranging from 13° F (-9° C) to 37° F (4° C). Summer days can be anything from balmy to boiling, averaging 69° F (22° C) to 84° F (30° C). Extremes, like winter blizzards, heavy spring rains, and summer heat waves are not uncommon, with spring-time weather being particularly changeable. Despite the winds that can gust off Lake Michigan, Chicago's "Windy City" moniker is actually attributed to the verbose bid the city made to host the 1893 World's Columbian Exposition (see p19).

3 What to Pack
Pack lightly for summer, and bring layers for the unpredictable spring and fall conditions. Layers are best for the often desperately cold winters, in order to cope with centrally heated environments. A hat, gloves, and suitable footwear are essential then too. While casual clothes are acceptable in most places, men should bring a jacket and tie, since they are required at many upscale restaurants.

4 Insurance
It is strongly recommended to have a comprehensive travel insurance policy including coverage for trip cancellation, lost luggage, car rental insurance and, most of all, medical expenses, which are very high in America.

5 Passports & Visas
Citizens of EU countries, New Zealand, Australia, and Japan can spend up to 90 days in the US without a visa, so long as they have a valid passport and a round-trip ticket. They will also need to register and pay a fee online at https://esta.cbp.dhs.gov prior to departure. Canadian citizens must show a valid passport. Citizens of other countries should contact their local US embassy well in advance of their trip to obtain the relevant visa.

6 Money
Do bring some dollars with you for essentials on arrival. But from then on, most places accept major credit cards. ATMs abound, but check with your own bank to avoid the fee charged for using ATMs of non-affiliated US banks. It's also worthwhile bringing a few US dollar traveler's checks in case of emergency. These can be changed at most banks and foreign exchange on showing photo ID, and can also be used in stores and restaurants.

7 Driver's License
Foreign or out-of-state driver's licenses are valid in Chicago – if they are in English. Bring your picture license even if you don't plan to rent a car: it's a good alternative to a passport if you are asked for proof of age in a bar.

8 Electric Current & Phone Adapters
Electrical appliances in the US operate on 110–120 volts and use two-prong plugs. Non-US, single-voltage appliances need a transformer and adapter, available in airport shops, electrical stores, and large department stores.

9 Discounts
If you have student or senior ID, it's a good idea to carry it with you to make the best of discounts offered on everything from public transit and hotels to admission to the main attractions.

10 Time Zone
Chicago operates on Central Time (six hours behind GMT). Daylight saving begins at 3am on the first Sunday in April and reverts to standard time at 1am on the last Sunday in October.

Left **Blue Line Train sign** Center **Amtrak train** Right **O'Hare Airport**

Arriving in Chicago

1 O'Hare International Airport

One of the world's busiest airports, O'Hare lies 20 miles (32 km) northwest of downtown Chicago. Serving most major airlines, this airport is big and spread out. Use the free Airport Transport System (ATS) to access the three domestic terminals, the international terminal, parking areas, and the Chicago Transit Authority (CTA) (see p108) station. Ⓢ 1-800-832-6352, www.ohare.com

2 Connections from O'Hare

Taxis are available on a first come first served basis from the lower level of the Arrivals terminal. Out of rush hours it can take around 45 minutes to reach Downtown. Car rental agencies are also at hand, near the baggage claim areas in terminals 1–3, and via courtesy telephones from terminal 5. Alternatively, shuttle buses, limos, and trains can take you into Chicago. For the latter, follow the "Trains to City" signs to the CTA Blue Line, the cheapest and – at 40 minutes – often the quickest way into town.

3 Midway Airport

Located 10 miles (16 km) southwest of Downtown, this airport serves mostly budget airlines, as well as a few major ones. Taxis are available from exit M5;

car rental agencies are located in the main terminal building; and shuttle buses leave from in front of it. Alternatively, follow signs from the terminal to the CTA station: the Orange Line brings you downtown in less than 30 minutes. Ⓢ 1-773-838-0600

4 Immigration

Landing cards and customs forms are distributed on the plane. Foreign nationals have to join a separate line to have these and their passports inspected after landing. Strict security checks, involving the taking of photographs and fingerprints, are now in place for those arriving in the US on a visa.

5 Shuttle Buses

These operate from both airports. Continental Airport Express will drop off at (and pick up from) any requested downtown location: Omega Airport Shuttle buses operate between the two airports. To catch a shuttle, go to the information counter at Baggage Claims. Ⓢ Continental Airport Express: 1-888-284-3826 • Omega Airport Shuttle: 1-773-483-6634

6 Limousines

Several limo companies, including Amm's and Chicago Express Limousine, offer private door-to-door services: book 24 hours in advance. Rates are higher than taxi

fares, and tips should be 10–15%. Ⓢ Amm's: 1-773-792-1126 • Chicago Limousine Service: 1-888-502-6224

7 Car Rental

You usually have to be over 25 with a valid license to rent a car. Reputable agencies such as Avis (800-331-1212) and Hertz (800-654-3131) are at both main airports and throughout the city. A deposit will be required. Collision damage waiver and liability insurance are highly recommended.

8 By Train

Over 40 Amtrak trains serve Union Station each day. The nearest "L" stop is at Clinton, but it's a good walk, so it is often better to take a cab or bus to your destination. Ⓢ 210 S. Canal St., 1-800-872-7245

9 By Bus

The inexpensive Megabus links Chicago with many other midwestern cities, and the bus stop is directly opposite Union Station. Tickets must be booked online. Ⓢ S. Canal St., www.us.megabus.com

10 By Car

Interstate highways into Chicago are I-55 from the southwest, I-57 from the south, I-88 from the west, I-90 from the east and northwest, and I-94 from the east and north. Route 66 from Santa Monica, CA joins I-55 before hitting Downtown.

Left **Water taxi** Center **"L" train** Right **Cyclists on the lakefront path**

🔟 Getting Around

1 The "L"
Short for elevated train, the "L" is nevertheless the name given to the entire CTA train network, including the sections that travel underground. The eight lines are identifiable by color: red, green, blue, brown, orange, pink, purple, and yellow. The red and blue lines run 24 hours a day (less often off-peak). Trains arrive every 5–20 minutes, and the service is fast and economical. ⊗ *CTA: 1-800-836-7000, www.transitchicago.com*

2 Buses
The CTA bus network covers the entire city and suburbs, and is especially useful for reaching the lakefront, which is not served by the "L." Look for the blue and white bus stop signs. PACE buses also cover the city suburbs and are numbered 208 and higher. ⊗ *CTA: as above • PACE: 1-847-364-7223, www.pacebus.com*

3 CTA transit cards & passes
A regular "L" or bus fare is $2.25, with an extra 25¢ for a transfer card (valid for two transfers within two hours of purchase), and you need exact change. You can buy a Transit card with a preset value or a top-up Transit card and charge it with the desired amount at an automated vending machine at any station. The relevant fare is then deducted from your pass each time you take a ride. One- to seven-day Visitor Passes are also available from stations, visitor centers, and selected tourist attractions.

4 Metra
Metra, the commuter rail system, serves the city's suburbs. Fares vary according to the journey's length. Downtown stops are Union Station, LaSalle Street Station, Ogilvie Transportation Center *(see p37)*, and Randolph Street Station. ⊗ *Metra: 312-322-6777 (Mon–Fri) or 773-836-7000 (RTA Travel Information), www.metrarail.com*

5 Taxis
It is usually easy to hail a cab Downtown; elsewhere it's better to call for one. There's an initial charge, then a fee per mile and per extra passenger. A 10–15% tip is expected. Companies include: ⊗ *Checker Taxi Assoc. 312-243-2537 • Flash Cab Co. 1-773-561-1444 • Yellow Cab Co. 312-829-4222*

6 Water Taxis
In summer, Wendella Riverbus (312-337-1446) runs water taxis between the Wrigley Building and both Union Station and the Ogilvie Transportaion Center. Shoreline Water Taxi (312-222-9328) also offers a service every 20 minutes from Navy Pier *(see pp20–21)* to the John G. Shedd Aquarium and near the Willis Tower.

7 Carshare
For getting out and about beyond the city limits, it's worth considering a carshare. Zipcar is a city-wide sharing effort. Choose the car you want online, and pick it up at one of many city locations. Rental is by the hour or day, with gas, reserved parking, and insurance included. Cars range from Mini Coopers to pick-ups. ⊗ *Zipcar: 1-866-4ZIPCAR, http://zipcar.com*

8 Walking
Exploring most Downtown and Northside areas (such as the Mag Mile or Lincoln Park) on foot is fine. However, avoid walking south of the South Loop after dark.

9 Cycling
Only confident cyclists should consider city travel as the roads are so busy. However, the 18 miles (29 km) of lakefront bike paths are very pleasant. To get a Chicago Bike Map call 312-742-2453. Bike Chicago rents bikes and conducts bike tours from Navy Pier: call 1-800-915-2453 or visit www.bikechicago.com.

10 Driving
Chicago's grid system *(see street index)* makes orientation relatively straightforward. However, expressways are often snarled, the Loop's one way streets can be very confusing, and finding parking Downtown can be a huge, costly problem.

Left **No smoking sign** Center **Visitors Information center** Right **Disabled sign**

🔟 Useful Information

1 Information Centers

Chicago has two main tourist information centers: in the Chicago Cultural Center *(see p69)* and in the Historic Pumping Station *(see p26)*. Opening hours are at least 10am–6pm. You can also get further information by calling the City of Chicago's Tourism Hotline (312-744-2400), the Chicago Convention and Tourism Bureau (312-201-8847), or the Illinois Bureau of Tourism (1-800-226-6632).

2 Websites

The city's official tourism website is www.explorechicago.org. For in-depth reviews of where to go and what to see, log onto www.metromix.com, affiliated to the *Chicago Tribune*. Internet cafés include the national chain Screenz (773-348-9300).

3 Media

The city's two main daily newspapers are the *Chicago Tribune* and the *Chicago Sun-Times*. The most popular radio stations include: WFMT (98.7 FM) for classical, WLUP (97.9 FM) for rock, and WGCI (107.5FM) for R&B. WBBM (780 AM) is a news station, as is Chicago Public Radio WBEZ (91.5 FM), and WSCR (670 AM) keeps you up to date on sports. For local TV, there's a wide range to choose from: CBS (Channel 2); NBC (Channel 5); ABC (Channel 7); WB (Channel 9); WTTW Public TV (Channel 11); and Fox (Channel 32).

4 Events

For a complete list of what's on in Chicago see www.choosechicago.com, or pick up the Chicago *Reader* – a free paper that comes out every Thursday, available in restaurants, bars, and other venues. Chicago is known for its conventions, some so large that conventioneers almost take over the city. Check the "Convention Calendar" at www.explore chicago.com, to see if your visit coincides with any.

5 Tipping

Plan to tip for most services: waitstaff expect 15–20%; bell hops and porters $1 per bag; hotel maids about $2 per night; bartenders up to $1 a drink.

6 Telephones

Most public phones accept coins or phone cards (calls to Directory Assistance are free). Chicago has two area codes: 312 for downtown and the immediate vicinity; 773 for the rest of the city. Dial 1 plus the area code for any US number outside the area code you are in. To dial abroad, key 011 + country code + city code (omitting any initial 0). If you need to rent a cell phone, try International Sound (1-800-353-2100). AT&T, Nextel, and Sprint are the largest mobile networks.

7 Families & Disabled Visitors

Chicago Parent magazine (www.chicagoparent.com) has a monthly calendar of kids' activities. Details of disabled accessibility to the city's main attractions are published by the Mayor's office at www.accessiblechicago.org.

8 Smoking & Drinking

Smoking is prohibited in all public spaces in Chicago. The legal age for the purchase or consumption of alcohol is 21, and the law requires photo ID as proof.

9 Consulates

In emergencies, your consulate may give assistance. ✪ *Australia: 123 N. Wacker Dr., 312-419-1480* • *Canada: 180 N. Stetson Ave., 312-616-1860* • *Great Britain: Wrigley Building, 400 N. Michigan Ave., 312-970-3800* • *Ireland: 400 N. Michigan Ave, 312-337-1868*

10 Public Holidays

The main public holidays are on the following dates: New Year's Day (Jan 1); Martin Luther King Day (3rd Mon in Jan); President's Day (3rd Mon in Feb); Casimir Pulaski Day (1st Mon in Mar); Memorial Day (last Mon in May); Independence Day (July 4); Labor Day (1st Mon in Sep); Thanksgiving (4th Thu in Nov); and Christmas Day (Dec 25).

Left **Lakefront recreation** Center **Hot Tix sign** Right **Public art, North Michigan Avenue**

TOP 10 Chicago on a Budget

1 Free Admission Days

Several city attractions such as Lincoln Park Zoo *(see p24–5)* never charge admission. Others often have one free day per week: bear in mind it might be cheaper, but the crowds can be greater.

2 Free Events

Summer in Chicago brings sunshine and lots of free outdoor happenings, especially in Grant Park *(see p71)*. Arrive early to get a good spot, and bring a picnic and warm clothing for after the sun goes down. The Mayor's Office of Special Events and other sources of information *(see p109)* will have details of concerts, neighborhood festivals, parades, and more. ◊ *Mayor's Office of Special Events (recorded info)* • *312-744-3370* • *www.cityofchicago.org/specialevents*

3 Free Tours

The Chicago Office of Tourism *(see p109)* provides information on a range of great free tours, such as the Cultural Center Tour and the Loop Tour Train *(see p111)*. The volunteer-run Chicago Greeters also offers an insider's take on the city at no charge *(see p111)*.

4 Dining Deals

Many restaurants have good-value "Early Bird Specials" or "pre-theater menus." Look for signs advertising deals.

5 Hot Tix

Half-price tickets for same-day theater performances can be bought in person at Hot Tix booths around the city. There is a slight discount for cash payment and a small fee for ticket processing. To save time fruitlessly waiting in line, check the website for daily listings of availability. ◊ *Hot Tix: Chicago Cultural Center, 72 E. Randolph St.*
• *Hot Tix: Waterworks Visitor Center 163 E. Pearson St.*
• *Both closed Mon*
• *www.hottix.org*

6 Public Art

Many famous artists, such as Pablo Picasso and Marc Chagall, have left their artistic mark on the city. Details of public art Downtown are included in a booklet, the *Loop Sculpture Guide*, which is available at the Chicago Cultural Center and the Waterworks Visitor Center. The University of Chicago *(see pp28–9)* also has notable works on campus, while Navy Pier has sculpture displays during summer.

7 Parks & Recreation

Chicago's many beautiful parks are run by the Chicago Park District. Their excellent facilities include skating areas, beaches, pools, golf courses, tennis courts, and walking and cycling paths. Contact Bike Chicago *(see p111)* at Navy Pier to rent bikes or in-line skates. ◊ *Chicago Park District: 312-742-7529, www.chicagoparkdistrict.com*

8 Improv Venues

Chicago is the place to catch the best rising comedy and improv stars. Comedy Sportz's totally improvised show sees two teams battle for your laughter. With over 25 shows a week, the iO theater is another great comedy venue. ◊ *Comedy Sportz, 929 W. Belmont St., 773-549-8080, www.comedysportzchicago.com*
• *iO Theater: 3541 N. Clark St., 773-880-0199, http://chicago.ioimprov.com*

9 Special Promotions

Throughout the year, the Chicago Office of Tourism *(see p109)* offers several promotions, such as Winter Delights, which include discounts on lodging, attractions, and meals.

10 CityPass

This pass grants entry to the Museum Campus trio *(see p93)*; The Art Institute of Chicago; John Hancock Observatory; Museum of Science & Industry; Field Museum; and Shedd Aquarium. It can be purchased online or at any of the participating venues, and is valid for nine days from the first day of use. It offers substantial savings, and you don't have to wait in line. ◊ *www.citypass.com*

Left **Uptown's Argyle Street neighborhood** Center **Carriage tours** Right **Lake Michigan tours**

Tours & Cruises

1 Chicago Neighborhood Tours

Apart from tours of neighborhoods such as Chinatown and Bronzeville, this company also runs special interest bus trips (on themes like Chicago's theaters). Tours begin at the Chicago Cultural Center (see p69): call ahead to book. ✪ *Chicago Neighborhood Tours: 312-742-1190, www.explorechicago.org*

2 Chicago Architectural Foundation Tours

Learn about the city's amazing architecture on a Chicago Architecture Foundation (CAF) walking, bike, bus, or (in summer) boat tour. The fascinating trips highlight both historic and modern buildings, including Frank Lloyd Wright's architectural legacy. ✪ *CAF: 224 S. Michigan Ave., 312-922-3432, www.architecture.org*

3 Bike Chicago Tours

Bike Chicago will guide you through the city's beautiful parks, neighborhoods, or along the stunning lakefront departing from either of its two locales. ✪ *Navy Pier: 600 E. Grand Ave., 312-595-9600 • North Avenue Beach: 312-729-1000 • www.bikechicago.com*

4 Untouchable Tours

Follow the trails of some of the city's most infamous 1920s and '30s gangster residents. Sites visited on this two-hour tour include that of the St. Valentine's Massacre, Little Italy, and other haunts of the likes of Al Capone and John Dillinger. ✪ *Untouchables: 1-773-881-1195, www.gangstertour.com*

5 Kayak Tours

Exercise your mind and your muscles by kayaking down the Chicago River while learning about the city's history and architecture. There are gangster and ghost themed tours for both beginners and advanced paddlers. ✪ *Wateriders Adventure Agents: 312-953-9287, www.wateriders.com*

6 Lake & River Boat Tours

Join a narrated tour from the Lake or Wendella boat tour to gain historical and architectural insight from a different perspective. Metro Ducks offer a wackier take with their tours onboard an amphibious WWII craft. ✪ *Lake Boat Tours: 312-527-1977, www.chicagoline.com • Wendella Boats: 312-337-1446, www.wendella boats.com*

7 Chicago Greeters

Run by the Chicago Office of Tourism (see p109), this free service gives groups of 1 to 6 visitors a chance to benefit from the wisdom of enthusiastic local residents who know and love the city. Choose from a range of themed or neighborhood tours, and preferably book online seven days in advance. ✪ *312-744-8000, www.chicagogreeter.com*

8 Loop Train Tour

While circling the Loop (see pp68–75) on a "L" train (see p69) an expert from the CAF explains the history of significant buildings and the "L" itself. This is a great opportunity to glimpse details of façades that are invisible from the sidewalks below. Tickets should be reserved online, in advance. ✪ *CAF: 224 S. Michigan Ave., www.caf. architecture.org, 10:30am Thu & Sat • limited DA*

9 Carriage Tours

For a romantic ride along the waterfront, the Mag Mile, or around the Gold Coast area, book a traditional horse-drawn carriage. A flat fee is charged for a half-hour tour. ✪ *Antique Coach & Carriage: 1-773-735-9400, www.antiquecoach-carriage.com*

10 Lake Cruises

Enjoy a meal or cocktails and dancing onboard the elegant *Odyssey* or *Spirit of Chicago* cruisers. In summer, schooners *Windy I* and *Windy II* also sail on the breeze. All depart from Navy Pier. ✪ *Odyssey: 1-866-305-2469, www.odysseycruises.com • Spirit of Chicago: 1-866-273-2469, www.spiritcruises.com • Windy I & II: 312-451-2900, www.tallshipwindy.com*

Check with tour operators as many tours are seasonal.

Left **Osco Drug store** Center **Lake front in winter** Right **Police**

Tips on Health & Security

1 Preventing Theft

As in most cities, the most common crimes are pickpocketing and purse snatching. Common sense can help deter these problems. Leave surplus cash, unnecessary credit cards, and valuables in a safe place at your hotel. Don't walk around with your wallet in a back pocket, and keep bags securely fastened and close to your body. Do keep a copy of your credit card numbers (and the number to call if they are lost) separate from the cards, and bring photocopies of important documents in case they are stolen.

2 Public Transport

It's best to avoid using public transportation late at night. Take a taxi instead. However, when you do take a train, stand well back on the platform until the train has stopped, never sit in an empty carriage, and do not lean against the train doors. Train platforms and trains usually have an intercom in case of emergency.

3 Knowing Your Surroundings

Plan your route before setting off so that you know where you are going. If you do get lost, try not to make a big show of consulting your map or guidebook. At night, avoid walking alone in dimly lit areas and in parks. Steer clear of areas beyond the south branch of the Chicago River (west of Downtown) and parts of the South Side where crime levels are higher.

4 Hotel Room Safety

Make yourself aware of the fire escape route from your room as soon as you arrive. Always keep the door locked, and be sure you know who is knocking before you let anyone in. Valuables are best kept locked in the in-room, or preferably hotel, safe.

5 Telephone Hotlines

For police, fire, and medical emergencies call 911. If you are not in a position to speak, the emergency locator should still be able to track you. For non-emergency police matters, such as theft, dial 311 to reach the City Helpline. Both numbers can be accessed by cell phones.

6 Hospitals

Hospitals and emergency rooms are listed in the Yellow Pages of the telephone directory. Your concierge will know which one is most convenient. Weiss Memorial Hospital and Northwestern Memorial Hospital are convenient to Downtown and the Northside of the city, while Bernard A. Mitchell Hospital, at The University of Chicago, serves the South Side. S *Weiss Memorial Hospital: 4646 N. Marine Dr., Map B3, 1-773-878-8700*

• *Northwestern Memorial Hospital: 251 E.Erie St., Map L2, 312-926-2000*
• *The University of Chicago's Bernard A. Mitchell Hospital: 5815 S. Maryland Ave., Map E6, 1-773-702-1000*

7 Medical Emergencies

In an emergency, call 911 or go directly to the nearest hospital. Even with medical insurance, you may have to pay for services yourself and claim reimbursement after. Contact your insurer before receiving any treatment.

8 Dental Emergencies

Many dental clinics are open 24 hours. Check with the hotel concierge or contact the Chicago Dental Society for a referral. S *Chicago Dental Society: 312-836-7300*

9 Pharmacies

Pharmacies are plentiful throughout the city. Many are open 24 hours. The most popular drug store chains (Walgreens, Osco, and CVS) all have pharmacies inside.

10 Seasonal Hazards

Chicago is a city of extreme seasons. Visitors should be prepared for cold, windy, and snowy winters, which can create hazardous conditions. In summer, the extreme heat can cause health problems: ensure you apply sunscreen, wear a hat, and drink plenty of water.

Left **Broadway Antique Market** Right **Water Tower Place**

🔟 Shopping Tips

Store Hours
Regular store and mall hours are usually 10am to 9pm, Monday to Saturday, and 11am to 6pm Sunday. However, Northside boutiques and stores along the Mag Mile *(see pp26–7)* often stay open until 7–8pm.

Taxes
Chicago state and local sales taxes are among the highest in the country at 10.25 per cent on all non-food items.

Sales Periods
Some Chicago stores have items on sale all year round, but expect real bargains after Christmas, on Presidents' Day, and on Labor Day *(see p109)*.

Department Stores
You're in shopper's heaven when it comes to department stores in Chicago, which are mostly located on North Michigan Avenue and State Street. They include traditional Macy's *(see p74)*, practical Sears *(see p74)*, upscale Nordstrom, and stylish Bloomingdale's Home & Furniture Store *(see p59)*. ✪ *Nordstrom, Westfield North Bridge Mall, 520 N. Michigan Ave. • Bloomingdale's: 900 N. Michigan Ave.*

Shopping Malls
There's no shortage of malls in the city, especially vertical ones on the Mag Mile. Here you'll find Water Tower Place *(see p26)*; Westfield North Bridge *(see pp56–7)*; Chicago Place – featuring the Midwest's flagship Saks Fifth Avenue – and 900 North Michigan Shops. Regular malls are scattered all around the city and its suburbs. ✪ *Chicago Place: 700 N. Michigan Ave.*

Chicago Souvenirs
Accent on Chicago and the Shop at the Cultural Center have shelves filled with Chicago mementos *(see p59)*, from kitsch to arty. Authentic local food such as pizza and Eli's cheesecake can be shipped anywhere in the US by Taste of Chicago. ✪ *Accent on Chicago: 875 N. Michigan Ave. • Shop at the Cultural Center, 78 E. Washington St. • Taste of Chicago: 1-877-908-2783, www.tastesofchicago.com*

Discount Outlets
Look for real bargains at Filene's Basement, while higher-end men's and women's clothing are discounted in the Mark Shale and Gap stores. Good value jewelery can be found at the Jeweler's Center *(see p74)*, and cheap housewares at Crate & Barrel. ✪ *Filene's Basement: 1 N. State St./ 830 N. Michigan Ave. • Mark Shale Outlet: 2593 Elston Ave. • Gap Outlet: 2778 N. Milwaukee Ave. • Crate & Barrel Outlet: 1864 N. Clybourn Ave.*

Music & Books
There are a few Barnes & Noble bookstores across the city. However, for specialty books and personal service, try Quimby's or Sandmeyer's Bookstore. Great-value CDs can be found on the back-wall racks of the legendary Rolling Stones shop, but Chicago is all about vinyl. Peruse vintage LPs at Reckless Records, or stop by Logan Hardware for new, used, and rare grooves. ✪ *Quimby's: 1854 W. North Ave. • Sandmeyer's Bookstore: 714 S. Dearborn St. • Rolling Stones: 7300 W. Irving Park Rd. • Reckless Records: 26 E. Madison St., 3161 N. Broadway, 1532 N. Milwaukee Ave. • Logan Hardware: 2410 W. Fullerton St.*

Art & Antiques
For information on art exhibitions, get a copy of *Chicago Gallery News*, which is available at visitor centers, or head to the River North Gallery District *(see p79)*. Taylor's *Guide to Antique Shops in Illinois and Southern Wisconsin* (available in bookstores or by calling 1-847-465-3311) will direct you to the best local antique dealers.

Size Conversions
Clothing and shoe sizes in the UK, Europe, and the US differ, and conversions are complicated. Look at www.onlineconversion.com for help with sizes.

Left **Continental breakfast, Chicago style** Right **Pizzeria Uno**

🔟 Accommodation & Dining Tips

1 Booking a Room

To book a room, contact the Chicago Convention and Tourism Bureau (CCVB). Discounted rates *(see below)* can be found by checking the Internet on sites such as www.choosechicago.com, calling the hotel directly, or contacting a reputable, no-fee reservation service such as Hot Rooms and Hotel Reservations Network. To hold a reservation, a credit card is usually necessary: no-shows will be charged. Be sure to specify if you want a smoking or non-smoking room. ⊗ *CCVB: 1-877-244-2246, www.choosechicago.com • Hot Rooms: 1-800-468-3500, www.hotrooms.com*

2 Rates

Hotel rates vary according to the hotel category, and the time of week and season. Peak rates are weekdays and from April–December. Rack rates, the basic room rates, are the ones used in this book to provide a guide price. Don't settle for them! It is almost always possible to get a better deal, so don't be too shy to ask.

3 Rooms

Usually, the larger the room, the higher the tab, and many, though not all, hotels charge more for a room with a view – so consider how much time you will want to spend in your room

before you pay the premium. Twin-bedded rooms are uncommon; most double rooms have either a queen- or king-sized bed or two double beds. If staying in a busy area, check to make sure rooms are soundproof.

4 Bed & Breakfasts

Bed & Breakfasts are a great way to see the city from a different perspective. For a list of homes offering guest rooms, check with At Home Inn Chicago, or Illinois Bed & Breakfast Association (ILBBA). Many require a minimum stay of two nights. ⊗ *At Home Inn Chicago: 1-800-375-7084 (toll free) • www.athomeinnchicago.com • ILBBA: 1-888-523-2406 • www.bbonline.com*

5 Taxes

Downtown restaurants add on a 10.25 per cent local sales tax to your check, and hotel tax in Chicago is quite high at 15.4 per cent (though the suburbs are slightly cheaper). Room rates tend to be quoted without tax.

6 Restaurant Reservations

Some restaurants do not take reservations (or only for groups of more than five), while for others, in particular the upscale ones, reservations well in advance are a must, especially on weekends. We indicate a recommendation for the restaurants

listed in this book, but it is always a good idea to call and check, especially if you have special needs or dietary requirements.

7 Meal Times

Breakfast is usually served in diners and coffee shops from about 6–10am. Lunch is normally available from 11:30am–2pm, and dinner takes place between approximately 5–10pm depending on the establishment. Early-bird dinners, normally served from 5–7pm, are usually a good bargain.

8 Chicago-Style & Ethnic Cuisine

Deep-dish pizza, hot dogs, and steaks are Chicago's main specialties. But in a city where a multitude of cultures meet, so do a multitude of cuisines, so check out the city's many ethnic restaurants *(see pp42–3)*.

9 Portions

You will find that portions vary hugely from place to place. Often portions at upscale restaurants are smaller, while steakhouses and ethnic eateries offer a more than generous serving.

10 Dress Codes

Few restaurants have strict dress codes, though some hotel and other upscale restaurants still expect men to wear jackets and ties.

Peninsula Chicago

Price Categories

For a standard, double room per night (with breakfast if included), taxes and extra charges.

$	under $100
$$	$100–200
$$$	$200–300
$$$$	$300–400
$$$$$	over $400

🔟 Luxury Hotels

1 Ritz-Carlton

The Ritz has it all – superior service, an award-winning dining room, spa, and state-of-the-art business facilities. Impressive views complement the classic furnishings and fine art in its spacious guest rooms, but it's the little things, like Bulgari toiletries and toys and cookies for the kids that puts it in a league of its own. ◈ *160 E. Pearson St. • Map L2 • 312-266-1000 • www.fourseasons.com • $$$$$*

2 Four Seasons

Expect the best in this grand hotel – possibly Chicago's most elegant. Lavish rooms command sweeping city and lake views, and the award-winning Seasons restaurant is a must-try. ◈ *120 E. Delaware Pl. • Map K2 • 312-280-8800 • www.fourseasons.com • $$$$$*

3 Peninsula Chicago

Understated elegance sums up this hotel. Large, earth-toned rooms have dressing areas, and a steam-free TV screen and hands-free telephone is found in every bathroom. Floor-to-ceiling windows dramatize the lobby, where afternoon tea is accompanied by live classical music. ◈ *108 E. Superior St. • Map L2 • 312-337-2888 • www.peninsula.com/chicago • $$$$$*

4 The Drake

Popular with visiting celebrities and royalty, this is the *grande dame* of Chicago hotels. It effortlessly blends modern convenience with the charm of days gone by. Each of the 535 rooms and suites is unique: many offer breathtaking views. ◈ *140 E. Walton Pl. • Map L2 • 312-787-2200 • www.thedrakehotel.com • $$$–$$$$$*

5 Sofitel Chicago Water Tower

This sleek, striking, ultra-modern hotel features spectacular views, sumptuous feather beds, and marble bathrooms in every room. There is also a 24-hour fitness center. ◈ *20 E. Chestnut St. • Map K2 • 312-324-4000 • www.sofitel.com • $$$–$$$$$*

6 Park Hyatt Chicago

Original contemporary art, rich woods, and warm tones create comfortable and tranquil public and private areas at this elegant boutique hotel. The state-of-the-art rooms feature furniture designed by Mies van der Rohe. ◈ *800 N. Michigan Ave. • Map L2 • 312-335-1234 • www.parkchicago.hyatt.com • $$$$$*

7 Fairmont

Overlooking Grant Park and Lake Michigan, the Fairmont features large, comfortable rooms that include high-speed Internet access, dressing areas, and marble bathrooms. ◈ *200 N. Columbus Dr. • Map L4 • 312-565-8000 • www.fairmont.com • $$–$$$$*

8 Trump International Hotel & Tower

Chicago's second-highest building (at 92 stories) houses this chic and state-of-the-art hotel. Stylish rooms have electronic amenities and floor-to-ceiling windows with views of Lake Michigan, the Chicago River, and the city skyline. ◈ *401 N. Wabash Ave. • Map K3 • 312-588-8000 • www.trumpchicagohotel.com • $$$$*

9 InterContinental Chicago

One of the city's most luxurious hotels mixes historic charm with contemporary elegance. This former men's club *(see p27)* has stunning public rooms, including a swimming pool, and very comfortable guest rooms. ◈ *505 N. Michigan Ave. • Map L2 • 312-944-4100 • www.icchicago.com • $$$$*

10 Conrad Chicago

Simple elegance and contemporary decor are features of this luxury hotel. In addition to 311 guestrooms and suites, there is The Restaurant at Conrad, The Terrace at Conrad, and Rendez-Vous (a stylish lounge). ◈ *521 N. Rush St. • Map L2 • 312-645-1500 • www.conradhotels.com • $$$*

Unless otherwise stated, all hotels accept credit cards, have private bathrooms, air con, non-smoking rooms, and rooms with DA.

Left **The Hilton Chicago** Right **Guest room, Hotel Burnham**

Historic Hotels

1 The Hilton Chicago

When it opened in 1927 The Hilton was the world's largest hotel. Popular with US presidents, it oozes opulence – especially the Versailles-inspired Grand Ballroom. The Executive Class King Lakeview rooms offer the best views. ✆ 720 S. Michigan Ave. • Map L6 • 312-922-4400 • www.chicagohilton.com • $$$

2 Palmer House Hilton

This has been an elegant fixture in the heart of the Loop for over 125 years. Extravagant frescoes decorate the ornate lobby's ceiling, while the guest rooms are subtly elegant. The hotel even has its own upscale shopping arcade. ✆ 17 E. Monroe St. • Map L4 • 312-726-7500 • www.chicagohilton.com • $$

3 Hotel Burnham

The Reliance Building – a handsome example of the Chicago School of architecture (see pp36–7) – was reborn as the boutique Hotel Burnham in 1999. Plush rooms are decorated in gold and blue, some with great views. A complimentary wine reception is held every evening. ✆ 1 W. Washington St. • Map J4 • 312-782-1111 • www.burnhamhotel.com • $$$$–$$$$$

4 The Ambassador East

In its heyday, this lavish hotel hosted stars such as Frank Sinatra and Liza Minelli. Comfortable rooms sport dark wood furniture and chintz furnishings; public areas, such as the Pump Room (see p83), are more impressive. ✆ 1301 N. State Pkwy. • Off map • 312-787-7200 • www.theambassadoreasthotel.com • $$

5 The Talbott

Enjoy the quiet elegance of this small, family-owned, European-style hotel. The Victorian parlor-like lobby and atmospheric Basil's bar and café offer a chance to unwind, and the 149 guest rooms and suites are large and welcoming. ✆ 20 E. Delaware Pl. • Map K2 • 312-944-4970 • www.talbotthotel.com • $$$

6 Allerton Hotel

Originally a residential hotel, the Allerton has a high-ceilinged, 1940s-inspired lobby, and large, traditional guest rooms with marble baths and lots of amenities. Don't miss the panorama from the 25th floor. ✆ 701 N. Michigan Ave. • Map L2 • 312-440-1500 • www.theallertonhotel.com • $$–$$$

7 The Whitehall

A quiet, understated European ambience has permeated this hotel since it opened in 1928. The 221 guest rooms combine elegant tradition with mod cons, and the Presidential Suite was a favorite of Katherine Hepburn. Check out the Fornetto Mei restaurant with its menu of neo-Milanese cuisine and thin-crust specialty pizzas. ✆ 105 E. Delaware Pl. • Map K2 • 312-944-6300 • www.thewhitehallhotel.com • $$–$$$

8 Silversmith Hotel & Suites

This boutique hotel close to the Magnificent Mile was built in the late 19th century. It features a Romanesque Revival façade and Arts and Crafts-style oak furniture in the large rooms. ✆ 10 S. Wabash Ave. • Map K4 • 312-372-7696 • www.silversmithchicagohotel.com • $$

9 The Tremont

An inviting fireplace welcomes you at this 1920s-built hotel, where guest rooms are small but comfortable; some have antique furniture and four-posters. Mike Ditka's restaurant is famous for its steaks and the collection of sports memorabilia. ✆ 100 E. Chestnut St. • Map K2 • 312-751-1900 • www.tremontchicago.com • $$

10 Millennium Knickerbocker

This hotel, once owned by Playboy Magazine, has hosted guests as famous as John Kennedy and Al Capone. Its 1930s lobby holds the Martini Bar (with live music most days), and the guest rooms exude a timeless elegance. ✆ 163 E. Walton Pl. • Map L2 • 312-751-8100 • www.millenniumhotels.com • $$$

Unless otherwise stated, all hotels accept credit cards, have private bathrooms, air con, non-smoking rooms, and rooms with DA.

Price Categories

For a standard,	
double room per	$ under $100
night (with breakfast	$$ $100–200
if included), taxes	$$$ $200–300
and extra charges.	$$$$ $300–400
	$$$$$ over $400

Left **Hotel Blake** Right **Wheeler Mansion**

Stylish Stays

1 W Chicago Lakeshore

A Zen water wall and "Leave me alone", rather than "Do not disturb" signs are indications of the W's hipper take on the hotel experience. The modern guest rooms have lovely views, as does the rooftop lounge, Whiskey Sky *(see p44)*. ◎ *644 N. Lake Shore Dr. • Map M3 • 312-943-9200 • www.whotels.com • $$$*

2 Wheeler Mansion

An immaculate 11-room hotel, this 130-year-old mansion is known for its great attention to detail. Soak up the lavish artwork, period features, and antique furniture, or take it easy in the tranquil garden. ◎ *2020 S. Calumet Ave. • Off map • 312-945-2020 • www.wheeler mansion.com • $$$*

3 Hotel Sax Chicago

This amazing hotel is much more than just somewhere to lay your head. State-of-the-art rooms offer hi-tech entertainment and eclectic decor. Guests can enjoy a drink in the atmospheric Crimson Lounge, surrounded by elegance and rich fabrics. ◎ *333 N. Dearborn St. • Map K3 • 312-245-0333 • www.hotelsaxchicago.com • $$*

4 W Chicago City Center

This hotel is trendy yet traditional, with comfy couches and board games in the lobby. Guest room decor is inspired by 1940s Hollywood glamor, with chaises longues and ostrich-leather headboards. ◎ *172 W. Adams St. • Map J4 • 312-332-1200 • www.whotels.com • $$$–$$$$*

5 Hotel Monaco

Most of the luxe rooms in this stylish 14-story hotel feature window seats (a.k.a "secluded meditation stations"), while the spirit is further calmed by aromatherapy oils in the bathrooms. Pep things up in the Party Like a Rock Star Suite, complete with jukebox and Jacuzzi tub. ◎ *225 N. Wabash Ave. • Map K3 • 312-960-8500 • www.monaco-chicago.com • $$*

6 Hotel Blake

This hotel contained printing presses before ever housing people. Now a National Historic Landmark, it offers large, light rooms. Savor Midwestern delicacies at the award-winning Custom House restaurant. ◎ *500 S. Dearborn St. • Map K5 • 312-986-1234 • www.hotelblake.com • $$$*

7 Dana Hotel & Spa

Chic and contemporary, this boutique hotel features rooms with modern furnishings, floor-to-ceiling windows, Wi-Fi, a state-of-the-art sound system, fine linens, and a double-sized shower. Guests can enjoy a list of services at the spa. The hotel restaurant, Ajasteak, provides a delectable range of Asian dishes. ◎ *660 N. State St. • Map K2 • 312-202-6000 • www.danahotelandspa.com • $$*

8 Hard Rock Hotel

This extravagant 381-room, musically themed hotel occupies the former Carbide and Carbon building – an Art Deco creation of 1929. Piped music and memorabilia are everywhere, and rooms are stylish but fun. ◎ *230 N. Michigan Ave. • Map L2 • 312-345-1000 • www.hardrock.com • $$$*

9 Hotel Allegro

Here, designer Cheryl Rowley has combined classic Art Deco features with contemporary colors and textures to great effect at this musically themed hotel. Complimentary wine is a standard nightly offering for guests. Fresh and fun. ◎ *171 W. Randolph St. • Map J4 • 312-236-0123 • www.allegrochicago.com • $$$*

10 The James

Modern and sleek, The James feels like a home away from home. Rooms have comfortable platform beds, a small dining area, plasma TV, stereo with MP3 dock, free Wi-Fi, and marble bathrooms. ◎ *55 E. Ontario St. • Map L2 • 312-337-1000 • www.jameshotels.com/chicago • $$*

Left **Homewood Suites** Right **Lobby, Hilton Garden Inn**

🔟 Budget Sleeps

1 Best Western River North

The location of this hotel, a little east of the Magnificent Mile, is excellent. Rooms are spacious, with free high-speed Internet access, in-room movies, and 30 minutes of local calls. There are also parking, fitness rooms, and an indoor pool. ⊗ *125 W. Ohio St. • Map K3 • 312-467-0800 or 1-800-727-0800 • www. rivernorthhotel.com • $*

2 Days Inn Lincoln Park North

This hotel is Chicago's highest-rated Days Inn. Free passes to the fitness center next door are part of the deal when you stay, as well as a continental breakfast and free Wi-Fi throughout the hotel. ⊗ *644 W. Diversey Pkwy. • Map E2 • 1-773-525-7010 • www.lpndaysinn.com • $$*

3 Belmont City Suites

A favorite of gangsters and mob bosses during Prohibition, this cozy, refurbished hotel now stands in the center of what makes Lakeview popular. Steps from Boystown's Halsted Strip, this is a great choice for those who like city nightlife. ⊗ *933 W. Belmont Ave. • Map E2 • 773-404-3400 • www.chicagocitysuites. com • $$*

4 Essex Inn Chicago

Experience spectacular views of Grant Park and Lake Michigan at this South Loop hotel. Rooms are spacious, with comfortable beds. There is a rooftop garden with swimming pool and a fitness center. The Savory Bar and Grill serves Greek, Mexican, and Italian food. ⊗ *800 S. Michigan Ave. • Map L6 • 312-939-2800 • www.essexinn.com • $*

5 The Inn at Lincoln Park

This hotel's Tudor-style exterior, Victorian lobby, and wagon-wheel trim are best described as eclectic. And while the rooms are definitely no-frills, the complimentary breakfast with views of Lincoln Park is a plus. ⊗ *601 W. Diversey Pkwy. • Map E2 • 1-773-348-2810 • www. innlp.com • $–$$*

6 Homewood Suites by Hilton

The two-room suites in this great-value hotel all have fully equipped kitchens, as well as living rooms with extra queen-size sofa beds. Use of the 19th-floor indoor pool and the fitness center all add to your stay here. ⊗ *40 E. Grand Ave. • Map L3 • 312-644-2222 • www.homewood suiteschicago.com • $$$*

7 Hilton Garden Inn

Each of this hotel's 357 functional and spacious rooms offers a large desk, complimentary high-speed Internet access, and many other amenities. Six corner suites offer the perfect setup for families and groups of friends: the hotel also has a pool and gym. ⊗ *10 E .Grand Ave. • Map L3 • 312-595-0000 • www. hiltongardeninn.com • $$$*

8 Hampton Inn & Suites

This centrally-located, family-friendly hotel offers two-room suites – with fully equipped kitchens – as well as many standard guest rooms. Bonuses include the fitness facility, indoor pool, complimentary breakfast buffet, and daily newspaper. ⊗ *33 W. Illinois St. • Map K3 • 312-832-0330 • www. hamptoninn.com • $$$*

9 Red Roof Inn Chicago

This is a great option for budget-minded travelers. Rooms at this centrally-located inn are small, but have all the essentials. A branch of the Coco Pazzo restaurant chain is on site. ⊗ *162 E. Ontario St. • Map L2 • 312-787-3580 • www.redroof.com • $$*

10 Hostelling International Chicago

This place is great value if you don't mind sleeping in a basic dormitory with local students, and you don't need to be a member in order to stay here. The facility includes lounges, fully equipped kitchens, and bed linen. ⊗ *24 E. Congress Pkwy. • Map L5 • 312-360-0300 • www.hichicago.org • $*

 Some budget accommodations offer weekday evening receptions with complimentary refreshments.

Price Categories

For a standard, double room per night (with breakfast if included), taxes and extra charges.

$	under $100
$$	$100–200
$$$	$200–300
$$$$	$300–400
$$$$$	over $400

View of Atrium, Embassy Suites Chicago Downtown

🔟 Business-Friendly Stays

1 Sheraton Chicago Hotel & Towers

The large, stylish guest rooms here offer fantastic lake, city, or river views. The hotel also has its own business center, boat dock, health club, and five restaurants. Popular with conventioneers. ✆ 301 E. North Water St. • Off map • 312-464-1000 • www.sheratonchicago.com • $$$

2 Westin Chicago River North

This sleek, four-star venue is home to a state-of-the-art Executive Business Center, fitness facility, and smoke-free guest rooms featuring the comfortable Westin Heavenly Bed. ✆ 320 N. Dearborn Ave. • Map K3 • 312-744-1900 • www.westinrivernorth.com • $$$

3 Hyatt Regency McCormick Place

Linked by a connecting walkway to McCormick Place convention center, the basic but modern rooms of the 32-story Hyatt Regency are an attractive stopover for conventioneers. The hotel also has a fitness facility. ✆ 2233 S. Martin Luther King Dr. • Map D5 • 312-567-1234 • www.mccormick place.hyatt.com • $$

4 Embassy Suites Hotel O'Hare-Rosemont

This hotel's seven-story garden atrium makes a pleasant retreat from the hustle and bustle of the nearby convention center and airport. Suites have all the necessary facilities; cooked breakfasts and an airport shuttle are complimentary. ✆ 5500 N. River Rd., Rosemont • Off map • 1-847-678-4000 • www.embassyohare.com • $$$

5 Swissôtel

Rising up where the Chicago River and Lake Michigan meet is this dramatic glass-and-steel creation. Oversized guest rooms contain every convenience for the business traveller and provide stellar views of the city. ✆ 323 E. Wacker Dr. • Map L3 • 312-565-0565 • www.swissotel.com • $$$

6 Hyatt Regency Chicago

A lobby full of greenery and fountains welcomes guests into this, the biggest hotel in the Hyatt chain. Although all guest rooms offer high speed Internet access, you can opt for a "Business Plan" upgrade to obtain more specific benefits during your stay. ✆ 151 E. Wacker Dr. • Map L3 • 312-565-1234 • www.hyatt.com • $$$–$$$$

7 Chicago Marriott Downtown

This 46-story hotel's contemporary rooms are designed to cater to every business need. Guests can also enjoy the hotel's five restaurants and lounges, or its on-site pool and fitness center. ✆ 540 N. Michigan Ave. • Map L2 • 312-836-0100 • www.marriott.com • $$$

8 Embassy Suites Hotel Chicago Downtown

The lofty atrium here is filled with plants, birds, and fountains; the two-room suites are spacious and well-equipped; service is personal; and cooked breakfasts plus other perks are included. ✆ 600 N. State St. • Map K2 • 312-943-3800 • www.embassysuites.com • $$

9 Courtyard by Marriott Chicago Downtown

Bright, modern rooms with high-speed Internet access, a spacious work area, and an extra sofa-bed make this centrally-located hotel a popular choice among leisure and business travelers alike. ✆ 30 E. Hubbard St. • Map K3 • 312-329-2500 • www.courtyard.com • $$

10 Hilton Chicago O'Hare Airport

The only hotel actually on airport grounds (conveniently linked to airport terminals via underground walkways) offers an enhanced business center, providing state-of-the-art telecommunications and multimedia conference facilities. Rooms are well soundproofed. ✆ O'Hare Airport • Map A3 • 1-773-686-8000 • www.hilton.com • $$$

Unless otherwise stated, all hotels accept credit cards, have private bathrooms, air con, non-smoking rooms, and rooms with DA.

General Index

Acknowledgements

The Authors
Chicago-based freelancer Elaine Glusac specializes in travel writing for an array of publications including *National Geographic Traveler* and the *International Herald Tribune*.

Elisa Kronish is a Chicago native who has written about the city's highlights and hidden finds for a variety of print and online travel guides such as Citysearch Chicago.

Roberta Sotonoff is a travel junkie. She writes about a variety of travel destinations, and her work has appeared worldwide in over 40 newspapers, magazines, on-line sites and guidebooks.

Produced by Departure Lounge, London
Editorial Director Naomi Peck
Art Director Lisa Kosky
Picture Researcher Debbie Woska
Editorial and Design Assistance Kelly Thompson, Davin Kuntze, Debbie Woska, Caroline Blake
Photographer Jim Warych
Additional Photography Andrew Leyerle
Illustrator Lee Redmond
Maps (DK India) Managing Editor: Aruna Ghose, Senior Cartographer: Uma Bhattacharya, Cartographers: Suresh Kumar, Alok Pathak
Proofreader Mary Sutherland
Factchecker Misty Tosh
Indexer Hilary Bird

AT DORLING KINDERSLEY
Publishing Managers Fay Franklin, Kate Poole
Senior Art Editor Marisa Renzullo
Publisher Douglas Amrine
Senior Cartographic Editor Casper Morris
DTP Jason Little, Conrad van Dyk
Production Controller Shane Higgins
Additional Contributions Emily Anderson, Marta Bescos Sanchez, Amy Bizzarri, D Clancy, Robert Devendorf, Emer FitzGerald, Anna Freiberger, Camilla Gersh, Laura Jones, Maite Lantaron, Alison McGill, Catherine Palmi, Rada Radojicic, Sands Publishing Solutions, Susana Smith, Brett Steel, Lauren Viera, Ros Walford

Playhouse, Riverside, Illinois, 1912 Frank Lloyd-Wright. © ARS, NY and DACS, London 2007 11tr; *Lampwork Paperweight: Clematis* c. 1848–55 Saint-Louis Factory, France 11cb; BUENA VISTA: 60bl; CHANT: 102tl; CHICAGO ARCHITECHTURE FOUNDATION: 58tc; CHICAGO OFFICE OF TOURISM: 85bl; Mark Montgomery 106tc; Willie Schmidt 112c; Peter J. Schulz 50tl, 92tr; CITY OF CHICAGO/GRC: 50tc; COLUMBIA PICTURES: 60tr; CORBIS: Alan Schein Photography 12–13c; Bettmann 35tl; Thomas A. Heinz 30clb; Jon Hicks1c; Sandy Felsenthal 30cla; COURT THEATRE: Mary Stuart by Friedrich Schiller. Translated by Robert David MacDonald. Directed by Joanne Akalaitis. Left to Right: Jenny Bacon and Barbara E. Robertson 48cla; DUSABLE MUSEUM: 99tr; ELKS MEMORIAL AND HEADQUARTERS: 87bl; THE FIELD MUSEUM: 6c, 14cla, 14c, 14br, 15tl, 15clb, 93c; FUNKY BUDDHA LOUNGE: 44tl; GENE SISKEL FILM CENTER: 48tr; GOLD COAST GUEST HOUSE: 114tl; THE GREATER NORTH MICHIGAN AVENUE ASSOCIATION: 58bl; Courtesy of HERSHEY'S CHICAGO: 81br; INTERNATIONAL MUSEUM OF SURGICAL SCIENCES: 39tl; iSTOCKPHOTO.COM: Grzegorz Kieca 108tc; JOHN HANDLEY: 50bl, 64tl, 106tr, 108tr; JAMES LEMASS: 31clb, 106–107; JOHN G. SHEDD AQUARIUM 22cb, 22bl, 22–23c, 23tr, 23cr, 23bl, 56c; Edward G. Lines, Jnr 92c; LEONARDO MEDIA LIMITED: 115tl, 116tl, 116tr; 117tl; LINCOLN PARK ZOO: 7tl, 24cla, 24bc, 24-25c,

25cr, 25clb; Todd Rosenberg 56tr; LITTLE BLACK PEARL WORKSHOP: 102tl; MARY EVANS PICTURE LIBRARY: 34t, 35d; MAYOR'S OFFICE OF SPECIAL EVENTS: 3tr, 50tr, 51tl; MEXICAN MUSEUM OF FINE ART: Work by Jesus Helguera Courtesy of Garrison and Rosslyn Valentine 38bl; MUSEUM OF CONTEMPORARY ART: *Memorial to the Idea of Man If He Was an Idea* H.C. Westermann © DACS, London/VAGA, New York 2007 79c; MUSEUM OF SCIENCE & INDUSTRY: 16bl, 16bcl, 17tr, 18tc, 18tr, 18c, 19c, 56tl; Scott Brownell 17cb; Dirk Fletcher 98cr; NATIONAL VIETNAM VETERANS MUSEUM: 95tl; *Goodbye Vietnam* David A. Sessions 38tl; NAVY PIER: 3bl, 6bl, 20cla, 20cb, 20–21c, 21tr, 21bl, 57tr; OLD TOWN SCHOOL OF FOLK MUSIC: 49tr; PARAMOUNT PICTURES: 60tl; PEGGY NOTEBAERT NATURE MUSEUM: 84tr; POSTER PLUS: 74tr; REGGIE'S ROCK CLUB: 96tr; RUSSIAN TEA-TIME: 75tl; SALPICON: 42bl; SOFITEL CHICAGO WATER TOWER: 45tl; SOUTH SHORE CULTURAL CENTER: Brook Collins/Chicago Rark District 98tl; STEPPENWOLF THEATRE: 48tl; TERRA FOUNDATION OF THE ARTS: 81tl; UNIVERSITY OF CHICAGO: 7b, 29tl, 29cla, 29clb, 98tr; WATER TOWER PALACE: 107tr; WHEELER MANSION: 117tr.

All other images are © Dorling Kindersley. For further information see *www.dkimages.com*

Special Editions of DK Travel Guides

DK Travel Guides can be purchased in bulk quantities at discounted prices for use in promotions or as premiums. We are also able to offer special editions and personalized jackets, corporate imprints, and excerpts from all of our books, tailored specifically to meet your own needs.

To find out more, please contact:
(in the United States) **SpecialSales@dk.com**
(in the UK) **TravelSpecialSales@uk.dk.com**
(in Canada) DK Special Sales at **general@tourmaline.ca**
(in Australia) **business.development@pearson.com.au**

Selected Street Index

Chicago's Grid System

Nearly all streets in Chicago run east-west or north–south. The zero point is at the intersection of Madison Street (running east-west) and State Street (running north-south). All streets are labelled in relation to this point: for example, the section of State Street north of Madison is known as North State Street. Numbering also begins at the zero point and odd numbers are on the east sides of north-south streets and the south sides of east-west streets.